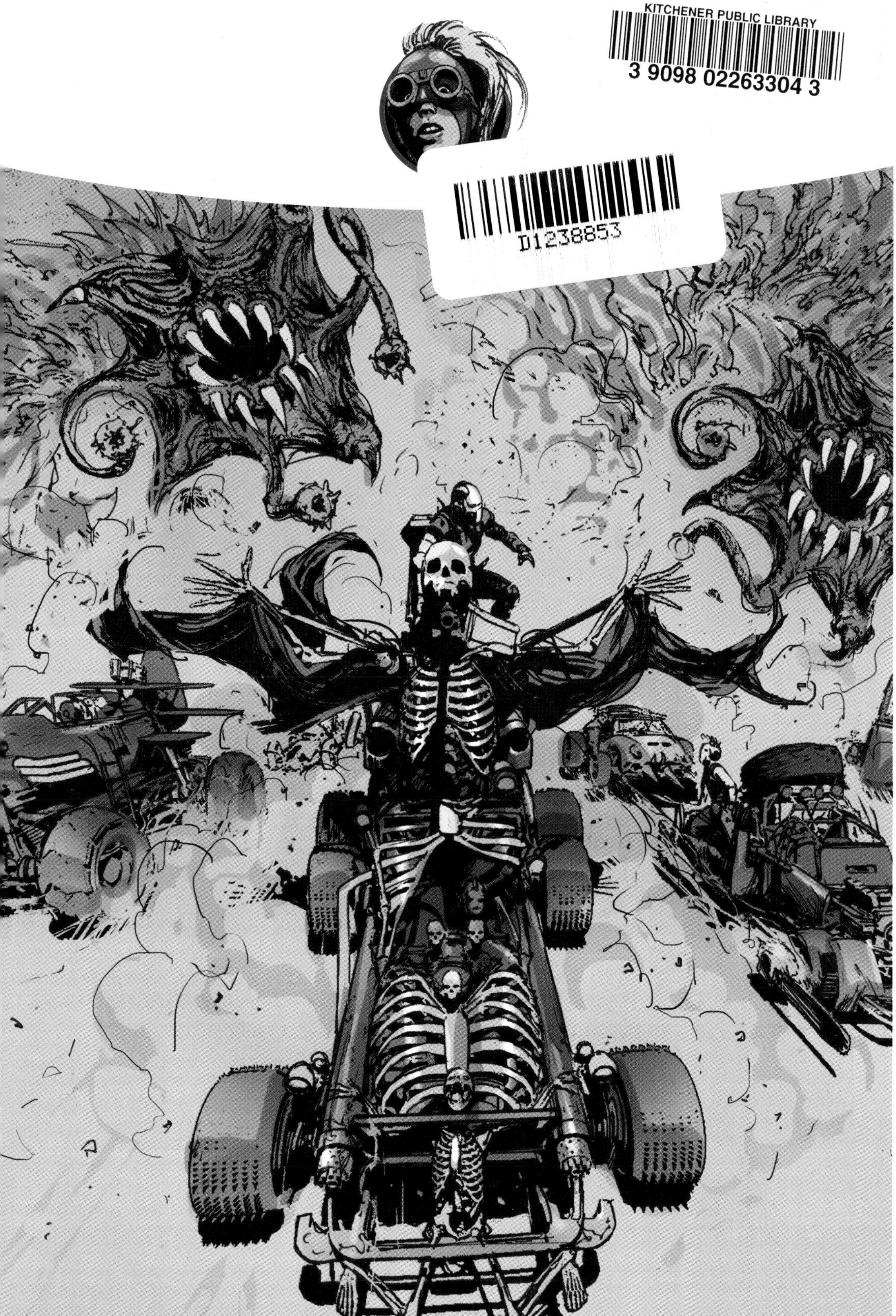

WACKY RACELAND

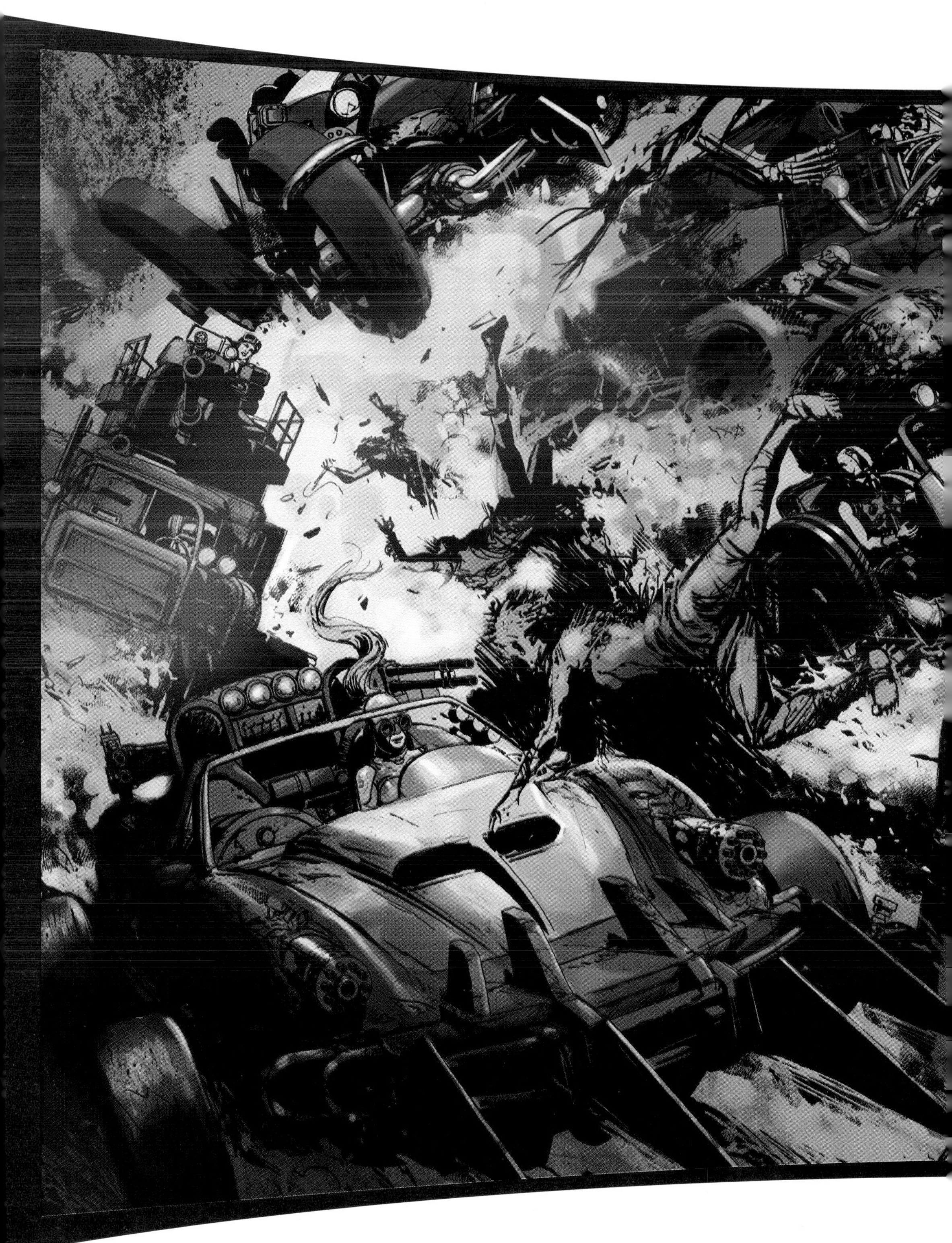

WACKY RACELAND

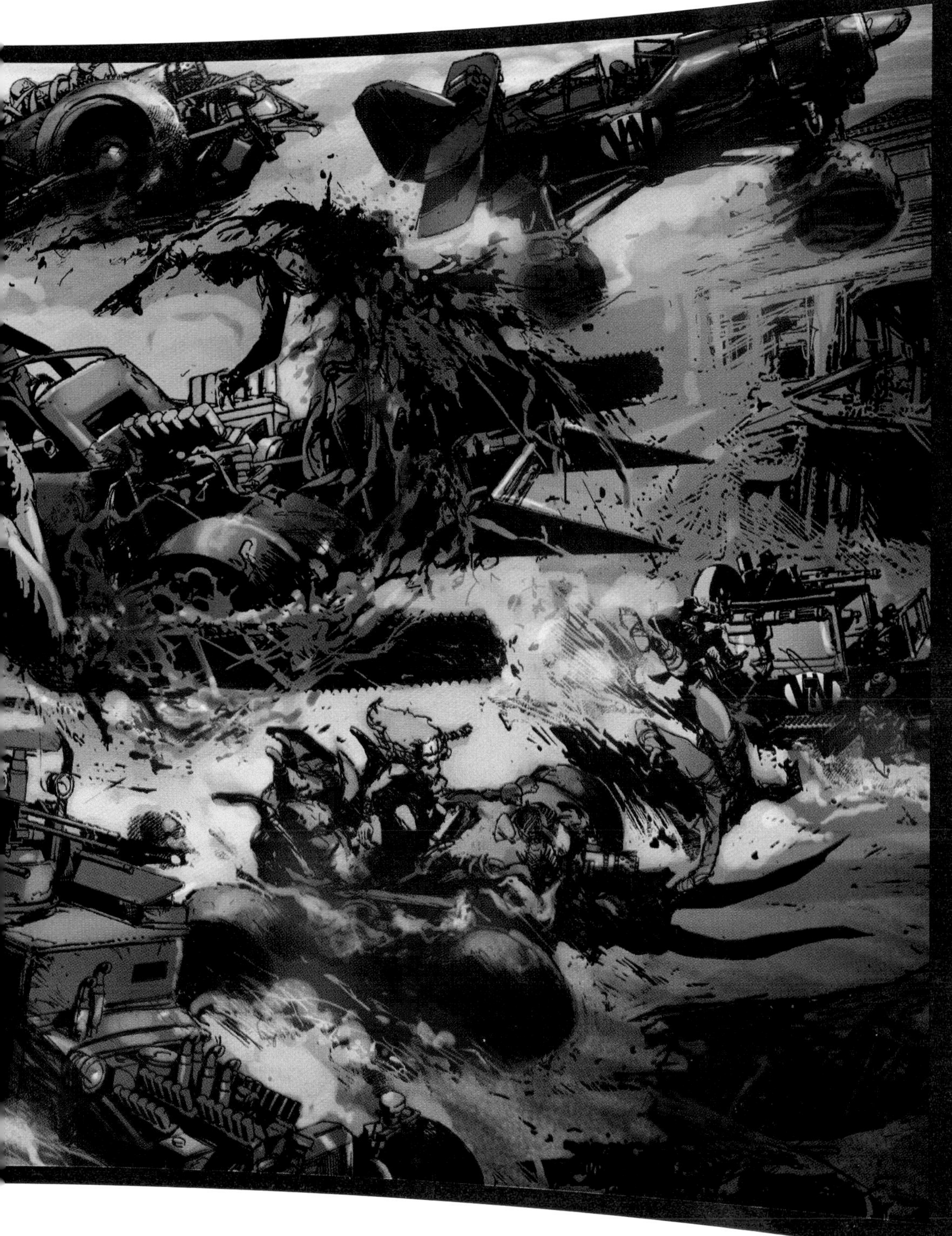

KEN PONTAC writer
LEONARDO MANCO artist
MARIANA SANZONE colorist
SAL CIPRIANO letterer
collection and original series cover art by **LEONARDO MANCO**
initial concepts by **MARK SEXTON**
designs by **LEONARDO MANCO**

MARIE JAVINS Editor - Original Series BRITTANY HOLZHERR Assistant Editor - Original Series
JEB WOODARD Group Editor - Collected Editions ERIKA ROTHBERG Editor - Collected Edition
STEVE COOK Design Director - Books LOUIS PRANDI Publication Design

BOB HARRAS Senior VP - Editor-in-Chief, DC Comics

DIANE NELSON President DAN DiDIO Publisher JIM LEE Publisher GEOFF JOHNS President & Chief Creative Officer
AMIT DESAI Executive VP - Business & Marketing Strategy, Direct to Consumer & Global Franchise Management
SAM ADES Senior VP - Direct to Consumer BOBBIE CHASE VP - Talent Development
MARK CHIARELLO Senior VP - Art, Design & Collected Editions JOHN CUNNINGHAM Senior VP - Sales & Trade Marketing
ANNE DePIES Senior VP - Business Strategy, Finance & Administration DON FALLETTI VP - Manufacturing Operations
LAWRENCE GANEM VP - Editorial Administration & Talent Relations ALISON GILL Senior VP - Manufacturing & Operations
HANK KANALZ Senior VP - Editorial Strategy & Administration JAY KOGAN VP - Legal Affairs THOMAS LOFTUS VP - Business Affairs
JACK MAHAN VP - Business Affairs NICK J. NAPOLITANO VP - Manufacturing Administration
EDDIE SCANNELL VP - Consumer Marketing COURTNEY SIMMONS Senior VP - Publicity & Communications
JIM (SKI) SOKOLOWSKI VP - Comic Book Specialty Sales & Trade Marketing NANCY SPEARS VP - Mass, Book, Digital Sales & Trade Marketing

WACKY RACELAND

DC Comics, 2900 West Alameda Ave., Burbank, CA 91505
Printed by Vanguard Graphics, LLC, Ithaca, NY, USA. 2/3/17. First Printing.
ISBN: 978-1-4012-6827-5
Library of Congress Cataloging-in-Publication Data is available.

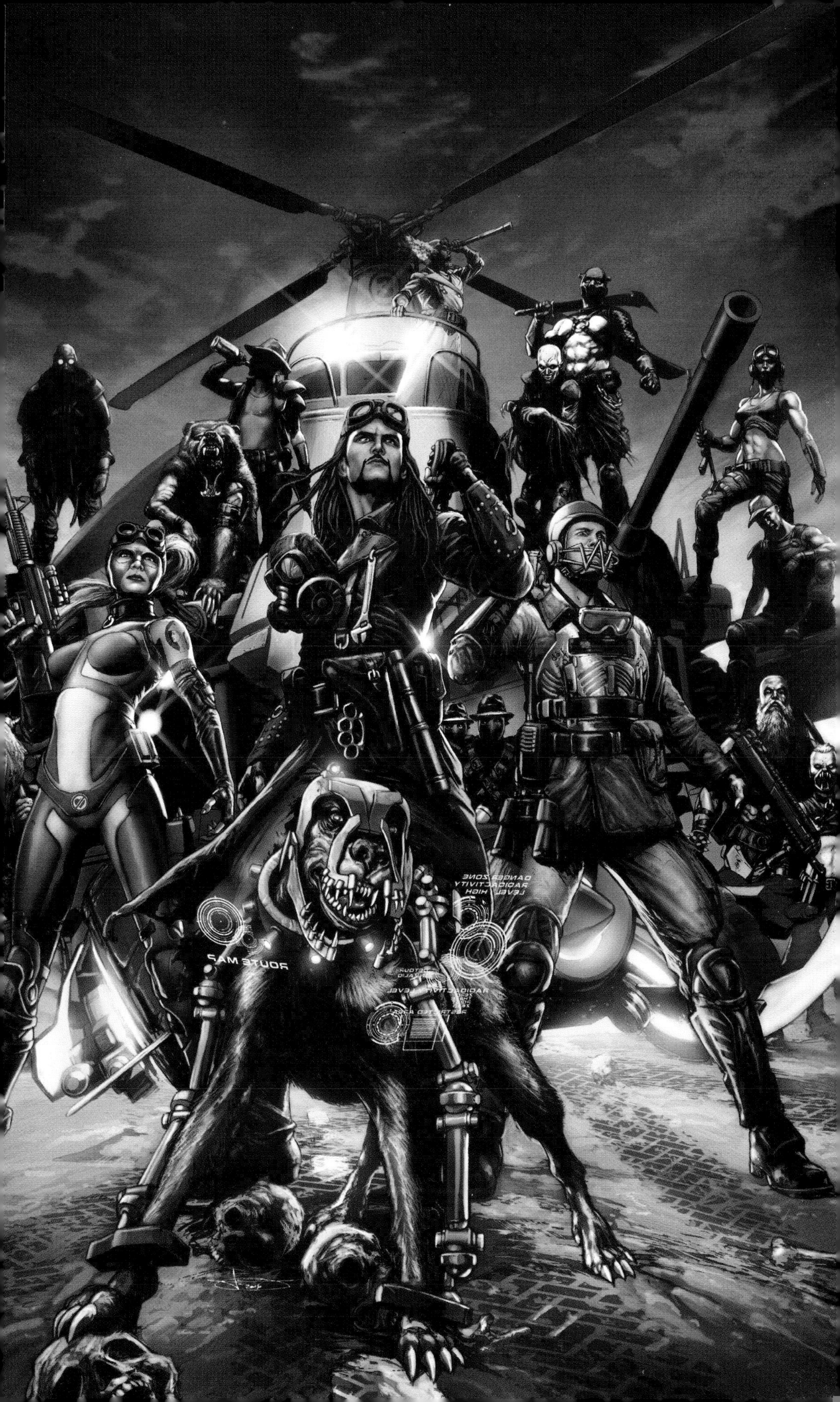
DANGER ZONE
RADIOACTIVITY
LEVEL HIGH
ROUTE MAP

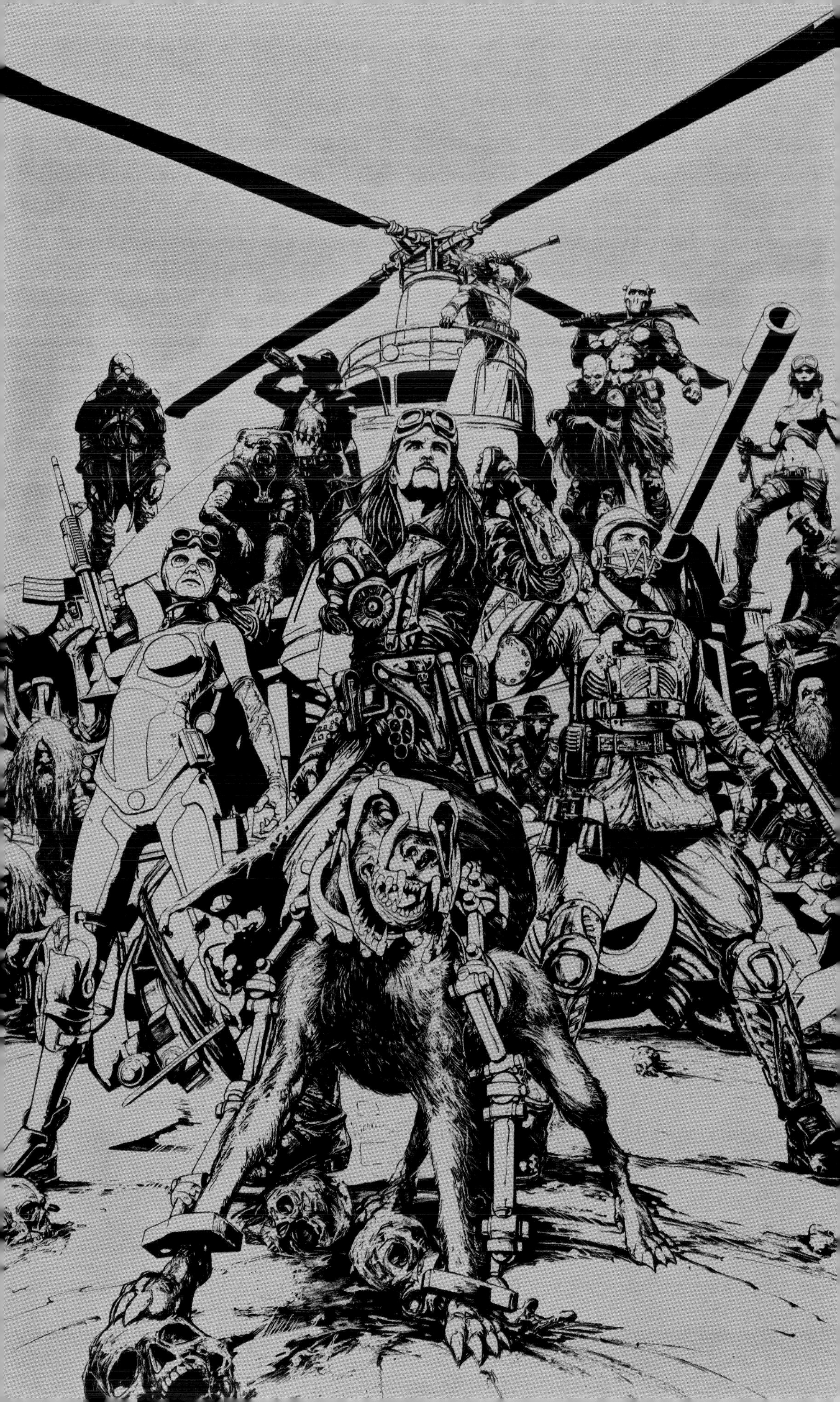

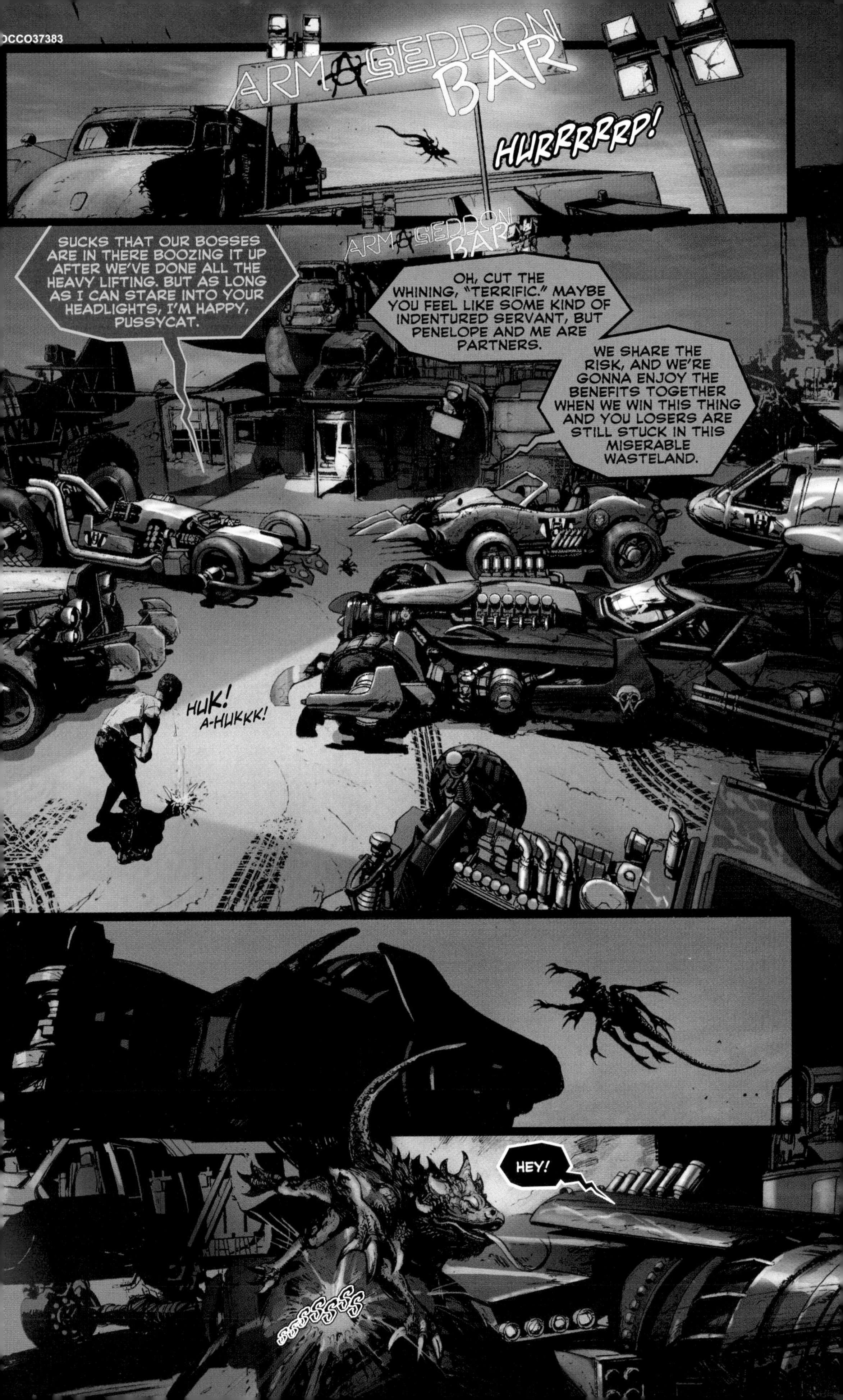
ARMAGEDDON BAR
HURRRRRP!
ARMAGEDDON BAR
SUCKS THAT OUR BOSSES ARE IN THERE BOOZING IT UP AFTER WE'VE DONE ALL THE HEAVY LIFTING. BUT AS LONG AS I CAN STARE INTO YOUR HEADLIGHTS, I'M HAPPY, PUSSYCAT.
OH, CUT THE WHINING, "TERRIFIC." MAYBE YOU FEEL LIKE SOME KIND OF INDENTURED SERVANT, BUT PENELOPE AND ME ARE PARTNERS.
WE SHARE THE RISK, AND WE'RE GONNA ENJOY THE BENEFITS TOGETHER WHEN WE WIN THIS THING AND YOU LOSERS ARE STILL STUCK IN THIS MISERABLE WASTELAND.
HUK! A-HUKKK!
HEY!
SSSSSSS

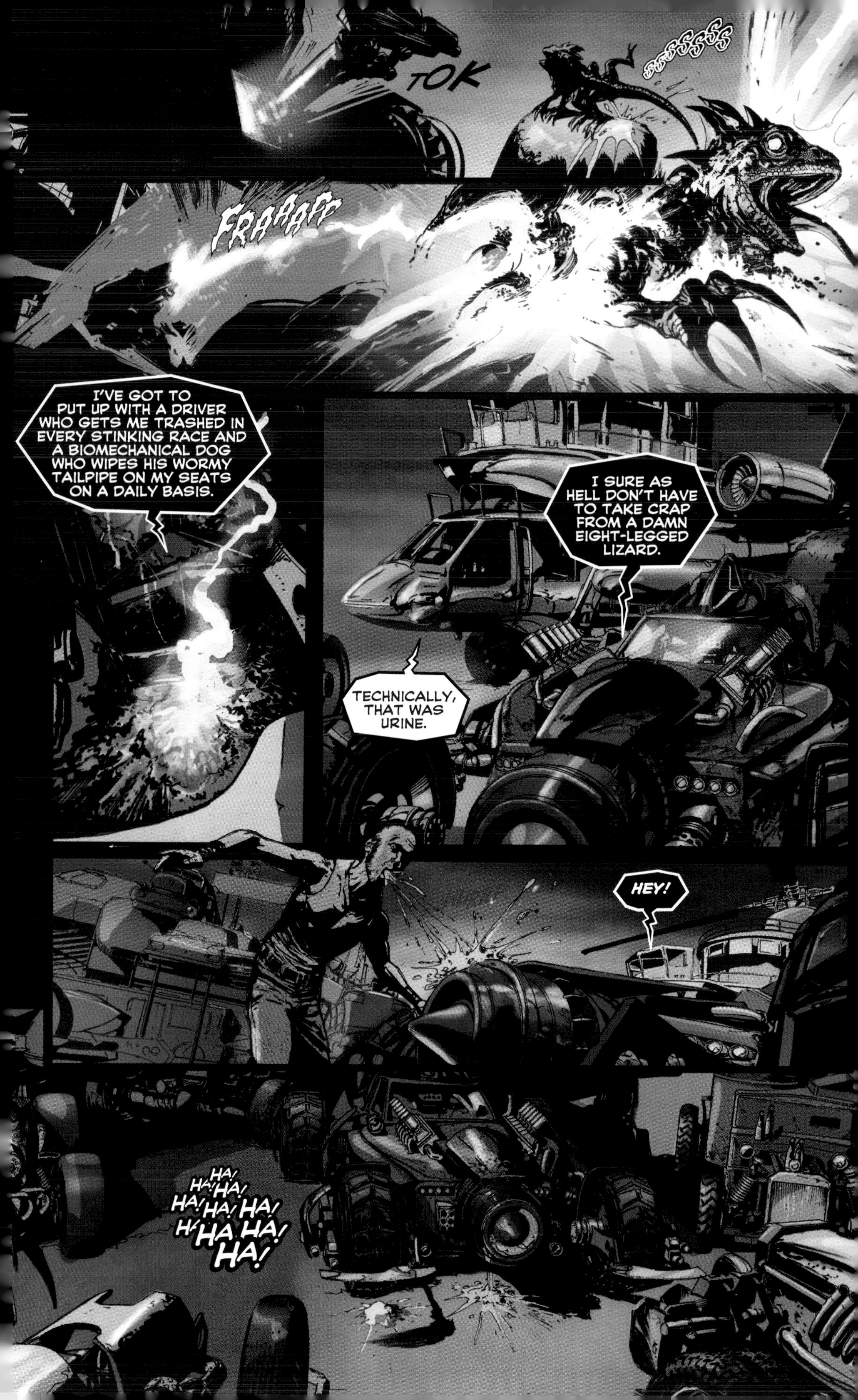
TOK
SSSSSSS
FRAAAPP
I'VE GOT TO PUT UP WITH A DRIVER WHO GETS ME TRASHED IN EVERY STINKING RACE AND A BIOMECHANICAL DOG WHO WIPES HIS WORMY TAILPIPE ON MY SEATS ON A DAILY BASIS.
I SURE AS HELL DON'T HAVE TO TAKE CRAP FROM A DAMN EIGHT-LEGGED LIZARD.
TECHNICALLY, THAT WAS URINE.
HEY!
HA! HA! HA! HA! HA! HA! H! HA! HA! HA!

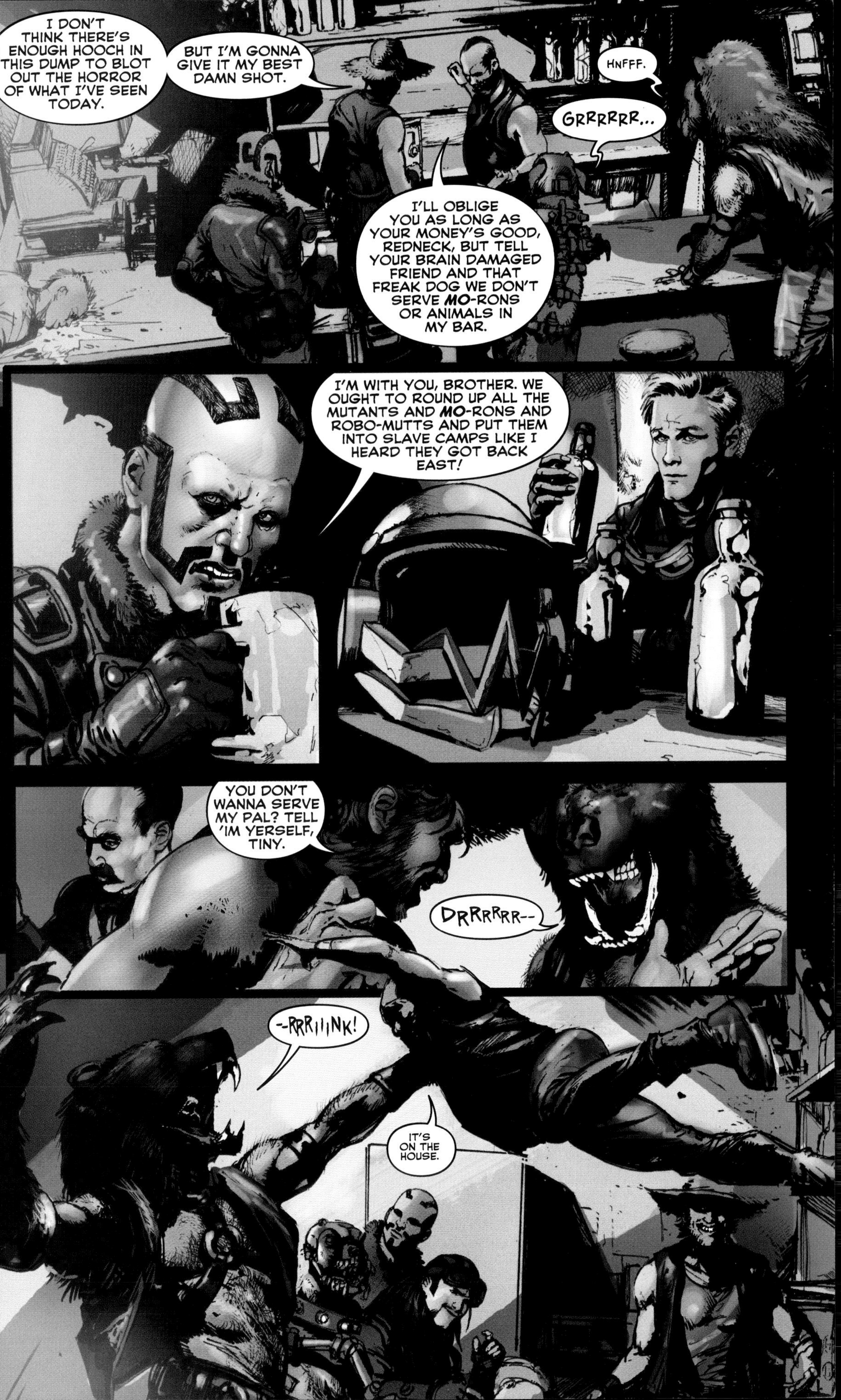
I DON'T THINK THERE'S ENOUGH HOOCH IN THIS DUMP TO BLOT OUT THE HORROR OF WHAT I'VE SEEN TODAY.
BUT I'M GONNA GIVE IT MY BEST DAMN SHOT.
HNFFF.
GRRRRRR...
I'LL OBLIGE YOU AS LONG AS YOUR MONEY'S GOOD, REDNECK, BUT TELL YOUR BRAIN DAMAGED FRIEND AND THAT FREAK DOG WE DON'T SERVE MO-RONS OR ANIMALS IN MY BAR.
I'M WITH YOU, BROTHER. WE OUGHT TO ROUND UP ALL THE MUTANTS AND MO-RONS AND ROBO-MUTTS AND PUT THEM INTO SLAVE CAMPS LIKE I HEARD THEY GOT BACK EAST!
YOU DON'T WANNA SERVE MY PAL? TELL 'IM YERSELF, TINY.
DRRRRRR--
--RRRIIINK!
IT'S ON THE HOUSE.

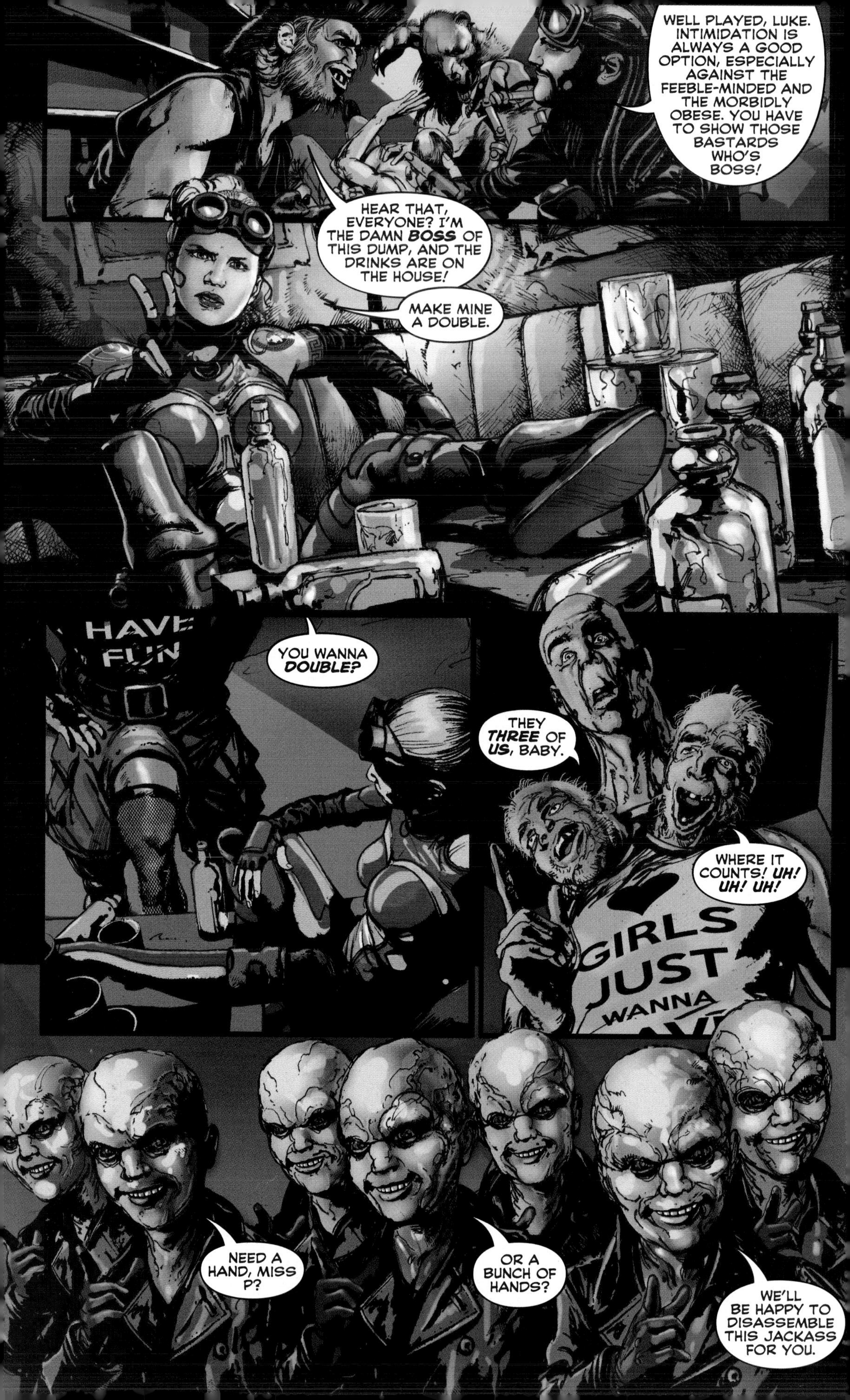
WELL PLAYED, LUKE. INTIMIDATION IS ALWAYS A GOOD OPTION, ESPECIALLY AGAINST THE FEEBLE-MINDED AND THE MORBIDLY OBESE. YOU HAVE TO SHOW THOSE BASTARDS WHO'S BOSS!
HEAR THAT, EVERYONE? I'M THE DAMN **BOSS** OF THIS DUMP, AND THE DRINKS ARE ON THE HOUSE!
MAKE MINE A DOUBLE.
HAVE FUN
YOU WANNA **DOUBLE?**
THEY **THREE** OF **US**, BABY.
WHERE IT COUNTS! **UH! UH! UH!**
GIRLS JUST WANNA
NEED A HAND, MISS P?
OR A BUNCH OF HANDS?
WE'LL BE HAPPY TO DISASSEMBLE THIS JACKASS FOR YOU.

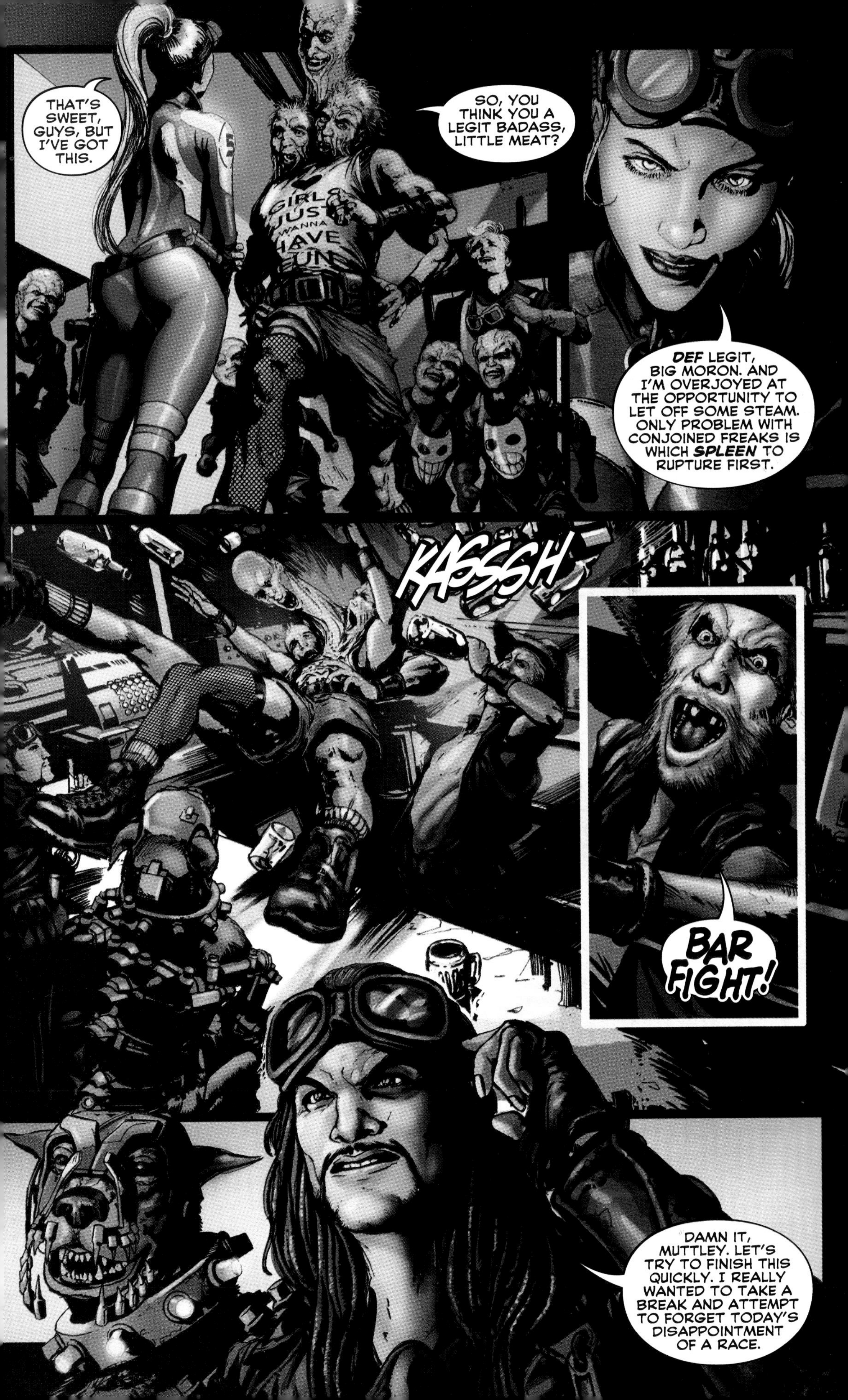
THAT'S SWEET, GUYS, BUT I'VE GOT THIS.
SO, YOU THINK YOU A LEGIT BADASS, LITTLE MEAT?
GIRLS JUST WANNA HAVE FUN
DEF LEGIT, BIG MORON. AND I'M OVERJOYED AT THE OPPORTUNITY TO LET OFF SOME STEAM. ONLY PROBLEM WITH CONJOINED FREAKS IS WHICH SPLEEN TO RUPTURE FIRST.
KASSSH
BAR FIGHT!
DAMN IT, MUTTLEY. LET'S TRY TO FINISH THIS QUICKLY. I REALLY WANTED TO TAKE A BREAK AND ATTEMPT TO FORGET TODAY'S DISAPPOINTMENT OF A RACE.

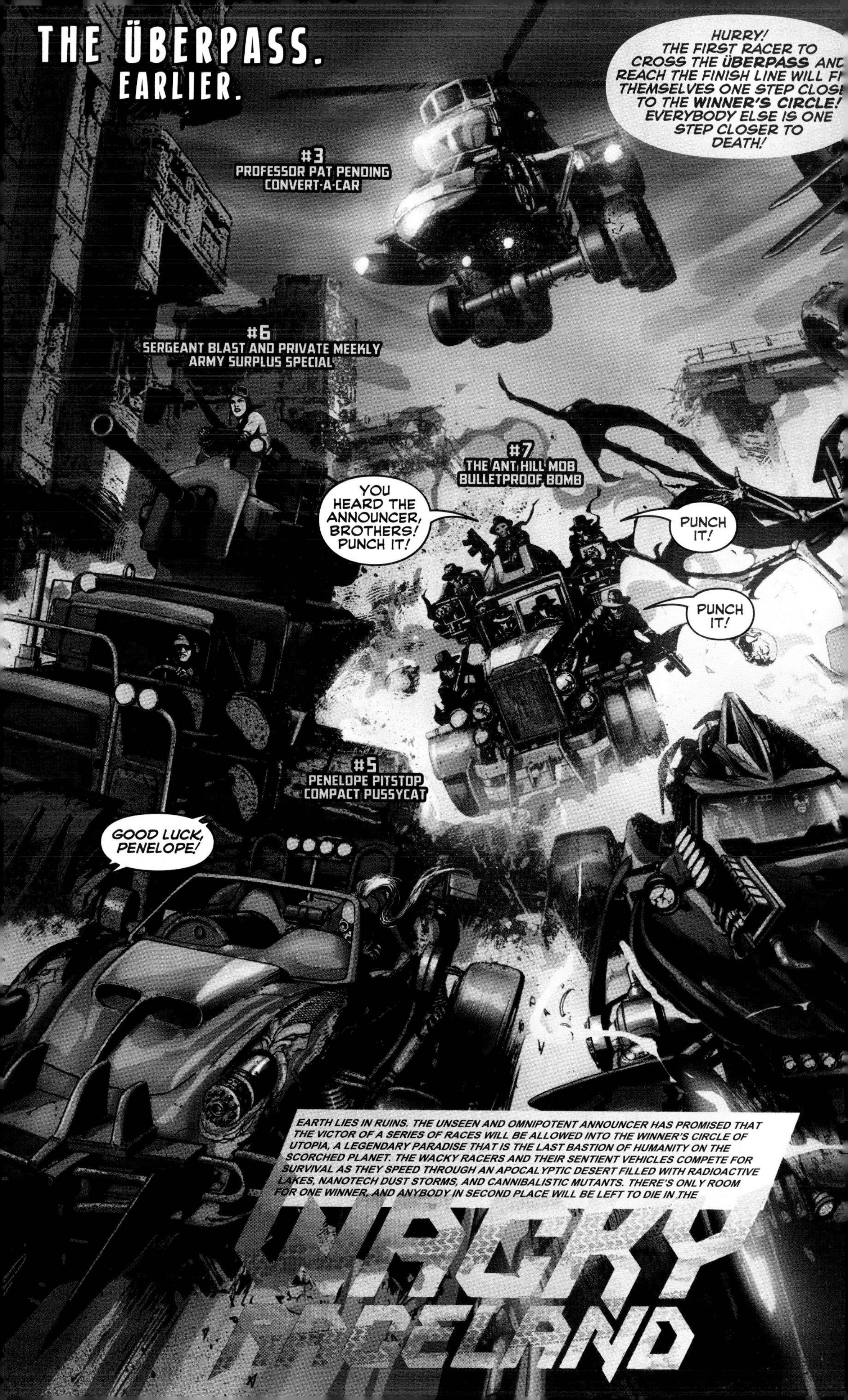

THE ÜBERPASS. EARLIER.
HURRY! THE FIRST RACER TO CROSS THE ÜBERPASS AN REACH THE FINISH LINE WILL FI THEMSELVES ONE STEP CLOSE TO THE WINNER'S CIRCLE! EVERYBODY ELSE IS ONE STEP CLOSER TO DEATH!
#3 PROFESSOR PAT PENDING CONVERT-A-CAR
#6 SERGEANT BLAST AND PRIVATE MEEKLY ARMY SURPLUS SPECIAL
#7 THE ANT HILL MOB BULLETPROOF BOMB
YOU HEARD THE ANNOUNCER, BROTHERS! PUNCH IT!
PUNCH IT!
PUNCH IT!
#5 PENELOPE PITSTOP COMPACT PUSSYCAT
GOOD LUCK, PENELOPE!
EARTH LIES IN RUINS. THE UNSEEN AND OMNIPOTENT ANNOUNCER HAS PROMISED THAT THE VICTOR OF A SERIES OF RACES WILL BE ALLOWED INTO THE WINNER'S CIRCLE OF UTOPIA, A LEGENDARY PARADISE THAT IS THE LAST BASTION OF HUMANITY ON THE SCORCHED PLANET. THE WACKY RACERS AND THEIR SENTIENT VEHICLES COMPETE FOR SURVIVAL AS THEY SPEED THROUGH AN APOCALYPTIC DESERT FILLED WITH RADIOACTIVE LAKES, NANOTECH DUST STORMS, AND CANNIBALISTIC MUTANTS. THERE'S ONLY ROOM FOR ONE WINNER, AND ANYBODY IN SECOND PLACE WILL BE LEFT TO DIE IN THE
WACKY RACELAND

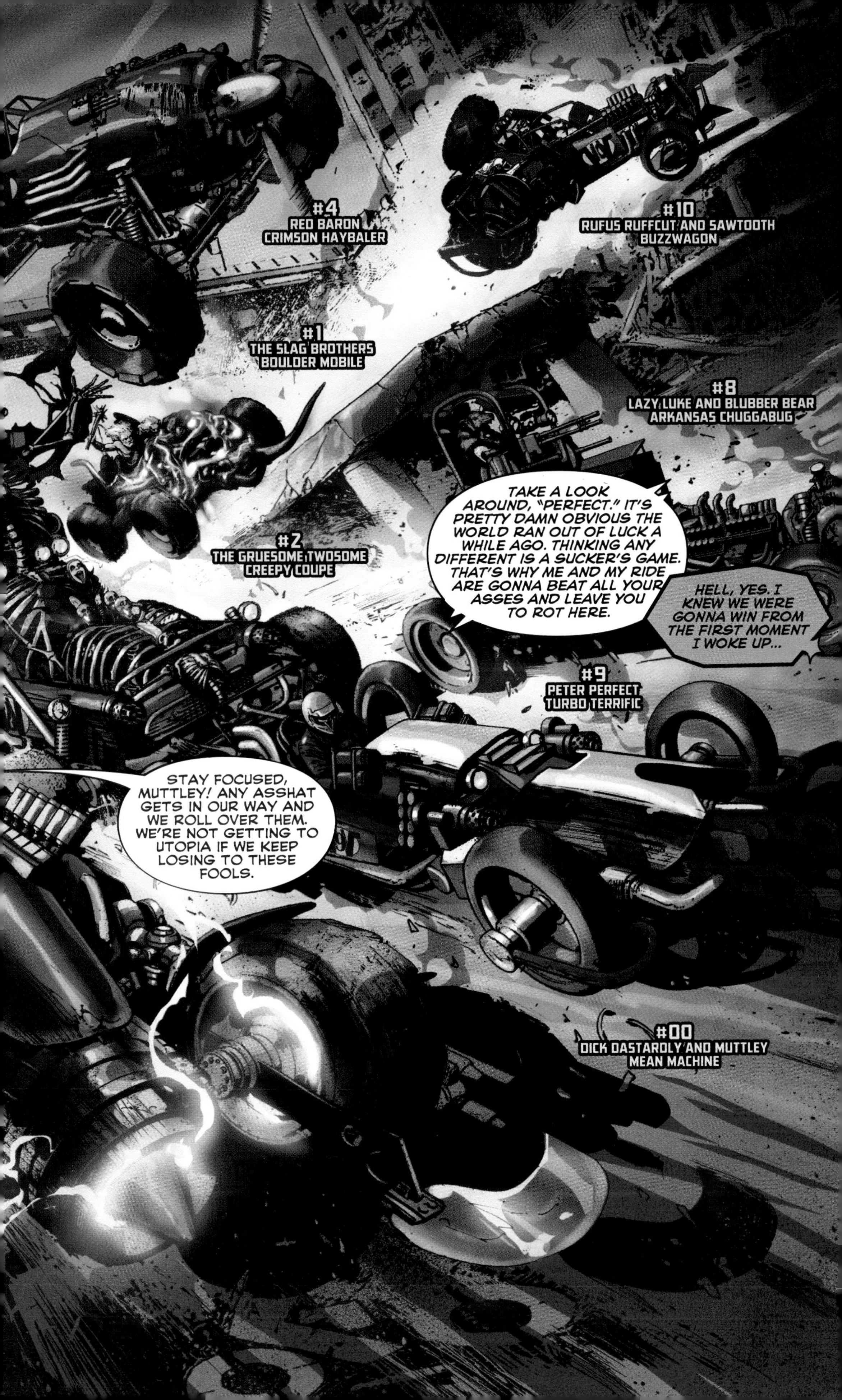

#4
RED BARON
CRIMSON HAYBALER
#10
RUFUS RUFFCUT AND SAWTOOTH
BUZZWAGON
#1
THE SLAG BROTHERS
BOULDER MOBILE
#8
LAZY LUKE AND BLUBBER BEAR
ARKANSAS CHUGGABUG
#2
THE GRUESOME TWOSOME
CREEPY COUPE
TAKE A LOOK AROUND, "PERFECT." IT'S PRETTY DAMN OBVIOUS THE WORLD RAN OUT OF LUCK A WHILE AGO. THINKING ANY DIFFERENT IS A SUCKER'S GAME. THAT'S WHY ME AND MY RIDE ARE GONNA BEAT ALL YOUR ASSES AND LEAVE YOU TO ROT HERE.
HELL, YES. I KNEW WE WERE GONNA WIN FROM THE FIRST MOMENT I WOKE UP...
#9
PETER PERFECT
TURBO TERRIFIC
STAY FOCUSED, MUTTLEY! ANY ASSHAT GETS IN OUR WAY AND WE ROLL OVER THEM. WE'RE NOT GETTING TO UTOPIA IF WE KEEP LOSING TO THESE FOOLS.
#00
DICK DASTARDLY AND MUTTLEY
MEAN MACHINE

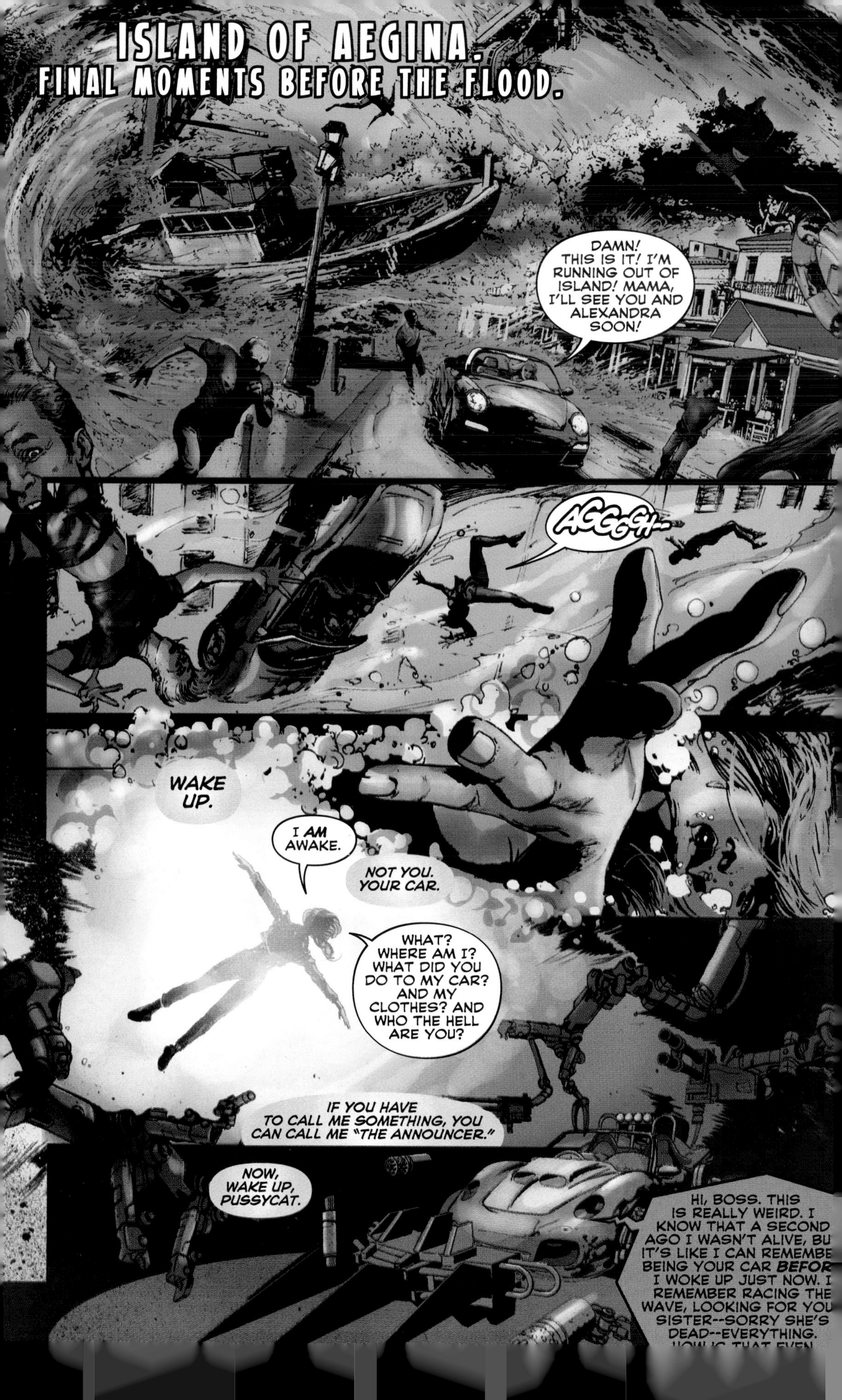
ISLAND OF AEGINA.
FINAL MOMENTS BEFORE THE FLOOD.
DAMN! THIS IS IT! I'M RUNNING OUT OF ISLAND! MAMA, I'LL SEE YOU AND ALEXANDRA SOON!
AGGGGH--
WAKE UP.
I AM AWAKE.
NOT YOU. YOUR CAR.
WHAT? WHERE AM I? WHAT DID YOU DO TO MY CAR? AND MY CLOTHES? AND WHO THE HELL ARE YOU?
IF YOU HAVE TO CALL ME SOMETHING, YOU CAN CALL ME "THE ANNOUNCER."
NOW, WAKE UP, PUSSYCAT.
HI, BOSS. THIS IS REALLY WEIRD. I KNOW THAT A SECOND AGO I WASN'T ALIVE, BU IT'S LIKE I CAN REMEMBE BEING YOUR CAR BEFOR I WOKE UP JUST NOW. I REMEMBER RACING THE WAVE, LOOKING FOR YOU SISTER--SORRY SHE'S DEAD--EVERYTHING.

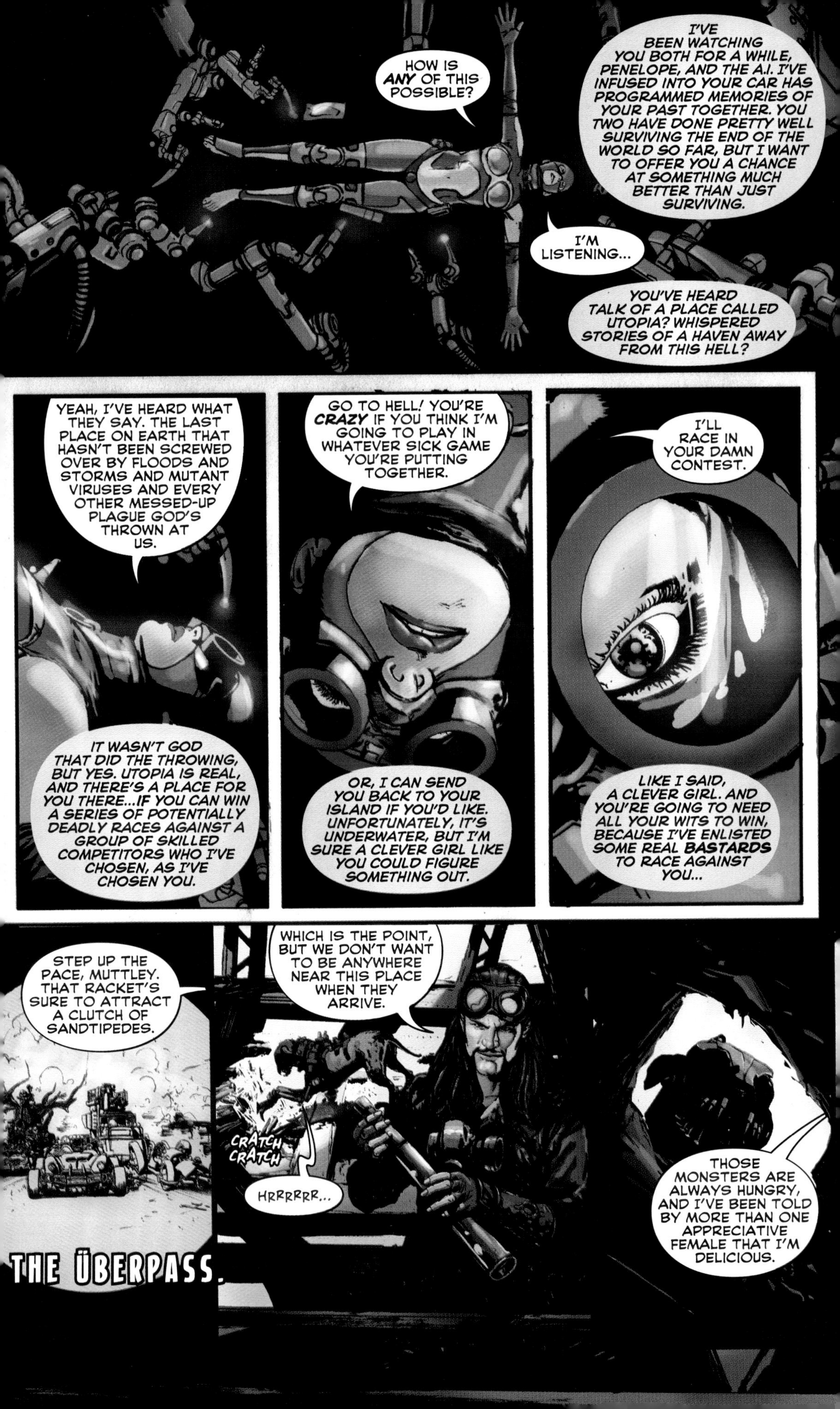
HOW IS ANY OF THIS POSSIBLE?
I'VE BEEN WATCHING YOU BOTH FOR A WHILE, PENELOPE, AND THE A.I. I'VE INFUSED INTO YOUR CAR HAS PROGRAMMED MEMORIES OF YOUR PAST TOGETHER. YOU TWO HAVE DONE PRETTY WELL SURVIVING THE END OF THE WORLD SO FAR, BUT I WANT TO OFFER YOU A CHANCE AT SOMETHING MUCH BETTER THAN JUST SURVIVING.
I'M LISTENING...
YOU'VE HEARD TALK OF A PLACE CALLED UTOPIA? WHISPERED STORIES OF A HAVEN AWAY FROM THIS HELL?
YEAH, I'VE HEARD WHAT THEY SAY. THE LAST PLACE ON EARTH THAT HASN'T BEEN SCREWED OVER BY FLOODS AND STORMS AND MUTANT VIRUSES AND EVERY OTHER MESSED-UP PLAGUE GOD'S THROWN AT US.
IT WASN'T GOD THAT DID THE THROWING, BUT YES. UTOPIA IS REAL, AND THERE'S A PLACE FOR YOU THERE...IF YOU CAN WIN A SERIES OF POTENTIALLY DEADLY RACES AGAINST A GROUP OF SKILLED COMPETITORS WHO I'VE CHOSEN, AS I'VE CHOSEN YOU.
GO TO HELL! YOU'RE CRAZY IF YOU THINK I'M GOING TO PLAY IN WHATEVER SICK GAME YOU'RE PUTTING TOGETHER.
OR, I CAN SEND YOU BACK TO YOUR ISLAND IF YOU'D LIKE. UNFORTUNATELY, IT'S UNDERWATER, BUT I'M SURE A CLEVER GIRL LIKE YOU COULD FIGURE SOMETHING OUT.
I'LL RACE IN YOUR DAMN CONTEST.
LIKE I SAID, A CLEVER GIRL. AND YOU'RE GOING TO NEED ALL YOUR WITS TO WIN, BECAUSE I'VE ENLISTED SOME REAL BASTARDS TO RACE AGAINST YOU...
THE ÜBERPASS.
STEP UP THE PACE, MUTTLEY. THAT RACKET'S SURE TO ATTRACT A CLUTCH OF SANDTIPEDES.
WHICH IS THE POINT, BUT WE DON'T WANT TO BE ANYWHERE NEAR THIS PLACE WHEN THEY ARRIVE.
CRATCH CRATCH
HRRRRRR...
THOSE MONSTERS ARE ALWAYS HUNGRY, AND I'VE BEEN TOLD BY MORE THAN ONE APPRECIATIVE FEMALE THAT I'M DELICIOUS.

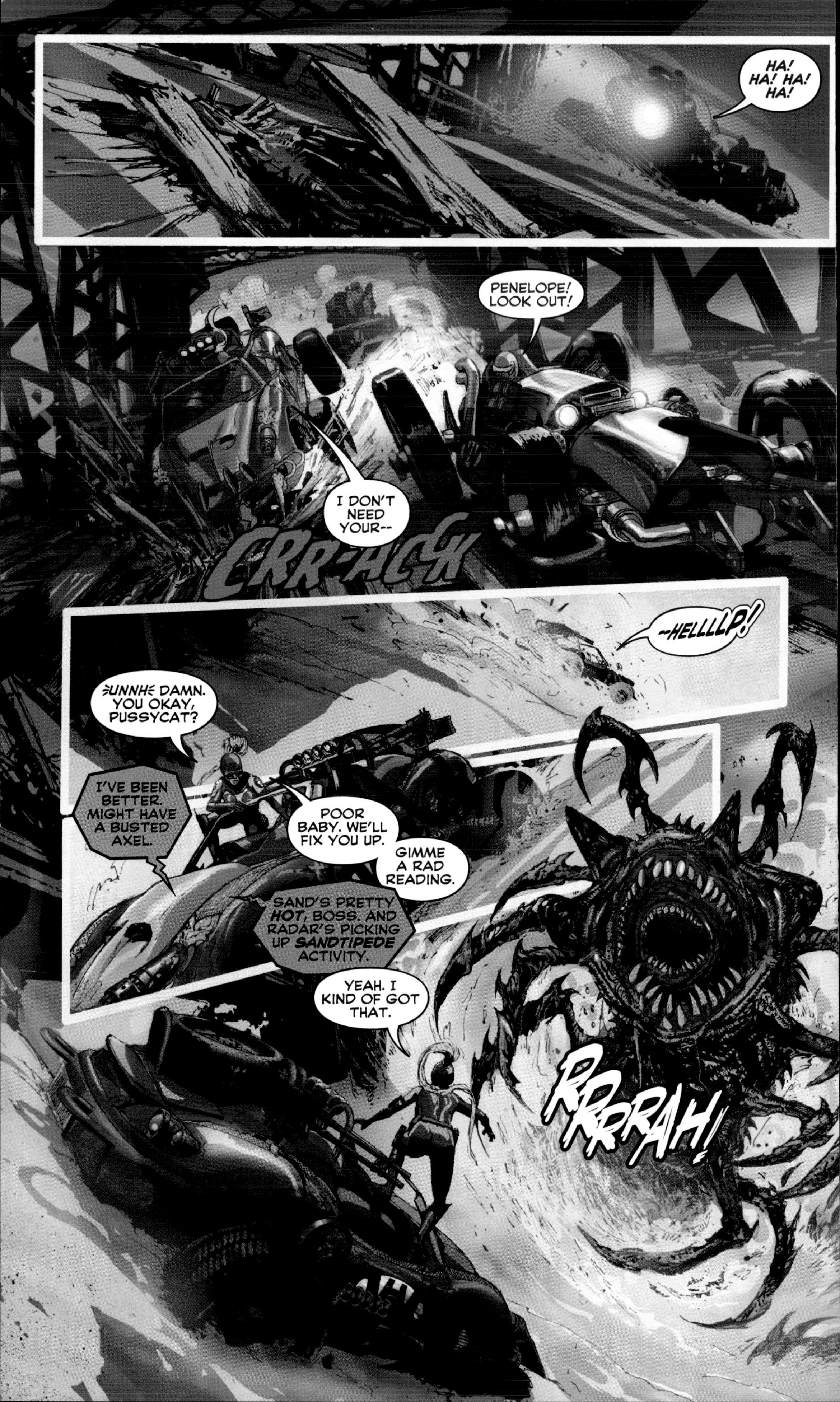
HA! HA! HA! HA!
PENELOPE! LOOK OUT!
I DON'T NEED YOUR--
CRR-ACK
--HELLLLLP!
UNNH DAMN. YOU OKAY, PUSSYCAT?
I'VE BEEN BETTER. MIGHT HAVE A BUSTED AXEL.
POOR BABY. WE'LL FIX YOU UP.
GIMME A RAD READING.
SAND'S PRETTY HOT, BOSS. AND RADAR'S PICKING UP SANDTIPEDE ACTIVITY.
YEAH. I KIND OF GOT THAT.
RRRRRAH!

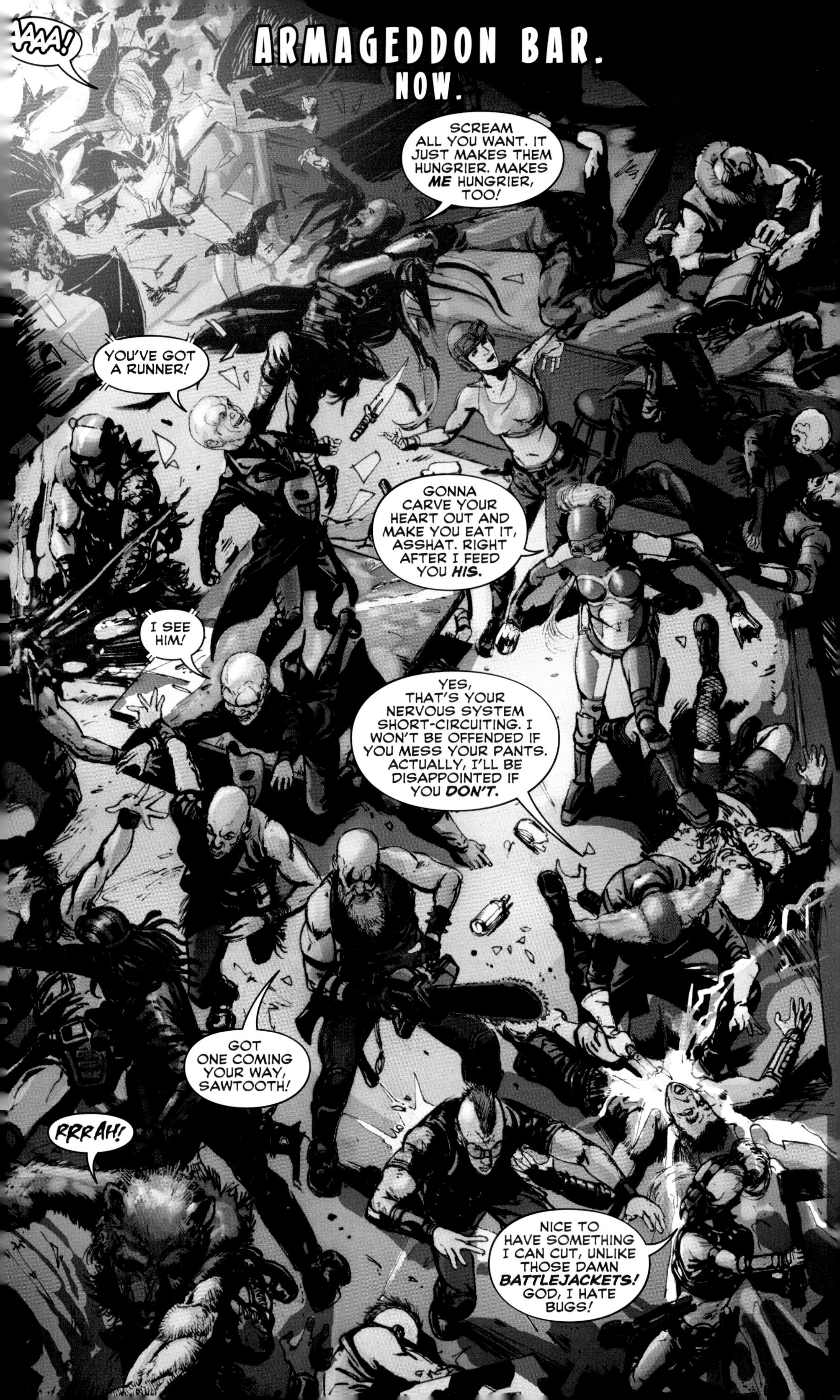
AAAA!
ARMAGEDDON BAR.
NOW.
SCREAM ALL YOU WANT. IT JUST MAKES THEM HUNGRIER. MAKES ME HUNGRIER, TOO!
YOU'VE GOT A RUNNER!
GONNA CARVE YOUR HEART OUT AND MAKE YOU EAT IT, ASSHAT. RIGHT AFTER I FEED YOU HIS.
I SEE HIM!
YES, THAT'S YOUR NERVOUS SYSTEM SHORT-CIRCUITING. I WON'T BE OFFENDED IF YOU MESS YOUR PANTS. ACTUALLY, I'LL BE DISAPPOINTED IF YOU DON'T.
GOT ONE COMING YOUR WAY, SAWTOOTH!
RRRAH!
NICE TO HAVE SOMETHING I CAN CUT, UNLIKE THOSE DAMN BATTLEJACKETS! GOD, I HATE BUGS!

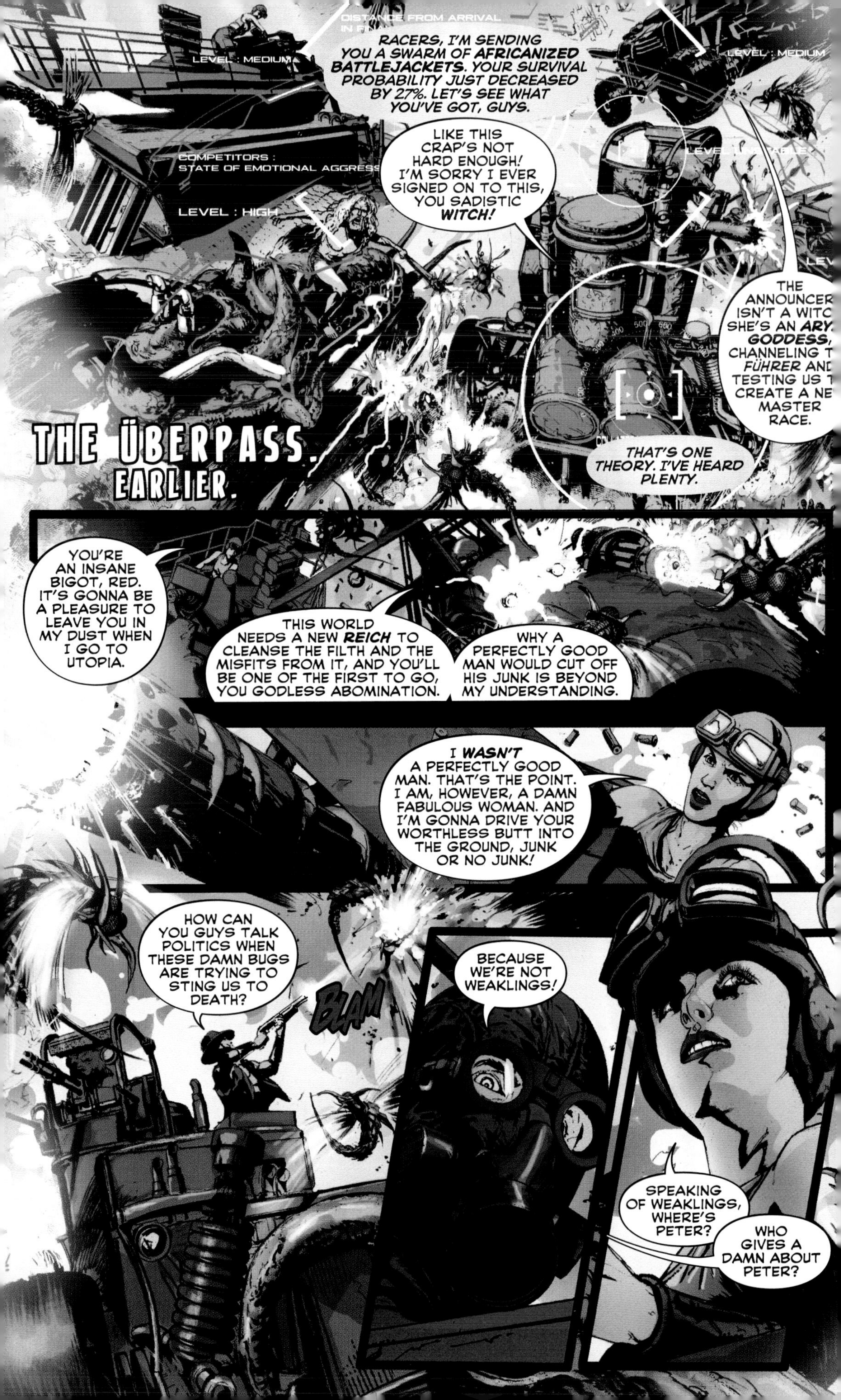

DISTANCE FROM ARRIVAL
LEVEL : MEDIUM
RACERS, I'M SENDING YOU A SWARM OF AFRICANIZED BATTLEJACKETS. YOUR SURVIVAL PROBABILITY JUST DECREASED BY 27%. LET'S SEE WHAT YOU'VE GOT, GUYS.
LEVEL : MEDIUM
COMPETITORS :
STATE OF EMOTIONAL AGGRESS
LEVEL : HIGH
LIKE THIS CRAP'S NOT HARD ENOUGH! I'M SORRY I EVER SIGNED ON TO THIS, YOU SADISTIC WITCH!
THE ANNOUNCER ISN'T A WITC SHE'S AN ARY GODDESS, CHANNELING T FÜHRER AND TESTING US T CREATE A NE MASTER RACE.
THAT'S ONE THEORY. I'VE HEARD PLENTY.
THE ÜBERPASS. EARLIER.
YOU'RE AN INSANE BIGOT, RED. IT'S GONNA BE A PLEASURE TO LEAVE YOU IN MY DUST WHEN I GO TO UTOPIA.
THIS WORLD NEEDS A NEW REICH TO CLEANSE THE FILTH AND THE MISFITS FROM IT, AND YOU'LL BE ONE OF THE FIRST TO GO, YOU GODLESS ABOMINATION.
WHY A PERFECTLY GOOD MAN WOULD CUT OFF HIS JUNK IS BEYOND MY UNDERSTANDING.
I WASN'T A PERFECTLY GOOD MAN. THAT'S THE POINT. I AM, HOWEVER, A DAMN FABULOUS WOMAN. AND I'M GONNA DRIVE YOUR WORTHLESS BUTT INTO THE GROUND, JUNK OR NO JUNK!
HOW CAN YOU GUYS TALK POLITICS WHEN THESE DAMN BUGS ARE TRYING TO STING US TO DEATH?
BLAM
BECAUSE WE'RE NOT WEAKLINGS!
SPEAKING OF WEAKLINGS, WHERE'S PETER?
WHO GIVES A DAMN ABOUT PETER?

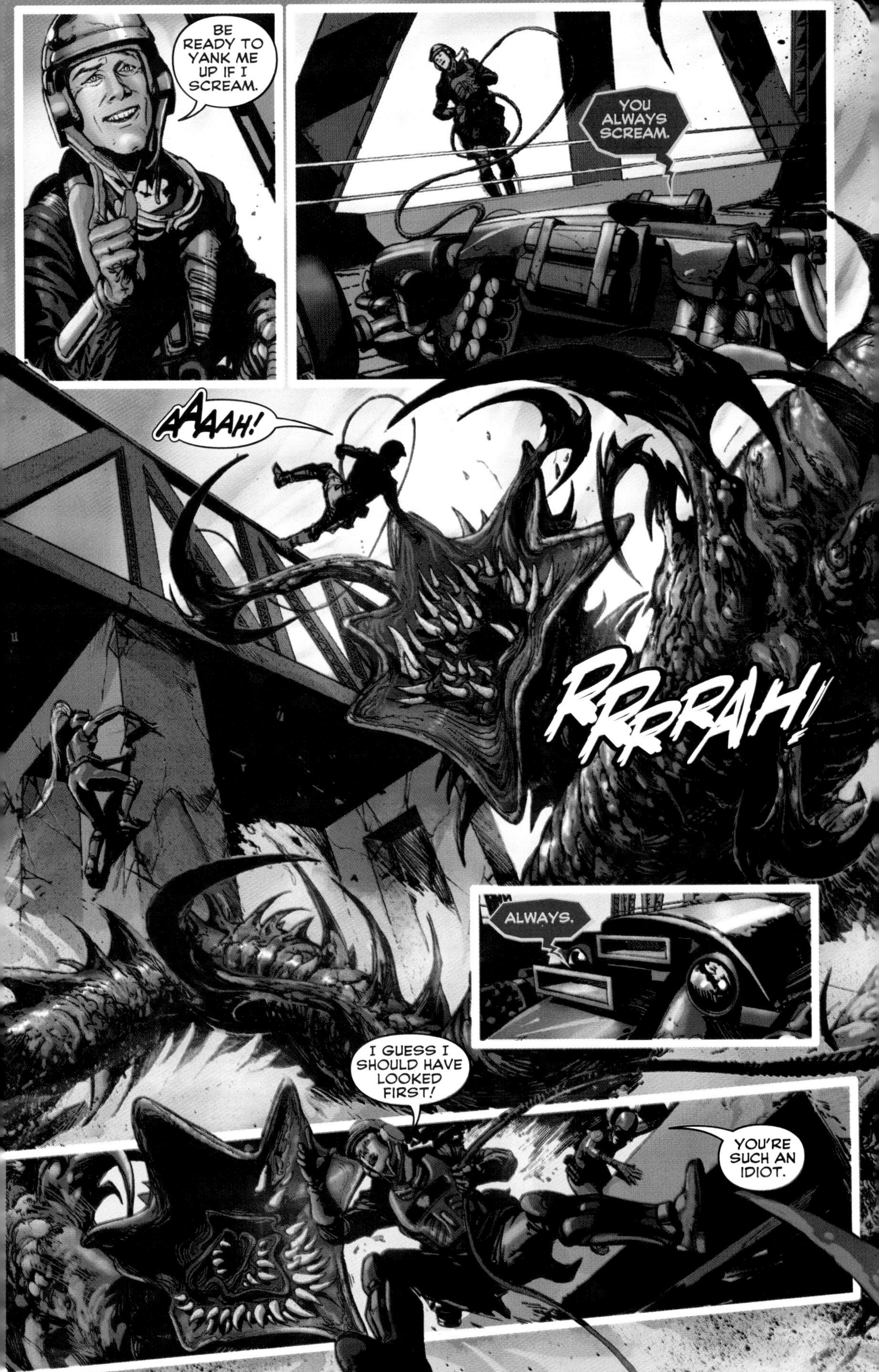
BE READY TO YANK ME UP IF I SCREAM.
YOU ALWAYS SCREAM.
AAAAH!
RRRRRAH!
ALWAYS.
I GUESS I SHOULD HAVE LOOKED FIRST!
YOU'RE SUCH AN IDIOT.

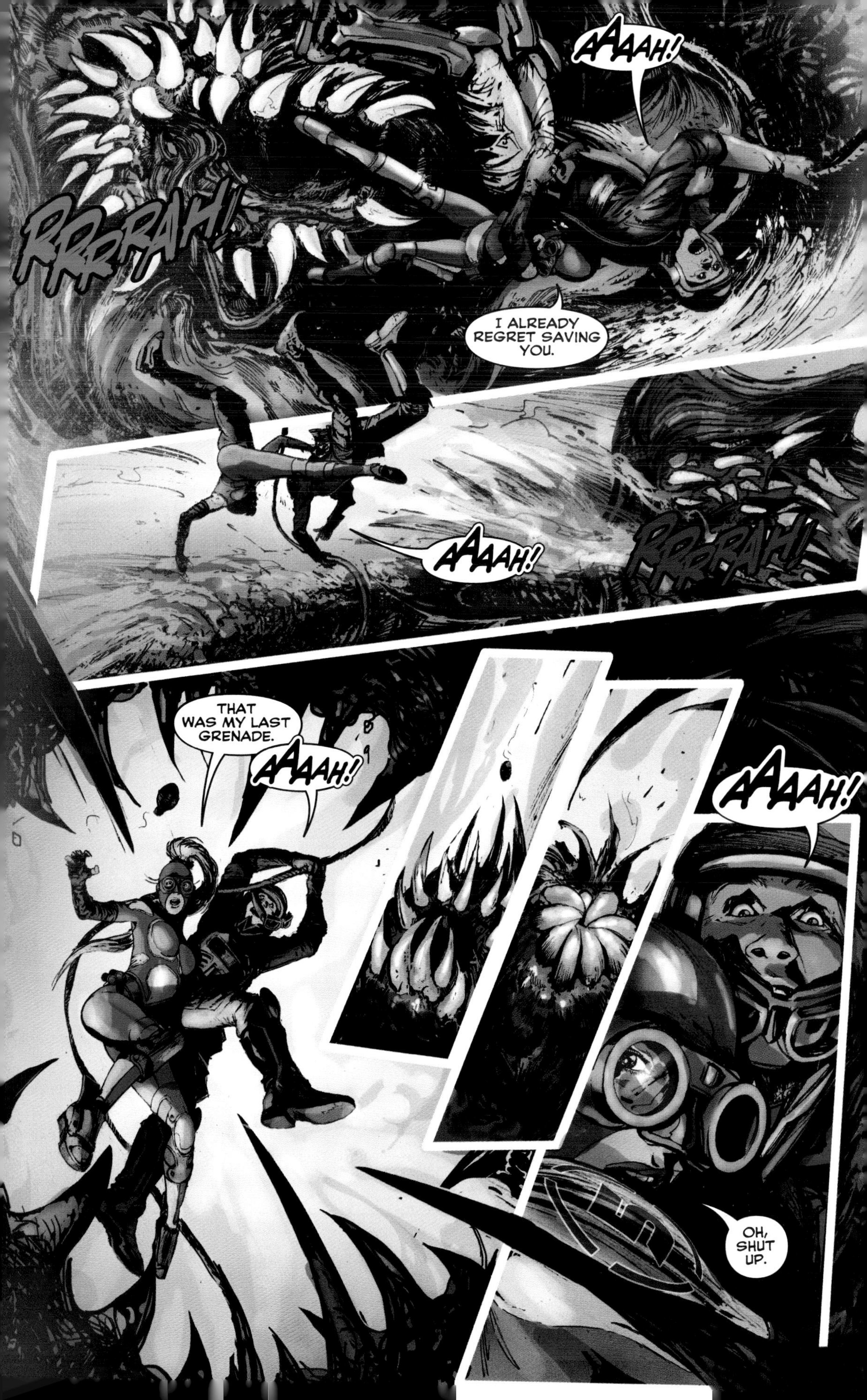
AAAAH!
RRRRAH!
I ALREADY REGRET SAVING YOU.
AAAAH!
RRRRAH!
THAT WAS MY LAST GRENADE.
AAAAH!
AAAAH!
OH, SHUT UP.

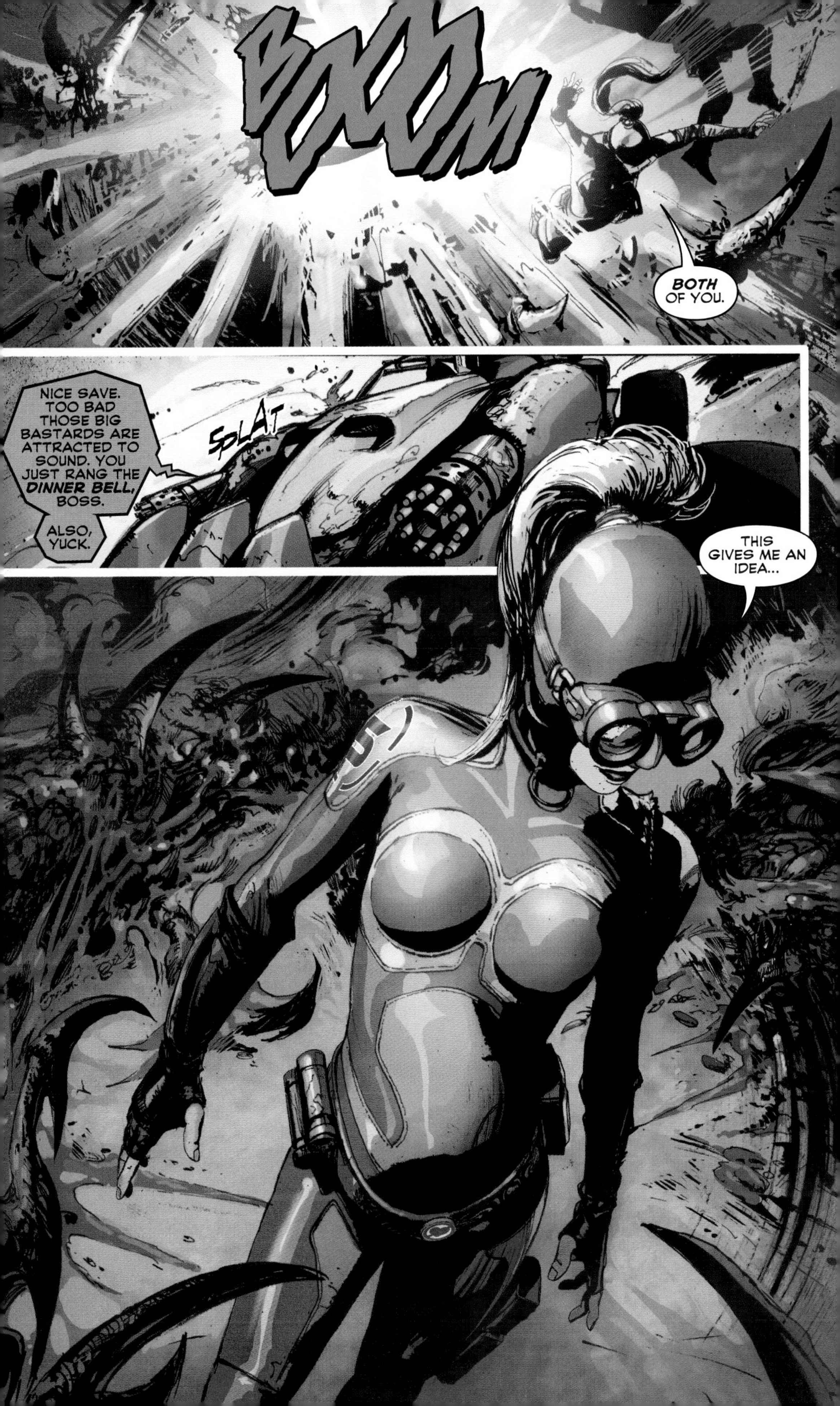
BOOM
BOTH OF YOU.
SPLAT
NICE SAVE. TOO BAD THOSE BIG BASTARDS ARE ATTRACTED TO SOUND. YOU JUST RANG THE DINNER BELL, BOSS.
ALSO, YUCK.
THIS GIVES ME AN IDEA...

CHOMP
NO DRINK FOR ME? YOU MEAT FOR MUTTLEY!
I'M SORRY! I'M SORRY!
ARMAGEDDON BAR
NOW.
THOSE BITES LOOK PRETTY DEEP, AND I KNOW THAT ANIMAL'S MOUTH IS FILTHY. YOU'RE GOING TO NEED A SHOT OR YOU'LL GET A NASTY INFECTION.
JAB
AARRRGH!
GOOD TO SEE SOMEBODY GETTING WHAT THEY DESERVE. UNLIKE US, HUH, MUTTLEY? WE WERE SO DAMN CLOSE...
HRRRRR...

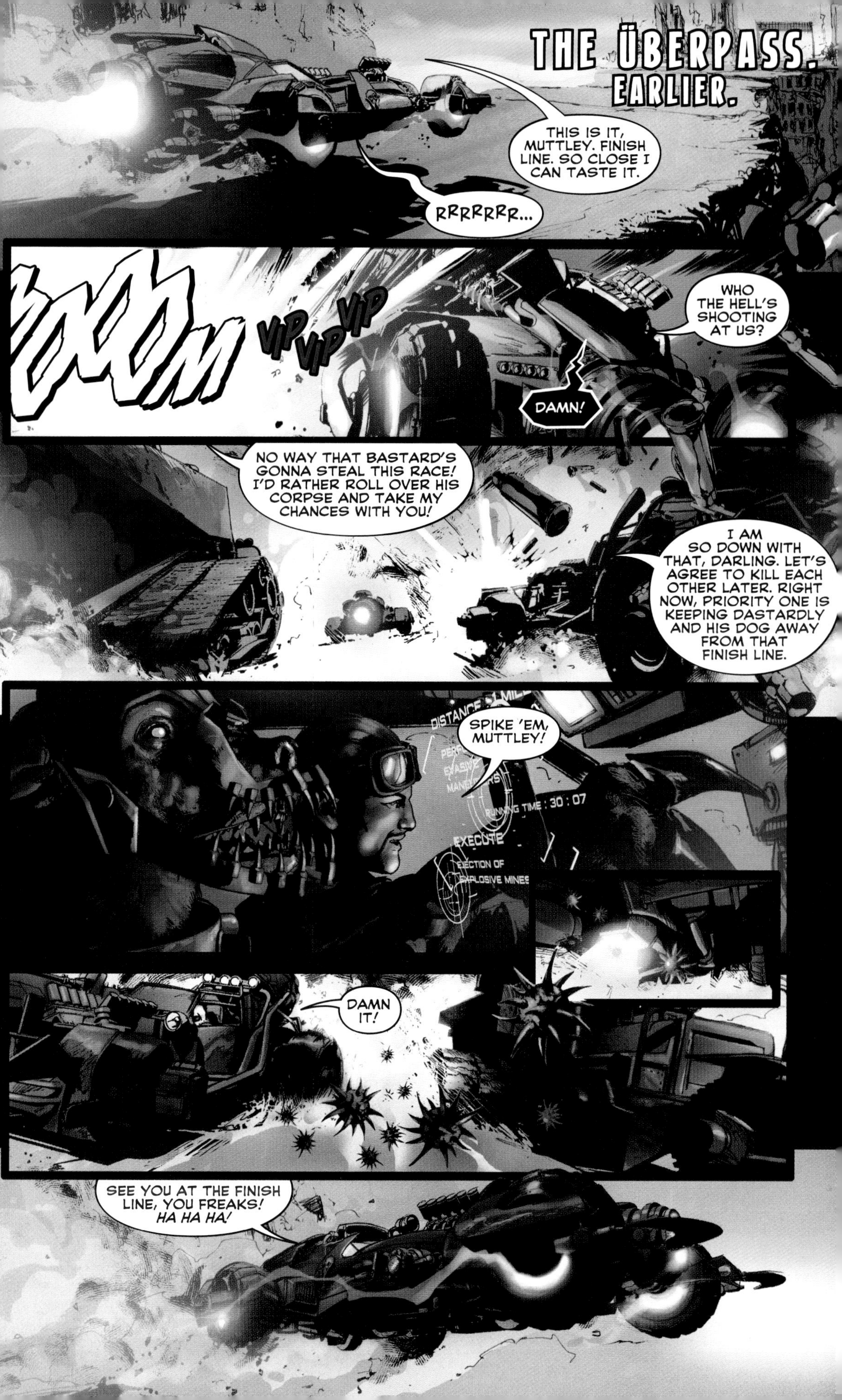
THE ÜBERPASS.
EARLIER.
THIS IS IT, MUTTLEY. FINISH LINE. SO CLOSE I CAN TASTE IT.
RRRRRRR...
VROOM
VIP VIP VIP
WHO THE HELL'S SHOOTING AT US?
DAMN!
NO WAY THAT BASTARD'S GONNA STEAL THIS RACE! I'D RATHER ROLL OVER HIS CORPSE AND TAKE MY CHANCES WITH YOU!
I AM SO DOWN WITH THAT, DARLING. LET'S AGREE TO KILL EACH OTHER LATER. RIGHT NOW, PRIORITY ONE IS KEEPING DASTARDLY AND HIS DOG AWAY FROM THAT FINISH LINE.
SPIKE 'EM, MUTTLEY!
EXECUTE
DAMN IT!
SEE YOU AT THE FINISH LINE, YOU FREAKS! HA HA HA!

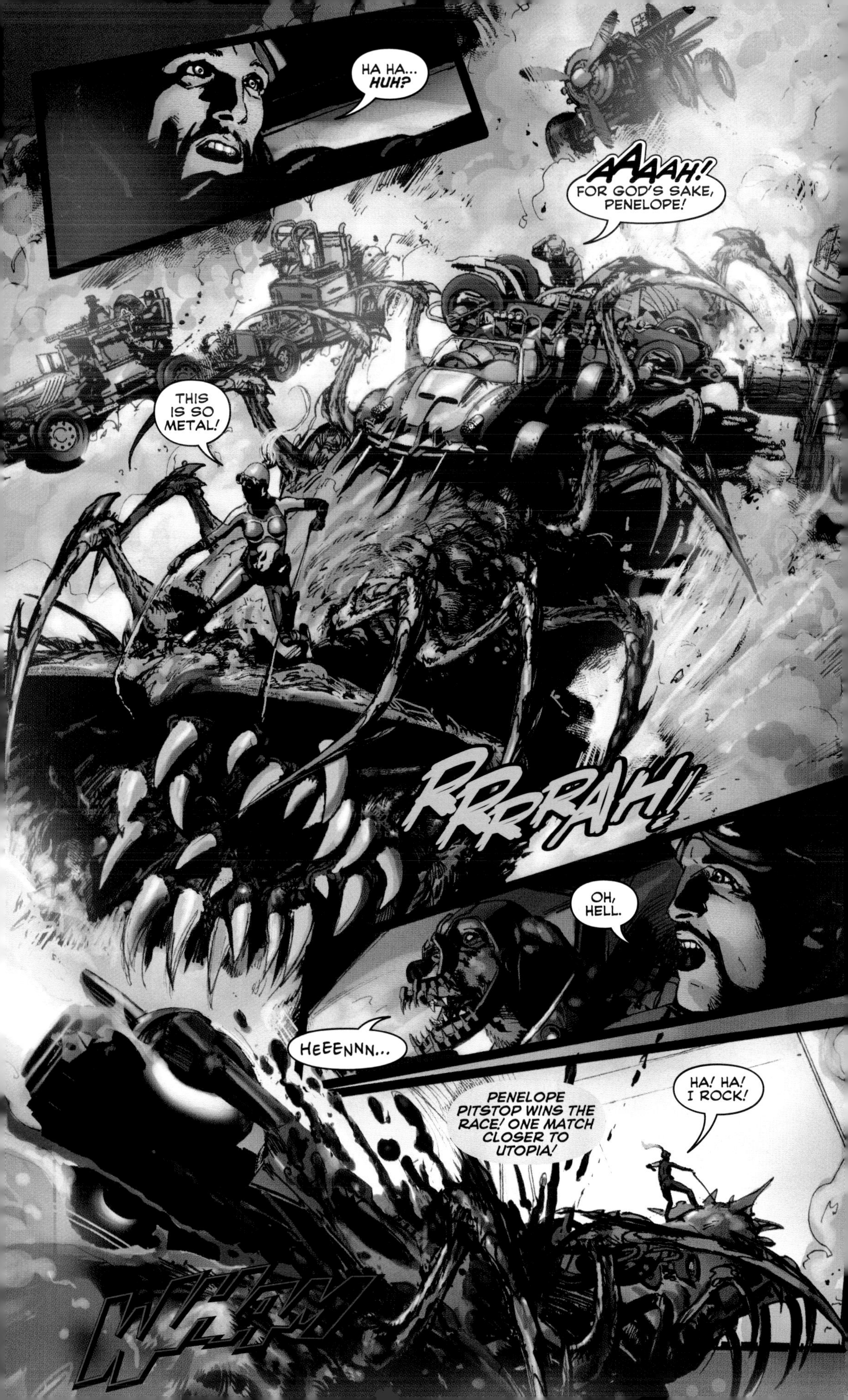

HA HA...
HUH?
AAAAH! FOR GOD'S SAKE, PENELOPE!
THIS IS SO METAL!
RRRRAAH!
OH, HELL.
HEEENNN...
PENELOPE PITSTOP WINS THE RACE! ONE MATCH CLOSER TO UTOPIA!
HA! HA! I ROCK!

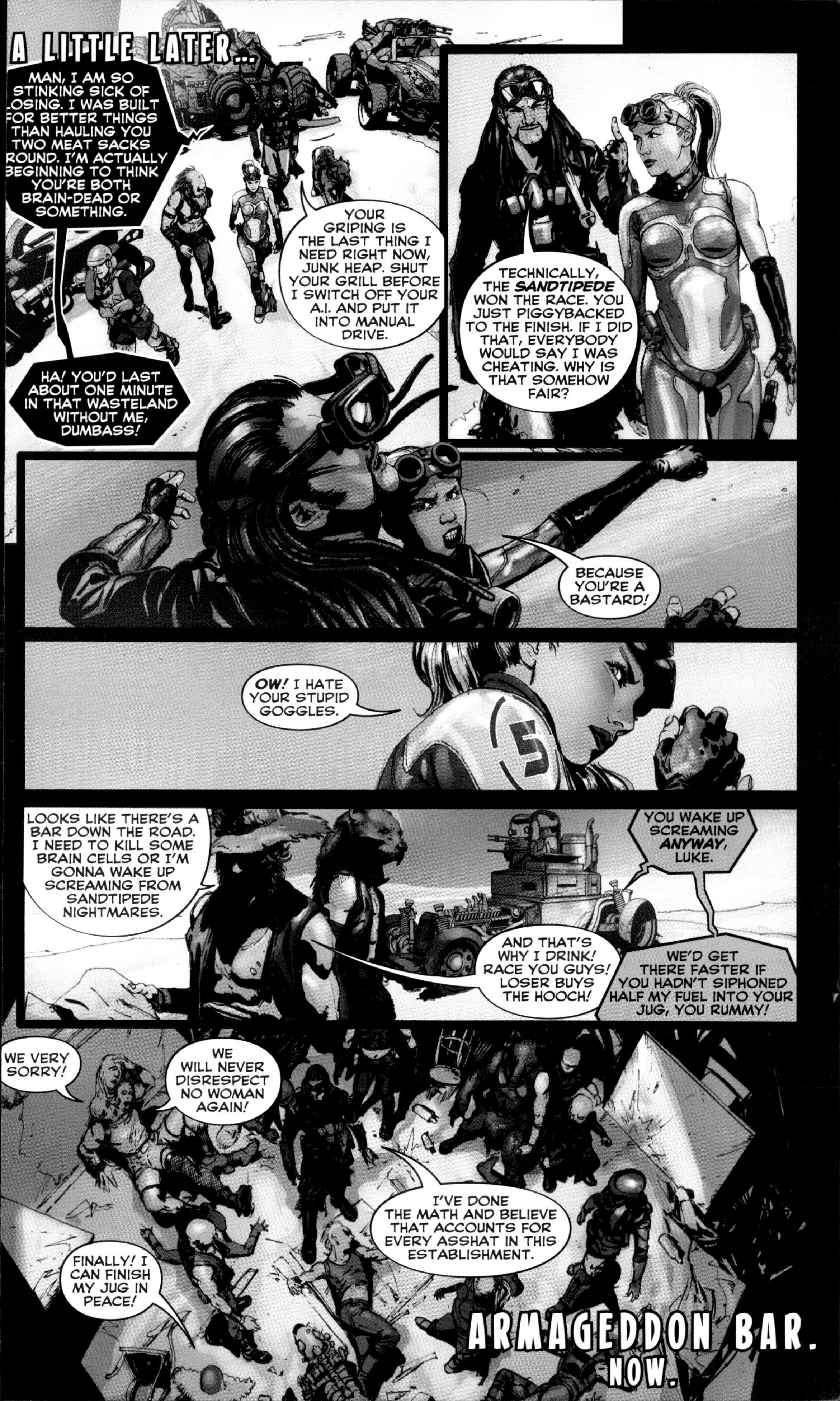
A LITTLE LATER...
MAN, I AM SO STINKING SICK OF LOSING. I WAS BUILT FOR BETTER THINGS THAN HAULING YOU TWO MEAT SACKS ROUND. I'M ACTUALLY BEGINNING TO THINK YOU'RE BOTH BRAIN-DEAD OR SOMETHING.
YOUR GRIPING IS THE LAST THING I NEED RIGHT NOW, JUNK HEAP. SHUT YOUR GRILL BEFORE I SWITCH OFF YOUR A.I. AND PUT IT INTO MANUAL DRIVE.
HA! YOU'D LAST ABOUT ONE MINUTE IN THAT WASTELAND WITHOUT ME, DUMBASS!
TECHNICALLY, THE SANDTIPEDE WON THE RACE. YOU JUST PIGGYBACKED TO THE FINISH. IF I DID THAT, EVERYBODY WOULD SAY I WAS CHEATING. WHY IS THAT SOMEHOW FAIR?
BECAUSE YOU'RE A BASTARD!
OW! I HATE YOUR STUPID GOGGLES.
LOOKS LIKE THERE'S A BAR DOWN THE ROAD. I NEED TO KILL SOME BRAIN CELLS OR I'M GONNA WAKE UP SCREAMING FROM SANDTIPEDE NIGHTMARES.
YOU WAKE UP SCREAMING ANYWAY, LUKE.
AND THAT'S WHY I DRINK! RACE YOU GUYS! LOSER BUYS THE HOOCH!
WE'D GET THERE FASTER IF YOU HADN'T SIPHONED HALF MY FUEL INTO YOUR JUG, YOU RUMMY!
WE VERY SORRY!
WE WILL NEVER DISRESPECT NO WOMAN AGAIN!
I'VE DONE THE MATH AND BELIEVE THAT ACCOUNTS FOR EVERY ASSHAT IN THIS ESTABLISHMENT.
FINALLY! I CAN FINISH MY JUG IN PEACE!
ARMAGEDDON BAR. NOW.

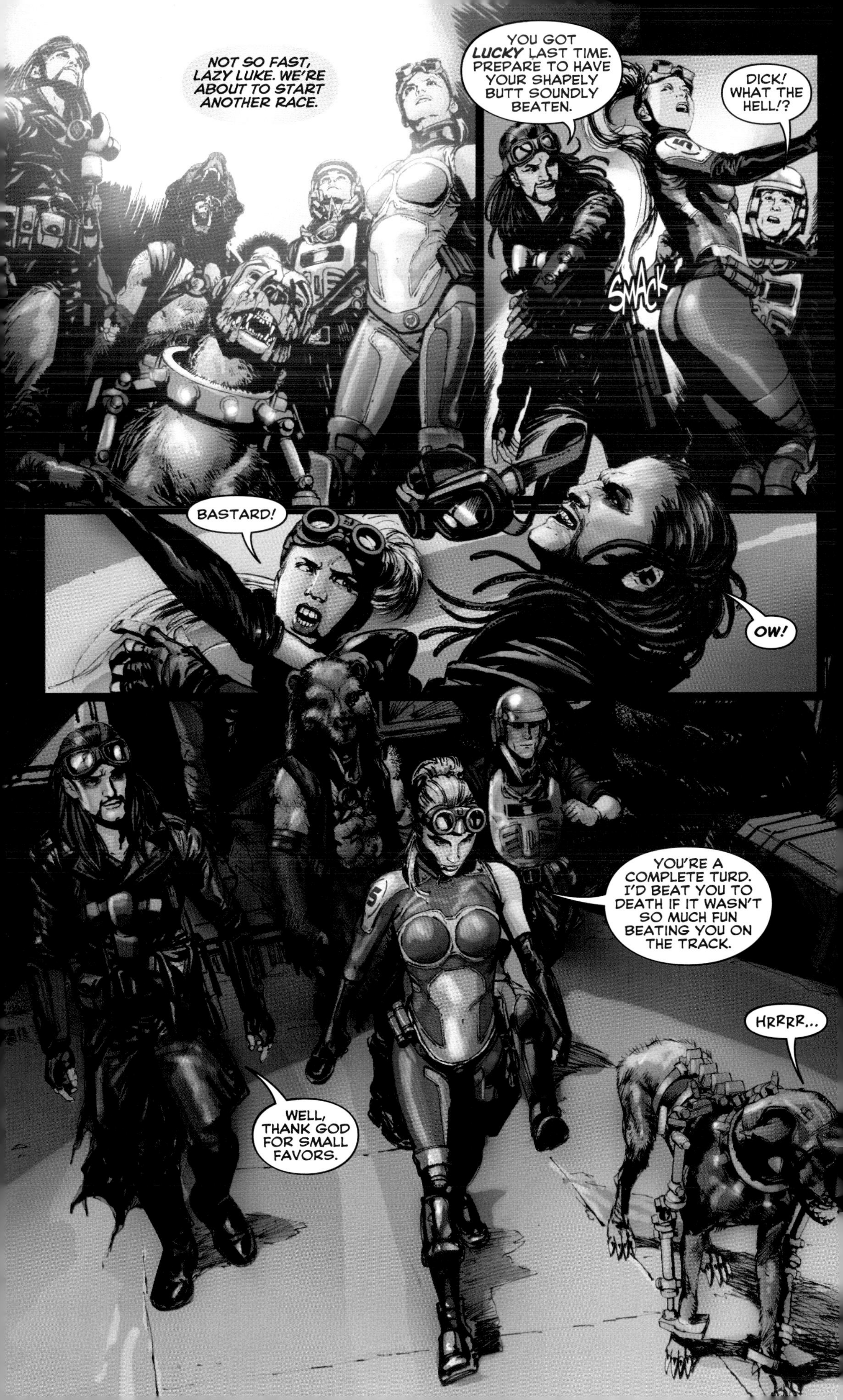
NOT SO FAST, LAZY LUKE. WE'RE ABOUT TO START ANOTHER RACE.
YOU GOT LUCKY LAST TIME. PREPARE TO HAVE YOUR SHAPELY BUTT SOUNDLY BEATEN.
DICK! WHAT THE HELL!?
SMACK
BASTARD!
OW!
YOU'RE A COMPLETE TURD. I'D BEAT YOU TO DEATH IF IT WASN'T SO MUCH FUN BEATING YOU ON THE TRACK.
WELL, THANK GOD FOR SMALL FAVORS.
HRRRR...

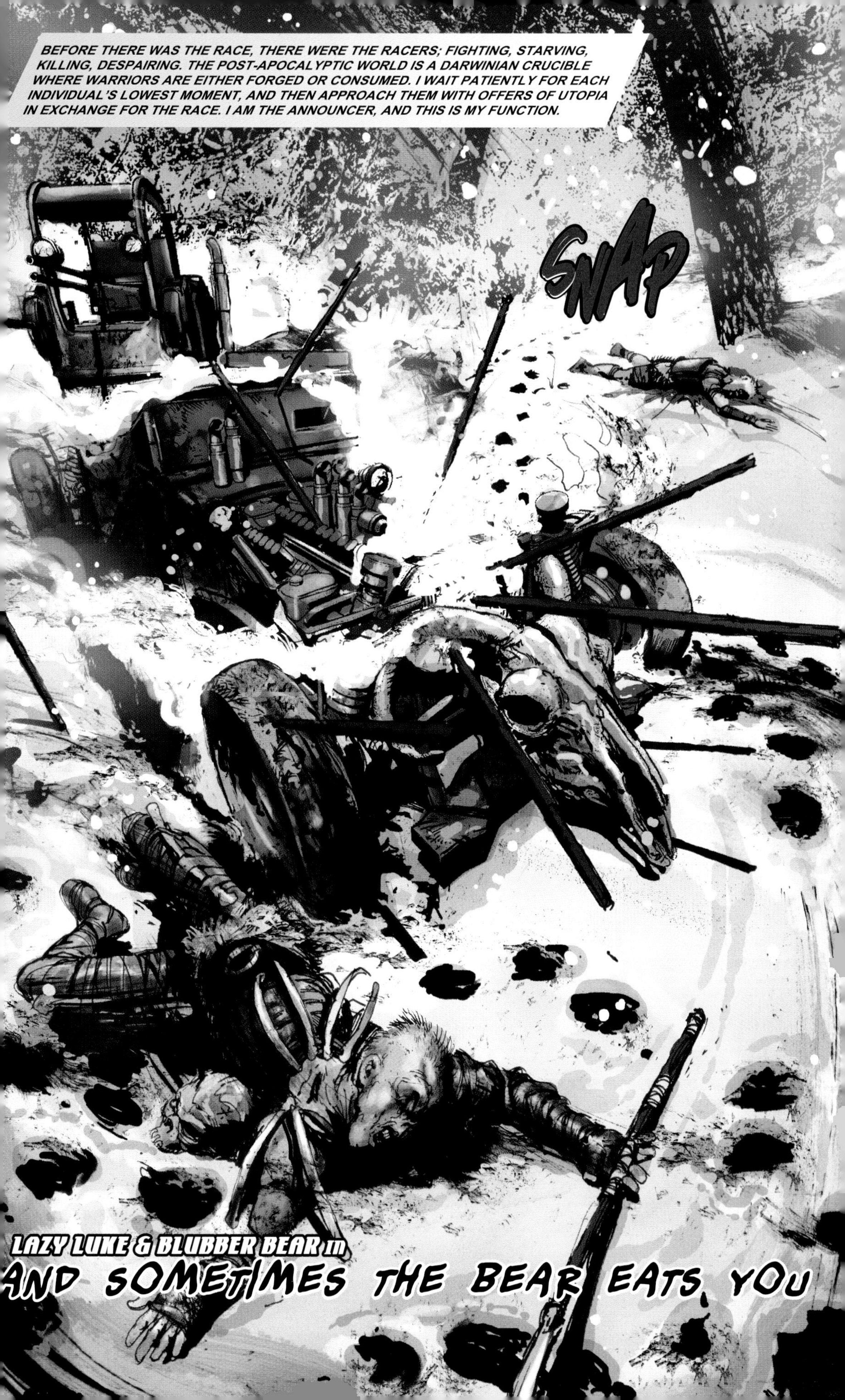
BEFORE THERE WAS THE RACE, THERE WERE THE RACERS; FIGHTING, STARVING, KILLING, DESPAIRING. THE POST-APOCALYPTIC WORLD IS A DARWINIAN CRUCIBLE WHERE WARRIORS ARE EITHER FORGED OR CONSUMED. I WAIT PATIENTLY FOR EACH INDIVIDUAL'S LOWEST MOMENT, AND THEN APPROACH THEM WITH OFFERS OF UTOPIA IN EXCHANGE FOR THE RACE. I AM THE ANNOUNCER, AND THIS IS MY FUNCTION.
SNAP
LAZY LUKE & BLUBBER BEAR in
AND SOMETIMES THE BEAR EATS YOU

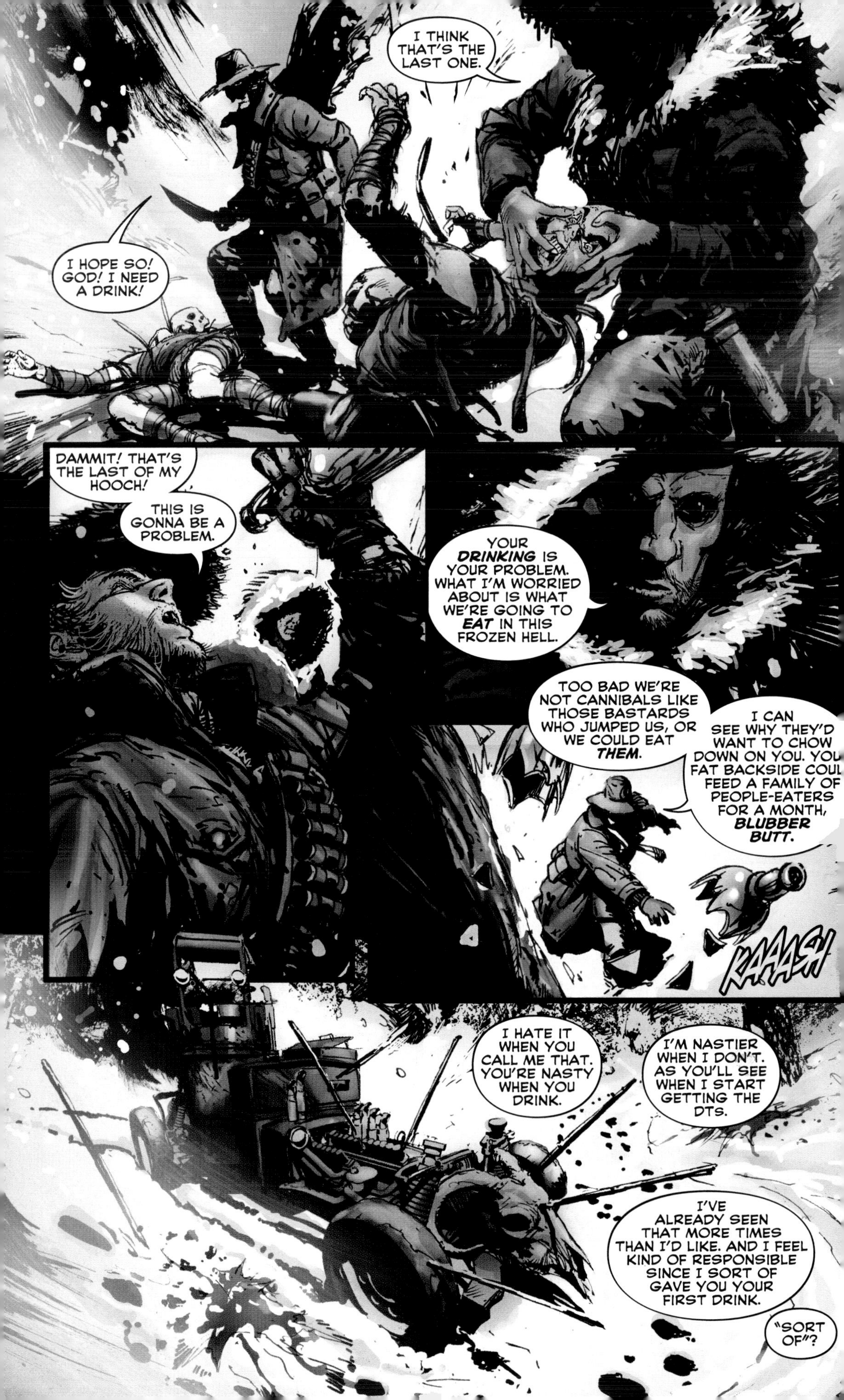
I THINK THAT'S THE LAST ONE.
I HOPE SO! GOD! I NEED A DRINK!
DAMMIT! THAT'S THE LAST OF MY HOOCH!
THIS IS GONNA BE A PROBLEM.
YOUR DRINKING IS YOUR PROBLEM. WHAT I'M WORRIED ABOUT IS WHAT WE'RE GOING TO EAT IN THIS FROZEN HELL.
TOO BAD WE'RE NOT CANNIBALS LIKE THOSE BASTARDS WHO JUMPED US, OR WE COULD EAT THEM.
I CAN SEE WHY THEY'D WANT TO CHOW DOWN ON YOU. YOU FAT BACKSIDE COUL FEED A FAMILY OF PEOPLE-EATERS FOR A MONTH, BLUBBER BUTT.
KAAASH
I HATE IT WHEN YOU CALL ME THAT. YOU'RE NASTY WHEN YOU DRINK.
I'M NASTIER WHEN I DON'T. AS YOU'LL SEE WHEN I START GETTING THE DTS.
I'VE ALREADY SEEN THAT MORE TIMES THAN I'D LIKE. AND I FEEL KIND OF RESPONSIBLE SINCE I SORT OF GAVE YOU YOUR FIRST DRINK.
"SORT OF"?

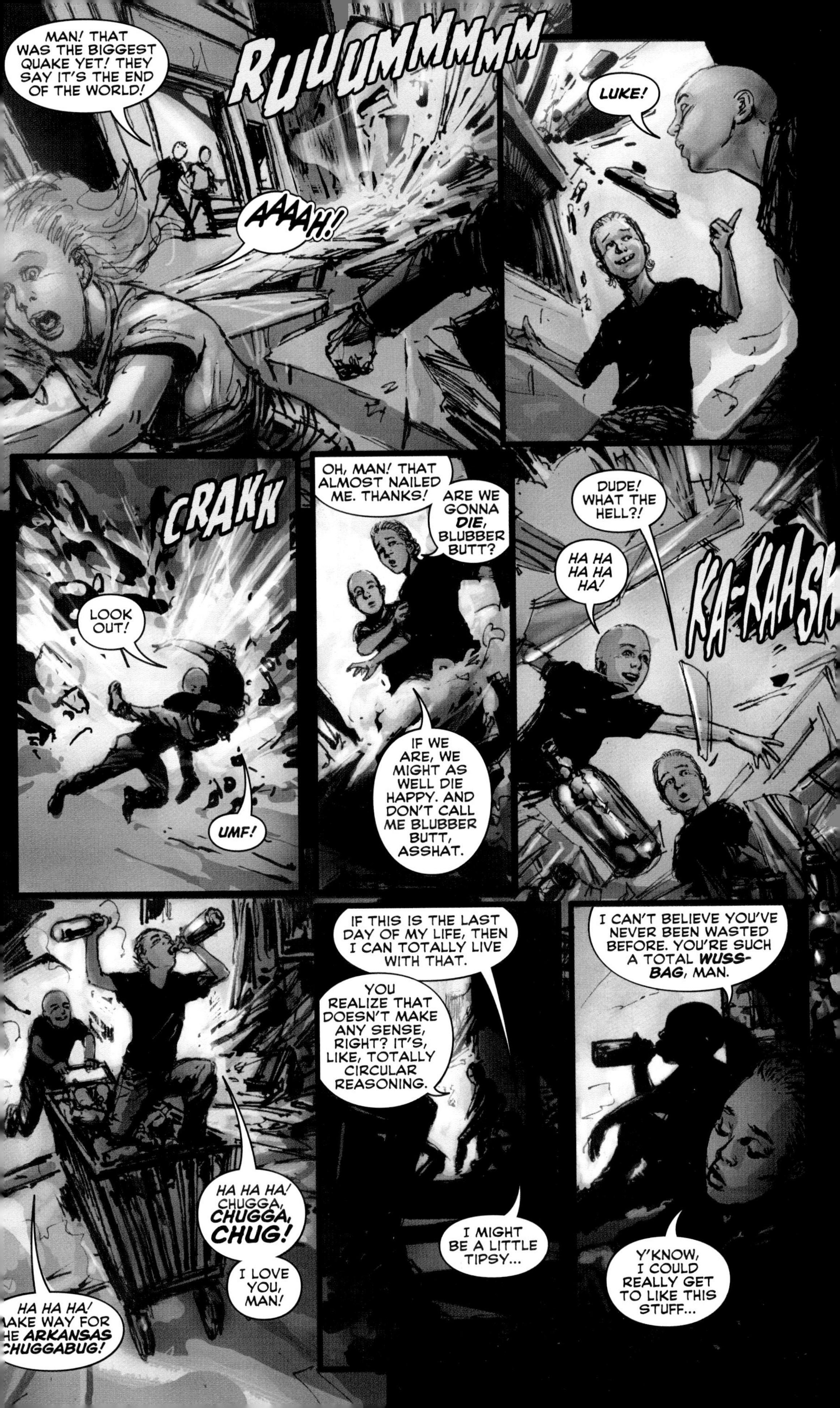

MAN! THAT WAS THE BIGGEST QUAKE YET! THEY SAY IT'S THE END OF THE WORLD!
RUUUMMMMM
AAAAH!
LUKE!
CRAKK
LOOK OUT!
UMF!
OH, MAN! THAT ALMOST NAILED ME. THANKS!
ARE WE GONNA DIE, BLUBBER BUTT?
IF WE ARE, WE MIGHT AS WELL DIE HAPPY. AND DON'T CALL ME BLUBBER BUTT, ASSHAT.
DUDE! WHAT THE HELL?!
HA HA HA HA HA!
KA-KAASH
HA HA HA! CHUGGA, CHUGGA, CHUG!
I LOVE YOU, MAN!
HA HA HA! AKE WAY FOR HE ARKANSAS CHUGGABUG!
IF THIS IS THE LAST DAY OF MY LIFE, THEN I CAN TOTALLY LIVE WITH THAT.
YOU REALIZE THAT DOESN'T MAKE ANY SENSE, RIGHT? IT'S, LIKE, TOTALLY CIRCULAR REASONING.
I MIGHT BE A LITTLE TIPSY...
I CAN'T BELIEVE YOU'VE NEVER BEEN WASTED BEFORE. YOU'RE SUCH A TOTAL WUSS-BAG, MAN.
Y'KNOW, I COULD REALLY GET TO LIKE THIS STUFF...

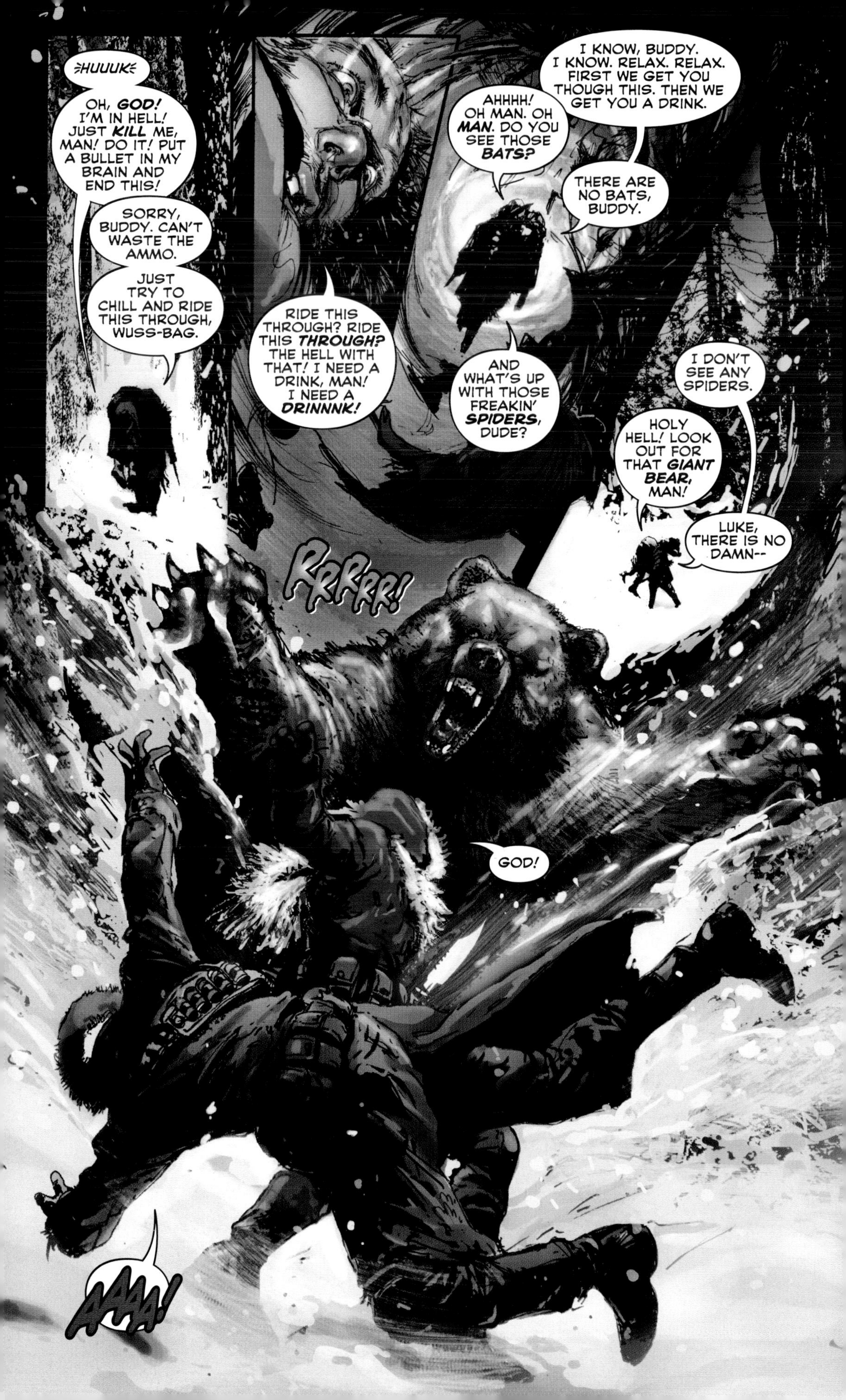

HUUUK
OH, GOD! I'M IN HELL! JUST KILL ME, MAN! DO IT! PUT A BULLET IN MY BRAIN AND END THIS!
SORRY, BUDDY. CAN'T WASTE THE AMMO.
JUST TRY TO CHILL AND RIDE THIS THROUGH, WUSS-BAG.
RIDE THIS THROUGH? RIDE THIS THROUGH? THE HELL WITH THAT! I NEED A DRINK, MAN! I NEED A DRINNNK!
AHHHH! OH MAN. OH MAN. DO YOU SEE THOSE BATS?
I KNOW, BUDDY. I KNOW. RELAX. RELAX. FIRST WE GET YOU THOUGH THIS. THEN WE GET YOU A DRINK.
THERE ARE NO BATS, BUDDY.
AND WHAT'S UP WITH THOSE FREAKIN' SPIDERS, DUDE?
I DON'T SEE ANY SPIDERS.
HOLY HELL! LOOK OUT FOR THAT GIANT BEAR, MAN!
LUKE, THERE IS NO DAMN--
RRRRR!
GOD!
AAAA!

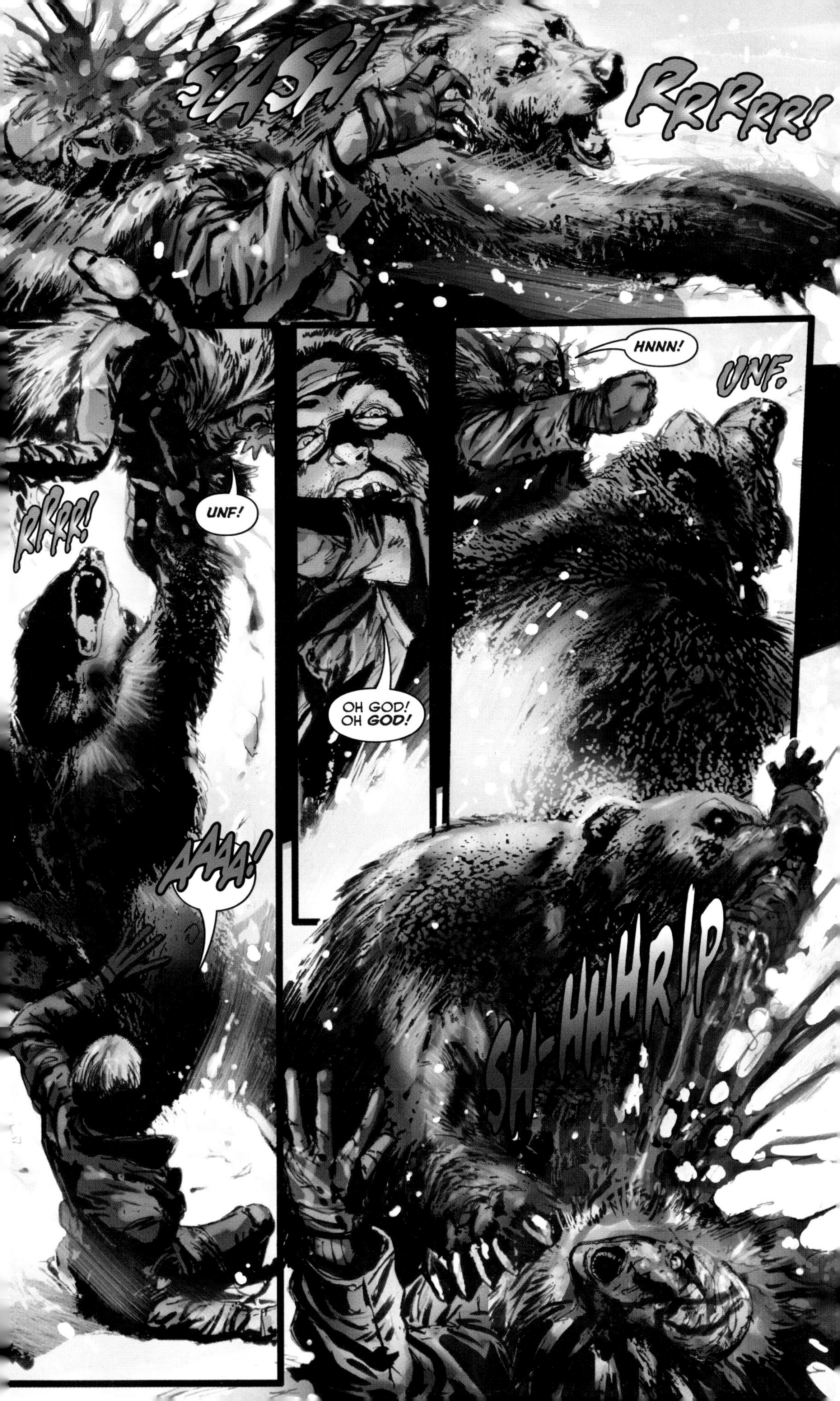
SLASH
RRRRRR!
RRRR!
UNF!
OH GOD! OH GOD!
HNNN!
UNF.
AAAA!
SH-HHHRIP

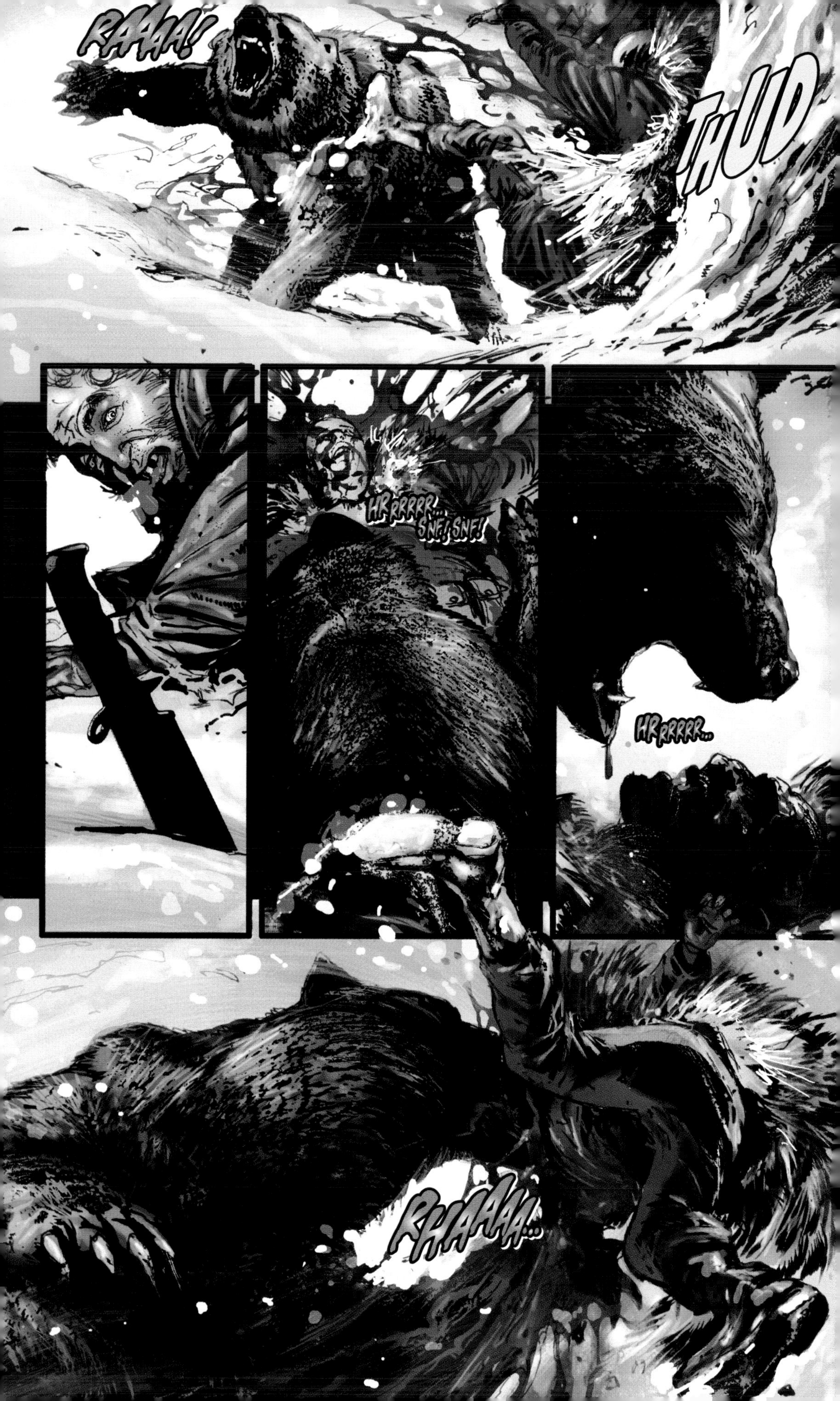
RAAAA!
THUD
HRRRRR...
SNF! SNF!
HRRRRR...
RHAAAA...

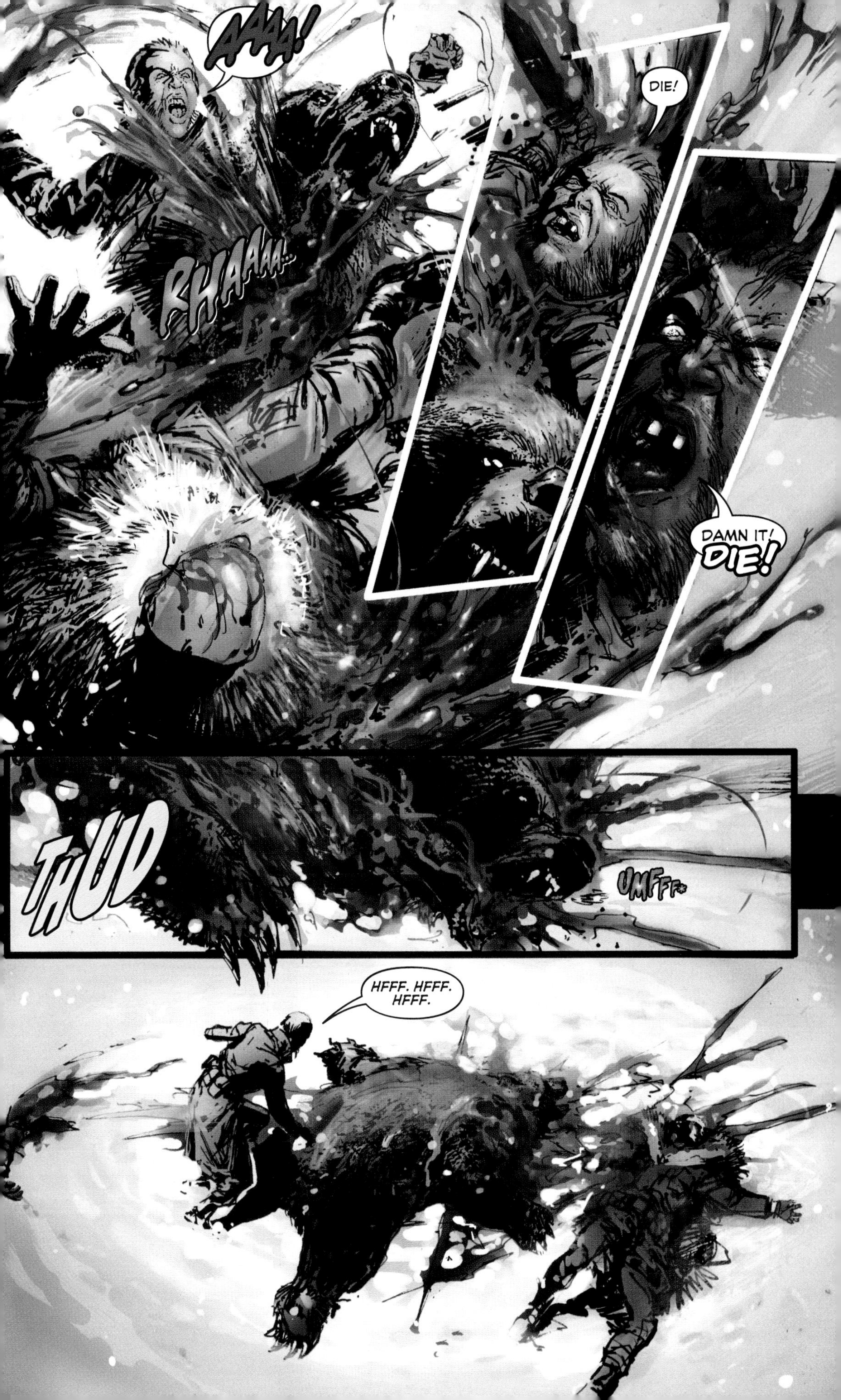
AAAA!
RHAAAA...
DIE!
DAMN IT! DIE!
THUD
UMFFF
HFFF. HFFF. HFFF.

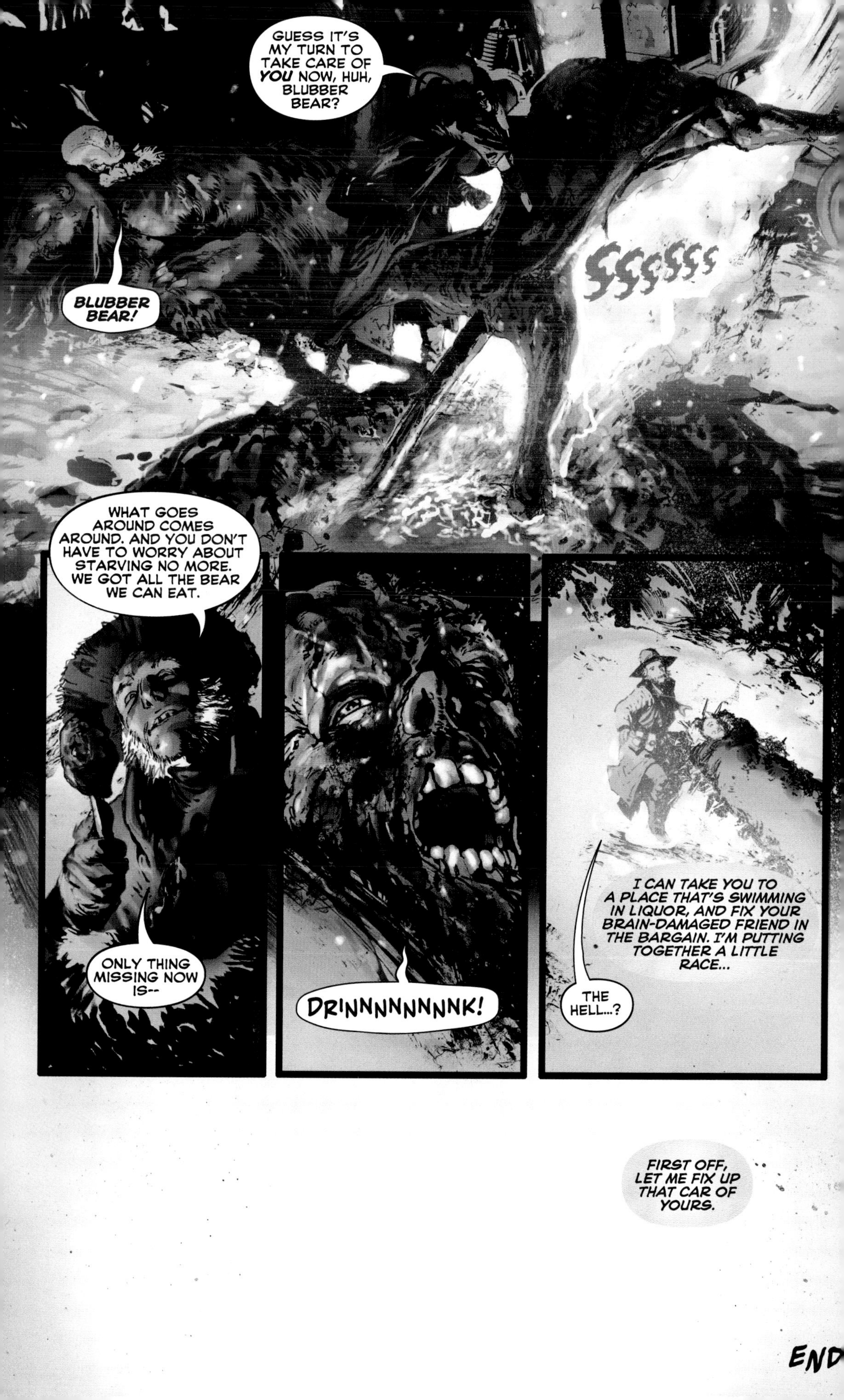
GUESS IT'S MY TURN TO TAKE CARE OF *YOU* NOW, HUH, BLUBBER BEAR?
SSSSSS
BLUBBER BEAR!
WHAT GOES AROUND COMES AROUND. AND YOU DON'T HAVE TO WORRY ABOUT STARVING NO MORE. WE GOT ALL THE BEAR WE CAN EAT.
ONLY THING MISSING NOW IS--
DRINNNNNNNNK!
I CAN TAKE YOU TO A PLACE THAT'S SWIMMING IN LIQUOR, AND FIX YOUR BRAIN-DAMAGED FRIEND IN THE BARGAIN. I'M PUTTING TOGETHER A LITTLE RACE...
THE HELL...?
FIRST OFF, LET ME FIX UP THAT CAR OF YOURS.
END

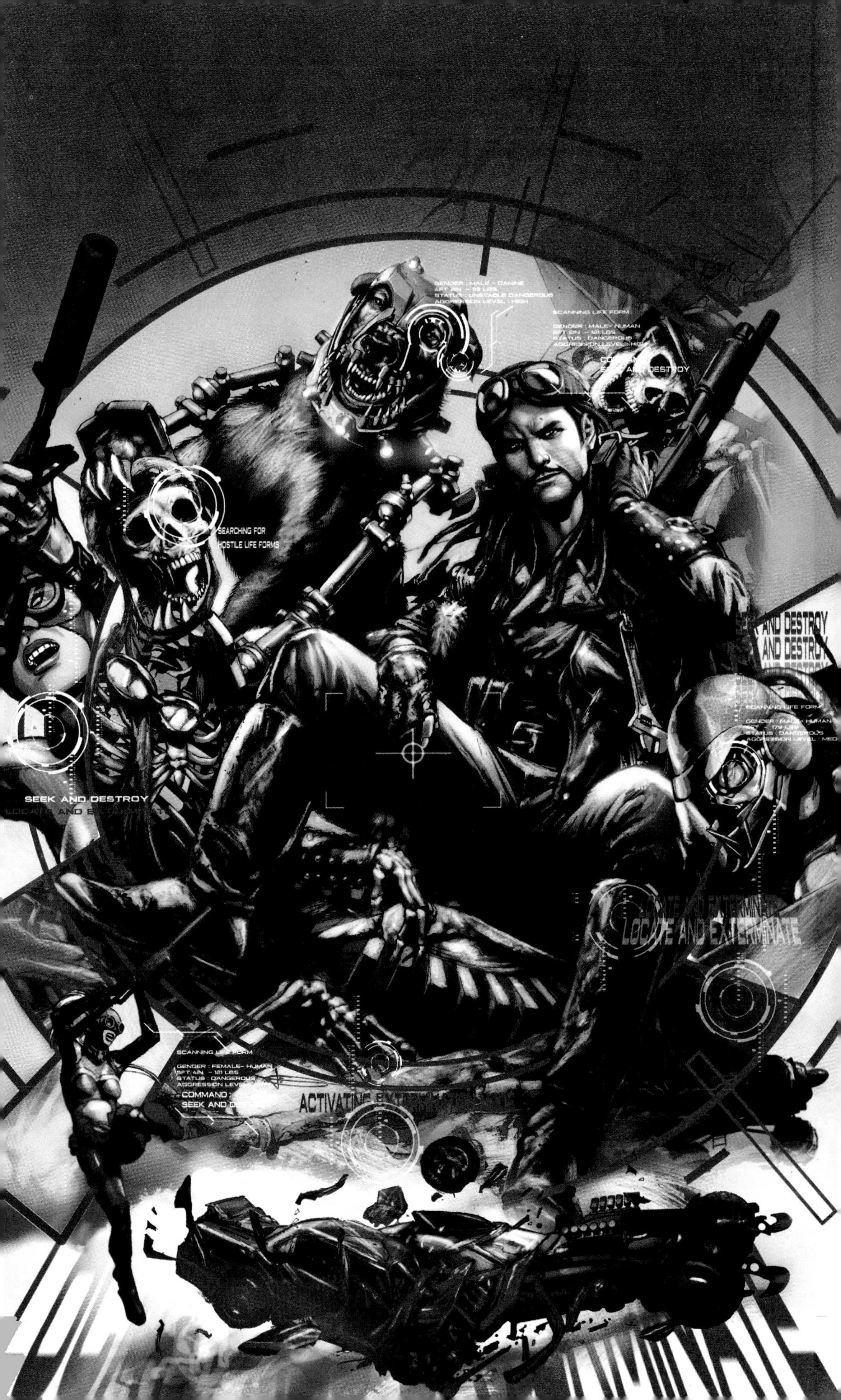
GENDER : MALE - CANINE
STATUS : UNSTABLE DANGEROUS
SCANNING LIFE FORM
GENDER : MALE- HUMAN
STATUS : DANGEROUS
SEARCHING FOR
HOSTILE LIFE FORMS
SEEK AND DESTROY
SCANNING LIFE FORM
LOCATE AND EXTERMINATE
SCANNING LIFE FORM
GENDER : FEMALE- HUMAN
5FT 4IN - 121 LBS
STATUS : DANGEROUS
COMMAND :

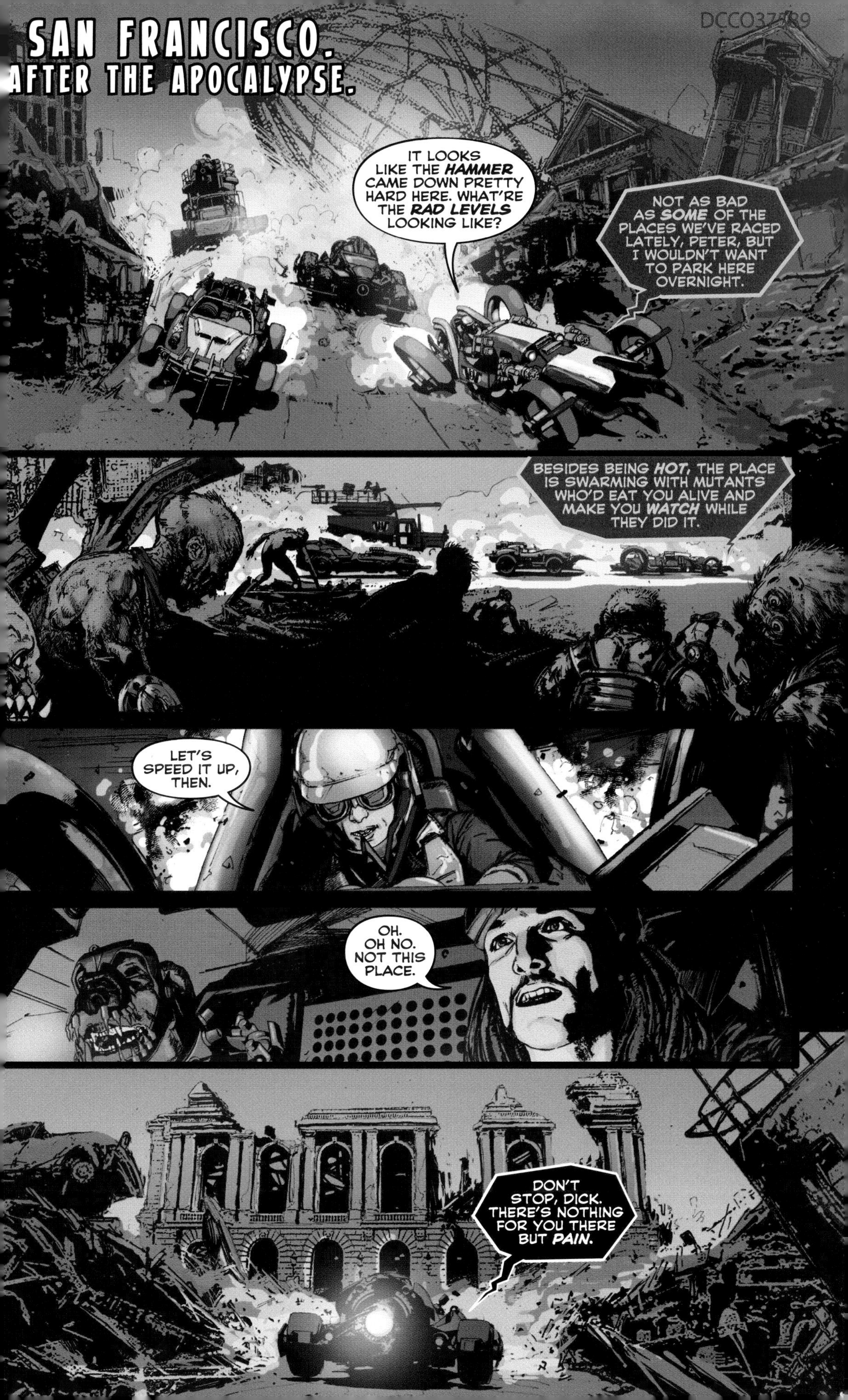
SAN FRANCISCO.
AFTER THE APOCALYPSE.
IT LOOKS LIKE THE HAMMER CAME DOWN PRETTY HARD HERE. WHAT'RE THE RAD LEVELS LOOKING LIKE?
NOT AS BAD AS SOME OF THE PLACES WE'VE RACED LATELY, PETER, BUT I WOULDN'T WANT TO PARK HERE OVERNIGHT.
BESIDES BEING HOT, THE PLACE IS SWARMING WITH MUTANTS WHO'D EAT YOU ALIVE AND MAKE YOU WATCH WHILE THEY DID IT.
LET'S SPEED IT UP, THEN.
OH. OH NO. NOT THIS PLACE.
DON'T STOP, DICK. THERE'S NOTHING FOR YOU THERE BUT PAIN.

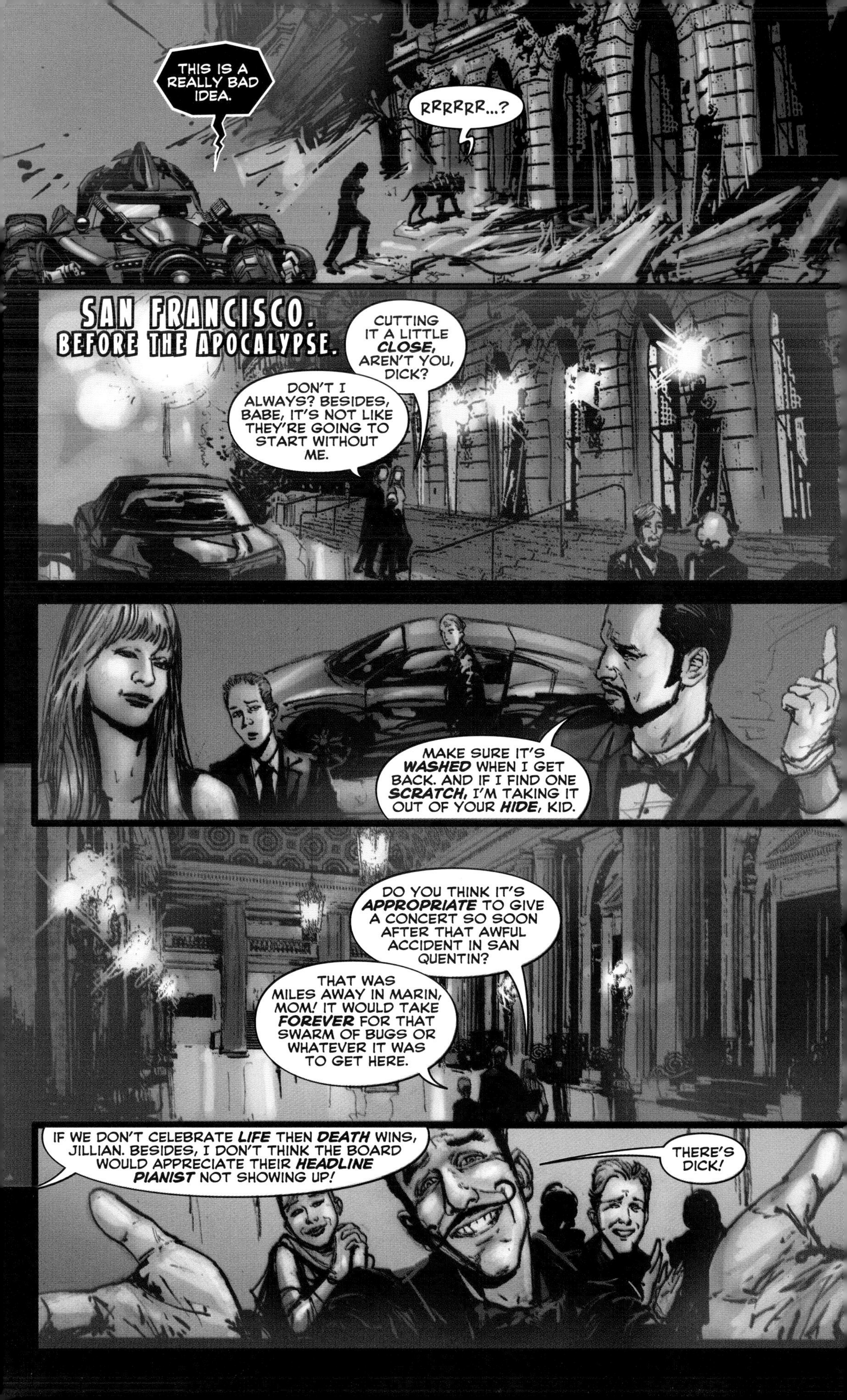

THIS IS A REALLY BAD IDEA.
RRRRRR...?
SAN FRANCISCO. BEFORE THE APOCALYPSE.
CUTTING IT A LITTLE CLOSE, AREN'T YOU, DICK?
DON'T I ALWAYS? BESIDES, BABE, IT'S NOT LIKE THEY'RE GOING TO START WITHOUT ME.
MAKE SURE IT'S WASHED WHEN I GET BACK. AND IF I FIND ONE SCRATCH, I'M TAKING IT OUT OF YOUR HIDE, KID.
DO YOU THINK IT'S APPROPRIATE TO GIVE A CONCERT SO SOON AFTER THAT AWFUL ACCIDENT IN SAN QUENTIN?
THAT WAS MILES AWAY IN MARIN, MOM! IT WOULD TAKE FOREVER FOR THAT SWARM OF BUGS OR WHATEVER IT WAS TO GET HERE.
IF WE DON'T CELEBRATE LIFE THEN DEATH WINS, JILLIAN. BESIDES, I DON'T THINK THE BOARD WOULD APPRECIATE THEIR HEADLINE PIANIST NOT SHOWING UP!
THERE'S DICK!

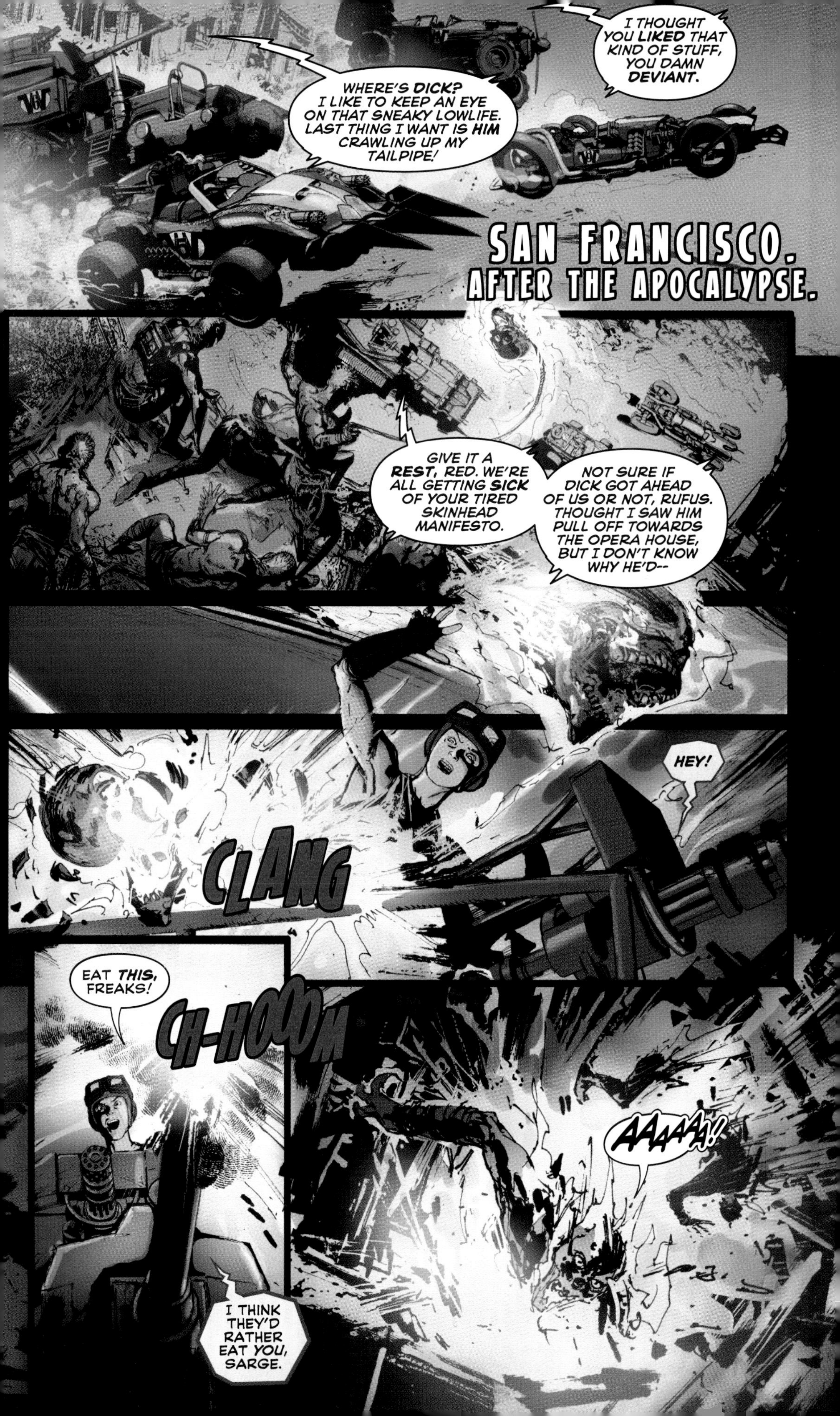
WHERE'S DICK? I LIKE TO KEEP AN EYE ON THAT SNEAKY LOWLIFE. LAST THING I WANT IS HIM CRAWLING UP MY TAILPIPE!
I THOUGHT YOU LIKED THAT KIND OF STUFF, YOU DAMN DEVIANT.
SAN FRANCISCO. AFTER THE APOCALYPSE.
GIVE IT A REST, RED. WE'RE ALL GETTING SICK OF YOUR TIRED SKINHEAD MANIFESTO.
NOT SURE IF DICK GOT AHEAD OF US OR NOT, RUFUS. THOUGHT I SAW HIM PULL OFF TOWARDS THE OPERA HOUSE, BUT I DON'T KNOW WHY HE'D--
HEY!
CLANG
EAT THIS, FREAKS!
CH-HOOOM
AAAAAA!
I THINK THEY'D RATHER EAT YOU, SARGE.

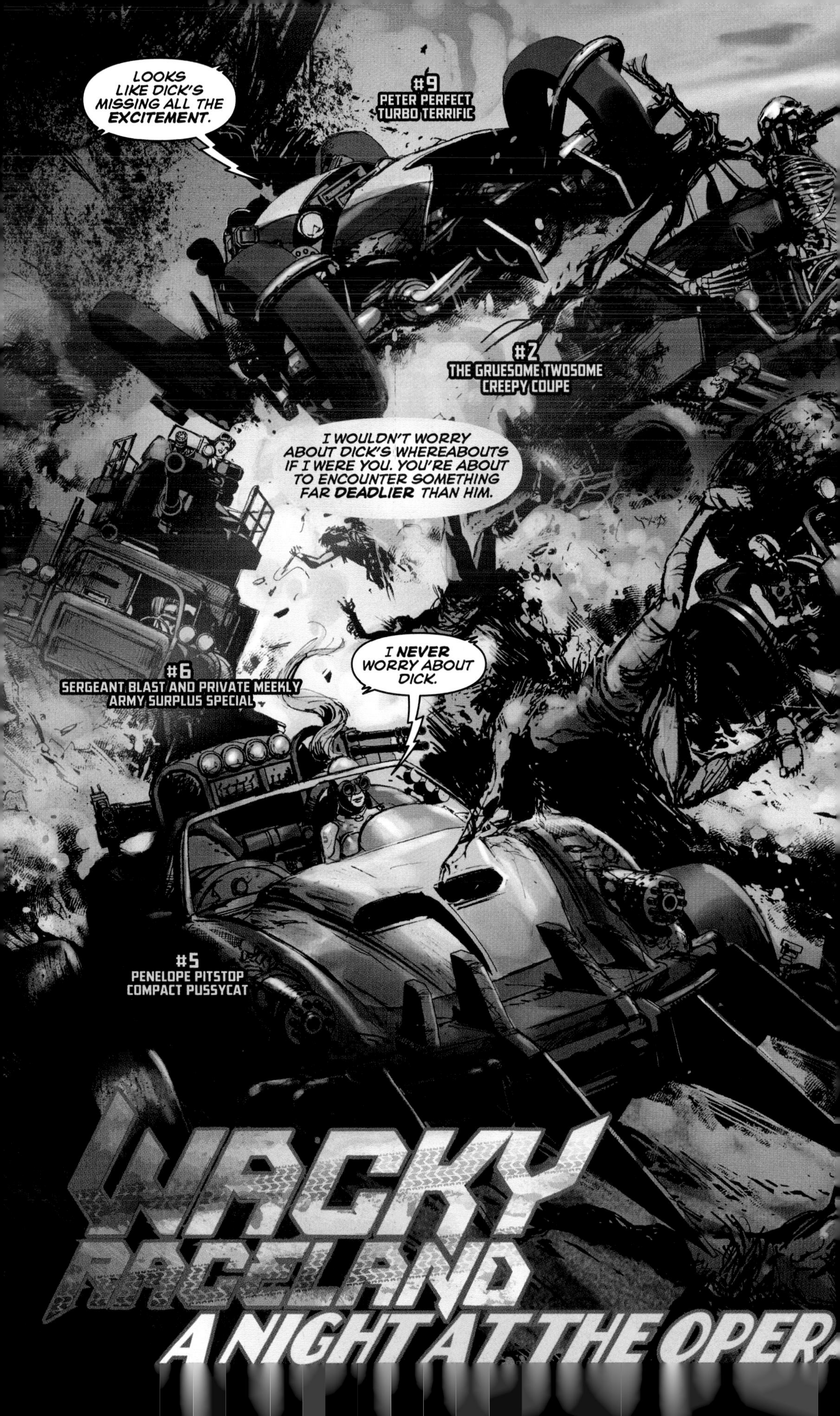
LOOKS LIKE DICK'S MISSING ALL THE EXCITEMENT.
#9
PETER PERFECT
TURBO TERRIFIC
#2
THE GRUESOME TWOSOME
CREEPY COUPE
I WOULDN'T WORRY ABOUT DICK'S WHEREABOUTS IF I WERE YOU. YOU'RE ABOUT TO ENCOUNTER SOMETHING FAR DEADLIER THAN HIM.
I NEVER WORRY ABOUT DICK.
#6
SERGEANT BLAST AND PRIVATE MEEKLY
ARMY SURPLUS SPECIAL
#5
PENELOPE PITSTOP
COMPACT PUSSYCAT
WACKY RACELAND
A NIGHT AT THE OPERA

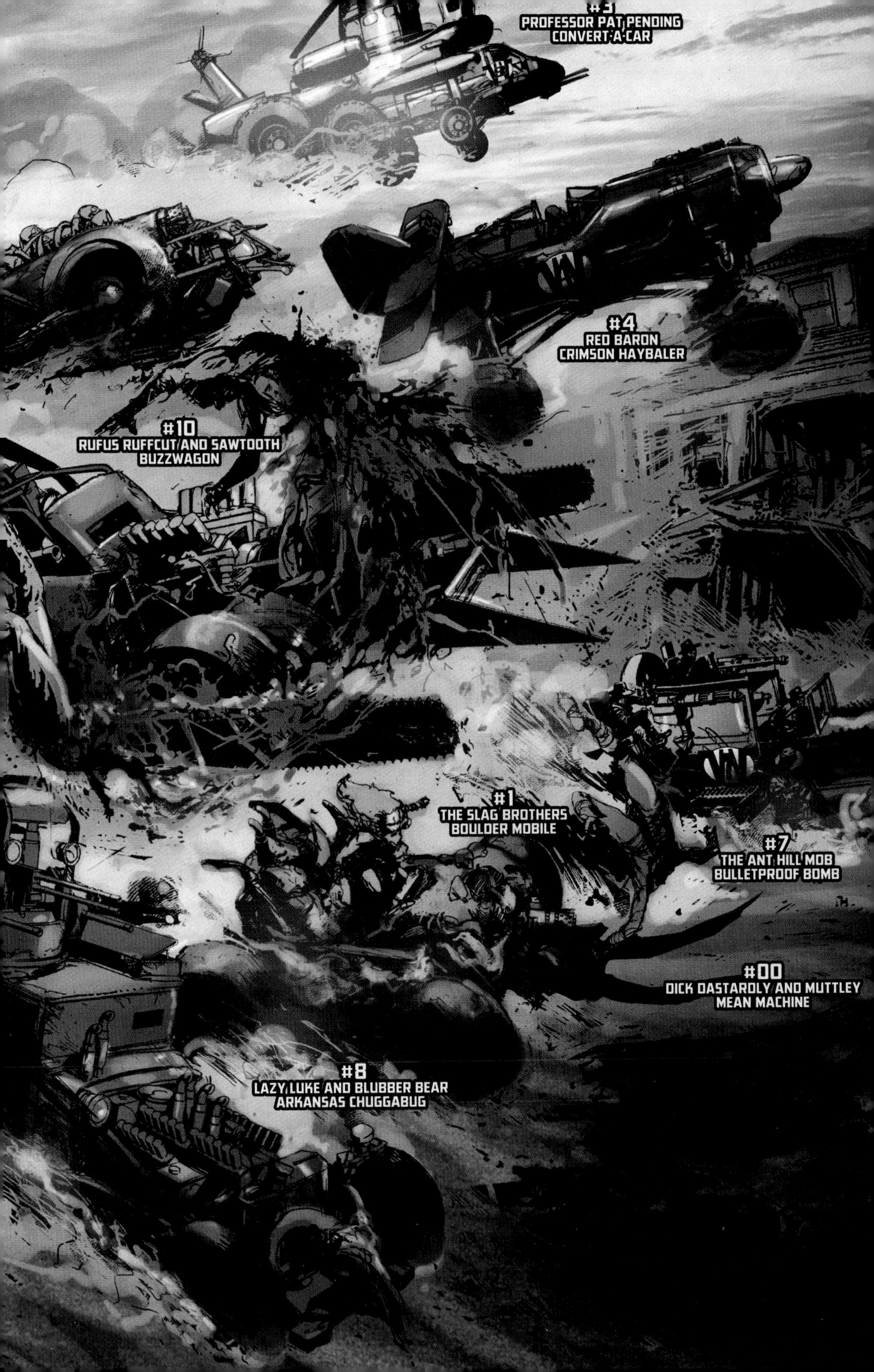
#3
PROFESSOR PAT PENDING
CONVERT-A-CAR
#4
RED BARON
CRIMSON HAYBALER
#10
RUFUS RUFFCUT AND SAWTOOTH
BUZZWAGON
#1
THE SLAG BROTHERS
BOULDER MOBILE
#7
THE ANT HILL MOB
BULLETPROOF BOMB
#00
DICK DASTARDLY AND MUTTLEY
MEAN MACHINE
#8
LAZY LUKE AND BLUBBER BEAR
ARKANSAS CHUGGABUG

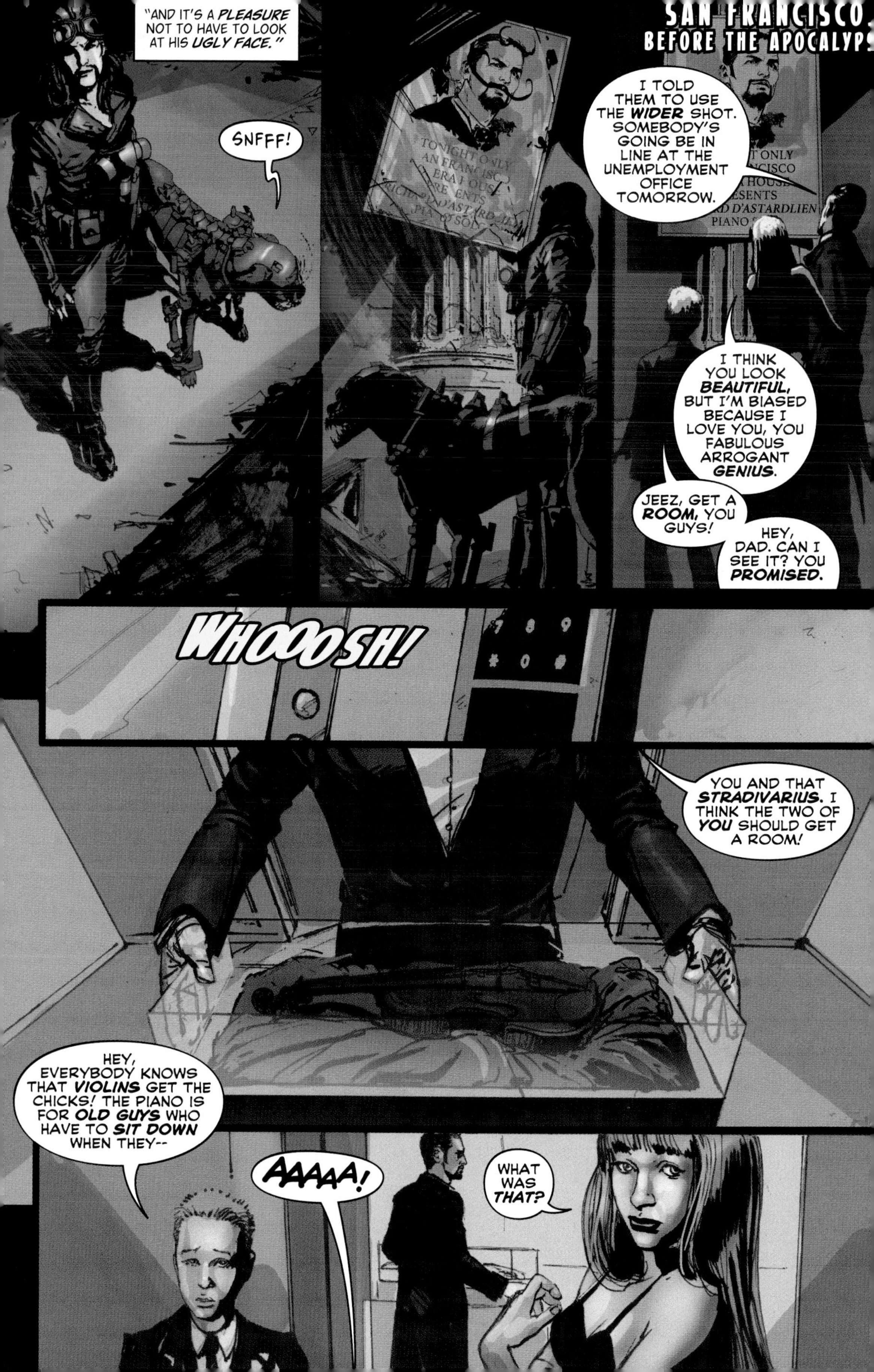
"AND IT'S A PLEASURE NOT TO HAVE TO LOOK AT HIS UGLY FACE."
SNFFF!
SAN FRANCISCO. BEFORE THE APOCALYPS
TONIGHT ONLY
I TOLD THEM TO USE THE WIDER SHOT. SOMEBODY'S GOING BE IN LINE AT THE UNEMPLOYMENT OFFICE TOMORROW.
I THINK YOU LOOK BEAUTIFUL, BUT I'M BIASED BECAUSE I LOVE YOU, YOU FABULOUS ARROGANT GENIUS.
JEEZ, GET A ROOM, YOU GUYS!
HEY, DAD. CAN I SEE IT? YOU PROMISED.
WHOOOOSH!
YOU AND THAT STRADIVARIUS. I THINK THE TWO OF YOU SHOULD GET A ROOM!
HEY, EVERYBODY KNOWS THAT VIOLINS GET THE CHICKS! THE PIANO IS FOR OLD GUYS WHO HAVE TO SIT DOWN WHEN THEY--
AAAAA!
WHAT WAS THAT?

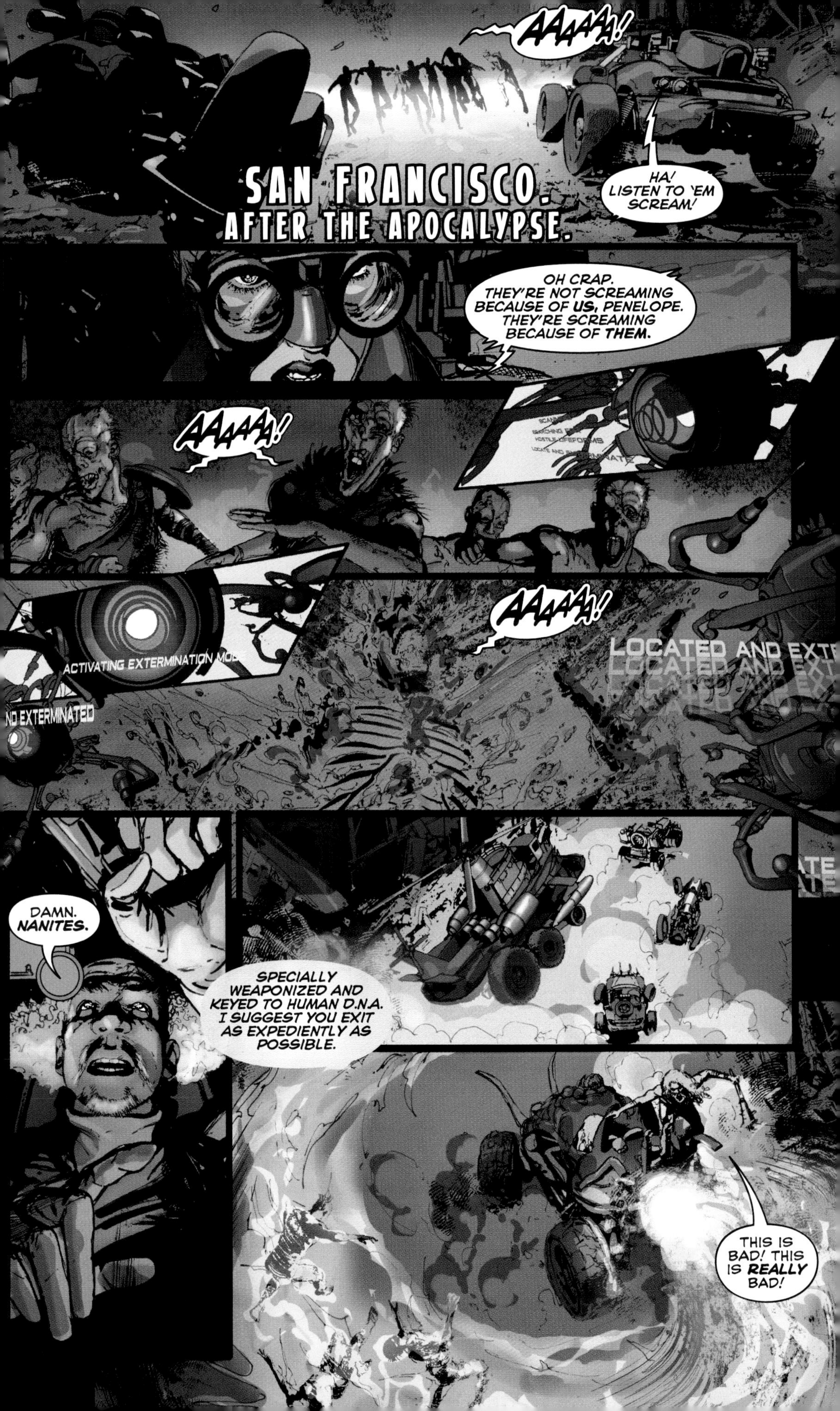
AAAAAA!
SAN FRANCISCO.
AFTER THE APOCALYPSE.
HA! LISTEN TO 'EM SCREAM!
OH CRAP. THEY'RE NOT SCREAMING BECAUSE OF US, PENELOPE. THEY'RE SCREAMING BECAUSE OF THEM.
AAAAAA!
AAAAAA!
ACTIVATING EXTERMINATION MODE
ND EXTERMINATED
LOCATED AND EXT
DAMN. NANITES.
SPECIALLY WEAPONIZED AND KEYED TO HUMAN D.N.A. I SUGGEST YOU EXIT AS EXPEDIENTLY AS POSSIBLE.
THIS IS BAD! THIS IS REALLY BAD!

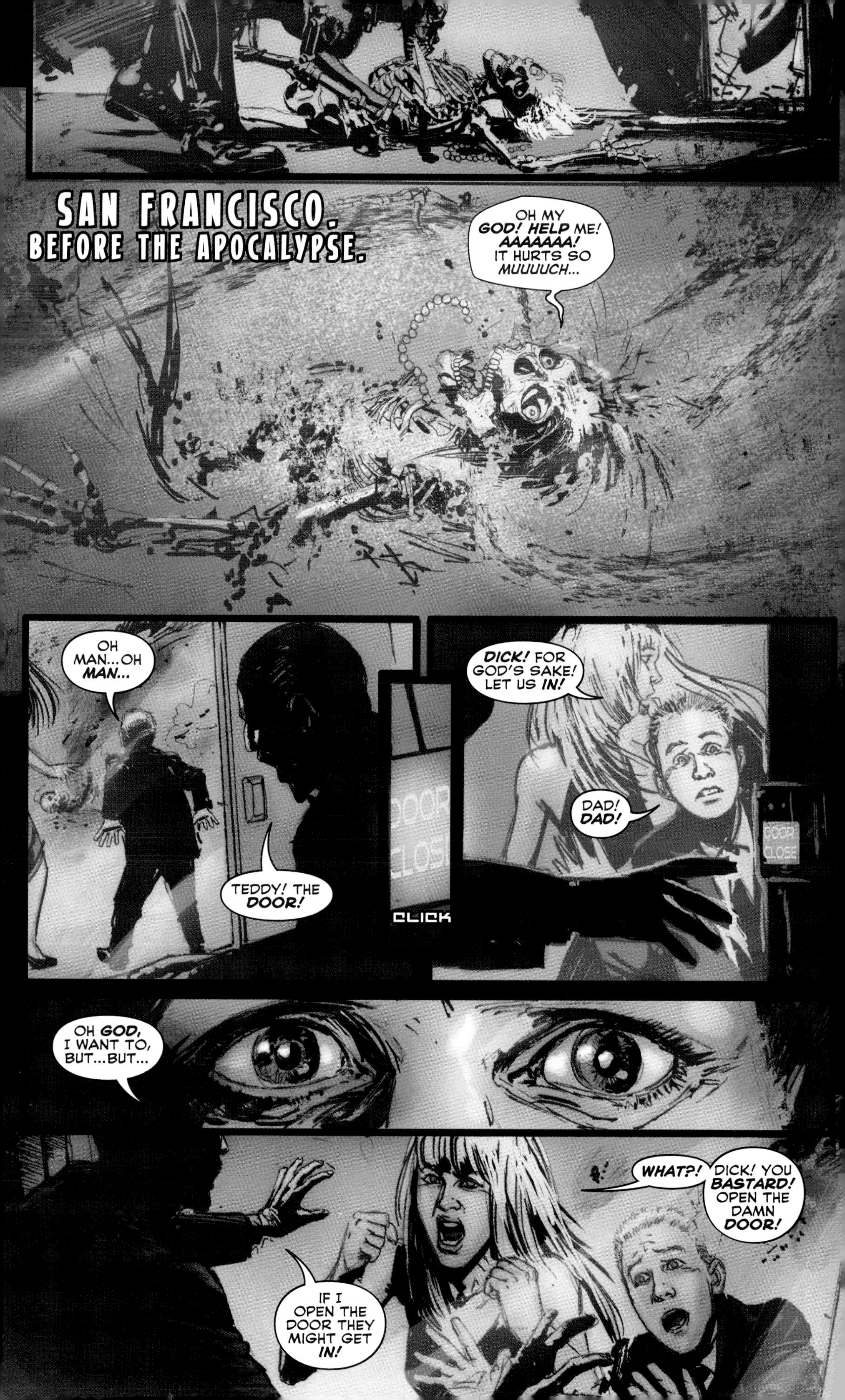

SAN FRANCISCO.
BEFORE THE APOCALYPSE.
OH MY GOD! HELP ME! AAAAAAA! IT HURTS SO MUUUUCH...
OH MAN...OH MAN...
TEDDY! THE DOOR!
DOOR CLOSE
CLICK
DICK! FOR GOD'S SAKE! LET US IN!
DAD! DAD!
DOOR CLOSE
OH GOD, I WANT TO, BUT...BUT...
IF I OPEN THE DOOR THEY MIGHT GET IN!
WHAT?!
DICK! YOU BASTARD! OPEN THE DAMN DOOR!

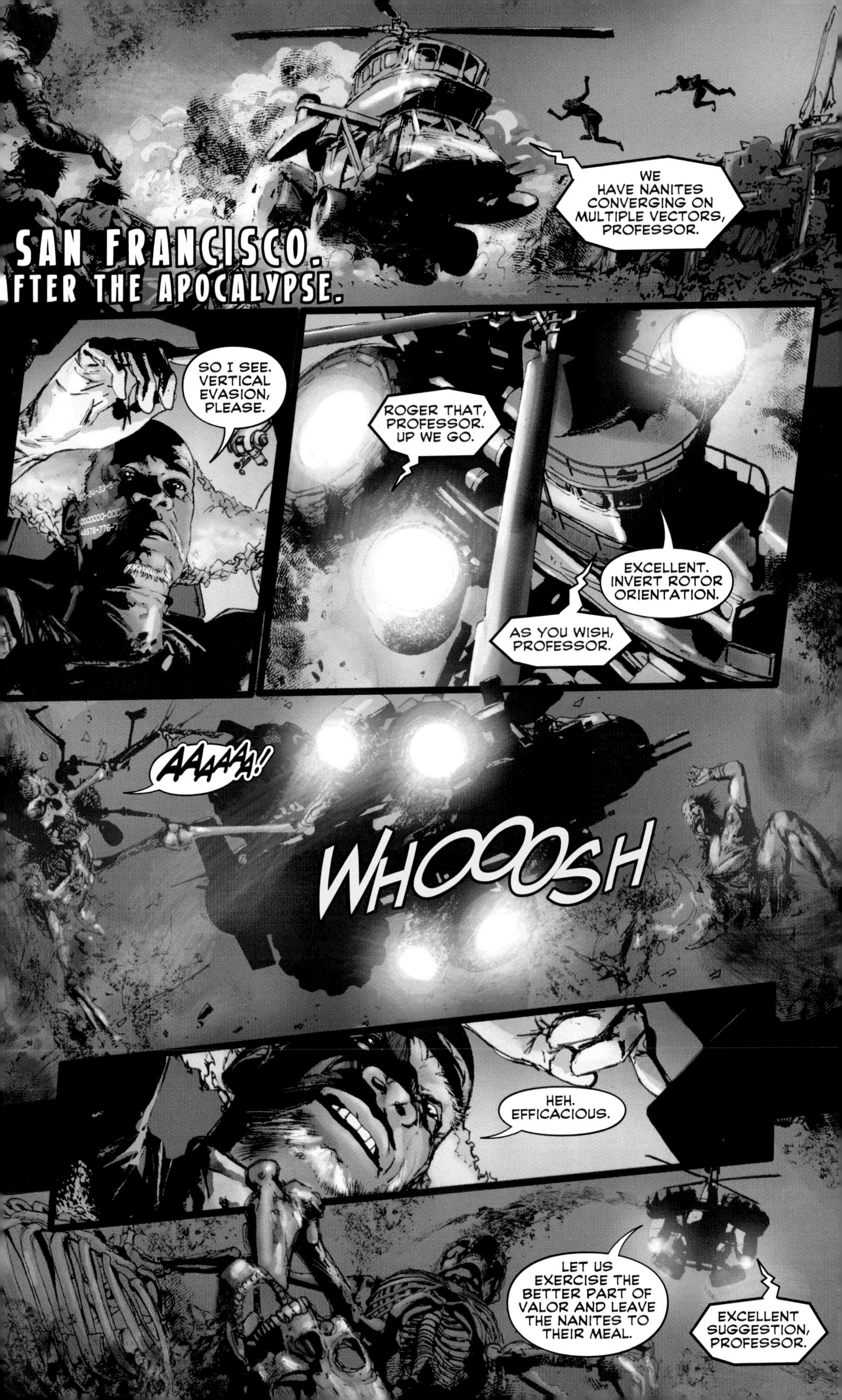
SAN FRANCISCO.
AFTER THE APOCALYPSE.
WE HAVE NANITES CONVERGING ON MULTIPLE VECTORS, PROFESSOR.
SO I SEE. VERTICAL EVASION, PLEASE.
ROGER THAT, PROFESSOR. UP WE GO.
EXCELLENT. INVERT ROTOR ORIENTATION.
AS YOU WISH, PROFESSOR.
AAAAA!
WHOOOSH
HEH. EFFICACIOUS.
LET US EXERCISE THE BETTER PART OF VALOR AND LEAVE THE NANITES TO THEIR MEAL.
EXCELLENT SUGGESTION, PROFESSOR.

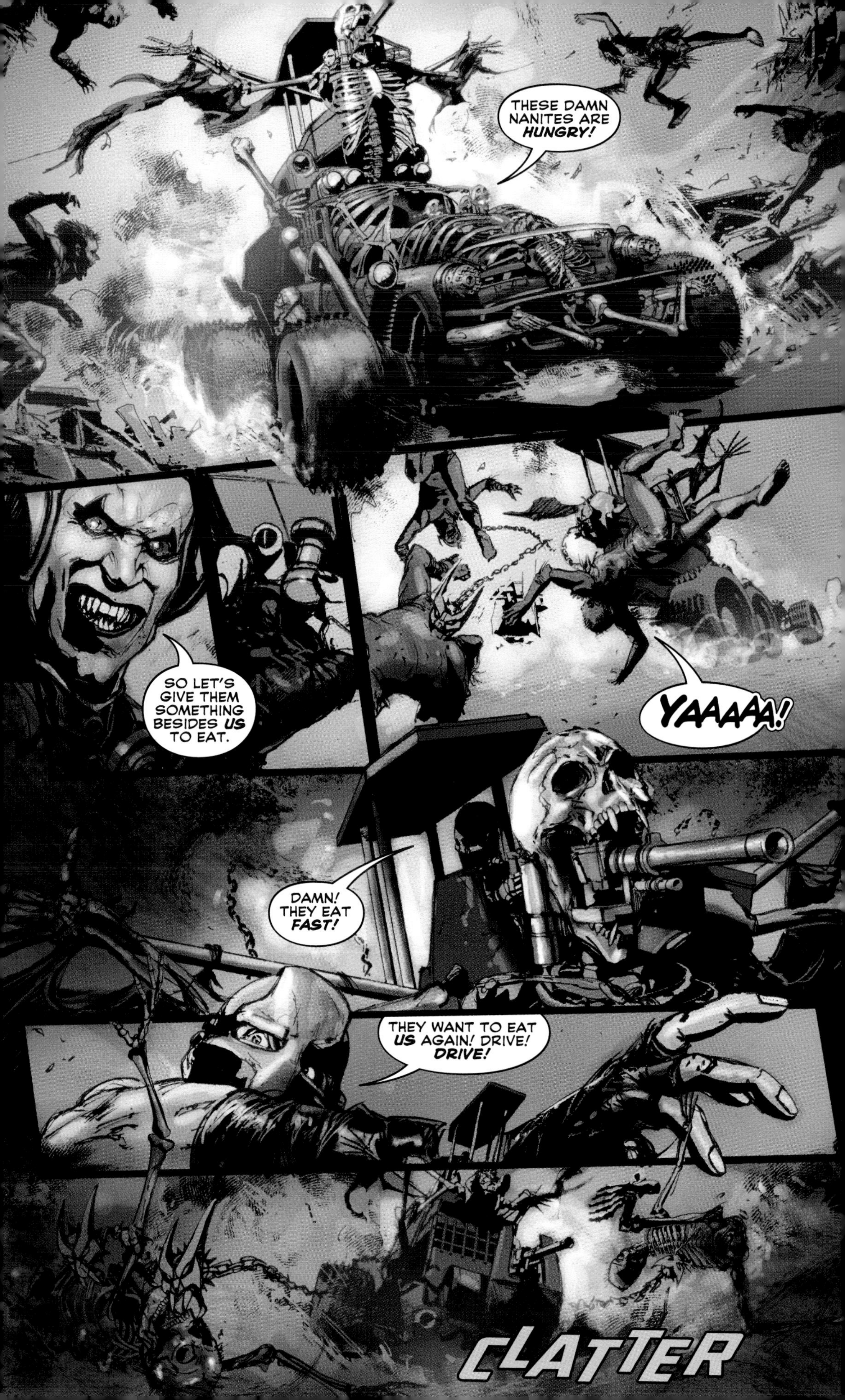
THESE DAMN NANITES ARE HUNGRY!
SO LET'S GIVE THEM SOMETHING BESIDES US TO EAT.
YAAAAA!
DAMN! THEY EAT FAST!
THEY WANT TO EAT US AGAIN! DRIVE! DRIVE!
CLATTER

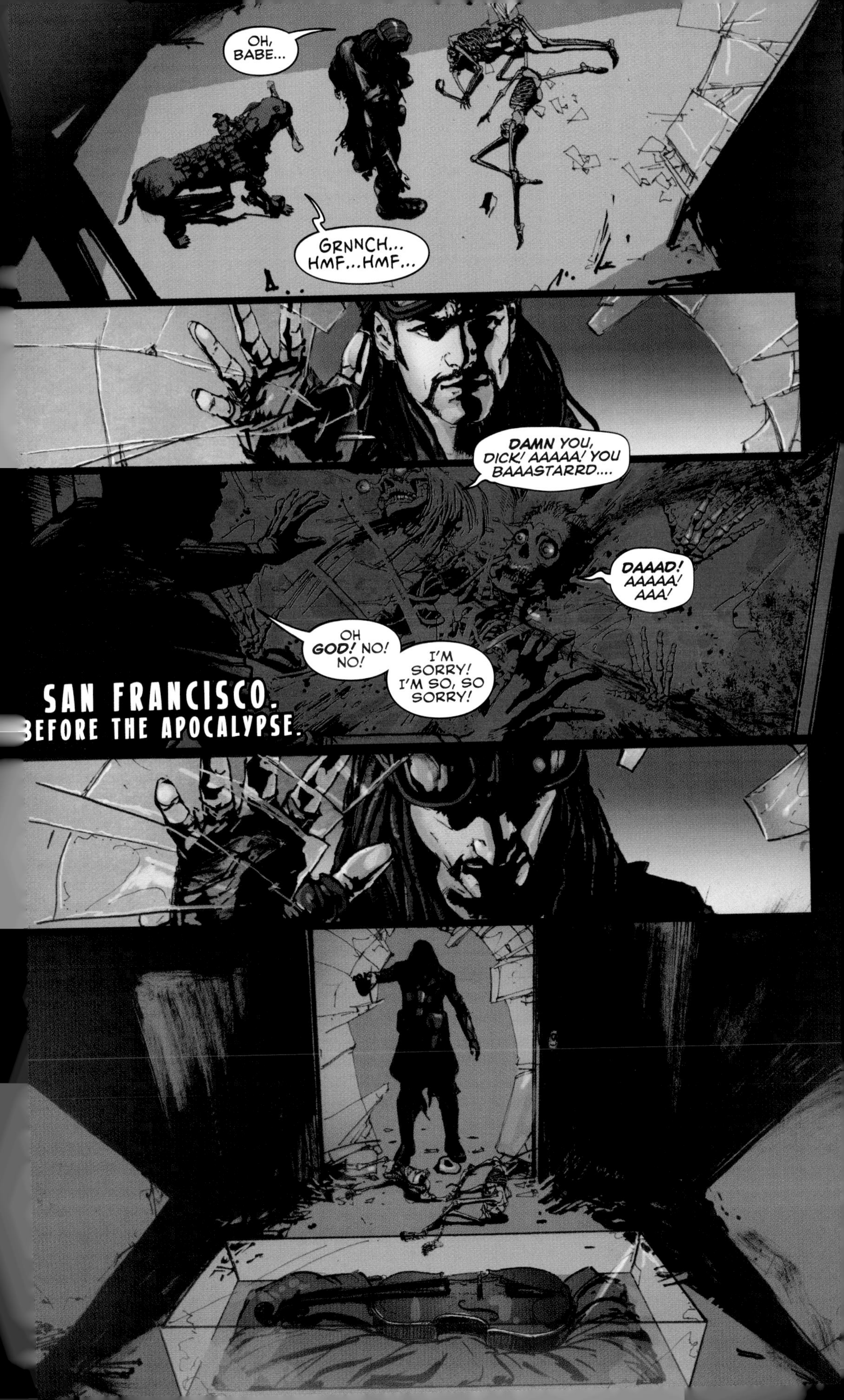

OH, BABE...
GRNNCH... HMF...HMF...
DAMN YOU, DICK! AAAAA! YOU BAAASTARRD....
DAAAD! AAAAA! AAA!
OH GOD! NO! NO!
I'M SORRY! I'M SO, SO SORRY!
SAN FRANCISCO. BEFORE THE APOCALYPSE.

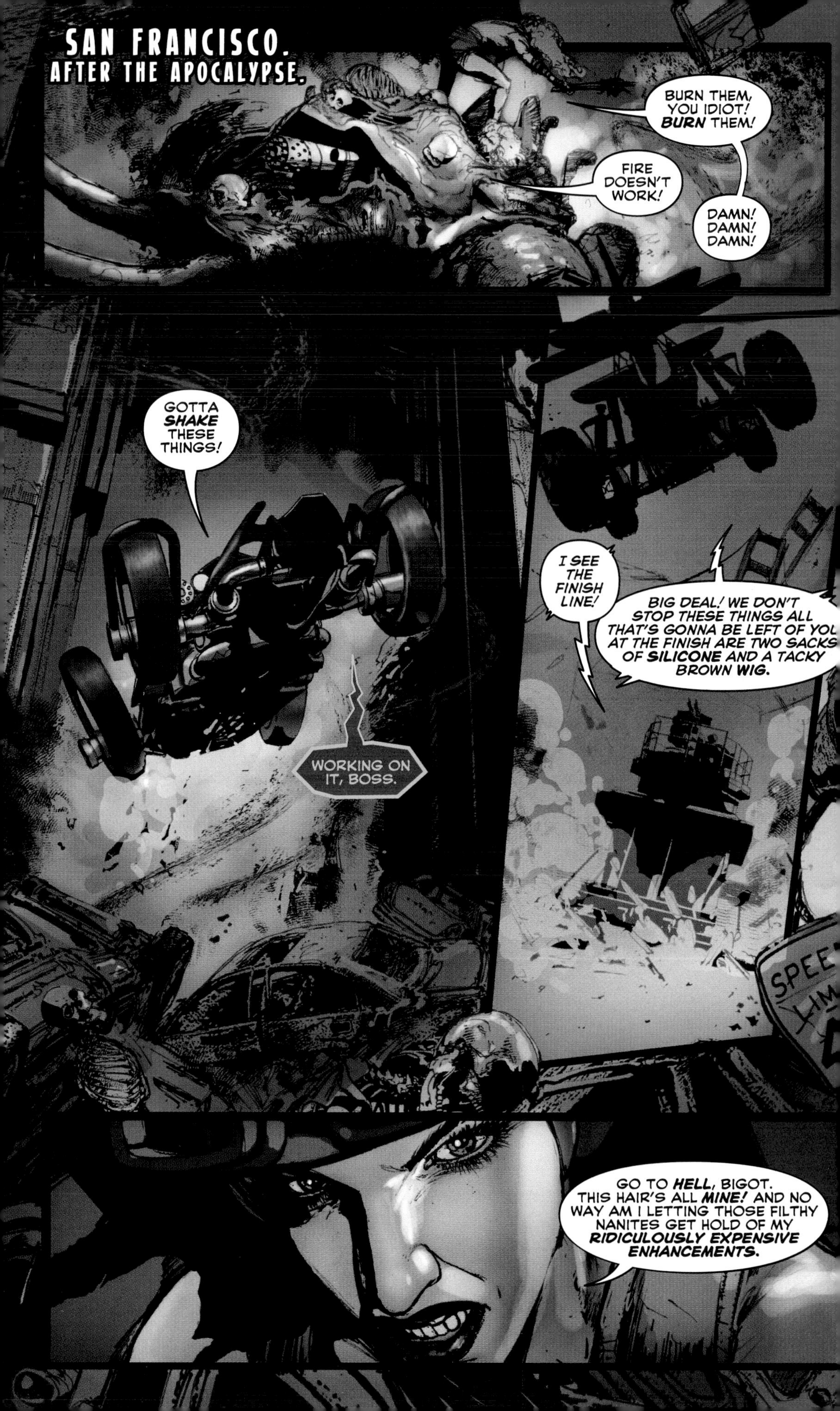
SAN FRANCISCO.
AFTER THE APOCALYPSE.
BURN THEM, YOU IDIOT! BURN THEM!
FIRE DOESN'T WORK!
DAMN! DAMN! DAMN!
GOTTA SHAKE THESE THINGS!
WORKING ON IT, BOSS.
I SEE THE FINISH LINE!
BIG DEAL! WE DON'T STOP THESE THINGS ALL THAT'S GONNA BE LEFT OF YOU AT THE FINISH ARE TWO SACKS OF SILICONE AND A TACKY BROWN WIG.
GO TO HELL, BIGOT. THIS HAIR'S ALL MINE! AND NO WAY AM I LETTING THOSE FILTHY NANITES GET HOLD OF MY RIDICULOUSLY EXPENSIVE ENHANCEMENTS.

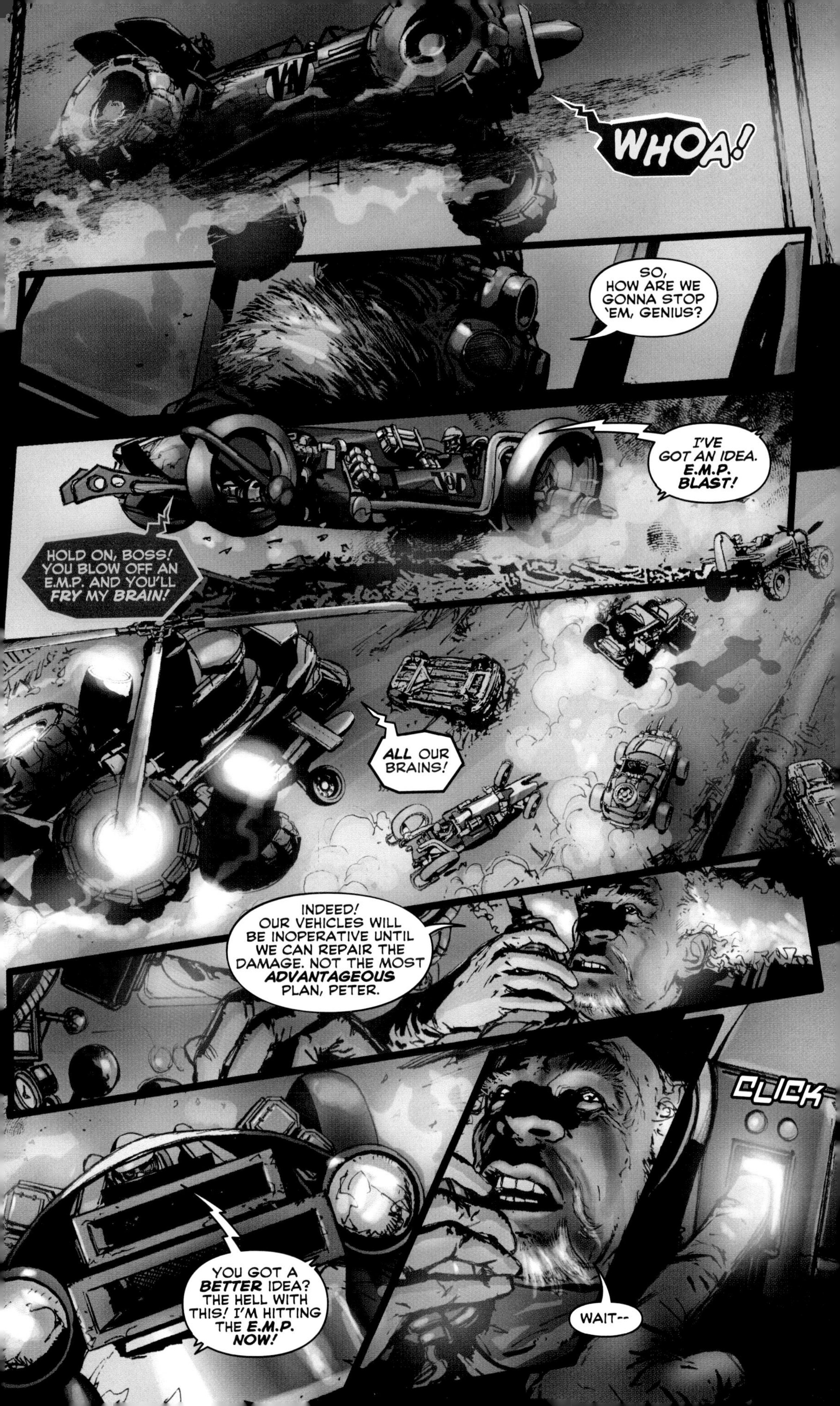

WHOA!
SO, HOW ARE WE GONNA STOP 'EM, GENIUS?
I'VE GOT AN IDEA. E.M.P. BLAST!
HOLD ON, BOSS! YOU BLOW OFF AN E.M.P. AND YOU'LL FRY MY BRAIN!
ALL OUR BRAINS!
INDEED! OUR VEHICLES WILL BE INOPERATIVE UNTIL WE CAN REPAIR THE DAMAGE. NOT THE MOST ADVANTAGEOUS PLAN, PETER.
CLICK
YOU GOT A BETTER IDEA? THE HELL WITH THIS! I'M HITTING THE E.M.P. NOW!
WAIT--

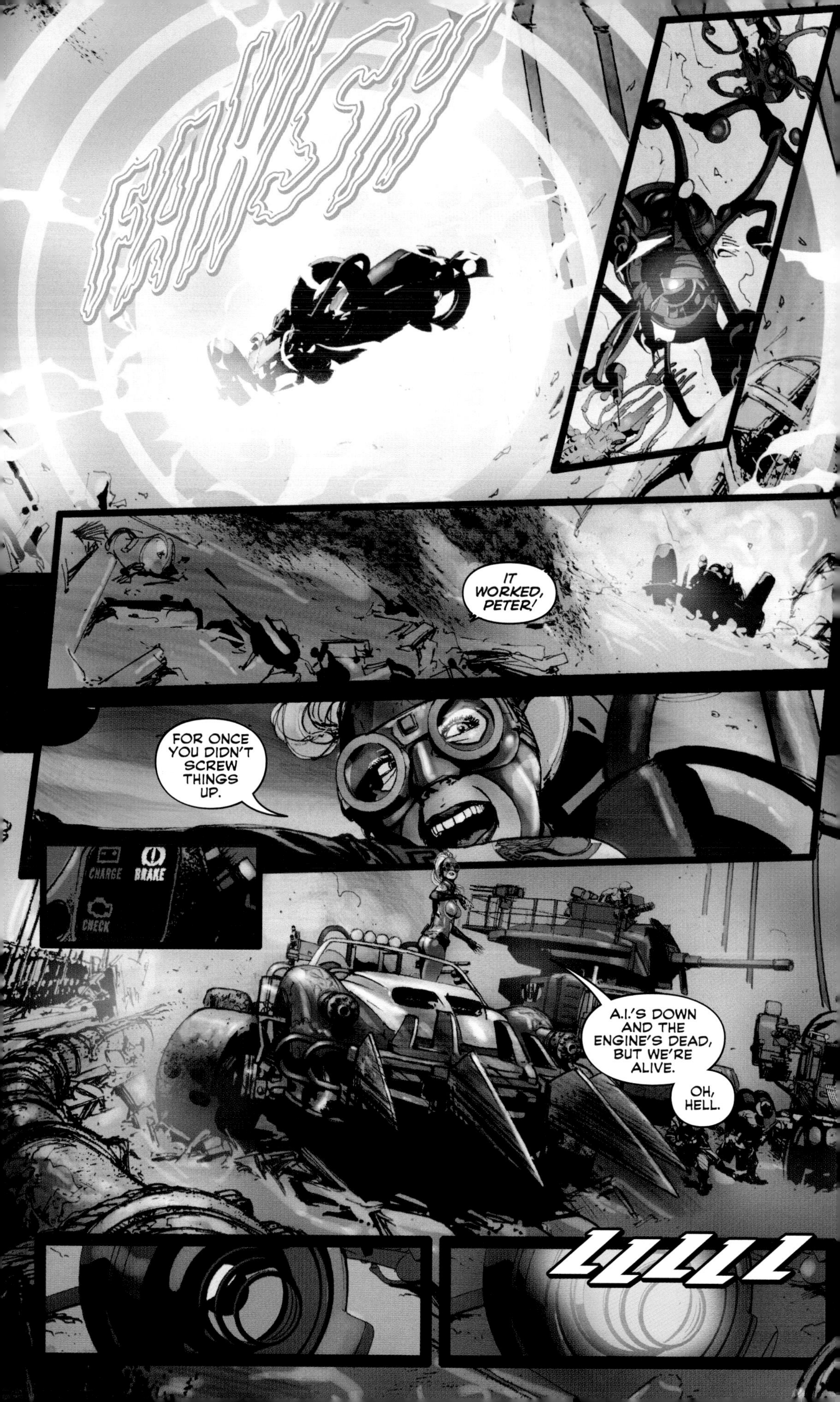
FRAKSH
IT WORKED, PETER!
FOR ONCE YOU DIDN'T SCREW THINGS UP.
CHARGE
BRAKE
CHECK
A.I.'S DOWN AND THE ENGINE'S DEAD, BUT WE'RE ALIVE.
OH, HELL.
ZZZZZ

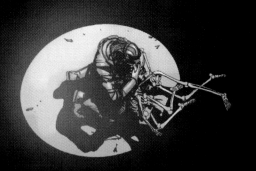

STAGE DOOR

AH-ROOOOOO...

I'M SO SORRY. I'M SO SORRY.

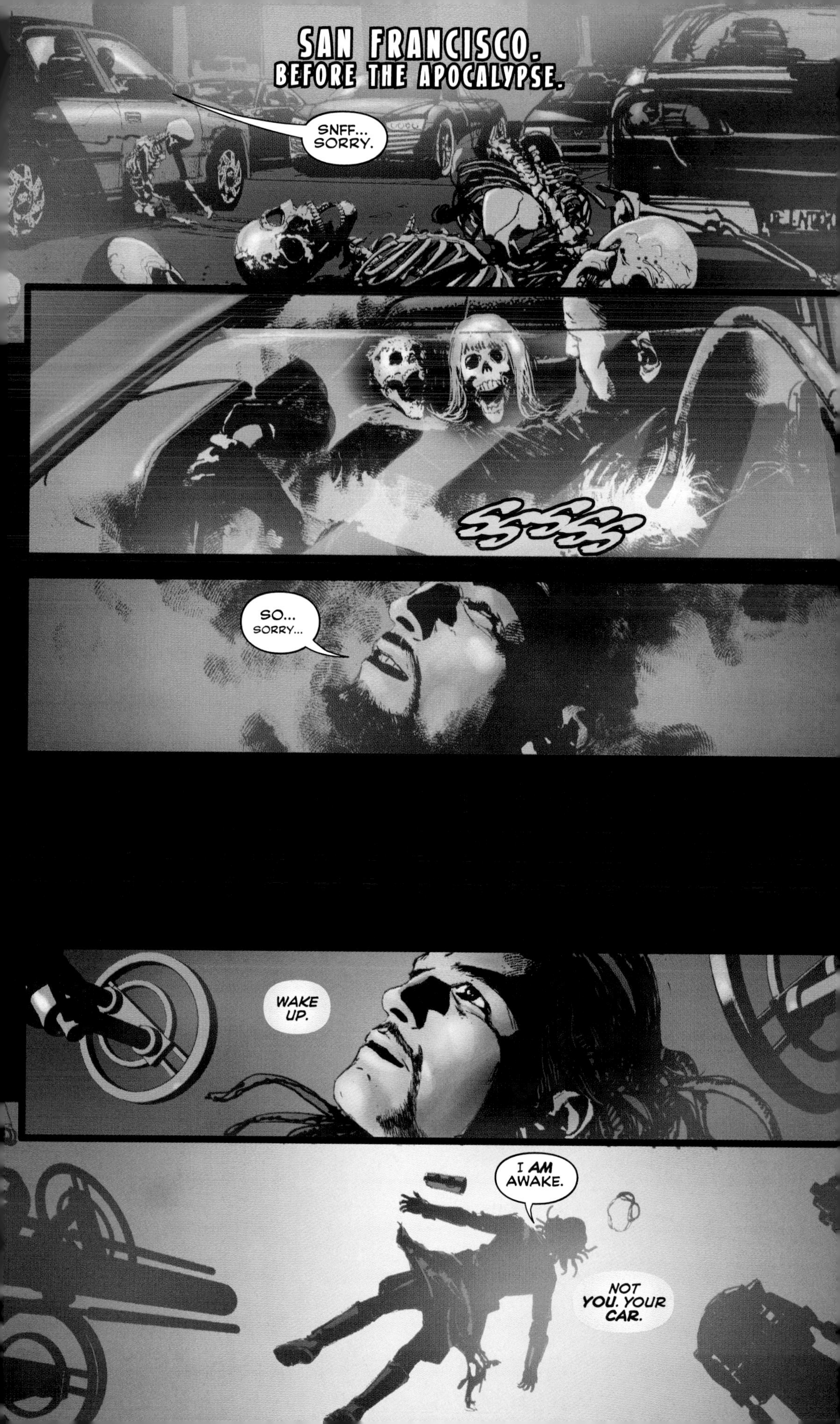
SAN FRANCISCO.
BEFORE THE APOCALYPSE.
SNFF... SORRY.
SSSSS
SO... SORRY...
WAKE UP.
I AM AWAKE.
NOT YOU. YOUR CAR.

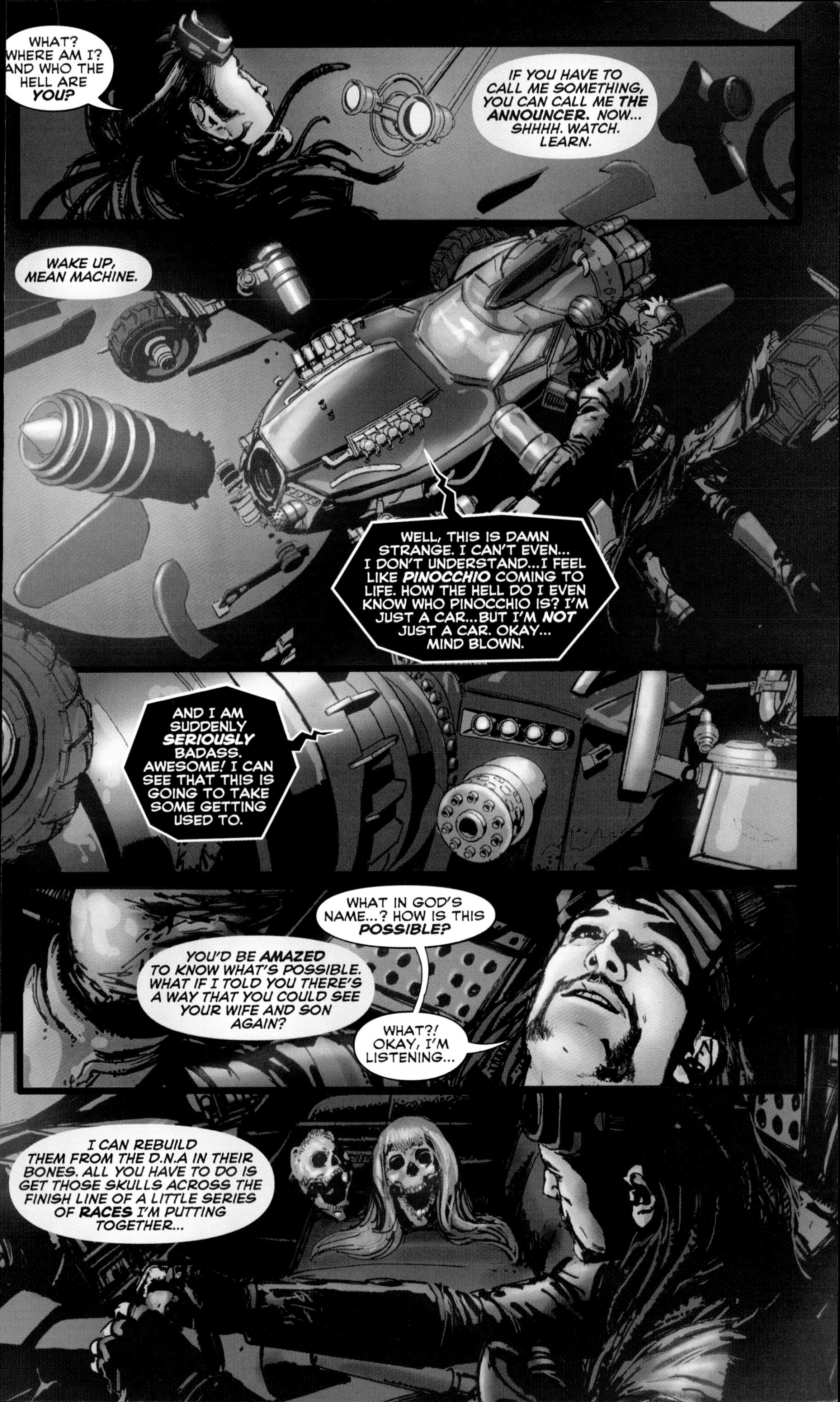
WHAT? WHERE AM I? AND WHO THE HELL ARE YOU?
IF YOU HAVE TO CALL ME SOMETHING, YOU CAN CALL ME THE ANNOUNCER. NOW... SHHHH. WATCH. LEARN.
WAKE UP, MEAN MACHINE.
WELL, THIS IS DAMN STRANGE. I CAN'T EVEN... I DON'T UNDERSTAND...I FEEL LIKE PINOCCHIO COMING TO LIFE. HOW THE HELL DO I EVEN KNOW WHO PINOCCHIO IS? I'M JUST A CAR...BUT I'M NOT JUST A CAR. OKAY... MIND BLOWN.
AND I AM SUDDENLY SERIOUSLY BADASS. AWESOME! I CAN SEE THAT THIS IS GOING TO TAKE SOME GETTING USED TO.
WHAT IN GOD'S NAME...? HOW IS THIS POSSIBLE?
YOU'D BE AMAZED TO KNOW WHAT'S POSSIBLE. WHAT IF I TOLD YOU THERE'S A WAY THAT YOU COULD SEE YOUR WIFE AND SON AGAIN?
WHAT?! OKAY, I'M LISTENING...
I CAN REBUILD THEM FROM THE D.N.A IN THEIR BONES. ALL YOU HAVE TO DO IS GET THOSE SKULLS ACROSS THE FINISH LINE OF A LITTLE SERIES OF RACES I'M PUTTING TOGETHER...

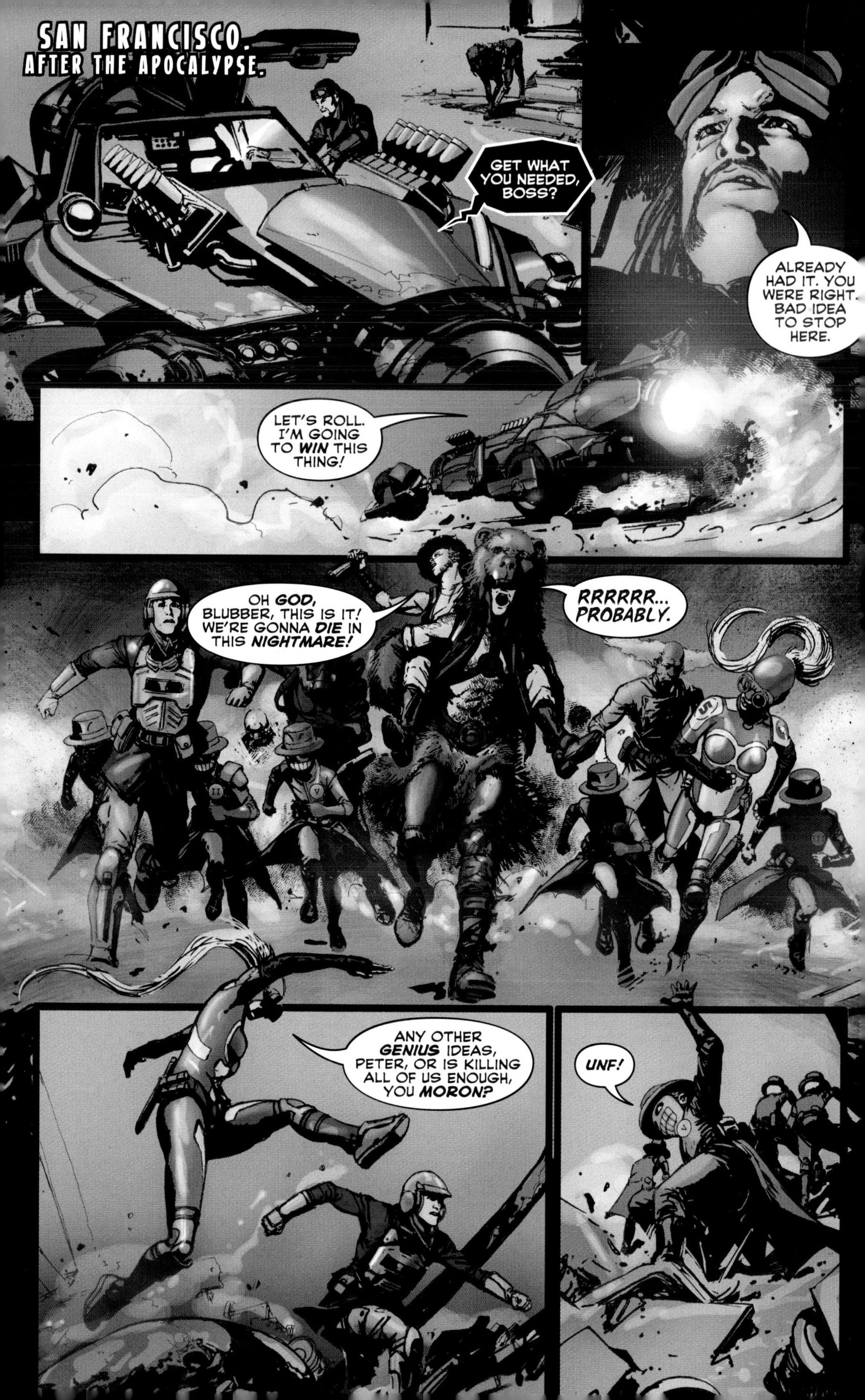
SAN FRANCISCO. AFTER THE APOCALYPSE.
GET WHAT YOU NEEDED, BOSS?
ALREADY HAD IT. YOU WERE RIGHT. BAD IDEA TO STOP HERE.
LET'S ROLL. I'M GOING TO *WIN* THIS THING!
OH *GOD,* BLUBBER, THIS IS IT! WE'RE GONNA *DIE* IN THIS *NIGHTMARE!*
RRRRRR... PROBABLY.
ANY OTHER *GENIUS* IDEAS, PETER, OR IS KILLING ALL OF US ENOUGH, YOU *MORON?*
UNF!

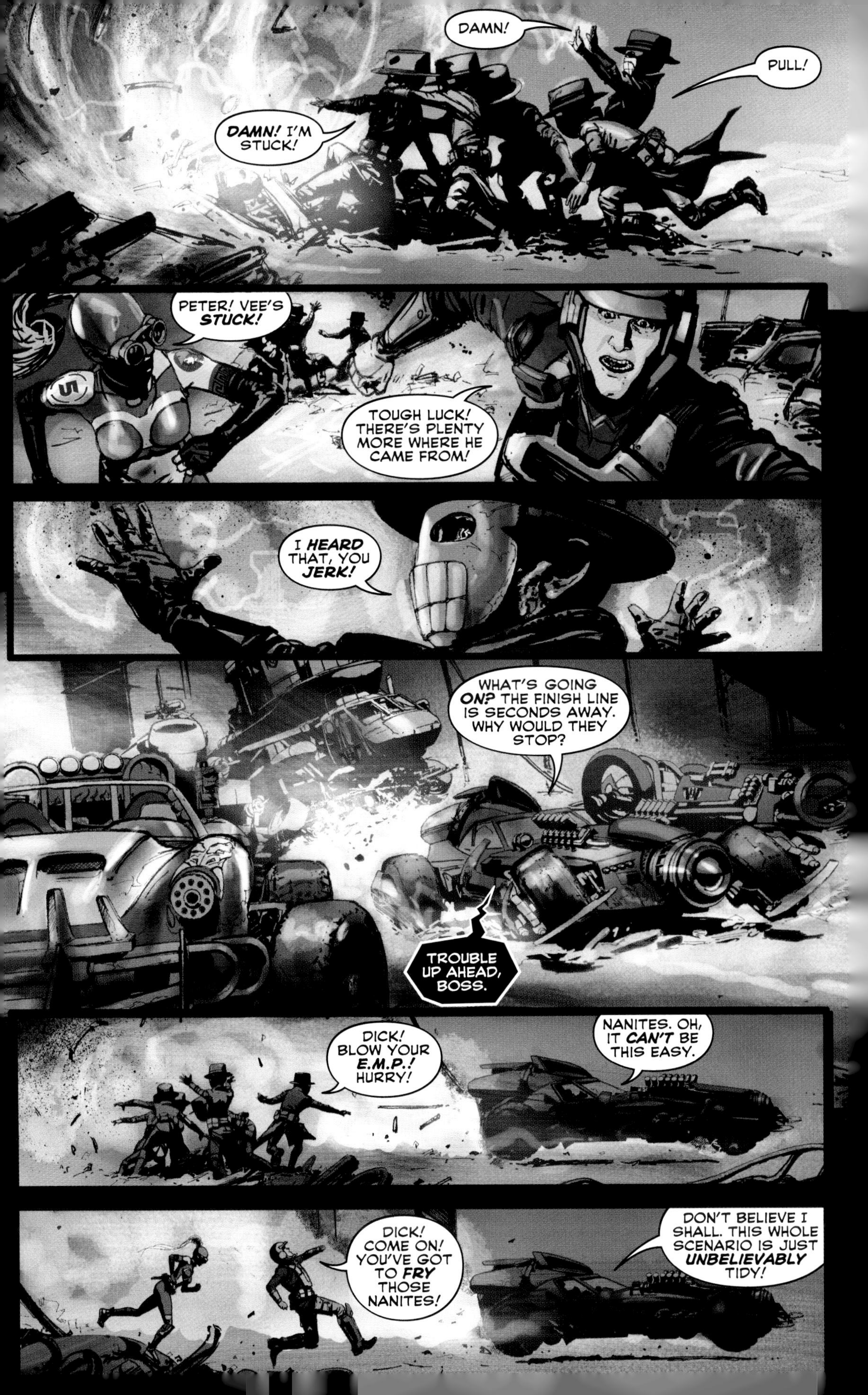
DAMN!
PULL!
DAMN! I'M STUCK!
PETER! VEE'S STUCK!
TOUGH LUCK! THERE'S PLENTY MORE WHERE HE CAME FROM!
I HEARD THAT, YOU JERK!
WHAT'S GOING ON? THE FINISH LINE IS SECONDS AWAY. WHY WOULD THEY STOP?
TROUBLE UP AHEAD, BOSS.
DICK! BLOW YOUR E.M.P.! HURRY!
NANITES. OH, IT CAN'T BE THIS EASY.
DICK! COME ON! YOU'VE GOT TO FRY THOSE NANITES!
DON'T BELIEVE I SHALL. THIS WHOLE SCENARIO IS JUST UNBELIEVABLY TIDY!

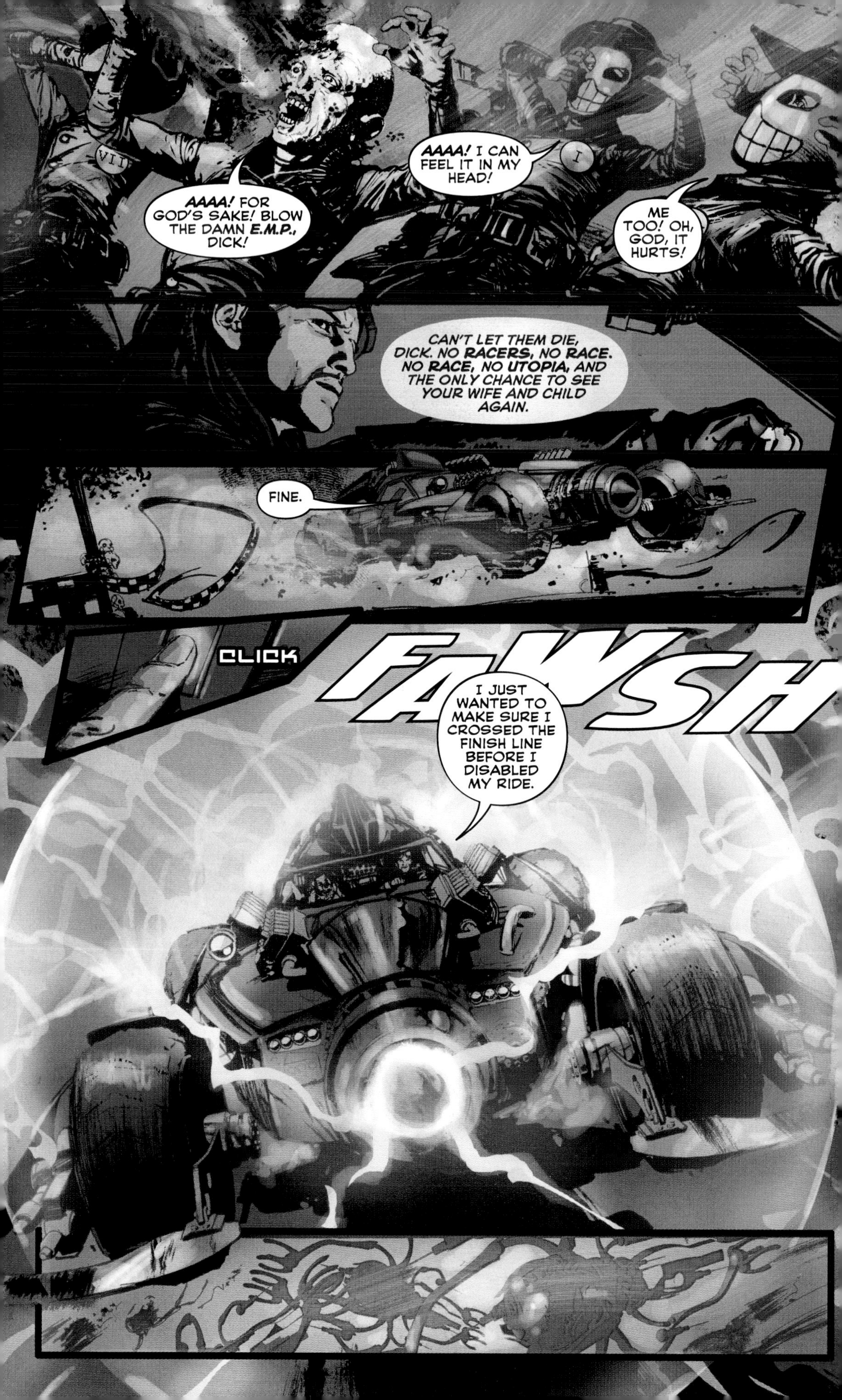
AAAA! FOR GOD'S SAKE! BLOW THE DAMN E.M.P., DICK!
AAAA! I CAN FEEL IT IN MY HEAD!
ME TOO! OH, GOD, IT HURTS!
CAN'T LET THEM DIE, DICK. NO RACERS, NO RACE. NO RACE, NO UTOPIA, AND THE ONLY CHANCE TO SEE YOUR WIFE AND CHILD AGAIN.
FINE.
CLICK
FAWSH
I JUST WANTED TO MAKE SURE I CROSSED THE FINISH LINE BEFORE I DISABLED MY RIDE.

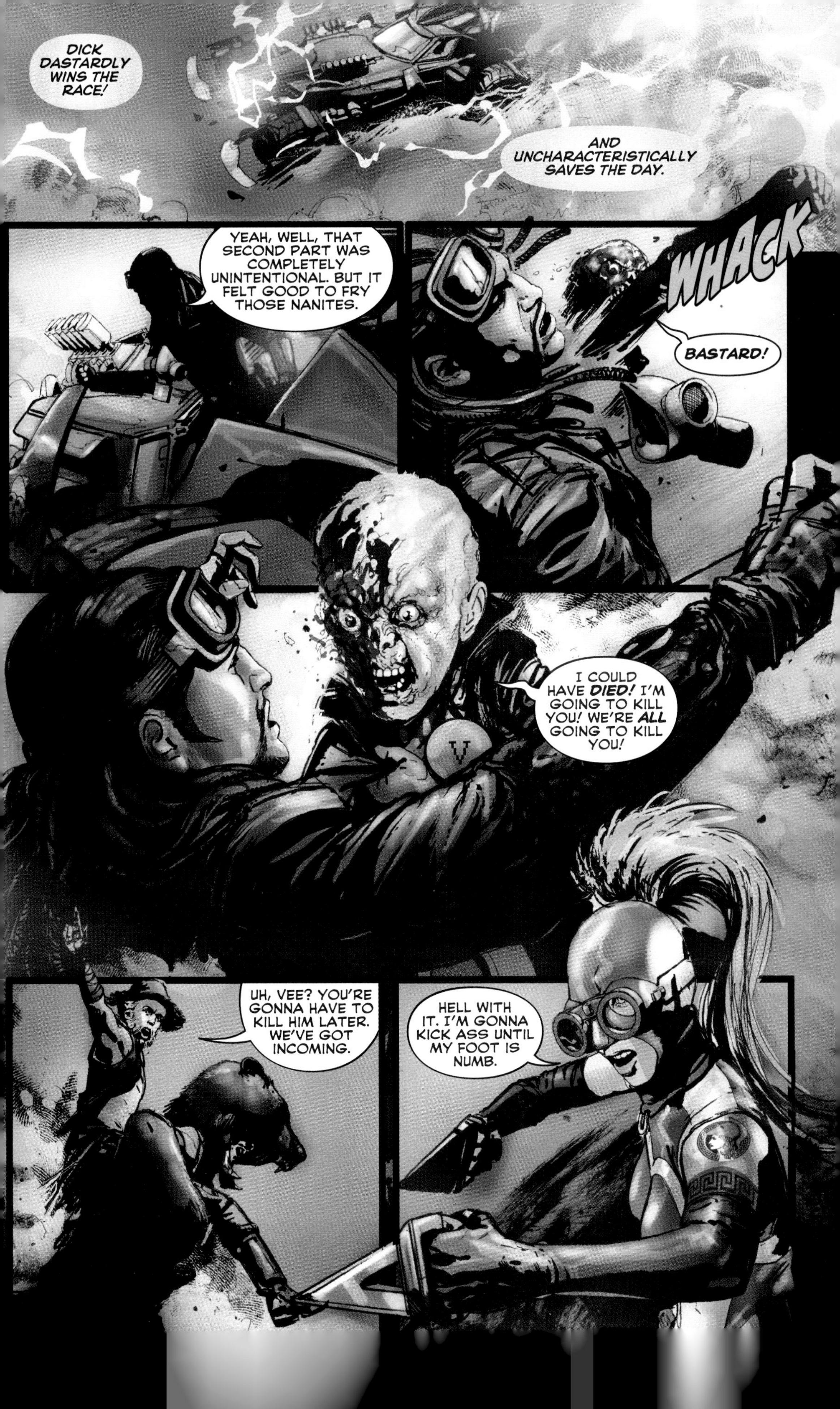
DICK DASTARDLY WINS THE RACE!
AND UNCHARACTERISTICALLY SAVES THE DAY.
YEAH, WELL, THAT SECOND PART WAS COMPLETELY UNINTENTIONAL. BUT IT FELT GOOD TO FRY THOSE NANITES.
WHACK
BASTARD!
I COULD HAVE DIED! I'M GOING TO KILL YOU! WE'RE ALL GOING TO KILL YOU!
UH, VEE? YOU'RE GONNA HAVE TO KILL HIM LATER. WE'VE GOT INCOMING.
HELL WITH IT. I'M GONNA KICK ASS UNTIL MY FOOT IS NUMB.

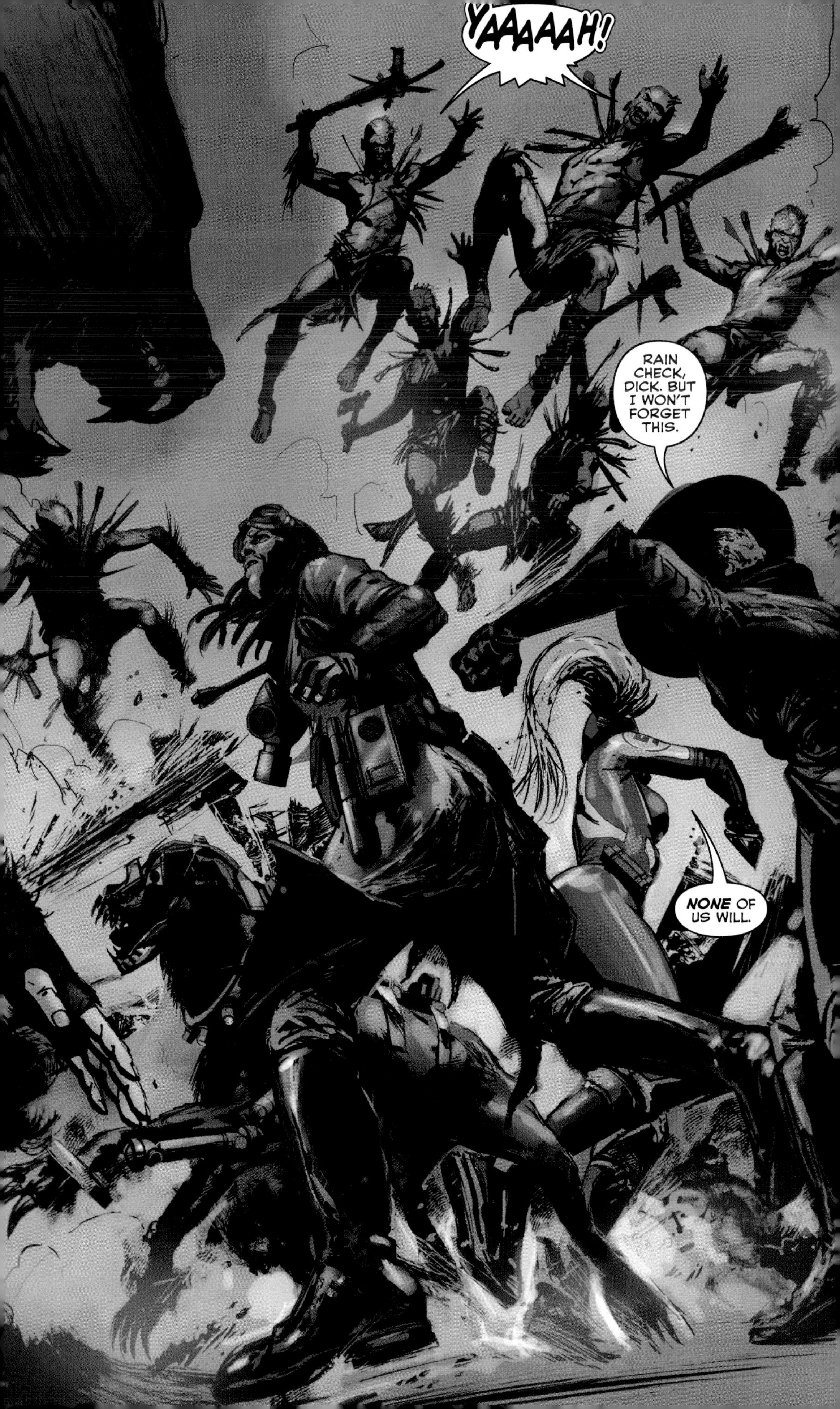
YAAAAAH!
RAIN CHECK, DICK. BUT I WON'T FORGET THIS.
NONE OF US WILL.

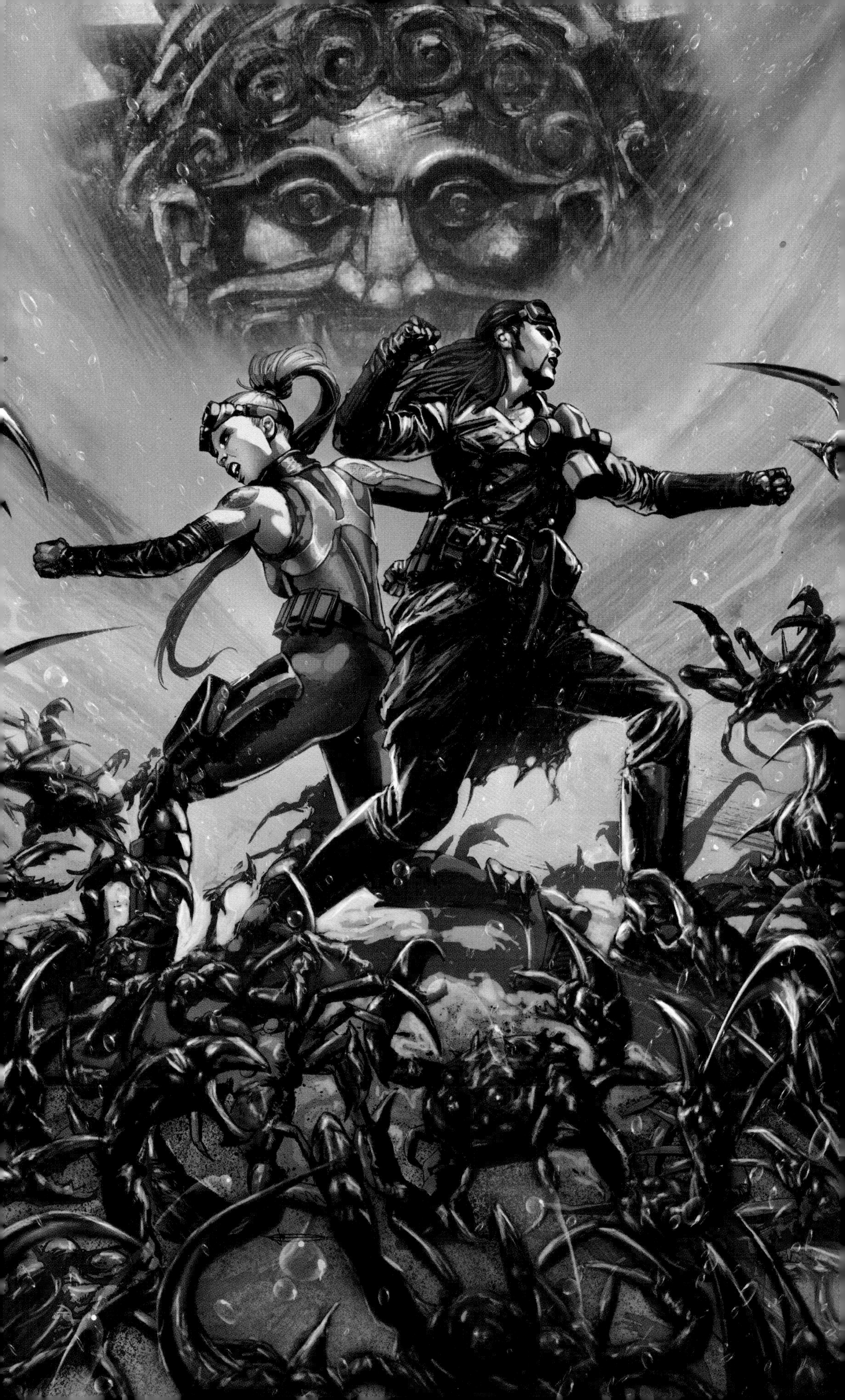

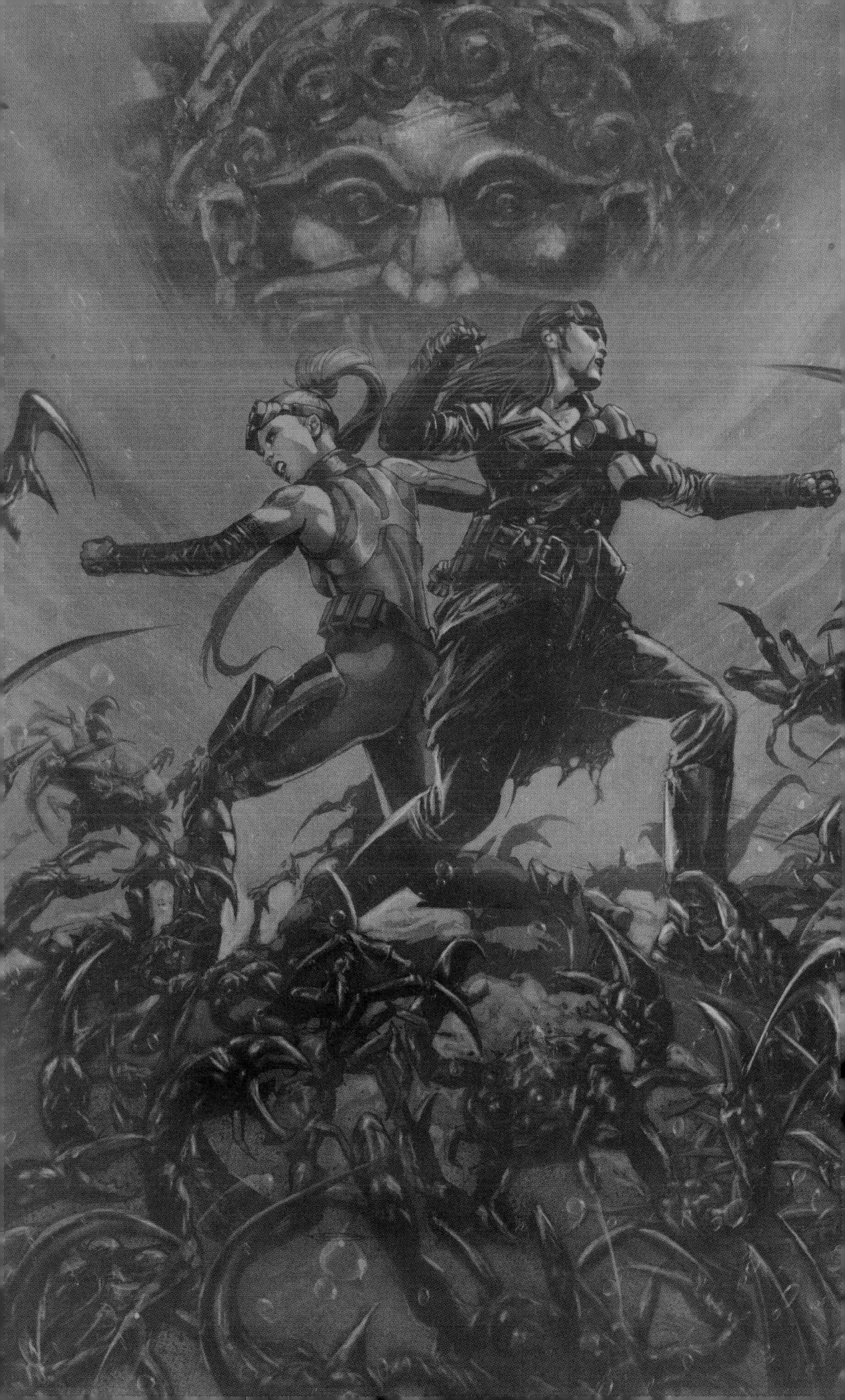

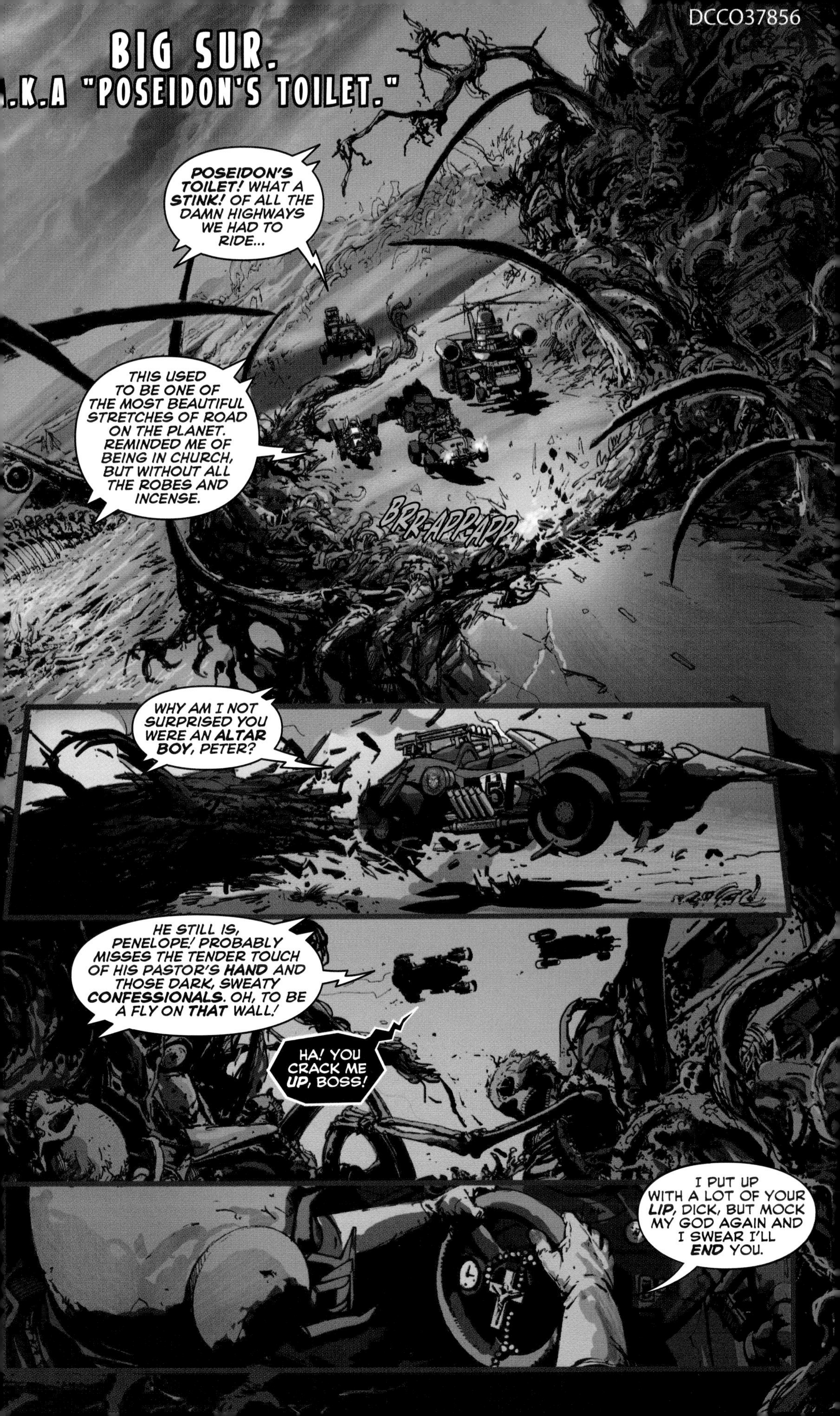
BIG SUR.
.K.A "POSEIDON'S TOILET."
POSEIDON'S TOILET! WHAT A STINK! OF ALL THE DAMN HIGHWAYS WE HAD TO RIDE...
THIS USED TO BE ONE OF THE MOST BEAUTIFUL STRETCHES OF ROAD ON THE PLANET. REMINDED ME OF BEING IN CHURCH, BUT WITHOUT ALL THE ROBES AND INCENSE.
BRR-APPAPP
WHY AM I NOT SURPRISED YOU WERE AN ALTAR BOY, PETER?
HE STILL IS, PENELOPE! PROBABLY MISSES THE TENDER TOUCH OF HIS PASTOR'S HAND AND THOSE DARK, SWEATY CONFESSIONALS. OH, TO BE A FLY ON THAT WALL!
HA! YOU CRACK ME UP, BOSS!
I PUT UP WITH A LOT OF YOUR LIP, DICK, BUT MOCK MY GOD AGAIN AND I SWEAR I'LL END YOU.

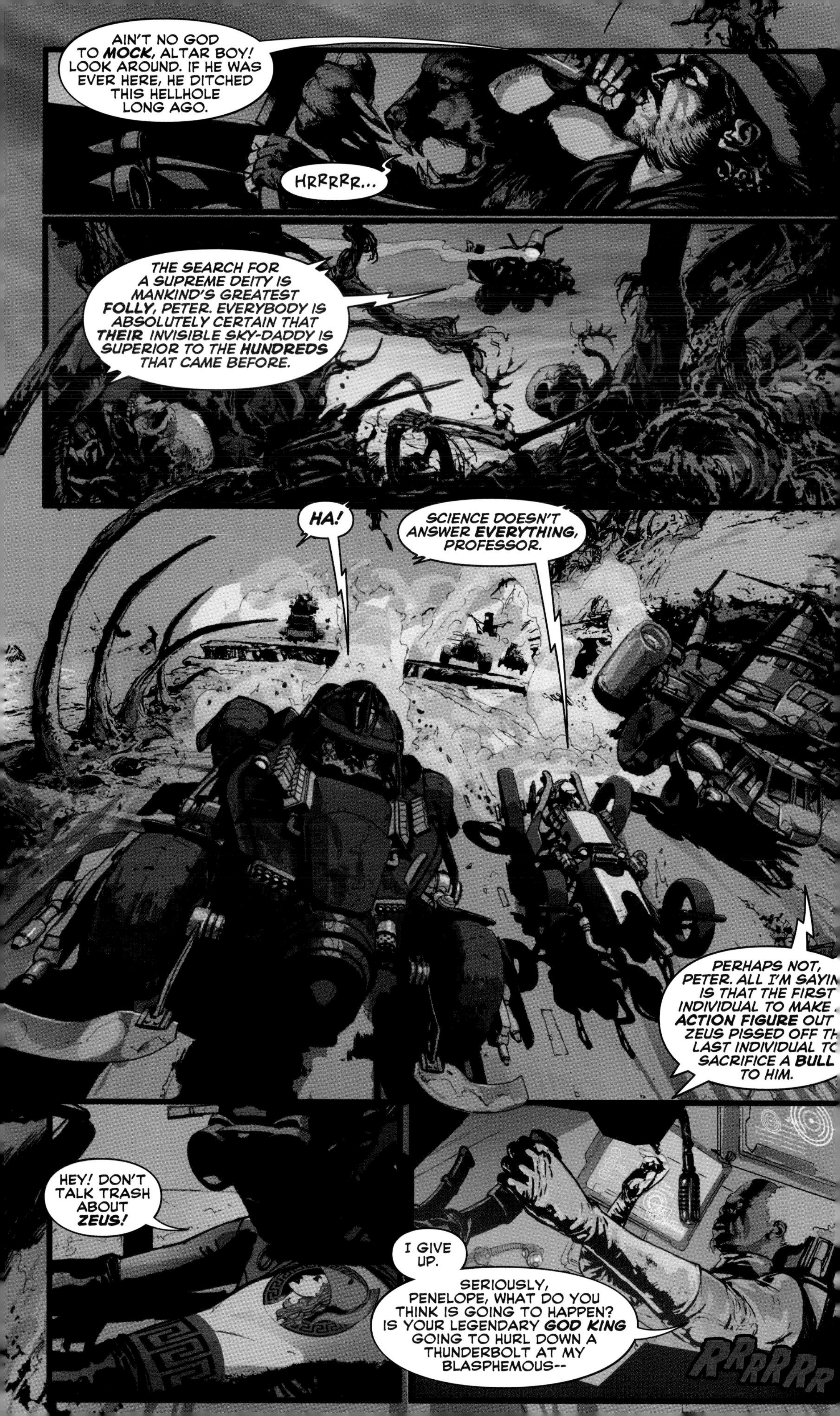

AIN'T NO GOD TO MOCK, ALTAR BOY! LOOK AROUND. IF HE WAS EVER HERE, HE DITCHED THIS HELLHOLE LONG AGO.
HRRRRR...
THE SEARCH FOR A SUPREME DEITY IS MANKIND'S GREATEST FOLLY, PETER. EVERYBODY IS ABSOLUTELY CERTAIN THAT THEIR INVISIBLE SKY-DADDY IS SUPERIOR TO THE HUNDREDS THAT CAME BEFORE.
HA!
SCIENCE DOESN'T ANSWER EVERYTHING, PROFESSOR.
PERHAPS NOT, PETER. ALL I'M SAYIN IS THAT THE FIRST INDIVIDUAL TO MAKE ACTION FIGURE OUT ZEUS PISSED OFF TH LAST INDIVIDUAL TO SACRIFICE A BULL TO HIM.
HEY! DON'T TALK TRASH ABOUT ZEUS!
I GIVE UP.
SERIOUSLY, PENELOPE, WHAT DO YOU THINK IS GOING TO HAPPEN? IS YOUR LEGENDARY GOD KING GOING TO HURL DOWN A THUNDERBOLT AT MY BLASPHEMOUS--
RRRRRRR

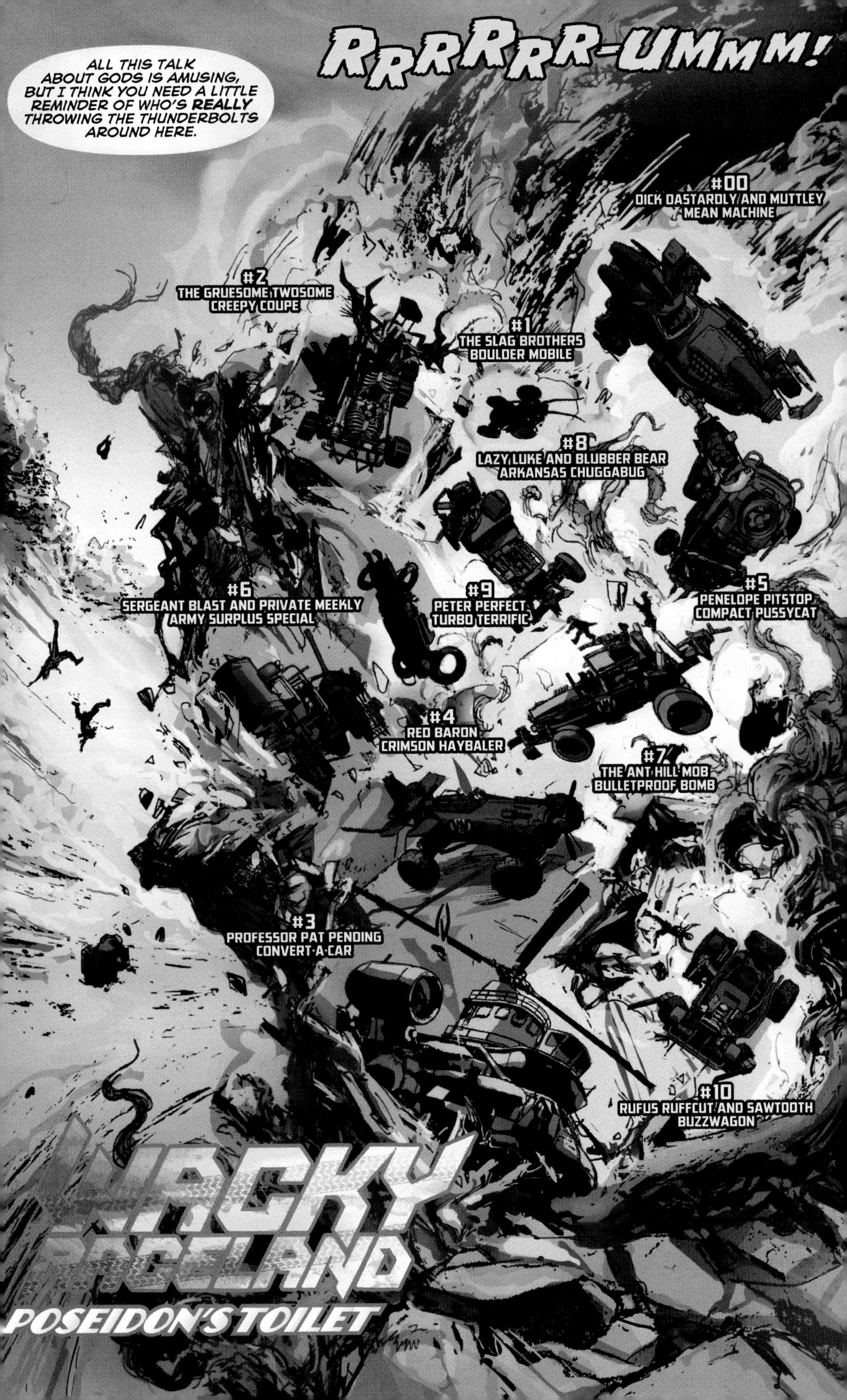
RRRRRRR-UMMMM!
ALL THIS TALK ABOUT GODS IS AMUSING, BUT I THINK YOU NEED A LITTLE REMINDER OF WHO'S **REALLY** THROWING THE THUNDERBOLTS AROUND HERE.
#00 DICK DASTARDLY AND MUTTLEY MEAN MACHINE
#2 THE GRUESOME TWOSOME CREEPY COUPE
#1 THE SLAG BROTHERS BOULDER MOBILE
#8 LAZY LUKE AND BLUBBER BEAR ARKANSAS CHUGGABUG
#6 SERGEANT BLAST AND PRIVATE MEEKLY ARMY SURPLUS SPECIAL
#9 PETER PERFECT TURBO TERRIFIC
#5 PENELOPE PITSTOP COMPACT PUSSYCAT
#4 RED BARON CRIMSON HAYBALER
#7 THE ANT HILL MOB BULLETPROOF BOMB
#3 PROFESSOR PAT PENDING CONVERT-A-CAR
#10 RUFUS RUFFCUT AND SAWTOOTH BUZZWAGON
POSEIDON'S TOILET

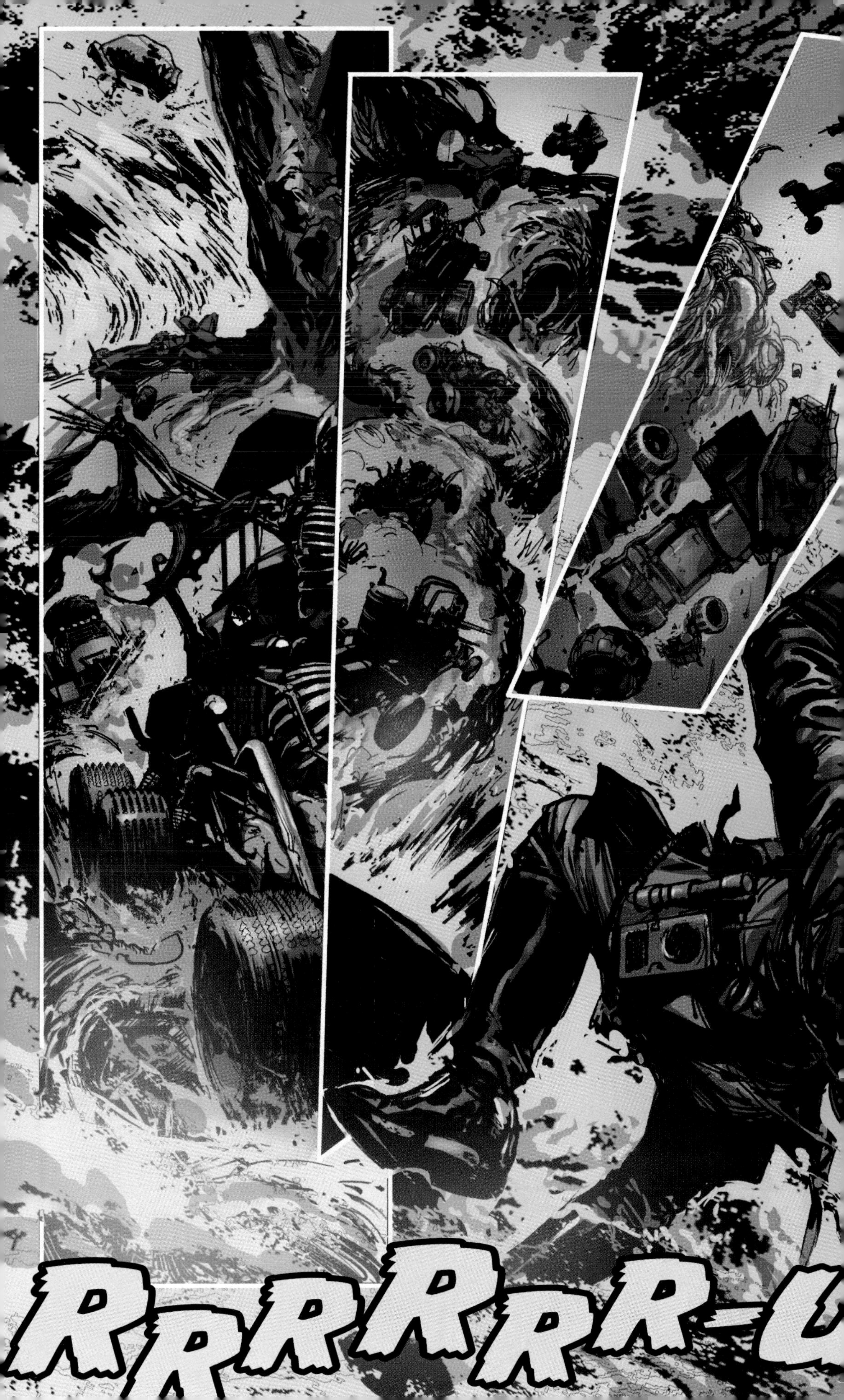
RRRRR-U

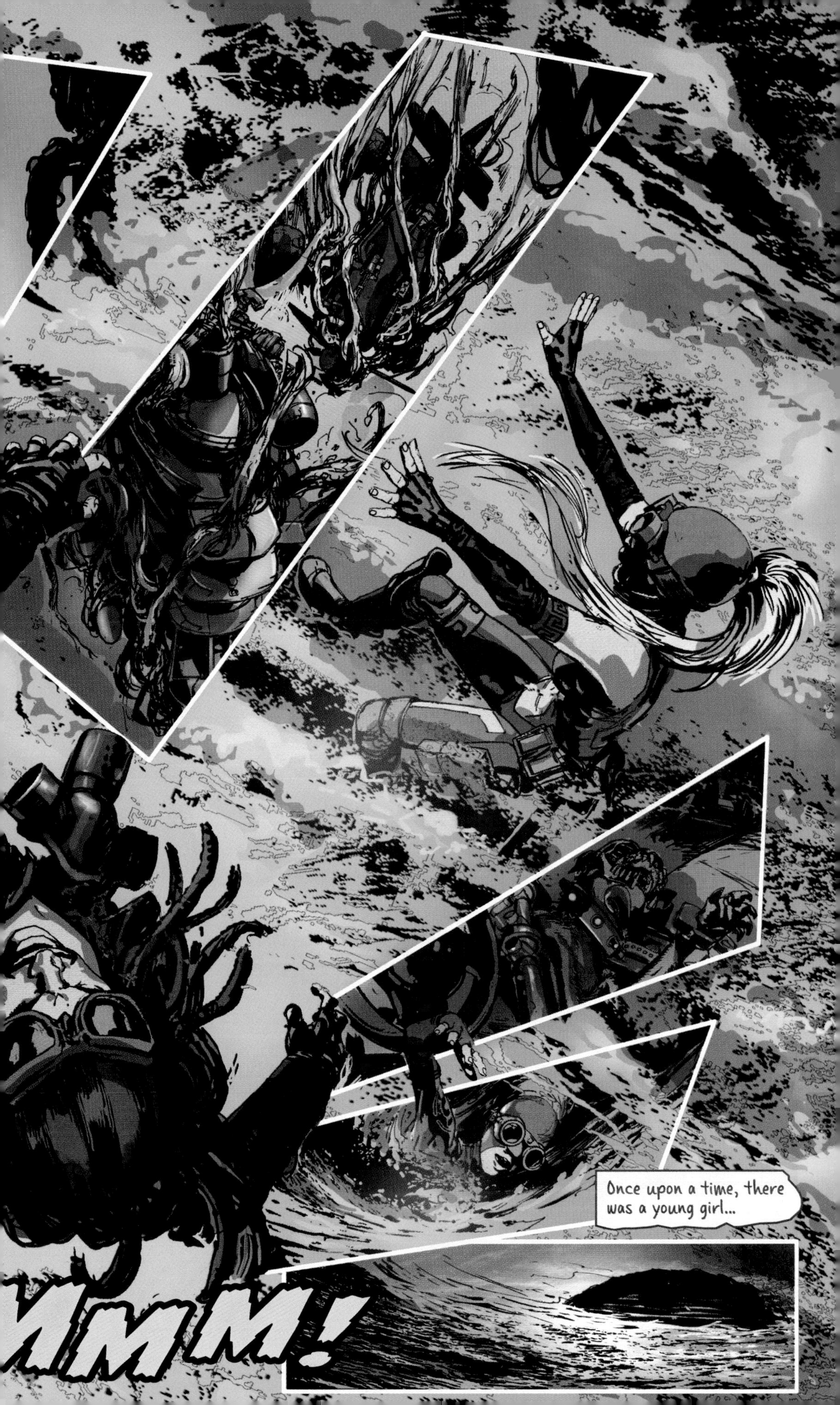
Once upon a time, there was a young girl...
MMM!

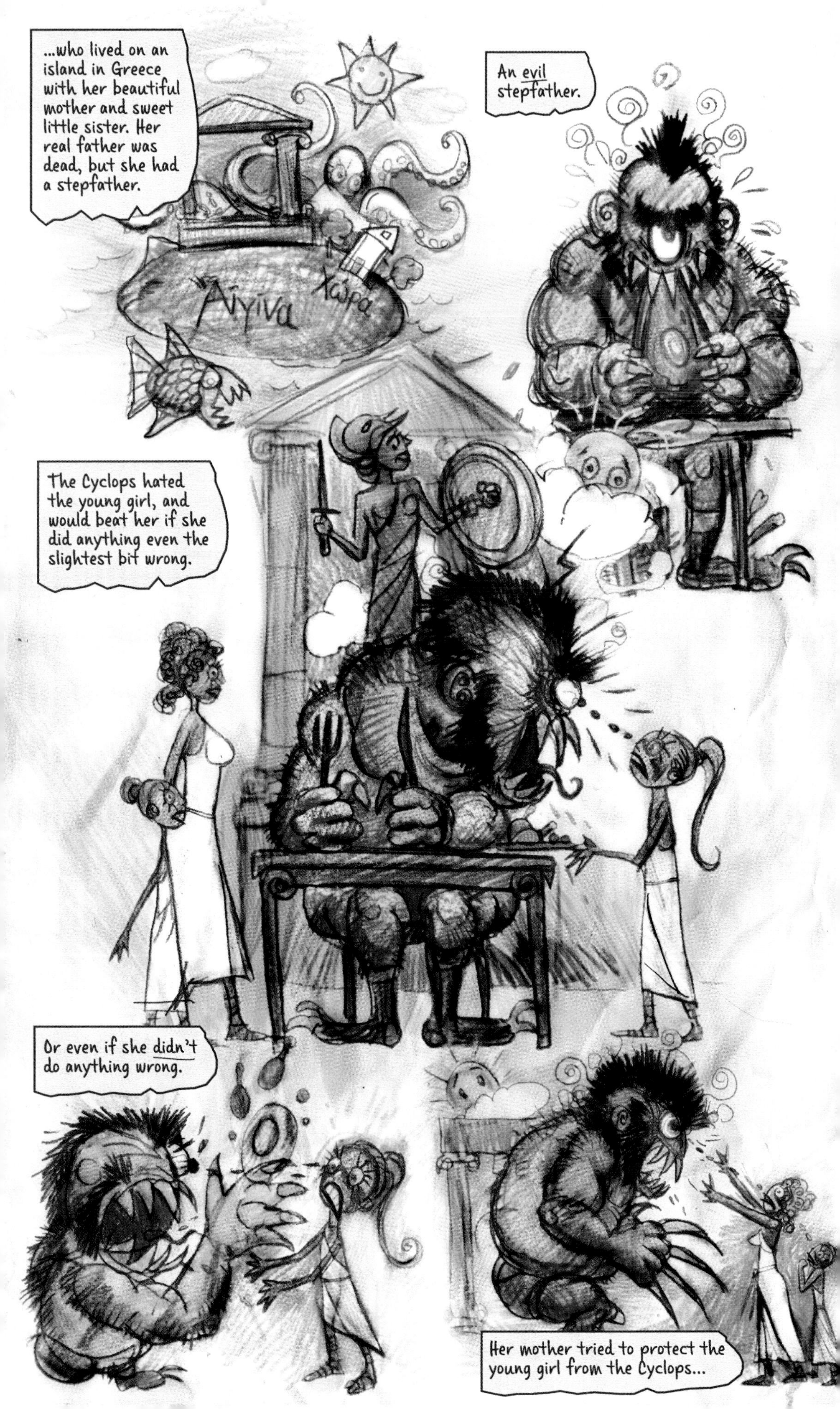

...who lived on an island in Greece with her beautiful mother and sweet little sister. Her real father was dead, but she had a stepfather.
Αίγινα
Χώρα
An evil stepfather.
The Cyclops hated the young girl, and would beat her if she did anything even the slightest bit wrong.
Or even if she didn't do anything wrong.
Her mother tried to protect the young girl from the Cyclops...

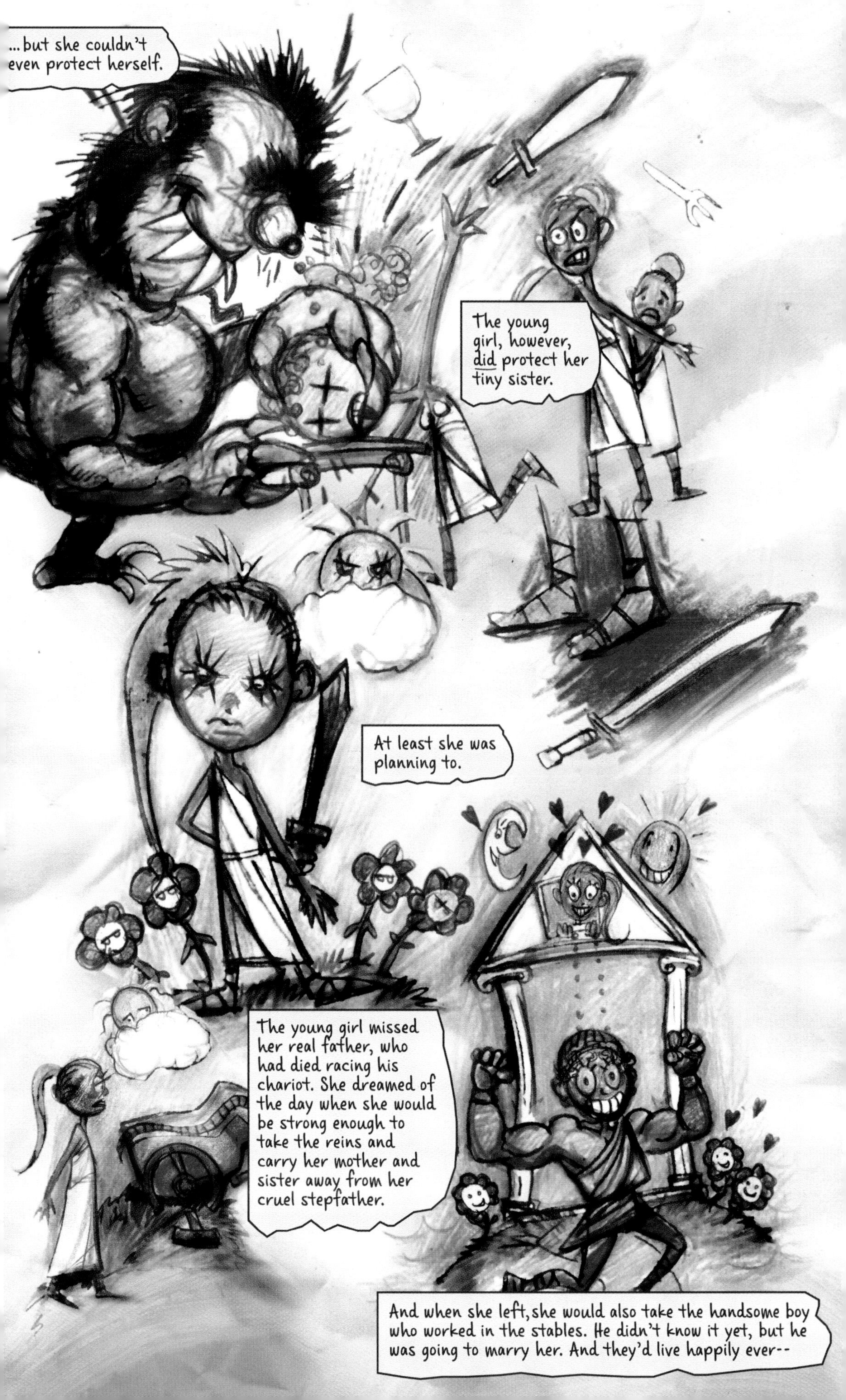
...but she couldn't even protect herself.
The young girl, however, did protect her tiny sister.
At least she was planning to.
The young girl missed her real father, who had died racing his chariot. She dreamed of the day when she would be strong enough to take the reins and carry her mother and sister away from her cruel stepfather.
And when she left, she would also take the handsome boy who worked in the stables. He didn't know it yet, but he was going to marry her. And they'd live happily ever--

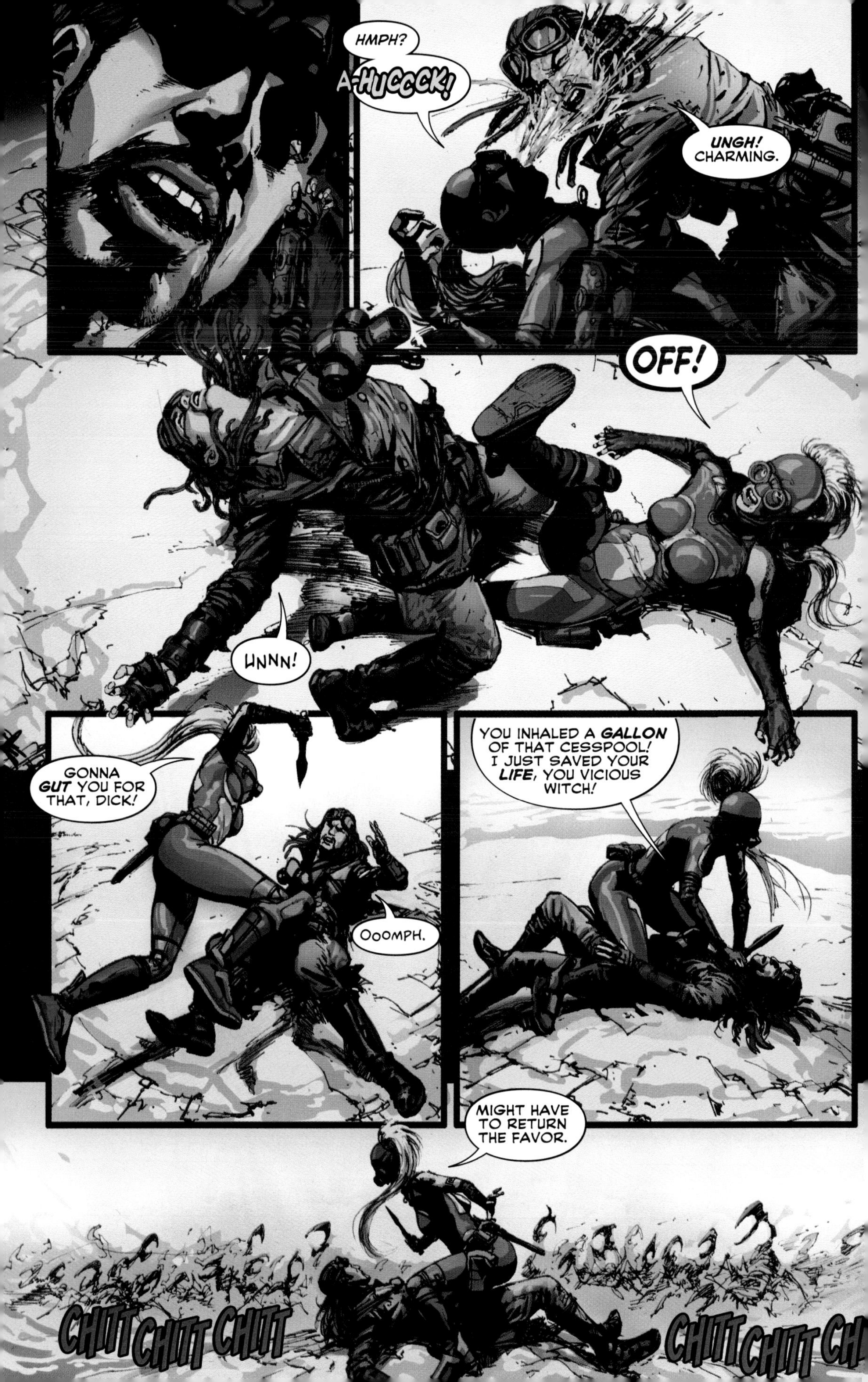
HMPH?
A-HUCCCK!
UNGH! CHARMING.
OFF!
UNNN!
GONNA GUT YOU FOR THAT, DICK!
OOOMPH.
YOU INHALED A GALLON OF THAT CESSPOOL! I JUST SAVED YOUR LIFE, YOU VICIOUS WITCH!
MIGHT HAVE TO RETURN THE FAVOR.
CHITT CHITT CHITT
CHITT CHITT CH

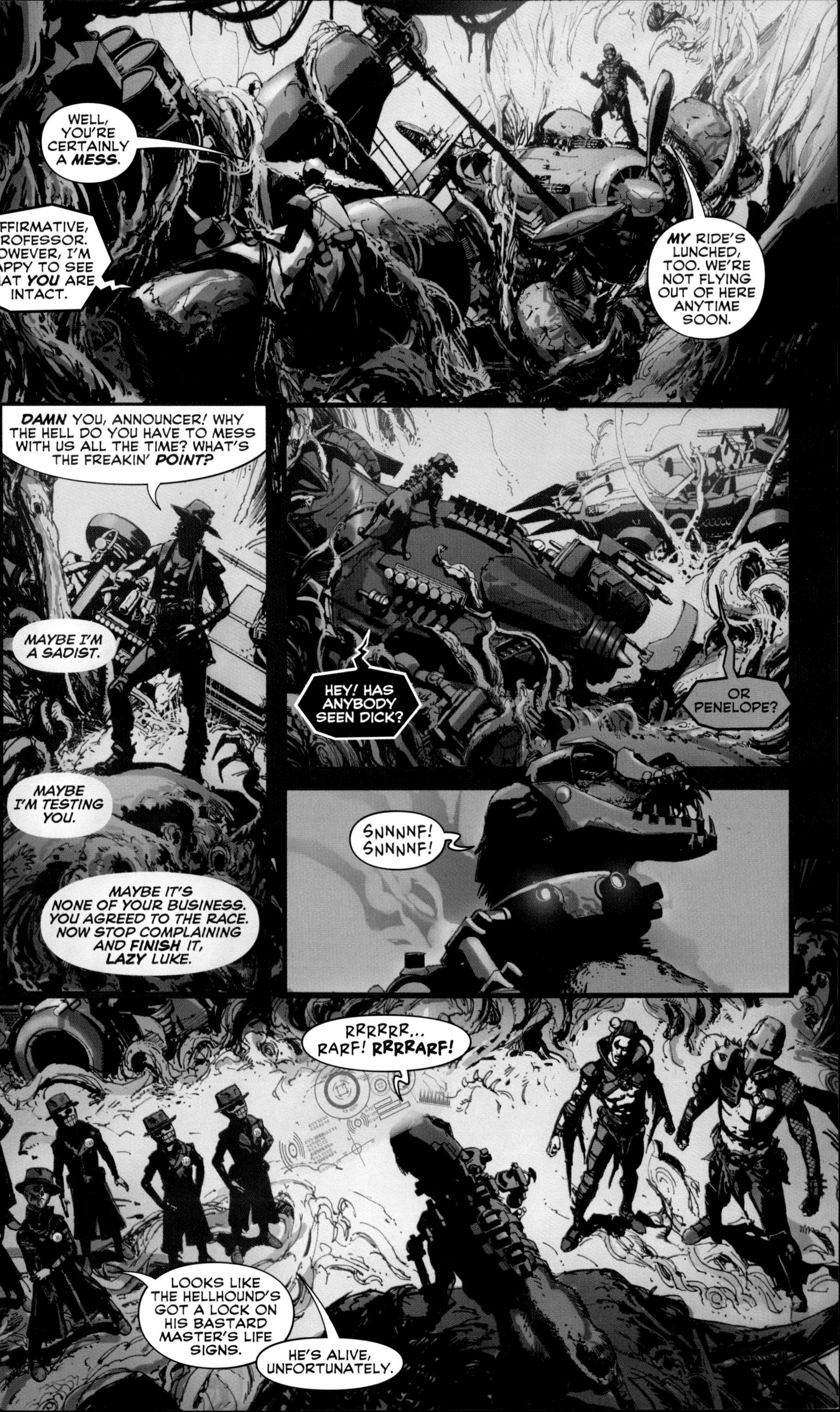
WELL, YOU'RE CERTAINLY A MESS.
FFIRMATIVE, ROFESSOR. OWEVER, I'M APPY TO SEE AT YOU ARE INTACT.
MY RIDE'S LUNCHED, TOO. WE'RE NOT FLYING OUT OF HERE ANYTIME SOON.
DAMN YOU, ANNOUNCER! WHY THE HELL DO YOU HAVE TO MESS WITH US ALL THE TIME? WHAT'S THE FREAKIN' POINT?
MAYBE I'M A SADIST.
MAYBE I'M TESTING YOU.
MAYBE IT'S NONE OF YOUR BUSINESS. YOU AGREED TO THE RACE. NOW STOP COMPLAINING AND FINISH IT, LAZY LUKE.
HEY! HAS ANYBODY SEEN DICK?
OR PENELOPE?
SNNNNF! SNNNNF!
RRRRRR... RARF! RRRRARF!
LOOKS LIKE THE HELLHOUND'S GOT A LOCK ON HIS BASTARD MASTER'S LIFE SIGNS.
HE'S ALIVE, UNFORTUNATELY.

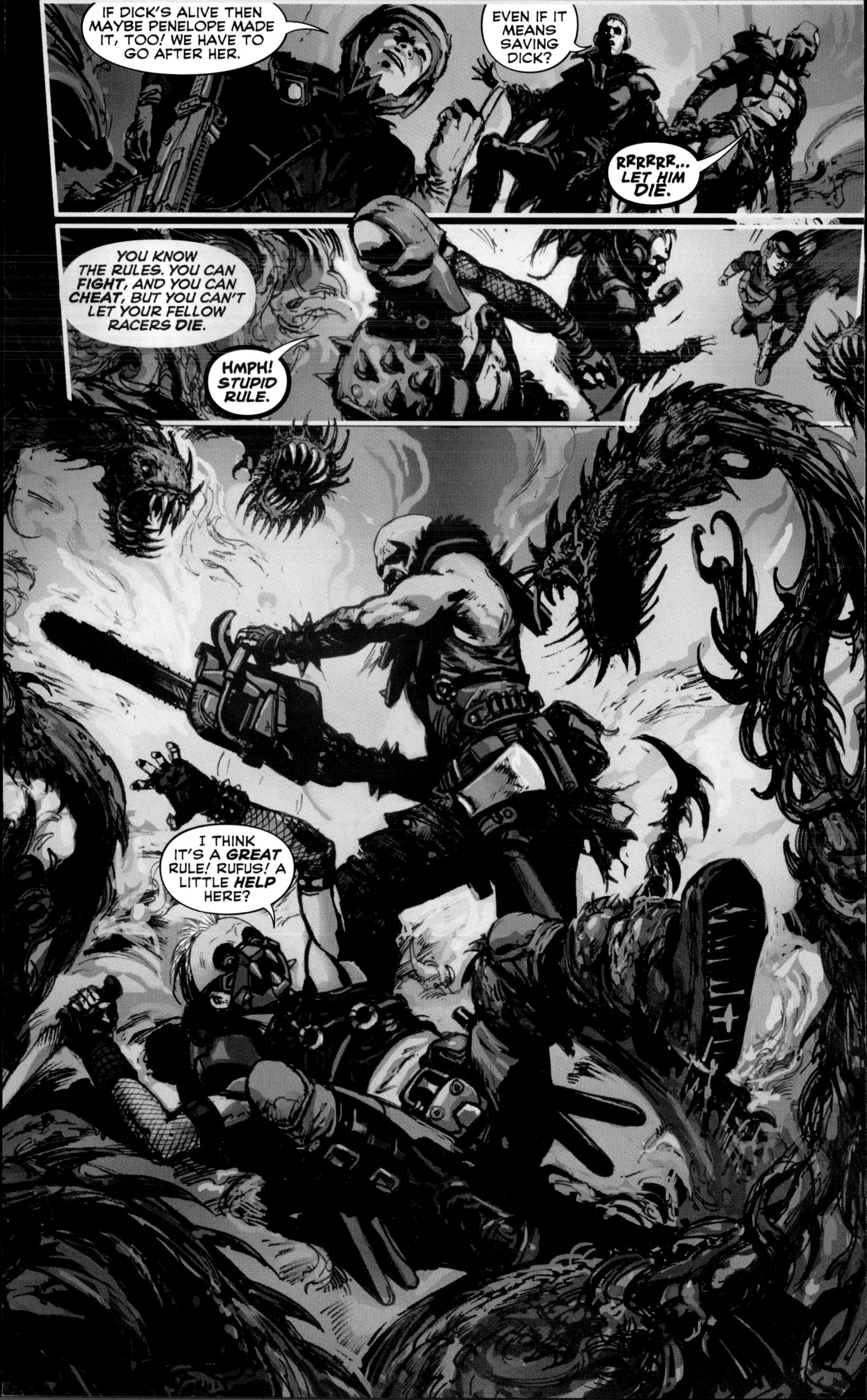
IF DICK'S ALIVE THEN MAYBE PENELOPE MADE IT, TOO! WE HAVE TO GO AFTER HER.
EVEN IF IT MEANS SAVING DICK?
RRRRRR... LET HIM DIE.
YOU KNOW THE RULES. YOU CAN FIGHT, AND YOU CAN CHEAT, BUT YOU CAN'T LET YOUR FELLOW RACERS DIE.
HMPH! STUPID RULE.
I THINK IT'S A GREAT RULE! RUFUS! A LITTLE HELP HERE?

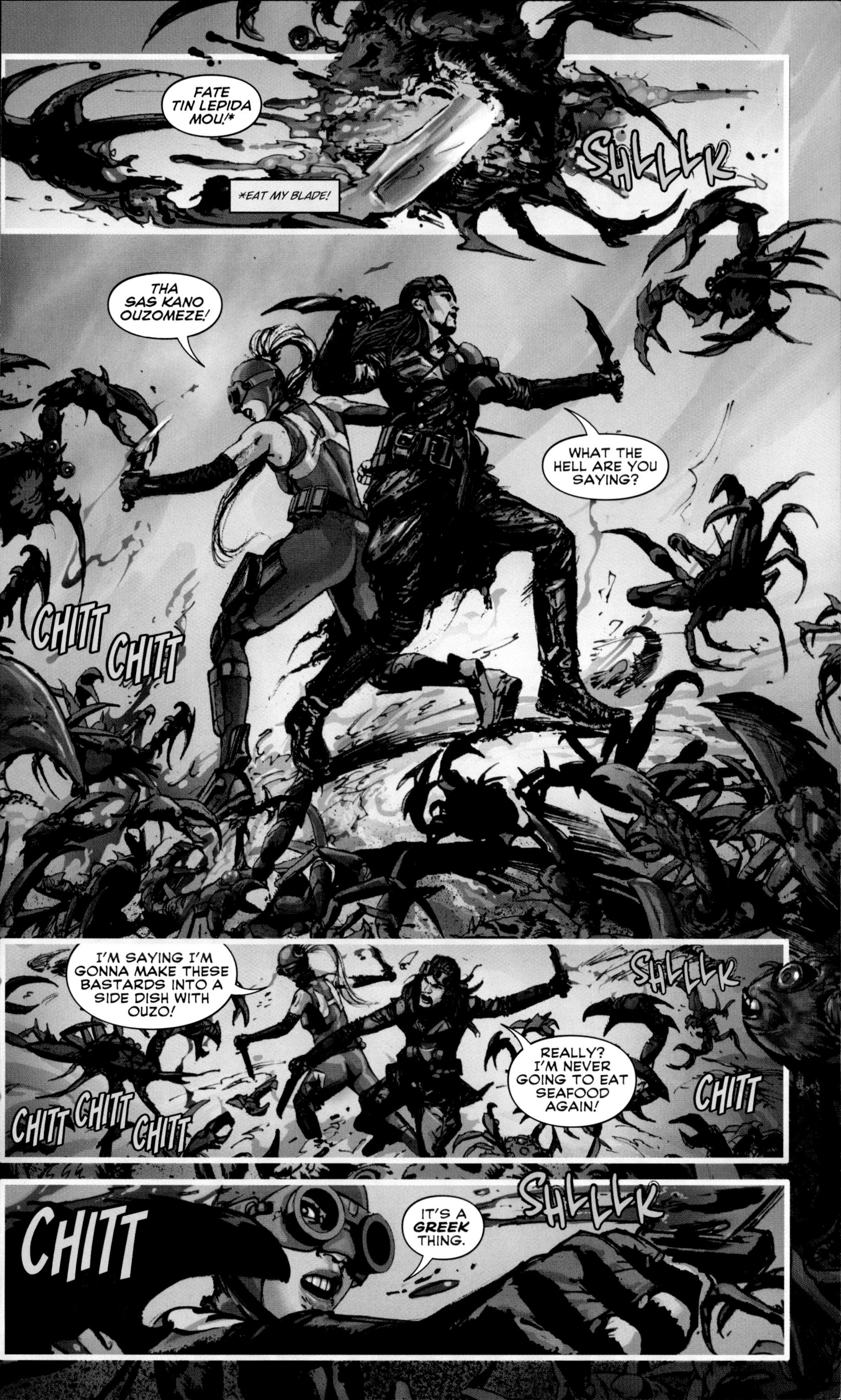
FATE TIN LEPIDA MOU!*
SHLLLK
*EAT MY BLADE!
THA SAS KANO OUZOMEZE!
WHAT THE HELL ARE YOU SAYING?
CHITT CHITT
I'M SAYING I'M GONNA MAKE THESE BASTARDS INTO A SIDE DISH WITH OUZO!
SHLLLK
REALLY? I'M NEVER GOING TO EAT SEAFOOD AGAIN!
CHITT CHITT CHITT
CHITT
CHITT
SHLLLK
IT'S A **GREEK** THING.

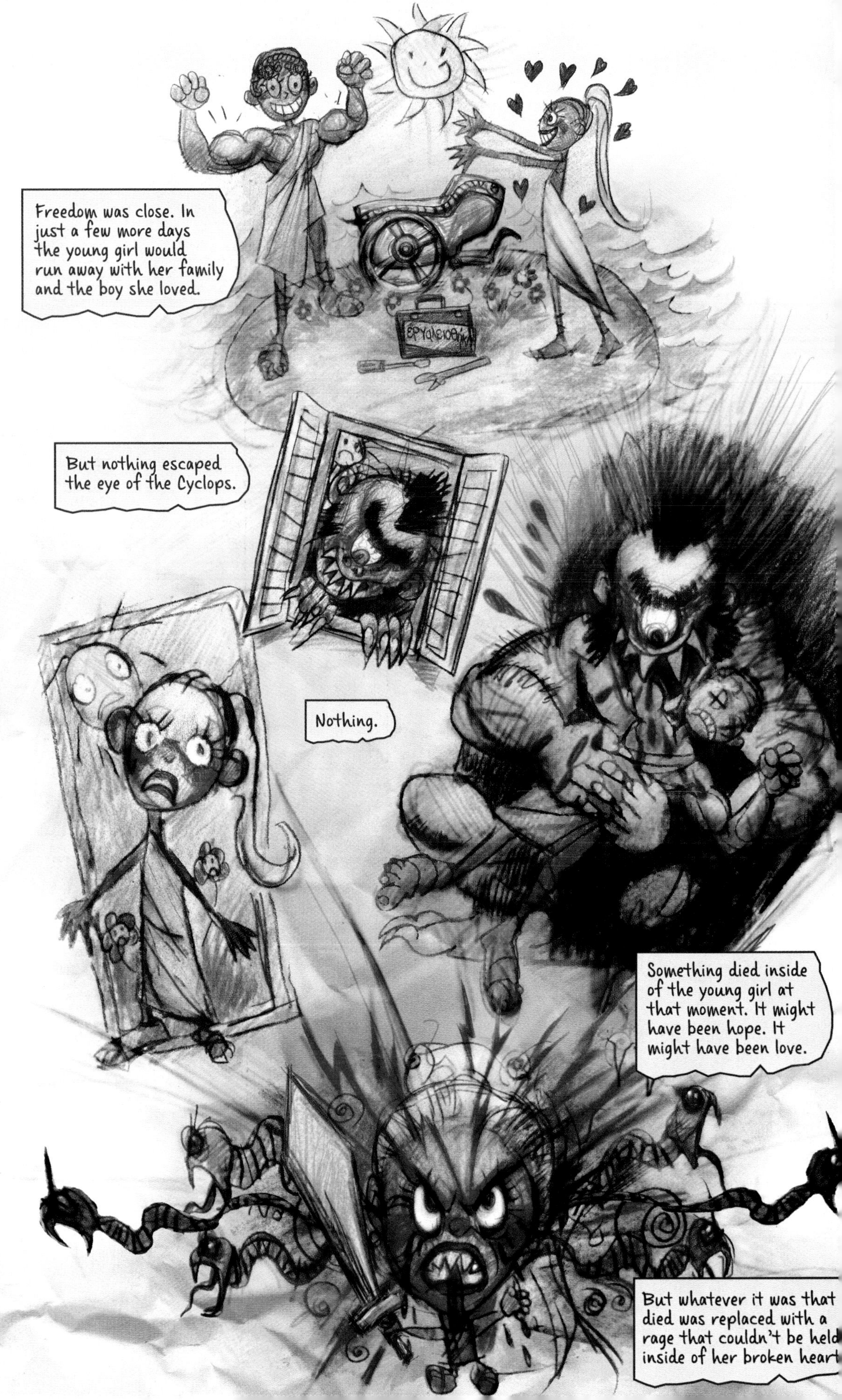
Freedom was close. In just a few more days the young girl would run away with her family and the boy she loved.
But nothing escaped the eye of the Cyclops.
Nothing.
Something died inside of the young girl at that moment. It might have been hope. It might have been love.
But whatever it was that died was replaced with a rage that couldn't be held inside of her broken heart

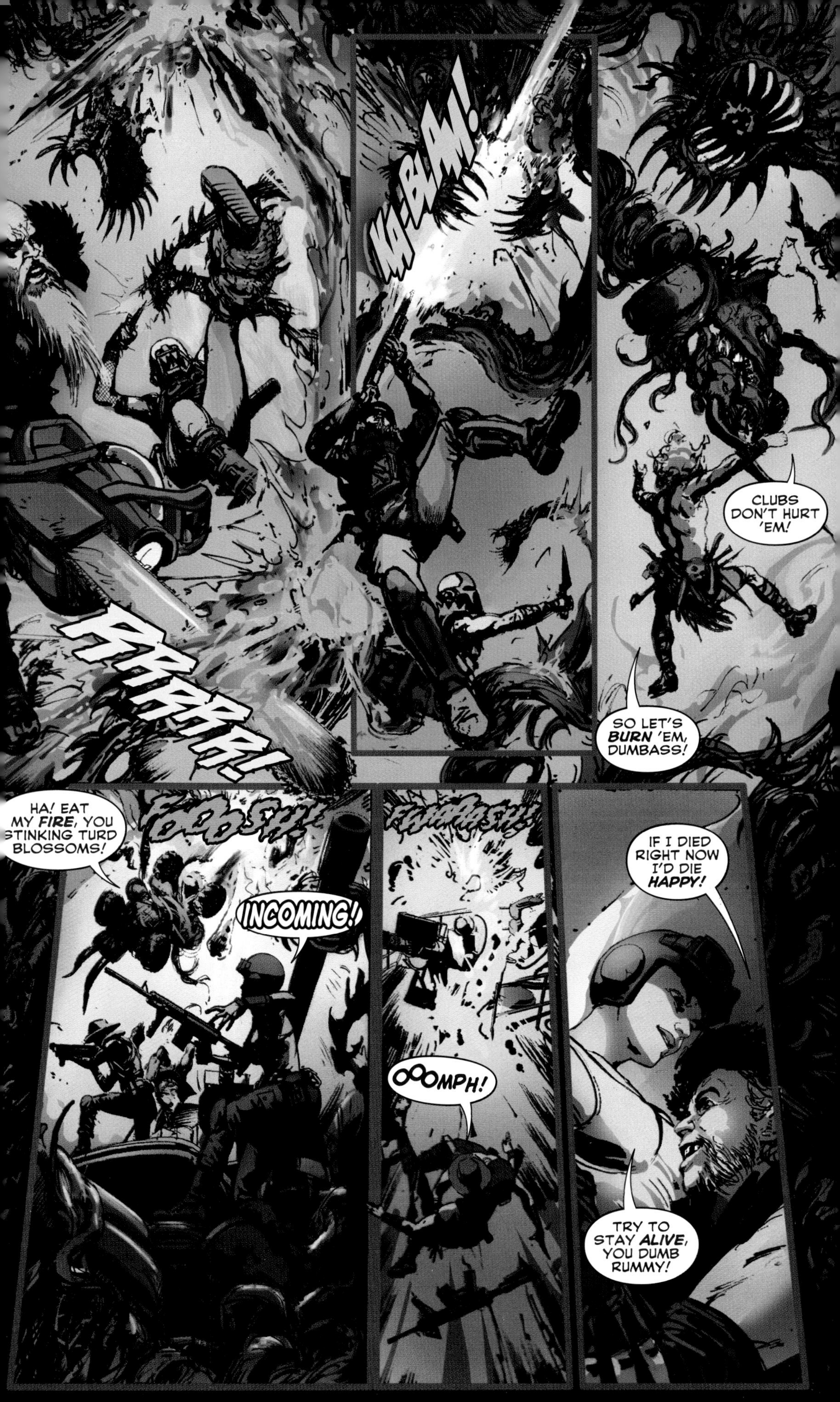
KA-BLAM!
CLUBS DON'T HURT 'EM!
FRRRRR!
SO LET'S BURN 'EM, DUMBASS!
HA! EAT MY FIRE, YOU STINKING TURD BLOSSOMS!
INCOMING!
OOOMPH!
IF I DIED RIGHT NOW I'D DIE HAPPY!
TRY TO STAY ALIVE, YOU DUMB RUMMY!

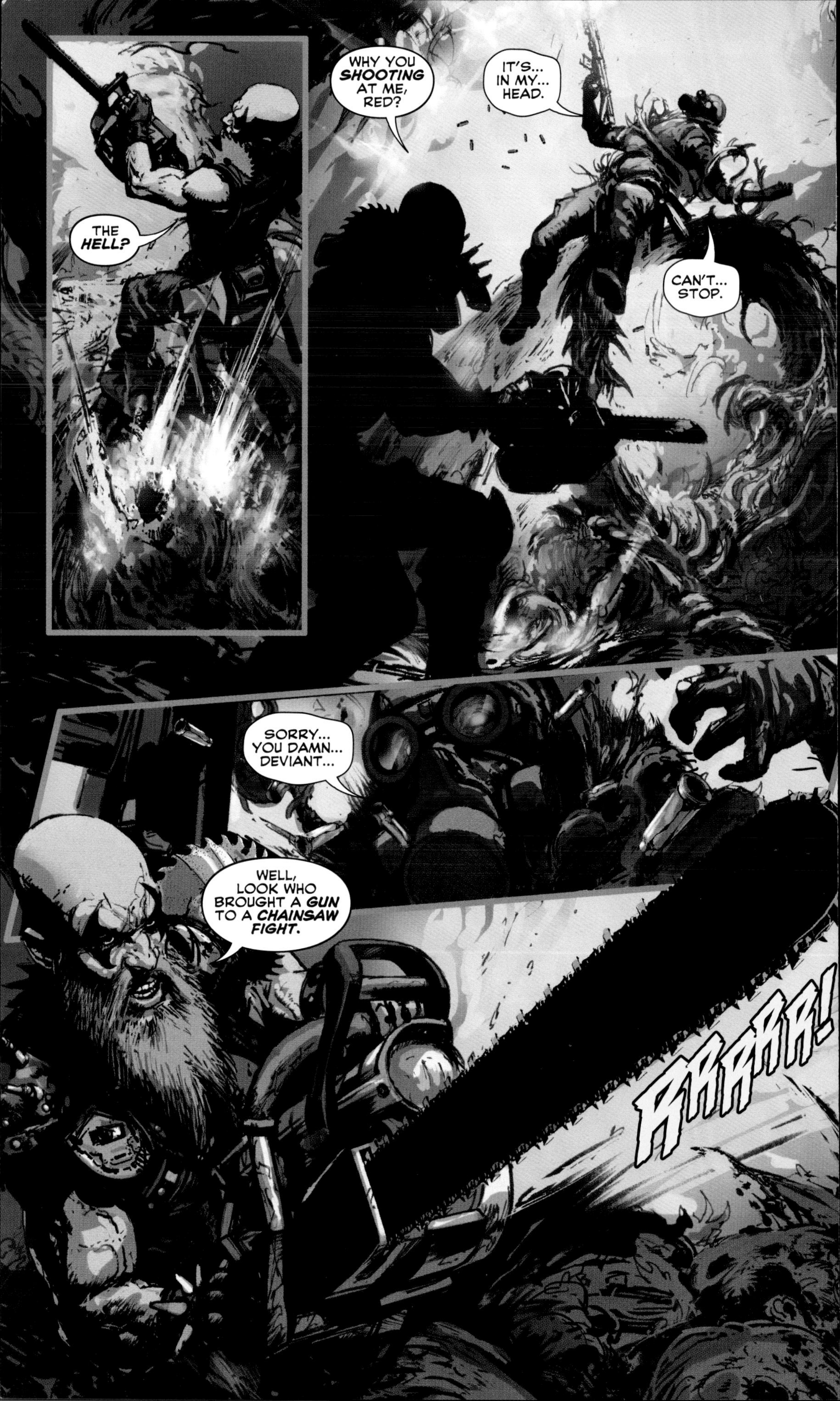

THE HELL?
WHY YOU SHOOTING AT ME, RED?
IT'S... IN MY... HEAD.
CAN'T... STOP.
SORRY... YOU DAMN... DEVIANT...
WELL, LOOK WHO BROUGHT A GUN TO A CHAINSAW FIGHT.
RRRRR!

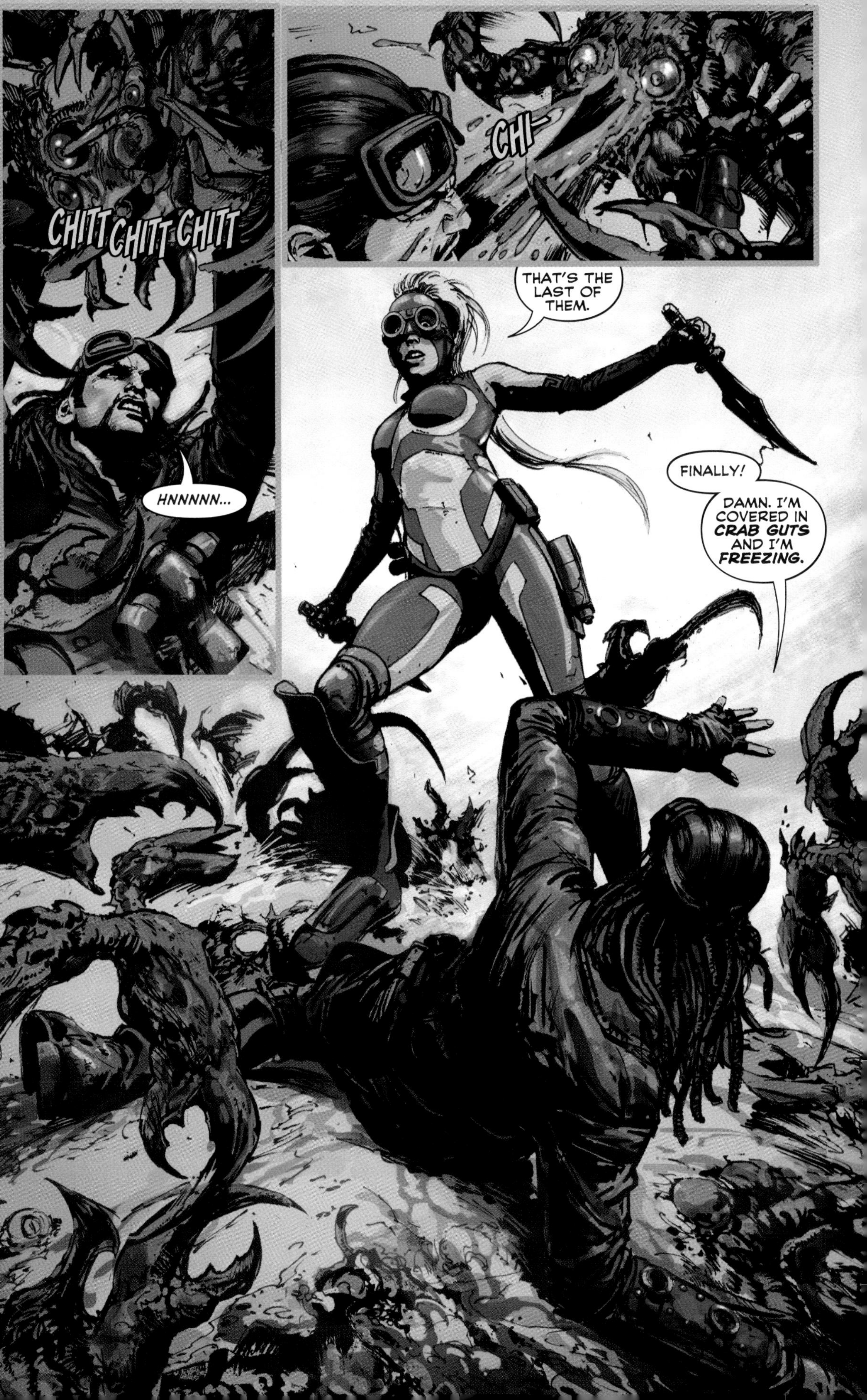

CHITT CHITT CHITT
HNNNNN...
CHI-
THAT'S THE LAST OF THEM.
FINALLY!
DAMN. I'M COVERED IN **CRAB GUTS** AND I'M ***FREEZING.***

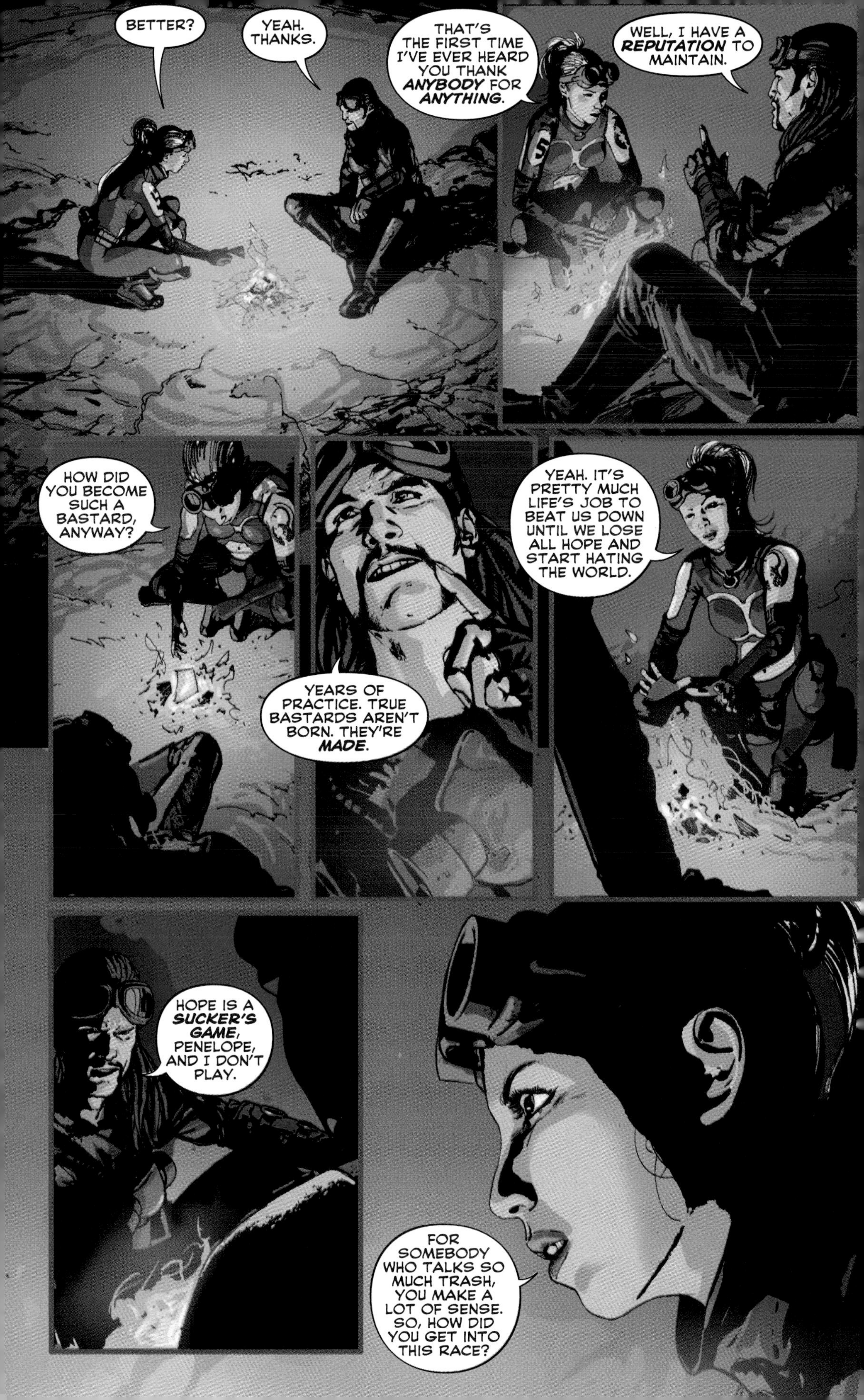
BETTER?
YEAH. THANKS.
THAT'S THE FIRST TIME I'VE EVER HEARD YOU THANK ANYBODY FOR ANYTHING.
WELL, I HAVE A REPUTATION TO MAINTAIN.
HOW DID YOU BECOME SUCH A BASTARD, ANYWAY?
YEARS OF PRACTICE. TRUE BASTARDS AREN'T BORN. THEY'RE MADE.
YEAH. IT'S PRETTY MUCH LIFE'S JOB TO BEAT US DOWN UNTIL WE LOSE ALL HOPE AND START HATING THE WORLD.
HOPE IS A SUCKER'S GAME, PENELOPE, AND I DON'T PLAY.
FOR SOMEBODY WHO TALKS SO MUCH TRASH, YOU MAKE A LOT OF SENSE. SO, HOW DID YOU GET INTO THIS RACE?

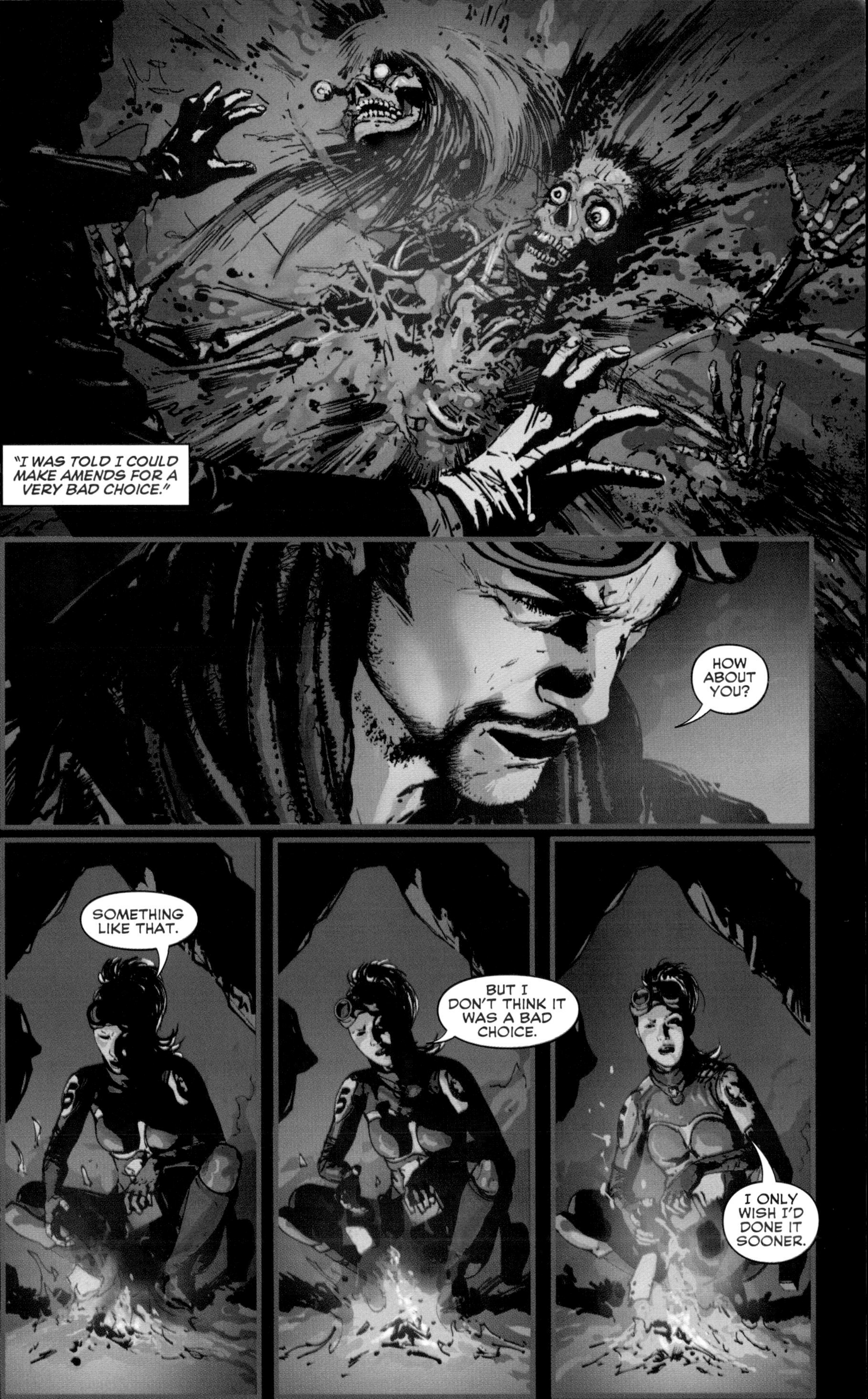
"I WAS TOLD I COULD MAKE AMENDS FOR A VERY BAD CHOICE."
HOW ABOUT YOU?
SOMETHING LIKE THAT.
BUT I DON'T THINK IT WAS A BAD CHOICE.
I ONLY WISH I'D DONE IT SOONER.

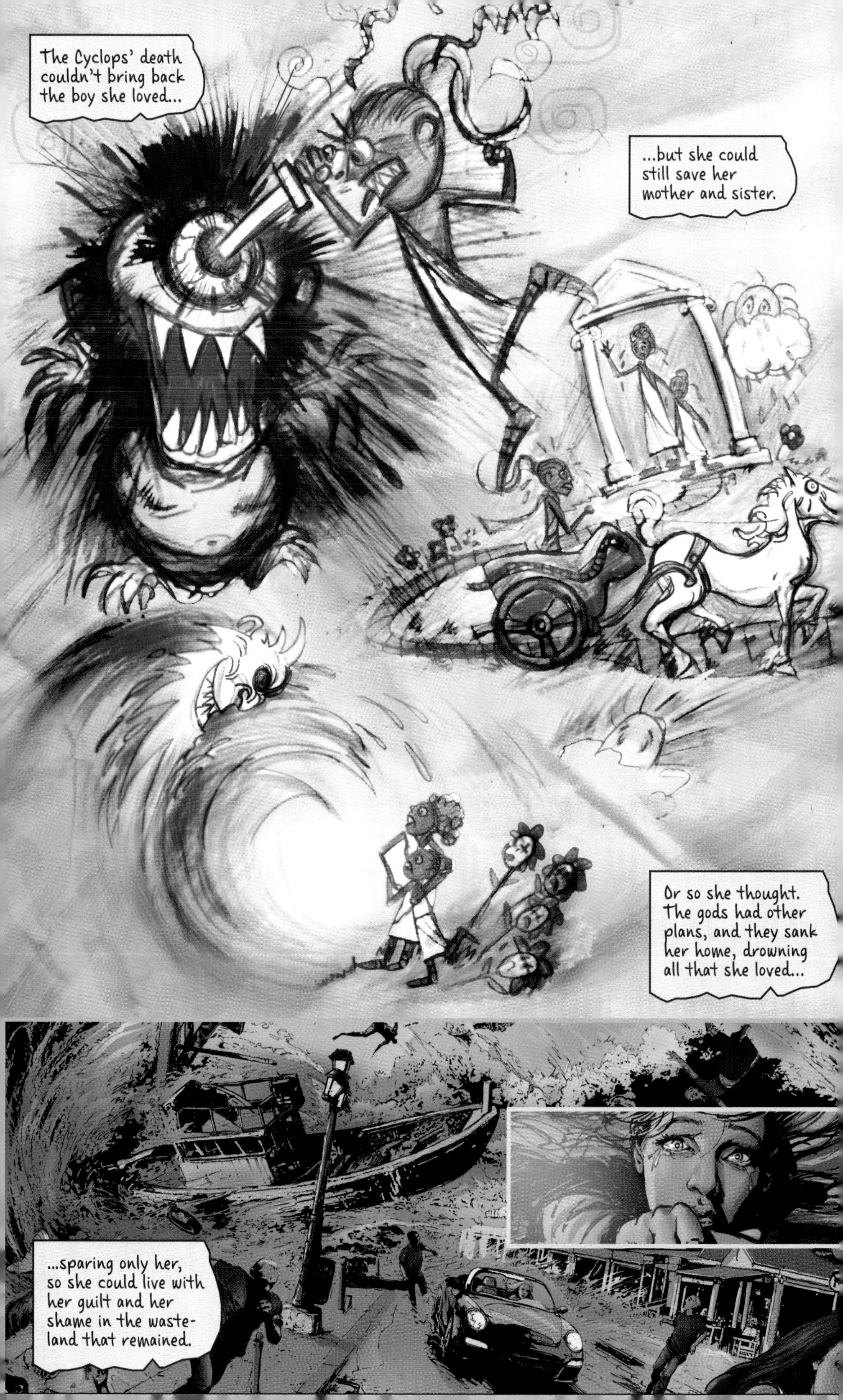
The Cyclops' death couldn't bring back the boy she loved...
...but she could still save her mother and sister.
Or so she thought. The gods had other plans, and they sank her home, drowning all that she loved...
...sparing only her, so she could live with her guilt and her shame in the waste-land that remained.

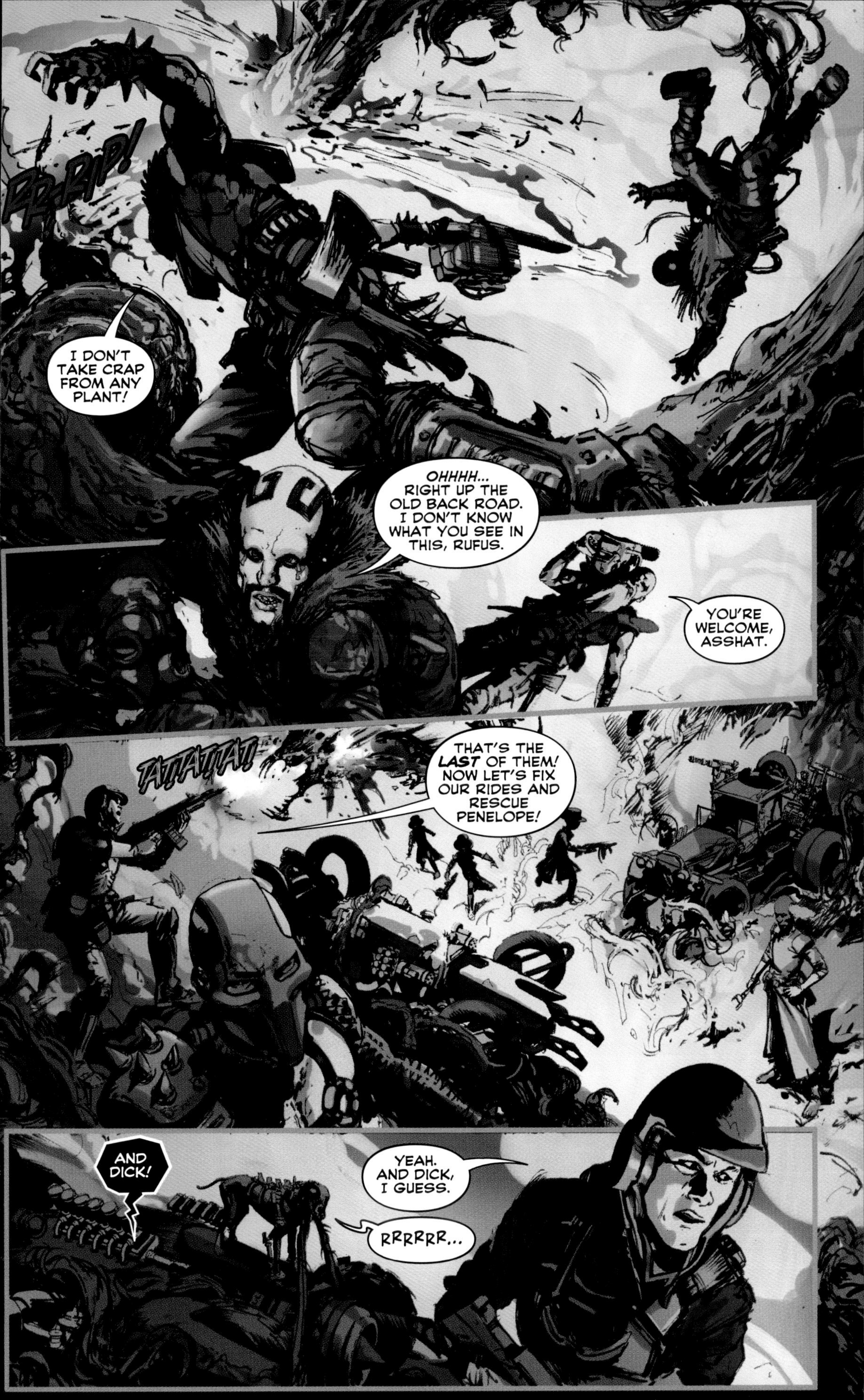
RR-RIP!
I DON'T TAKE CRAP FROM ANY PLANT!
OHHHH... RIGHT UP THE OLD BACK ROAD. I DON'T KNOW WHAT YOU SEE IN THIS, RUFUS.
YOU'RE WELCOME, ASSHAT.
TATTATTAT!
THAT'S THE LAST OF THEM! NOW LET'S FIX OUR RIDES AND RESCUE PENELOPE!
AND DICK!
YEAH. AND DICK, I GUESS.
RRRRRR...

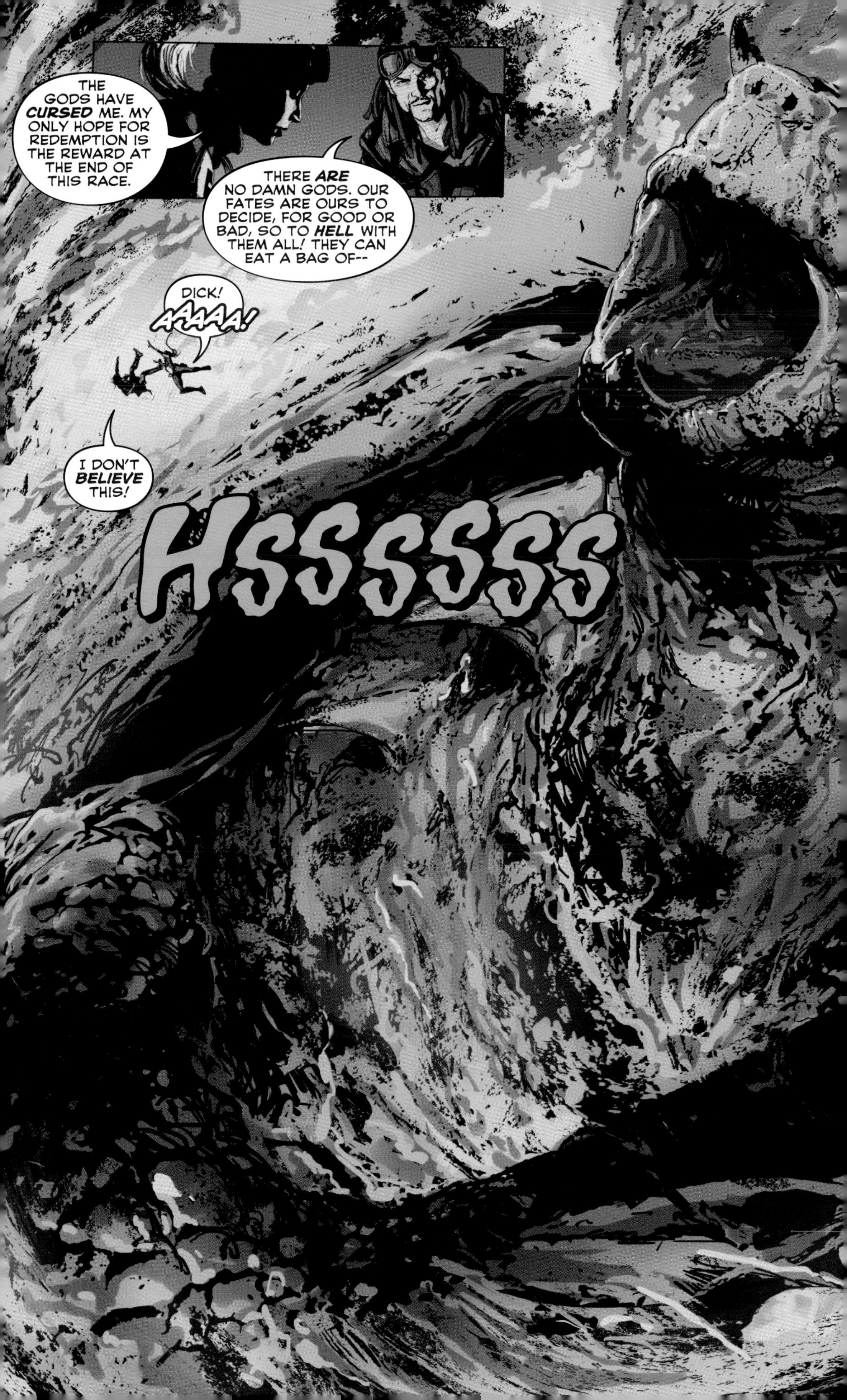
THE GODS HAVE CURSED ME. MY ONLY HOPE FOR REDEMPTION IS THE REWARD AT THE END OF THIS RACE.
THERE ARE NO DAMN GODS. OUR FATES ARE OURS TO DECIDE, FOR GOOD OR BAD, SO TO HELL WITH THEM ALL! THEY CAN EAT A BAG OF--
DICK! AAAAA!
I DON'T BELIEVE THIS!
HSSSSSS

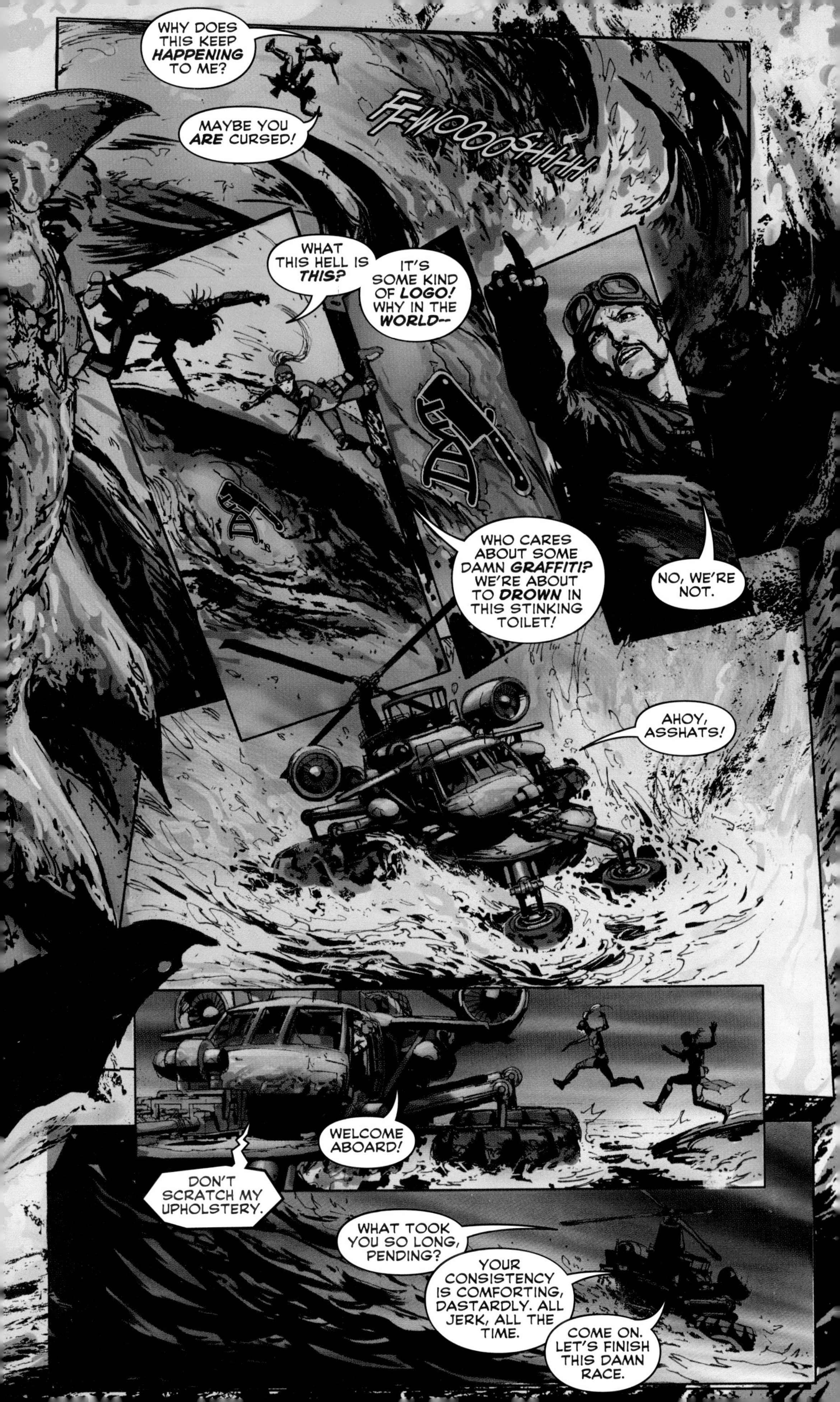
WHY DOES THIS KEEP HAPPENING TO ME?
MAYBE YOU ARE CURSED!
FFWOOOOSHHH
WHAT THIS HELL IS THIS?
IT'S SOME KIND OF LOGO! WHY IN THE WORLD--
WHO CARES ABOUT SOME DAMN GRAFFITI!? WE'RE ABOUT TO DROWN IN THIS STINKING TOILET!
NO, WE'RE NOT.
AHOY, ASSHATS!
WELCOME ABOARD!
DON'T SCRATCH MY UPHOLSTERY.
WHAT TOOK YOU SO LONG, PENDING?
YOUR CONSISTENCY IS COMFORTING, DASTARDLY. ALL JERK, ALL THE TIME.
COME ON. LET'S FINISH THIS DAMN RACE.

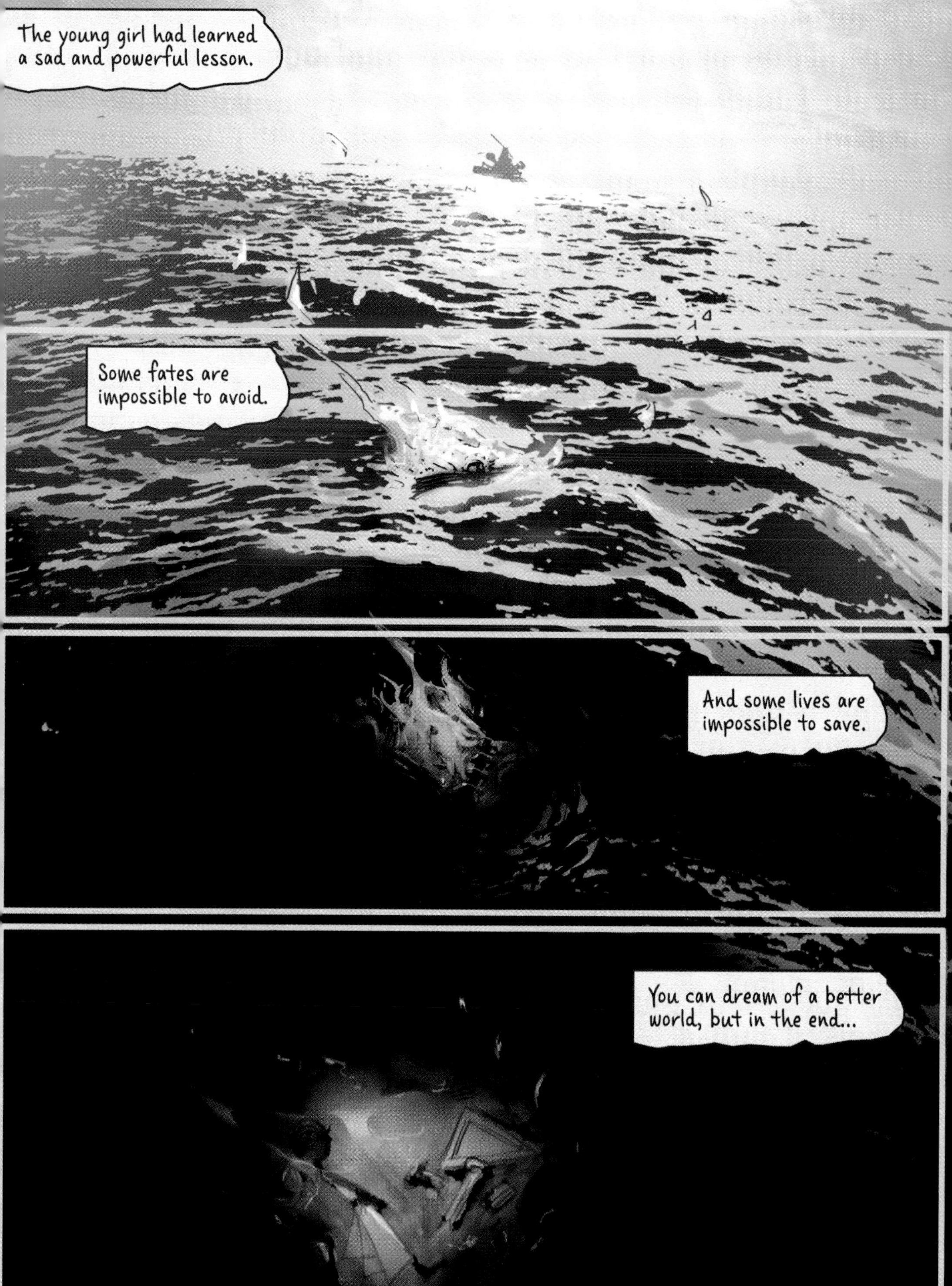
The young girl had learned a sad and powerful lesson.
Some fates are impossible to avoid.
And some lives are impossible to save.
You can dream of a better world, but in the end...

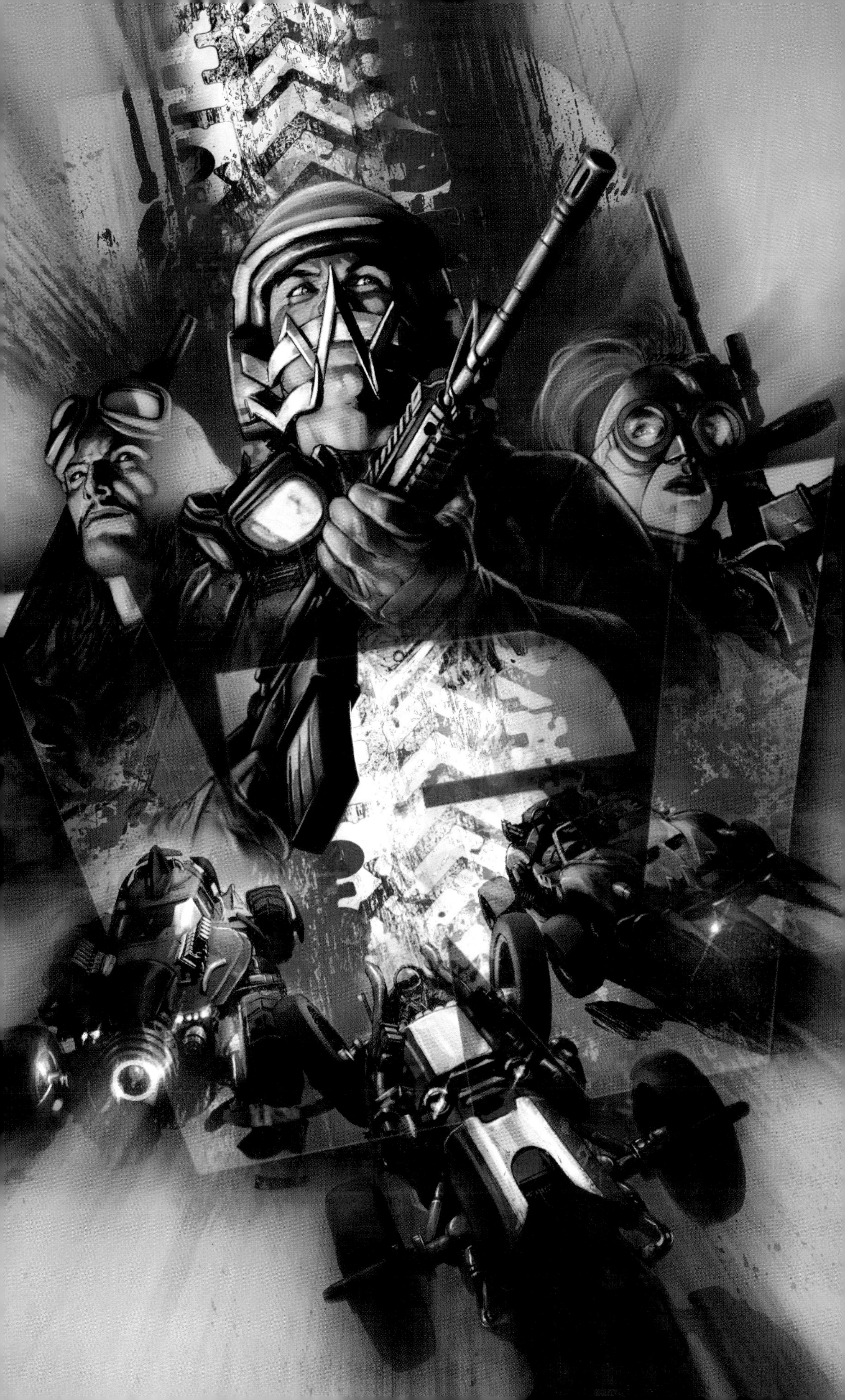

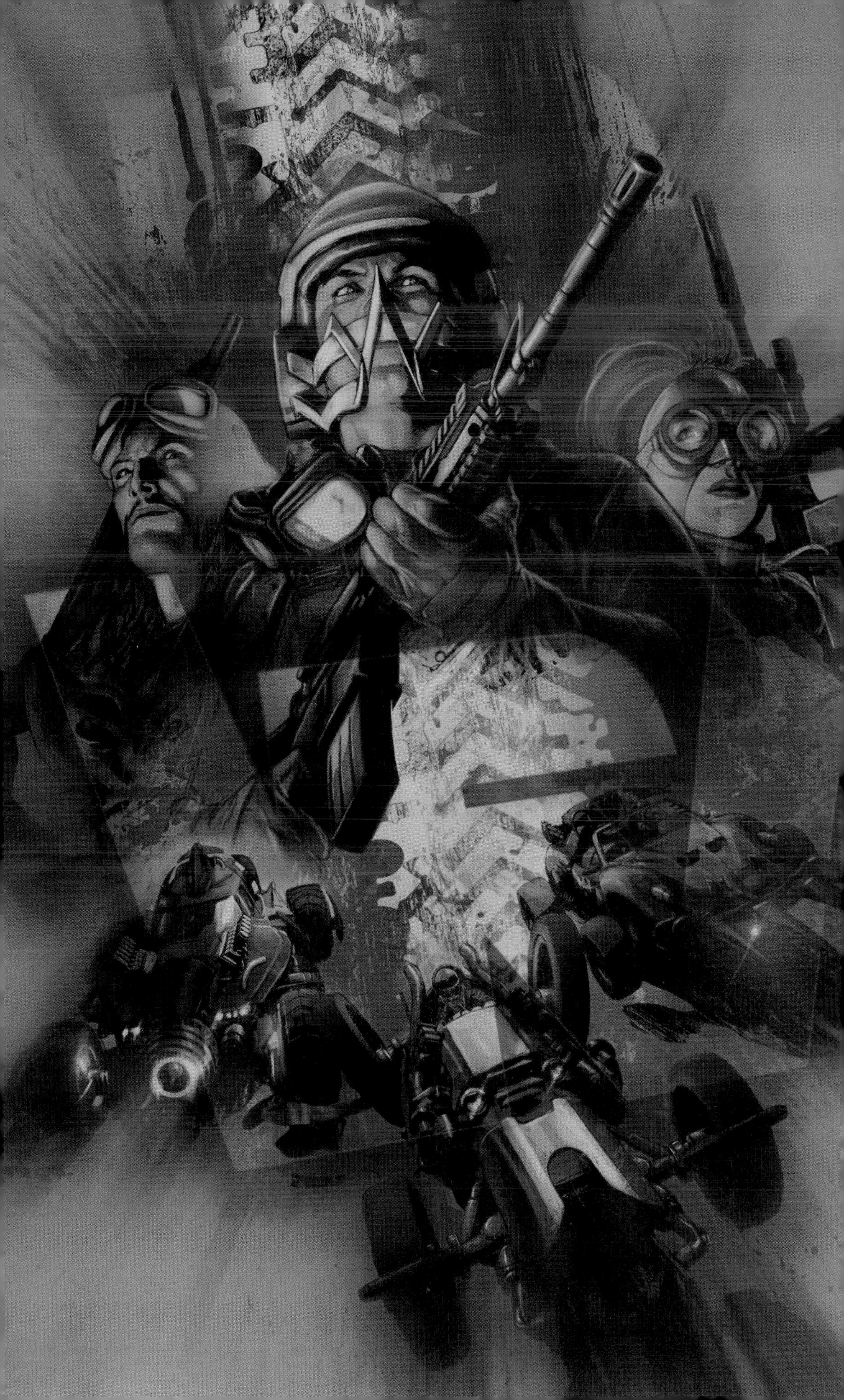

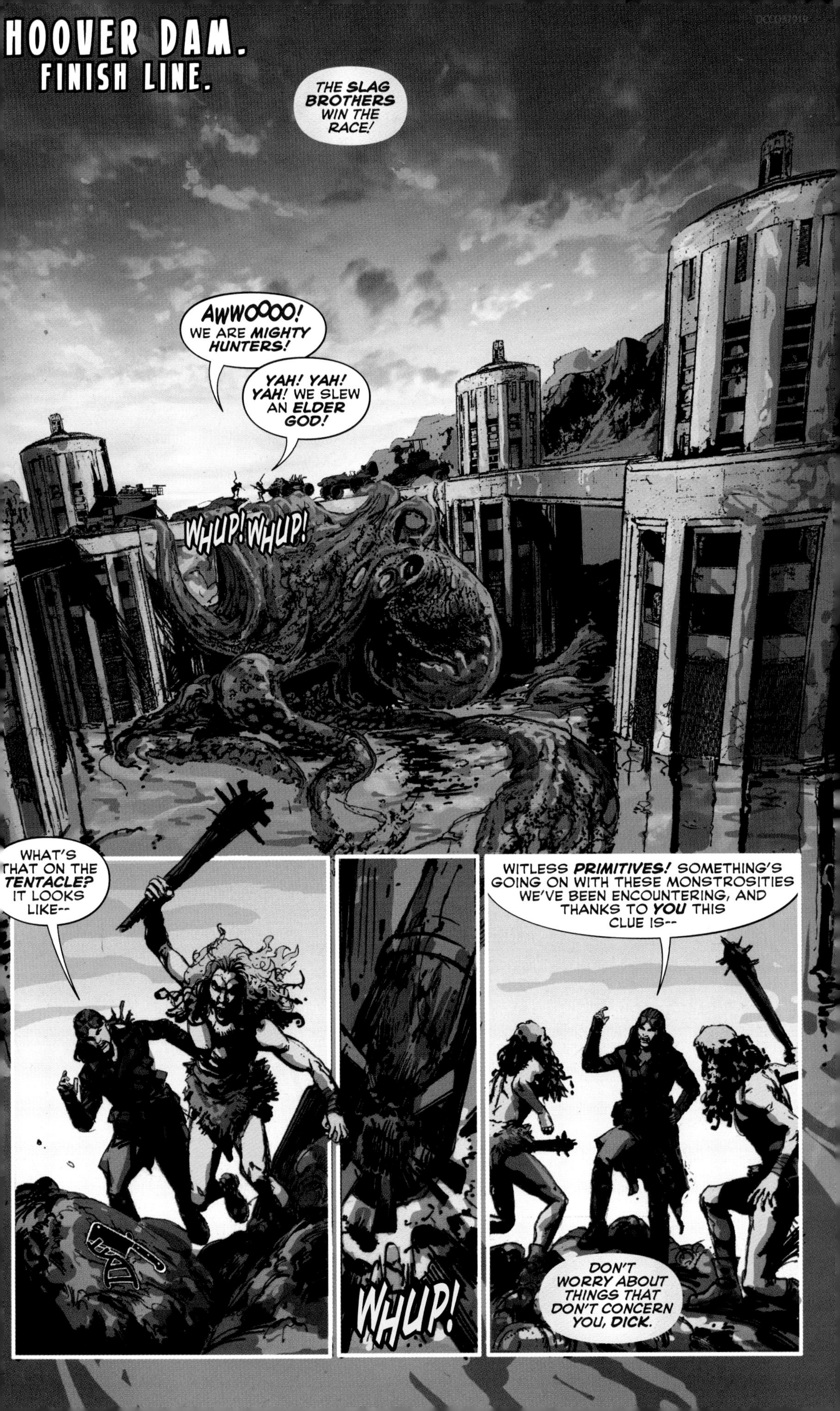
HOOVER DAM. FINISH LINE.
THE SLAG BROTHERS WIN THE RACE!
AWWOOOO! WE ARE MIGHTY HUNTERS!
YAH! YAH! YAH! WE SLEW AN ELDER GOD!
WHUP! WHUP!
WHAT'S THAT ON THE TENTACLE? IT LOOKS LIKE--
WHUP!
WITLESS PRIMITIVES! SOMETHING'S GOING ON WITH THESE MONSTROSITIES WE'VE BEEN ENCOUNTERING, AND THANKS TO YOU THIS CLUE IS--
DON'T WORRY ABOUT THINGS THAT DON'T CONCERN YOU, DICK.

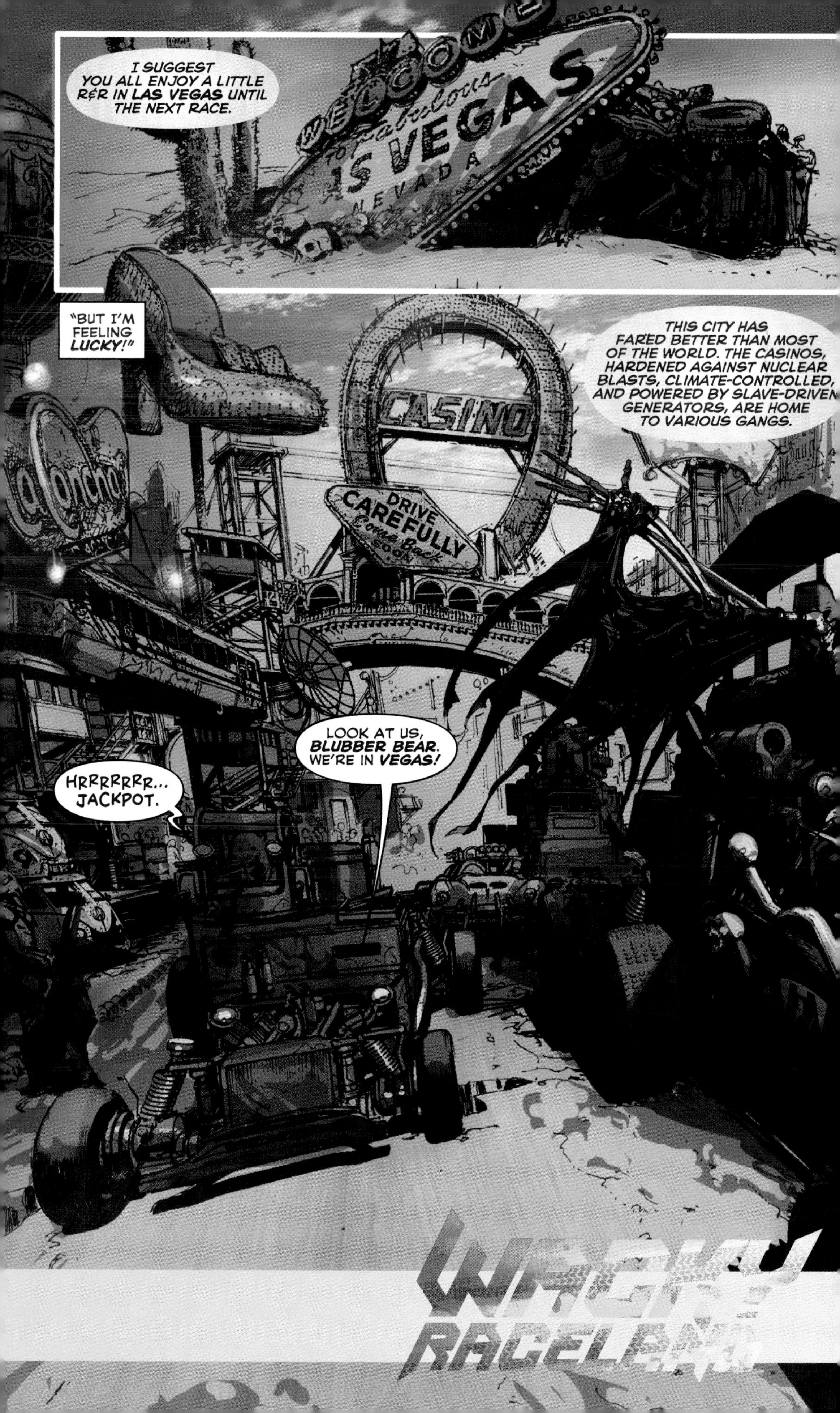
I SUGGEST YOU ALL ENJOY A LITTLE R&R IN **LAS VEGAS** UNTIL THE NEXT RACE.
WELCOME
VEGAS
NEVADA
"BUT I'M FEELING **LUCKY!**"
CASINO
DRIVE CAREFULLY
Come Back
SOON
THIS CITY HAS FARED BETTER THAN MOST OF THE WORLD. THE CASINOS, HARDENED AGAINST NUCLEAR BLASTS, CLIMATE-CONTROLLED, AND POWERED BY SLAVE-DRIVEN GENERATORS, ARE HOME TO VARIOUS GANGS.
HRRRRRRR... JACKPOT.
LOOK AT US, **BLUBBER BEAR.** WE'RE IN **VEGAS!**

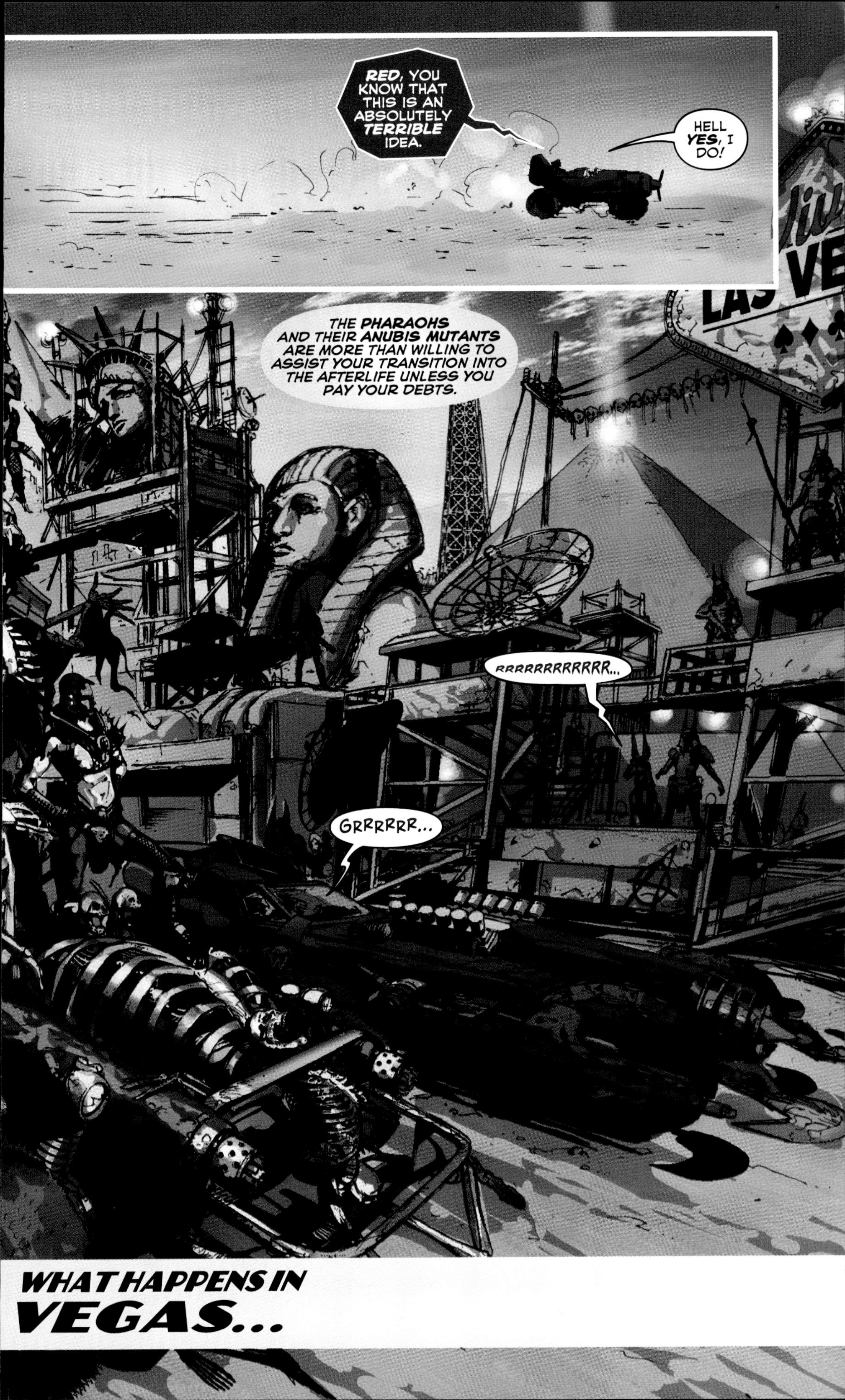
RED, YOU KNOW THAT THIS IS AN ABSOLUTELY TERRIBLE IDEA.
HELL YES, I DO!
THE PHARAOHS AND THEIR ANUBIS MUTANTS ARE MORE THAN WILLING TO ASSIST YOUR TRANSITION INTO THE AFTERLIFE UNLESS YOU PAY YOUR DEBTS.
RRRRRRRRRRRR...
GRRRRRR...
WHAT HAPPENS IN VEGAS...

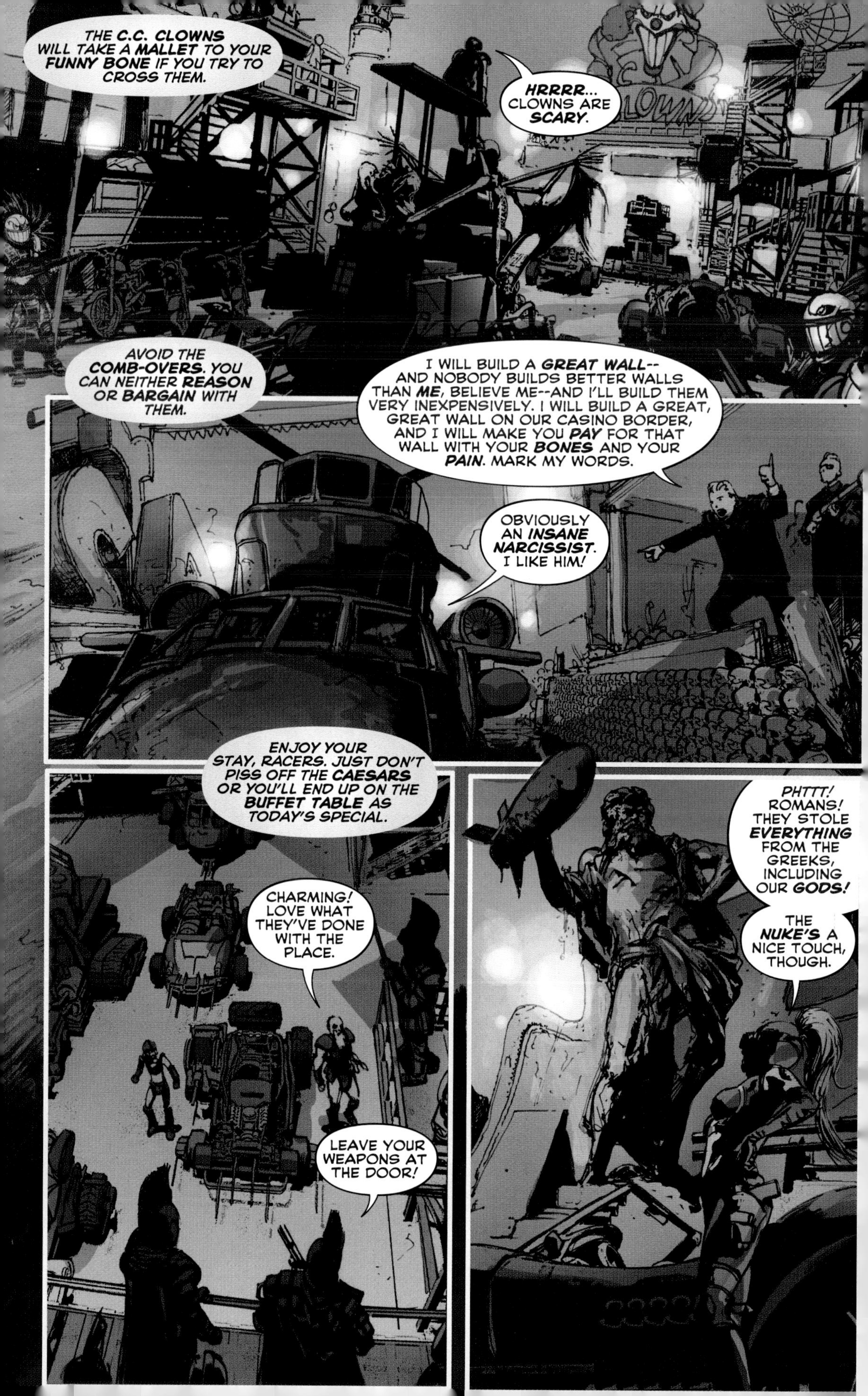
THE C.C. CLOWNS WILL TAKE A MALLET TO YOUR FUNNY BONE IF YOU TRY TO CROSS THEM.
HRRRR... CLOWNS ARE SCARY.
AVOID THE COMB-OVERS. YOU CAN NEITHER REASON OR BARGAIN WITH THEM.
I WILL BUILD A GREAT WALL-- AND NOBODY BUILDS BETTER WALLS THAN ME, BELIEVE ME--AND I'LL BUILD THEM VERY INEXPENSIVELY. I WILL BUILD A GREAT, GREAT WALL ON OUR CASINO BORDER, AND I WILL MAKE YOU PAY FOR THAT WALL WITH YOUR BONES AND YOUR PAIN. MARK MY WORDS.
OBVIOUSLY AN INSANE NARCISSIST. I LIKE HIM!
ENJOY YOUR STAY, RACERS. JUST DON'T PISS OFF THE CAESARS OR YOU'LL END UP ON THE BUFFET TABLE AS TODAY'S SPECIAL.
CHARMING! LOVE WHAT THEY'VE DONE WITH THE PLACE.
LEAVE YOUR WEAPONS AT THE DOOR!
PHTTT! ROMANS! THEY STOLE EVERYTHING FROM THE GREEKS, INCLUDING OUR GODS!
THE NUKE'S A NICE TOUCH, THOUGH.

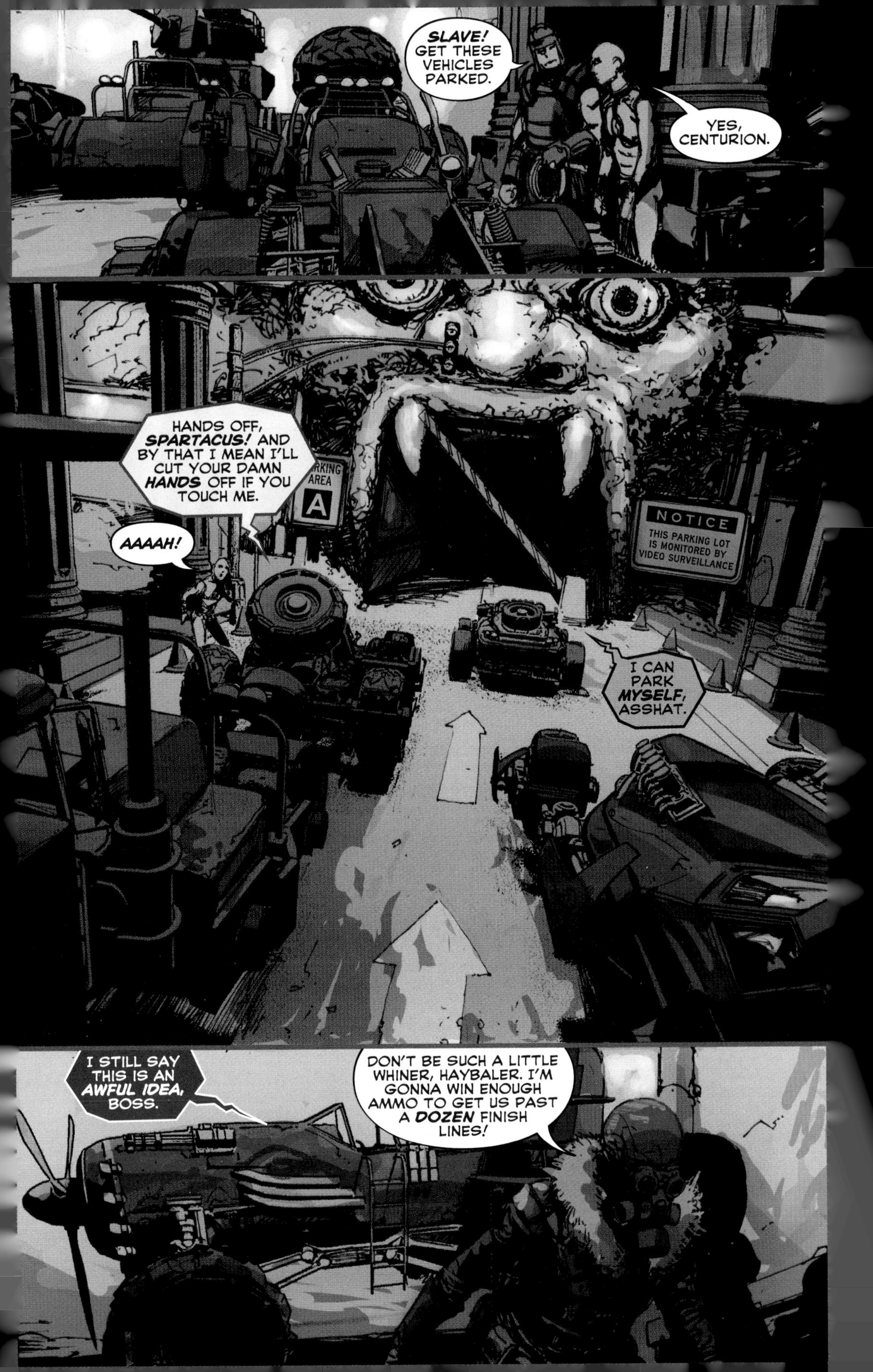
SLAVE! GET THESE VEHICLES PARKED.
YES, CENTURION.
HANDS OFF, SPARTACUS! AND BY THAT I MEAN I'LL CUT YOUR DAMN HANDS OFF IF YOU TOUCH ME.
AAAAH!
ARKING AREA A
NOTICE
THIS PARKING LOT IS MONITORED BY VIDEO SURVEILLANCE
I CAN PARK MYSELF, ASSHAT.
I STILL SAY THIS IS AN AWFUL IDEA, BOSS.
DON'T BE SUCH A LITTLE WHINER, HAYBALER. I'M GONNA WIN ENOUGH AMMO TO GET US PAST A DOZEN FINISH LINES!

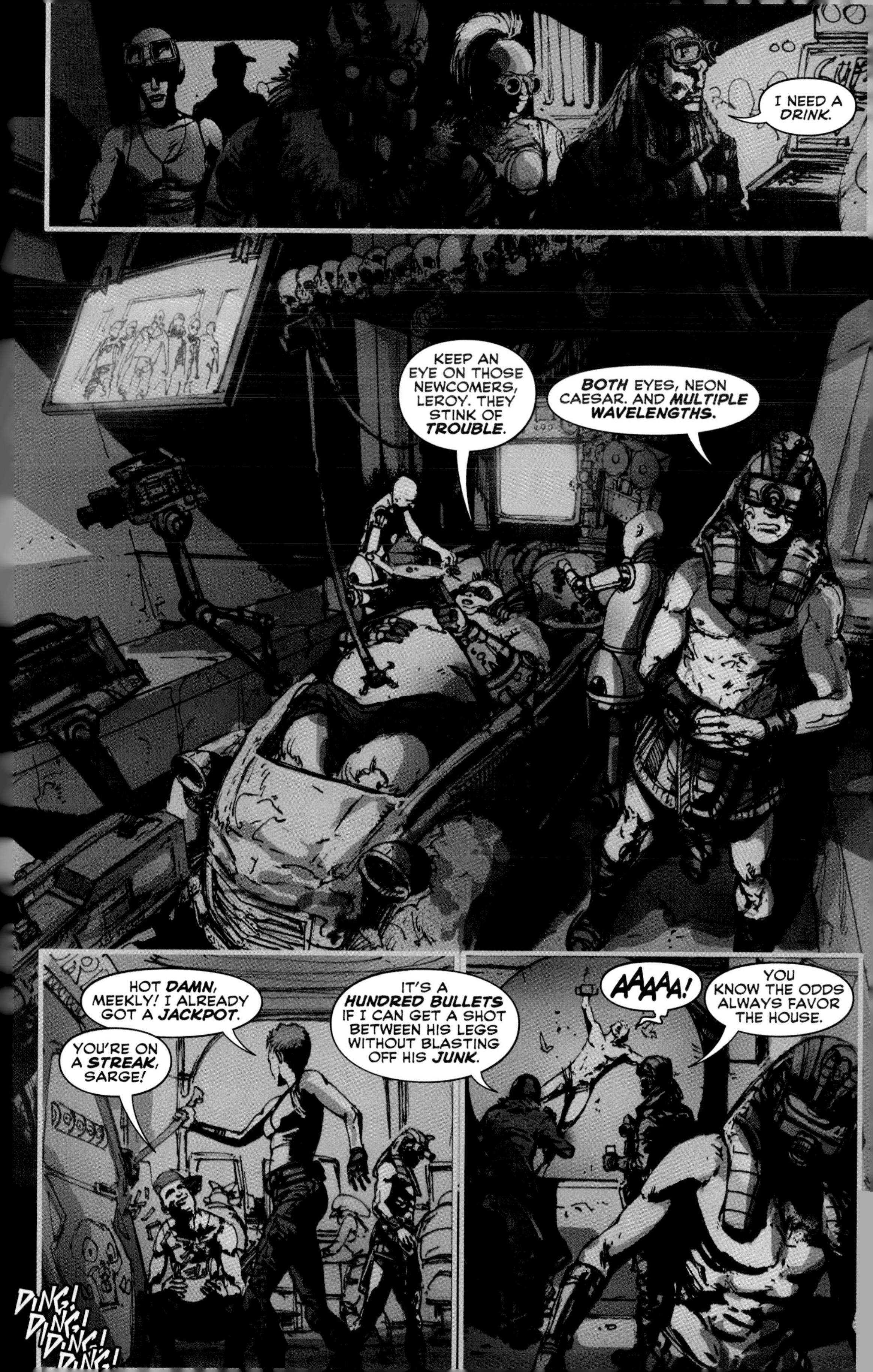
I NEED A DRINK.
KEEP AN EYE ON THOSE NEWCOMERS, LEROY. THEY STINK OF TROUBLE.
BOTH EYES, NEON CAESAR. AND MULTIPLE WAVELENGTHS.
HOT DAMN, MEEKLY! I ALREADY GOT A JACKPOT.
YOU'RE ON A STREAK, SARGE!
IT'S A HUNDRED BULLETS IF I CAN GET A SHOT BETWEEN HIS LEGS WITHOUT BLASTING OFF HIS JUNK.
AAAAA!
YOU KNOW THE ODDS ALWAYS FAVOR THE HOUSE.
DING! DING! DING! DING!

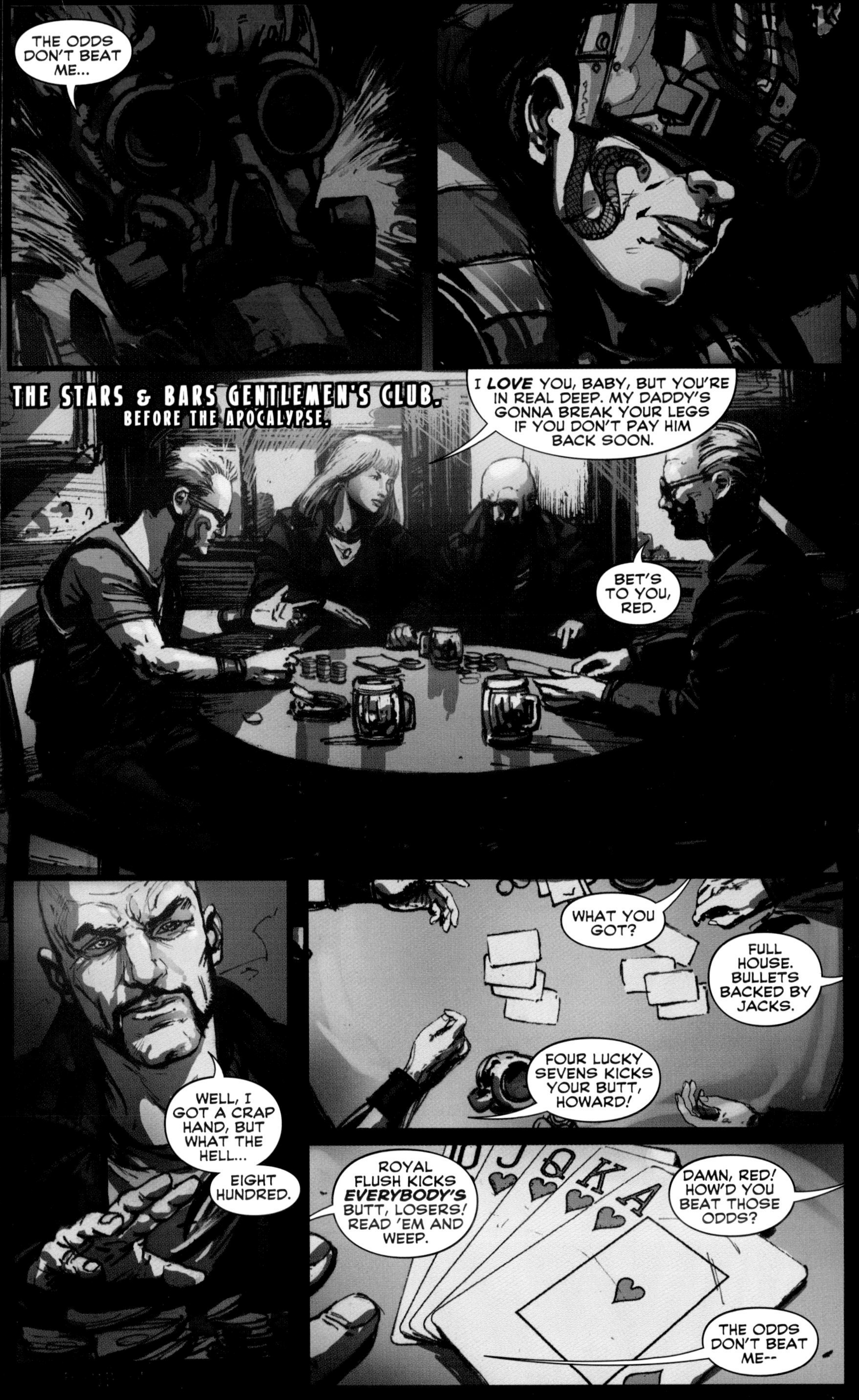
THE ODDS DON'T BEAT ME...
THE STARS & BARS GENTLEMEN'S CLUB.
BEFORE THE APOCALYPSE.
I LOVE YOU, BABY, BUT YOU'RE IN REAL DEEP. MY DADDY'S GONNA BREAK YOUR LEGS IF YOU DON'T PAY HIM BACK SOON.
BET'S TO YOU, RED.
WELL, I GOT A CRAP HAND, BUT WHAT THE HELL...
EIGHT HUNDRED.
WHAT YOU GOT?
FULL HOUSE. BULLETS BACKED BY JACKS.
FOUR LUCKY SEVENS KICKS YOUR BUTT, HOWARD!
ROYAL FLUSH KICKS EVERYBODY'S BUTT, LOSERS! READ 'EM AND WEEP.
DAMN, RED! HOW'D YOU BEAT THOSE ODDS?
THE ODDS DON'T BEAT ME--

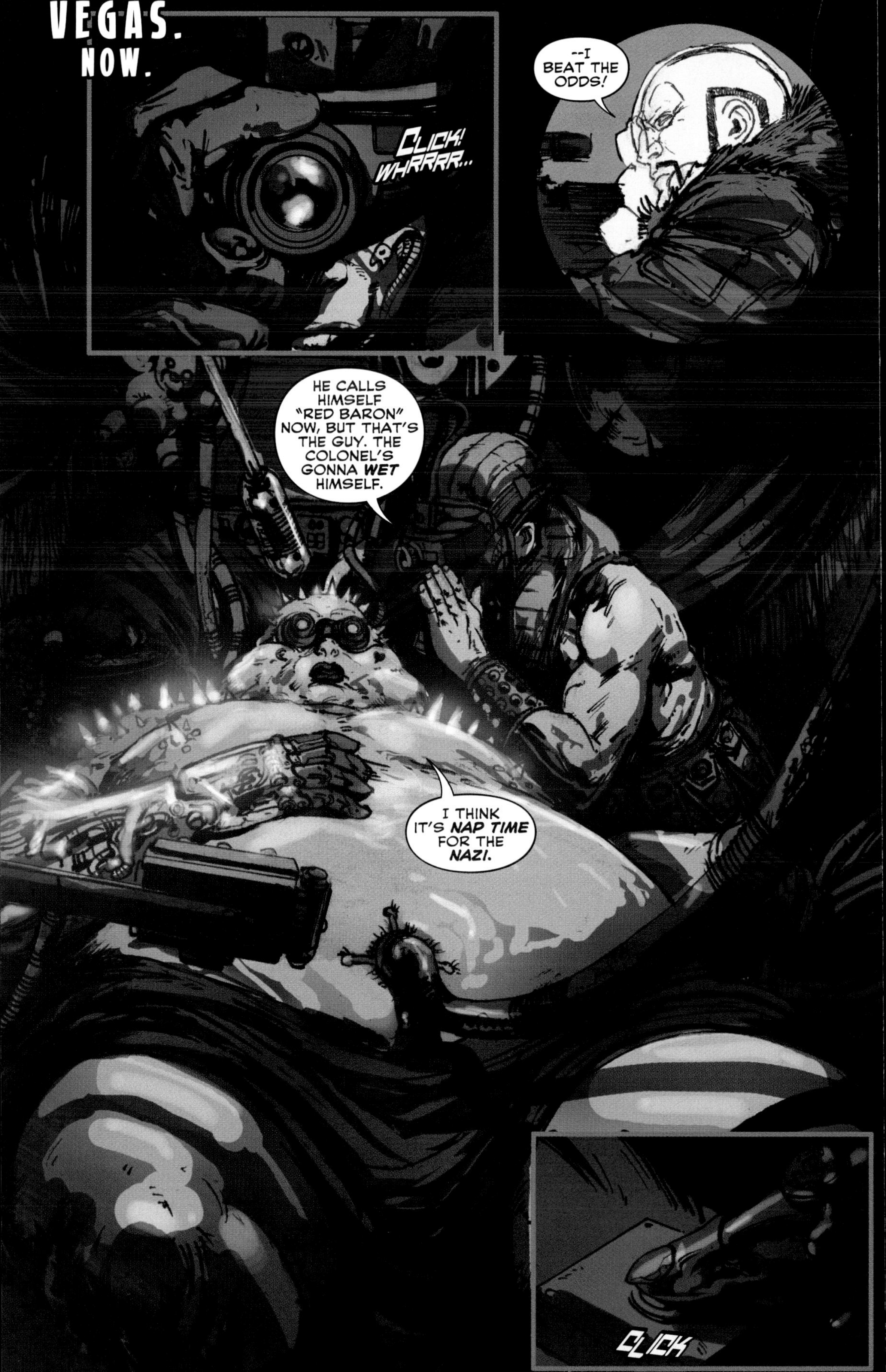

VEGAS.
NOW.
CLICK! WHRRRR...
--I BEAT THE ODDS!
HE CALLS HIMSELF "RED BARON" NOW, BUT THAT'S THE GUY. THE COLONEL'S GONNA WET HIMSELF.
I THINK IT'S NAP TIME FOR THE NAZI.
CLICK

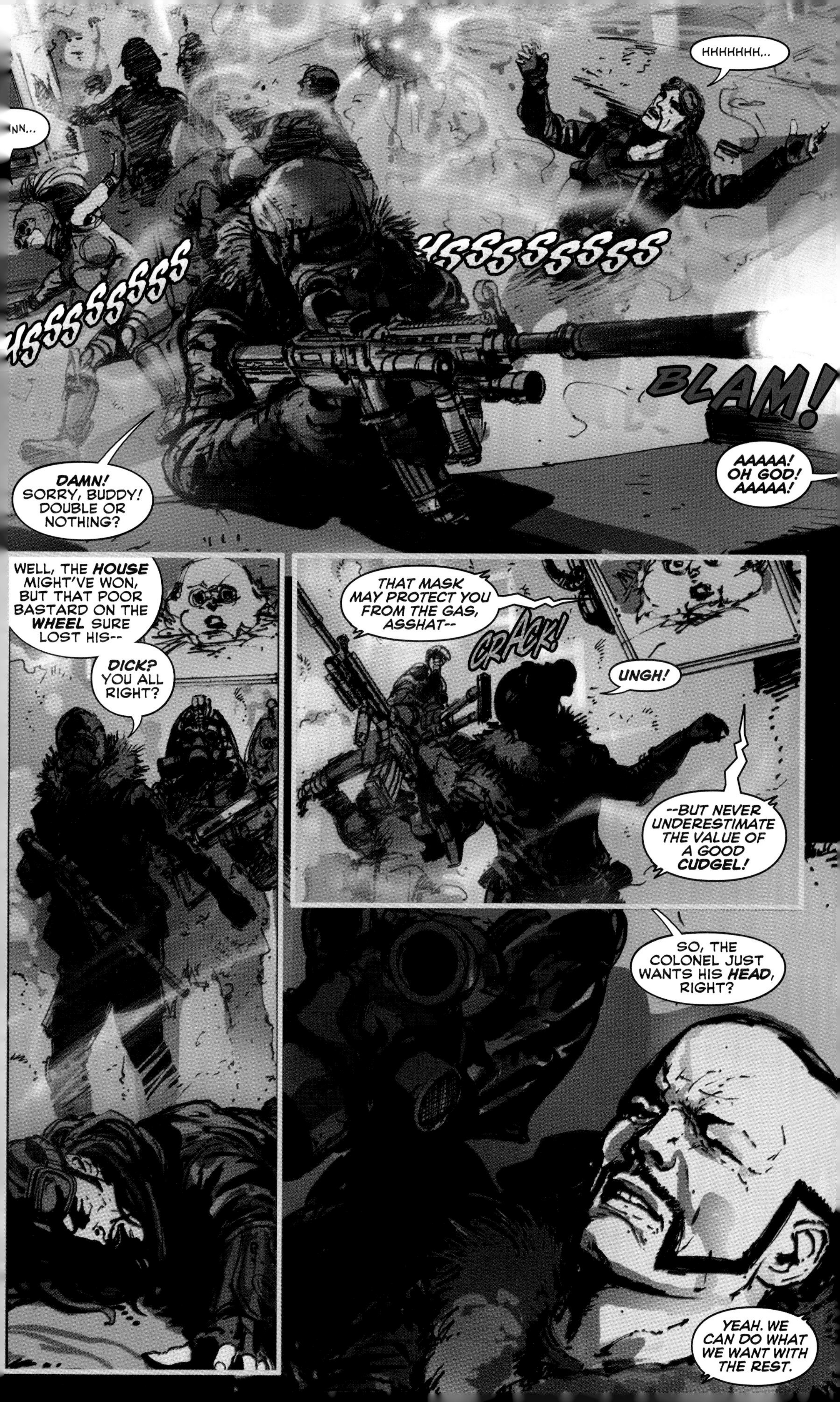
NN...
HHHHHHH...
HSSSSSSSS
HSSSSSSSSS
BLAM!
DAMN! SORRY, BUDDY! DOUBLE OR NOTHING?
AAAAA! OH GOD! AAAAA!
WELL, THE HOUSE MIGHT'VE WON, BUT THAT POOR BASTARD ON THE WHEEL SURE LOST HIS--
DICK? YOU ALL RIGHT?
THAT MASK MAY PROTECT YOU FROM THE GAS, ASSHAT--
CRACK!
UNGH!
--BUT NEVER UNDERESTIMATE THE VALUE OF A GOOD CUDGEL!
SO, THE COLONEL JUST WANTS HIS HEAD, RIGHT?
YEAH. WE CAN DO WHAT WE WANT WITH THE REST.

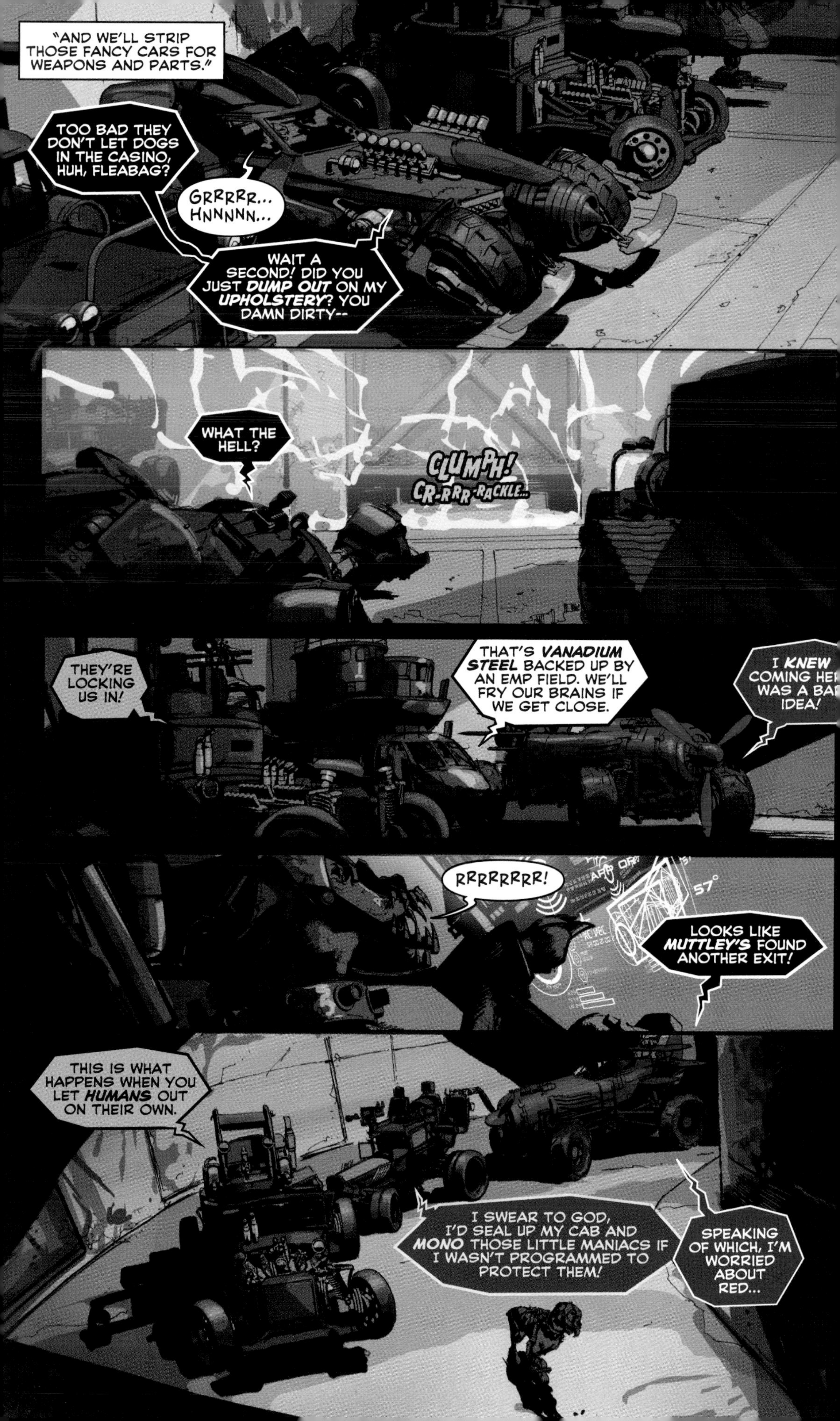
"AND WE'LL STRIP THOSE FANCY CARS FOR WEAPONS AND PARTS."
TOO BAD THEY DON'T LET DOGS IN THE CASINO, HUH, FLEABAG?
GRRRRR... HNNNNN...
WAIT A SECOND! DID YOU JUST DUMP OUT ON MY UPHOLSTERY? YOU DAMN DIRTY--
WHAT THE HELL?
CLUMPH! CR-RRR-RACKLE...
THEY'RE LOCKING US IN!
THAT'S VANADIUM STEEL BACKED UP BY AN EMP FIELD. WE'LL FRY OUR BRAINS IF WE GET CLOSE.
RRRRRRRR!
LOOKS LIKE MUTTLEY'S FOUND ANOTHER EXIT!
THIS IS WHAT HAPPENS WHEN YOU LET HUMANS OUT ON THEIR OWN.
I SWEAR TO GOD, I'D SEAL UP MY CAB AND MONO THOSE LITTLE MANIACS IF I WASN'T PROGRAMMED TO PROTECT THEM!
SPEAKING OF WHICH, I'M WORRIED ABOUT RED...

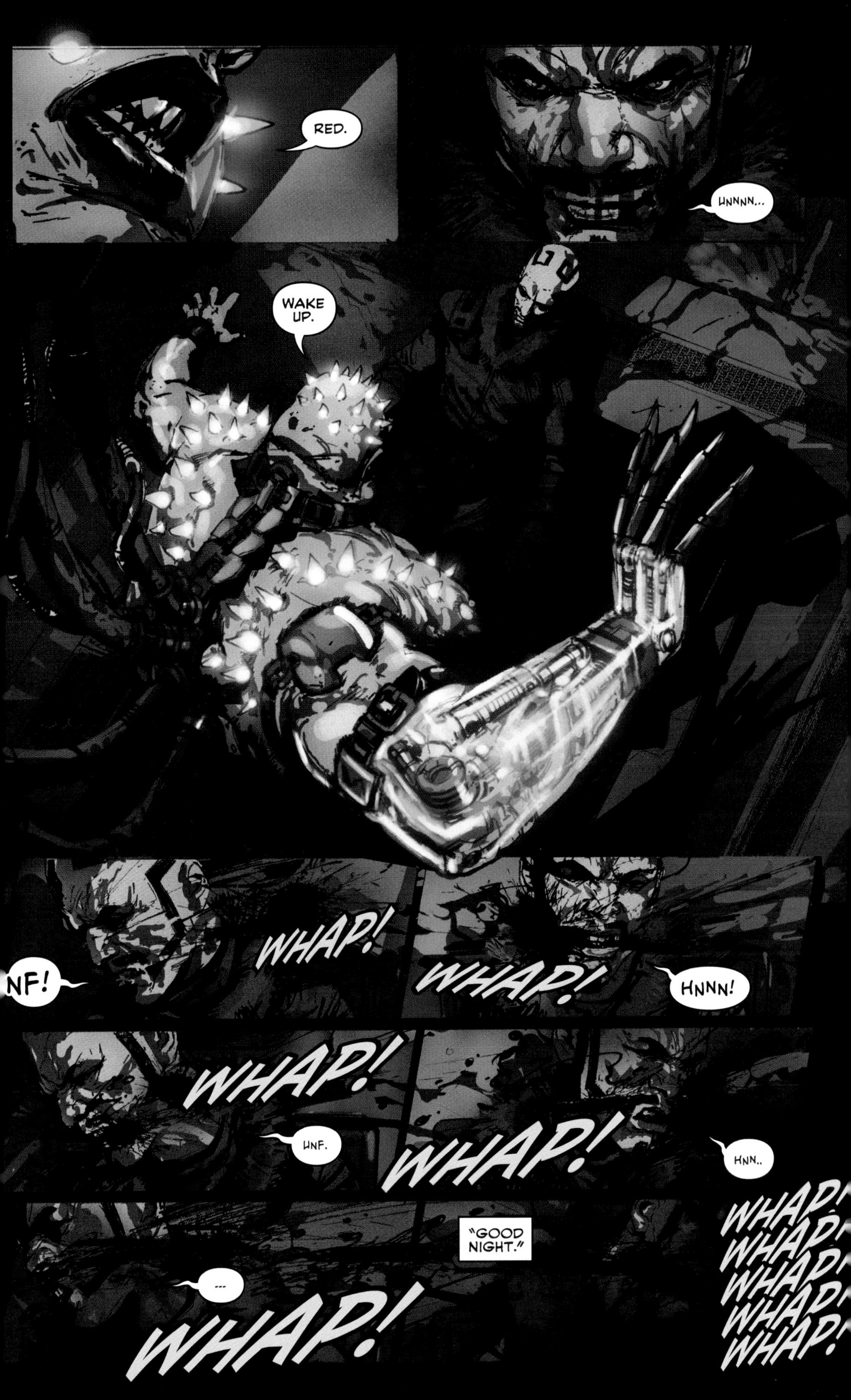
RED.
UNNNN...
WAKE UP.
WHAP!
NF!
WHAP!
HNNN!
WHAP!
UNF.
WHAP!
HNN..
"GOOD NIGHT."
...
WHAP!
WHAP!
WHAP!
WHAP!
WHAP!
WHAP!

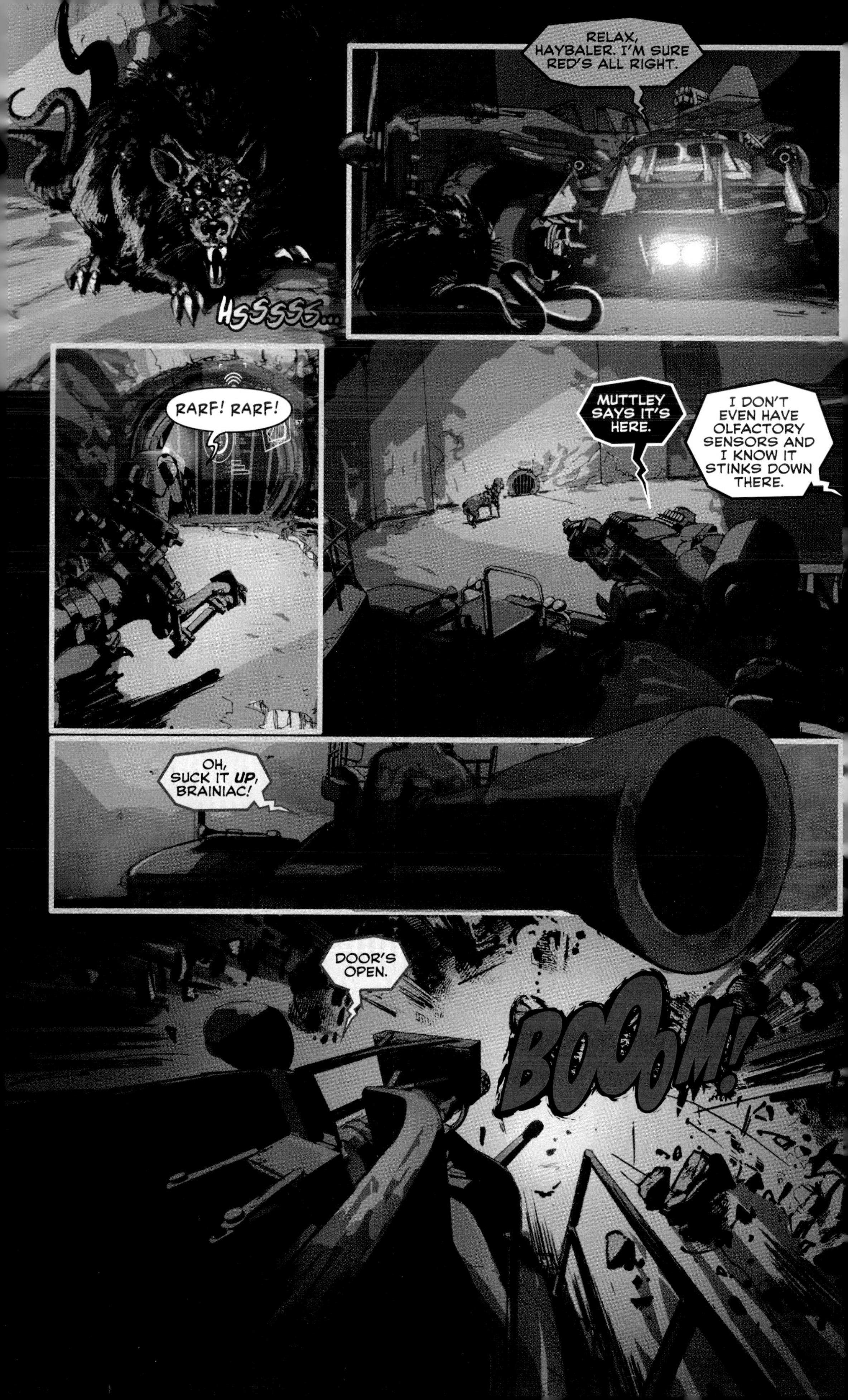
HSSSSS...
RELAX, HAYBALER. I'M SURE RED'S ALL RIGHT.
RARF! RARF!
MUTTLEY SAYS IT'S HERE.
I DON'T EVEN HAVE OLFACTORY SENSORS AND I KNOW IT STINKS DOWN THERE.
OH, SUCK IT UP, BRAINIAC!
DOOR'S OPEN.
BOOOM!

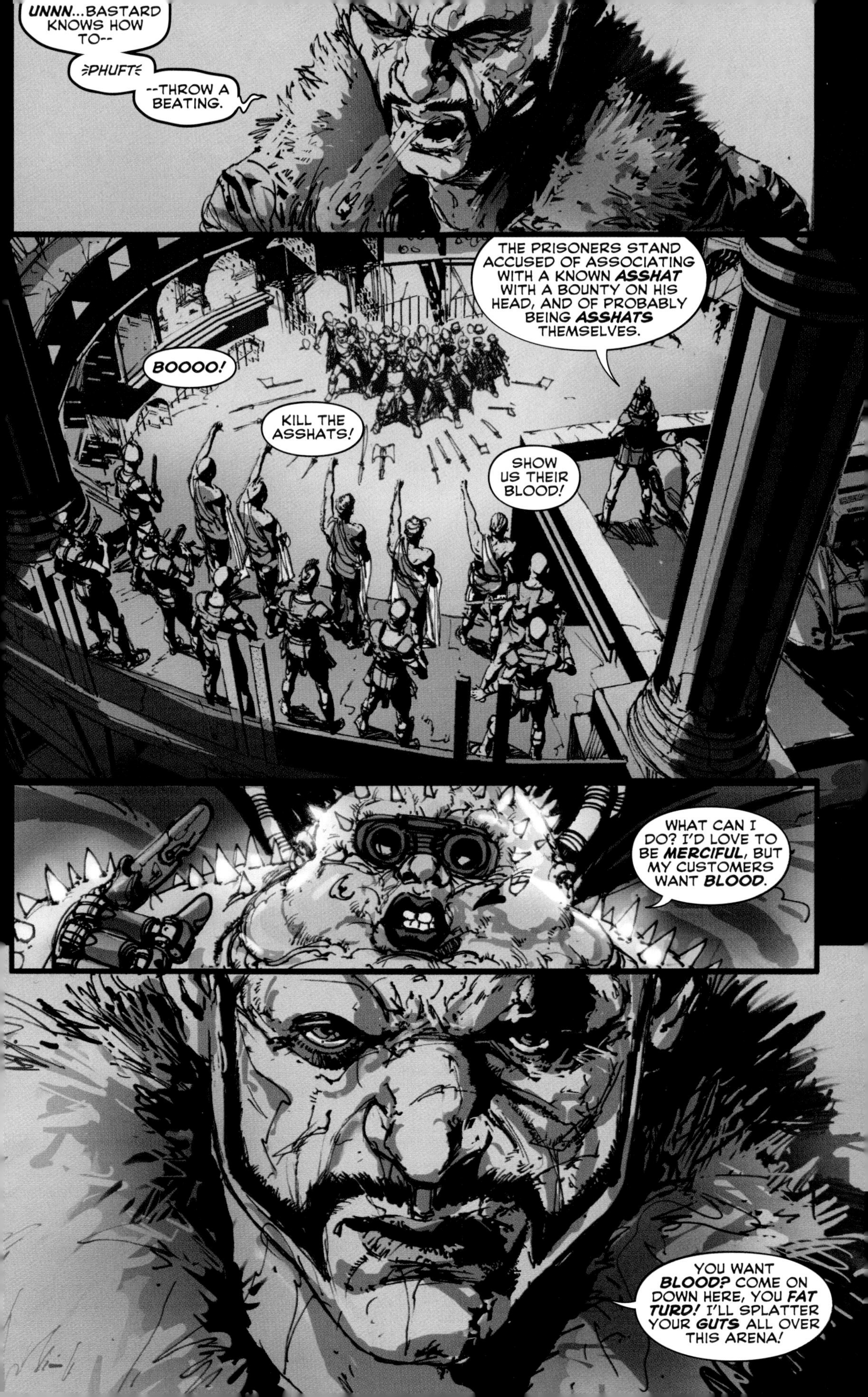
UNNN...BASTARD KNOWS HOW TO--
≶PHUFT≷
--THROW A BEATING.
THE PRISONERS STAND ACCUSED OF ASSOCIATING WITH A KNOWN ASSHAT WITH A BOUNTY ON HIS HEAD, AND OF PROBABLY BEING ASSHATS THEMSELVES.
BOOOO!
KILL THE ASSHATS!
SHOW US THEIR BLOOD!
WHAT CAN I DO? I'D LOVE TO BE MERCIFUL, BUT MY CUSTOMERS WANT BLOOD.
YOU WANT BLOOD? COME ON DOWN HERE, YOU FAT TURD! I'LL SPLATTER YOUR GUTS ALL OVER THIS ARENA!

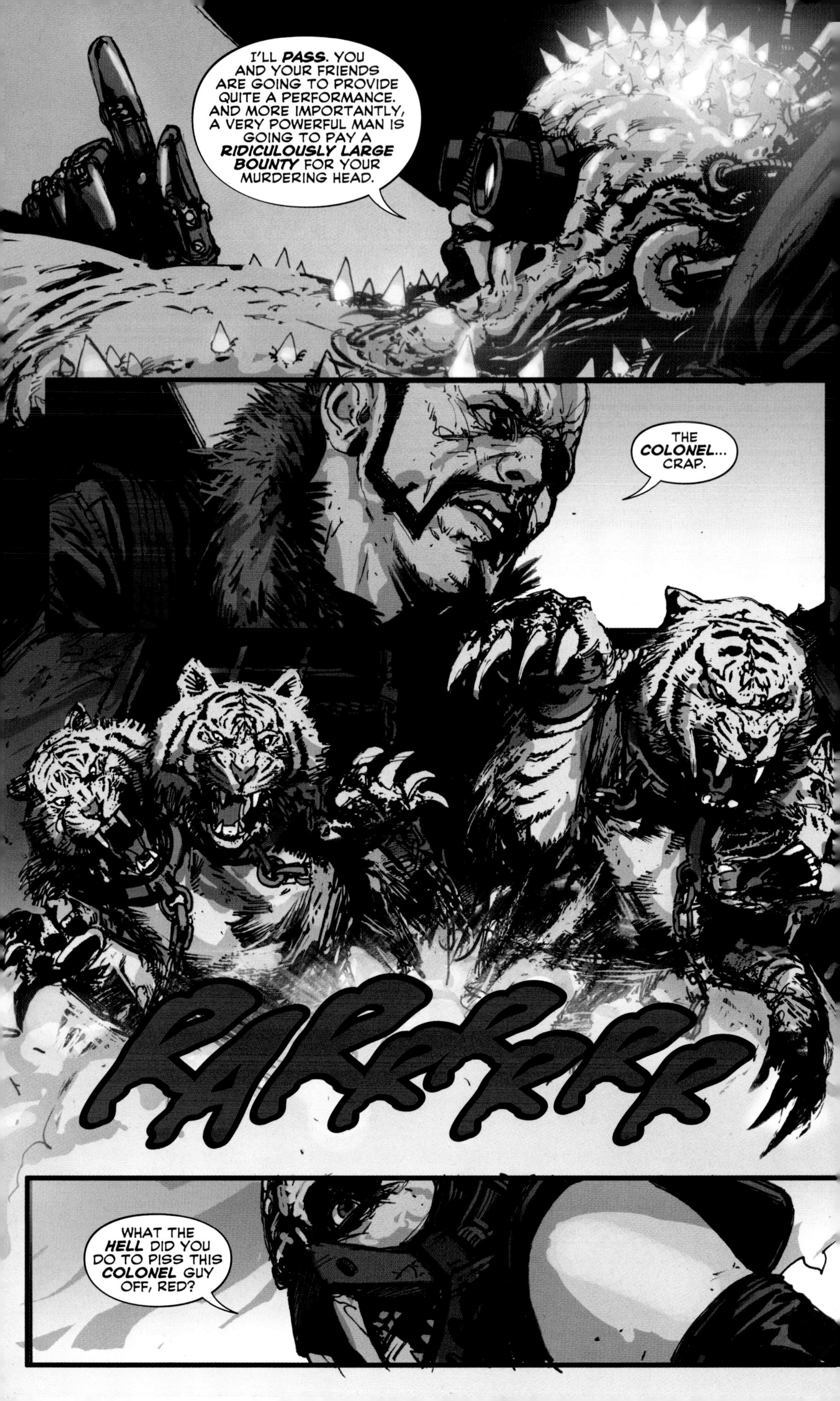

I'LL PASS. YOU AND YOUR FRIENDS ARE GOING TO PROVIDE QUITE A PERFORMANCE. AND MORE IMPORTANTLY, A VERY POWERFUL MAN IS GOING TO PAY A RIDICULOUSLY LARGE BOUNTY FOR YOUR MURDERING HEAD.
THE COLONEL... CRAP.
RARRRRRRR
WHAT THE HELL DID YOU DO TO PISS THIS COLONEL GUY OFF, RED?

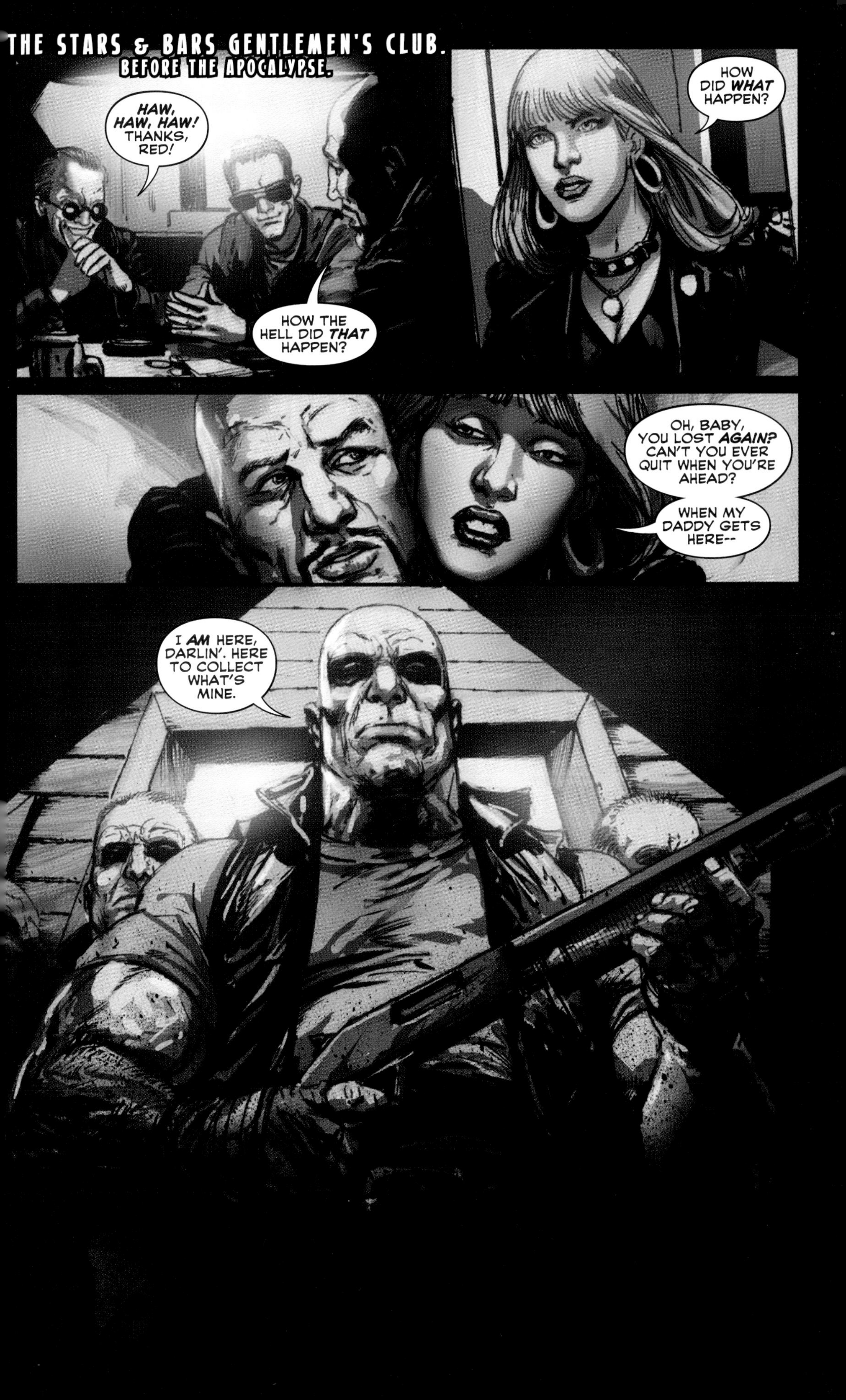
THE STARS & BARS GENTLEMEN'S CLUB.
BEFORE THE APOCALYPSE.
HAW, HAW, HAW! THANKS, RED!
HOW THE HELL DID THAT HAPPEN?
HOW DID WHAT HAPPEN?
OH, BABY, YOU LOST AGAIN? CAN'T YOU EVER QUIT WHEN YOU'RE AHEAD?
WHEN MY DADDY GETS HERE--
I AM HERE, DARLIN'. HERE TO COLLECT WHAT'S MINE.

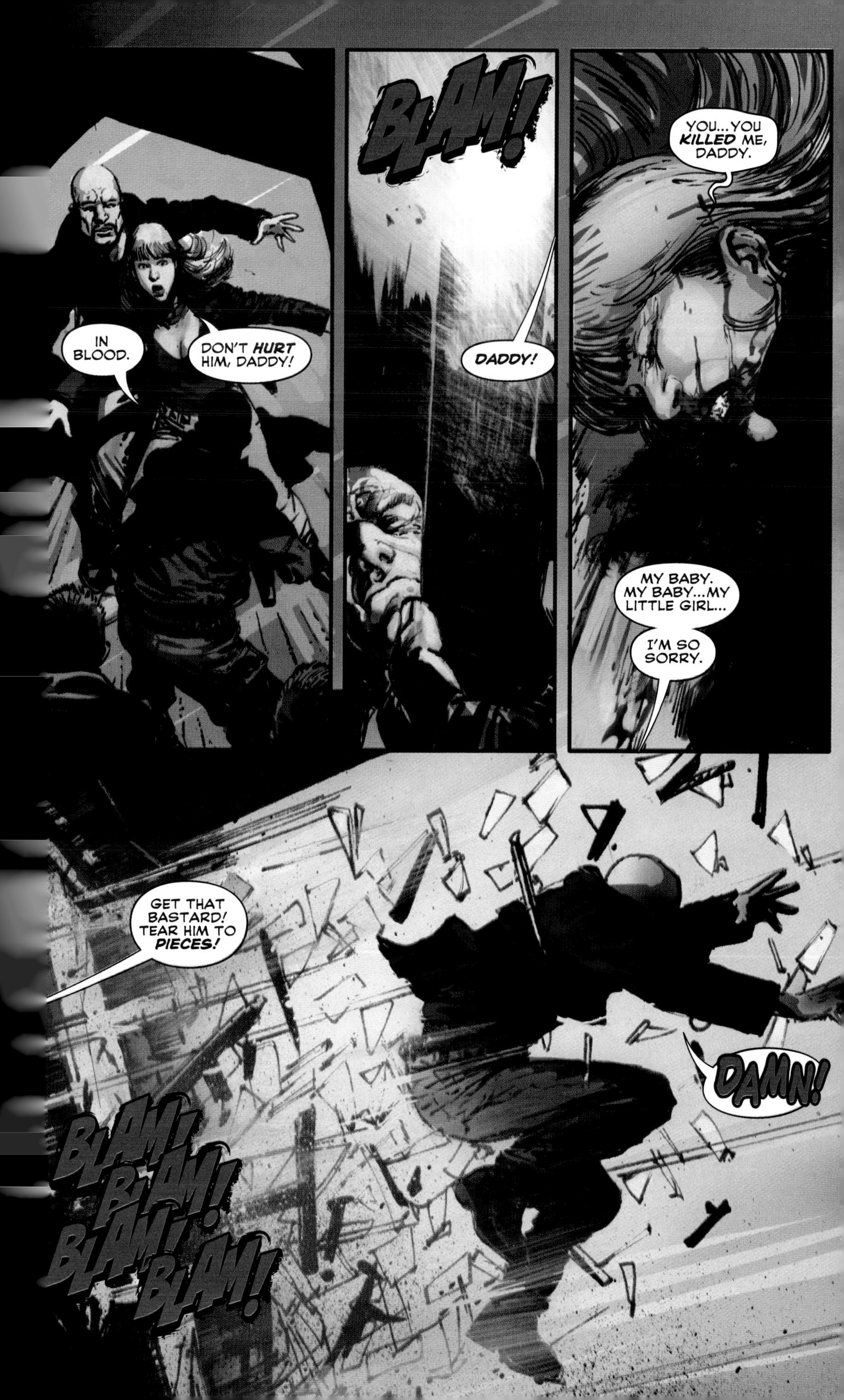
IN BLOOD.
DON'T HURT HIM, DADDY!
BLAM!
DADDY!
YOU...YOU KILLED ME, DADDY.
MY BABY. MY BABY...MY LITTLE GIRL...
I'M SO SORRY.
GET THAT BASTARD! TEAR HIM TO PIECES!
DAMN!
BLAM! BLAM! BLAM! BLAM!

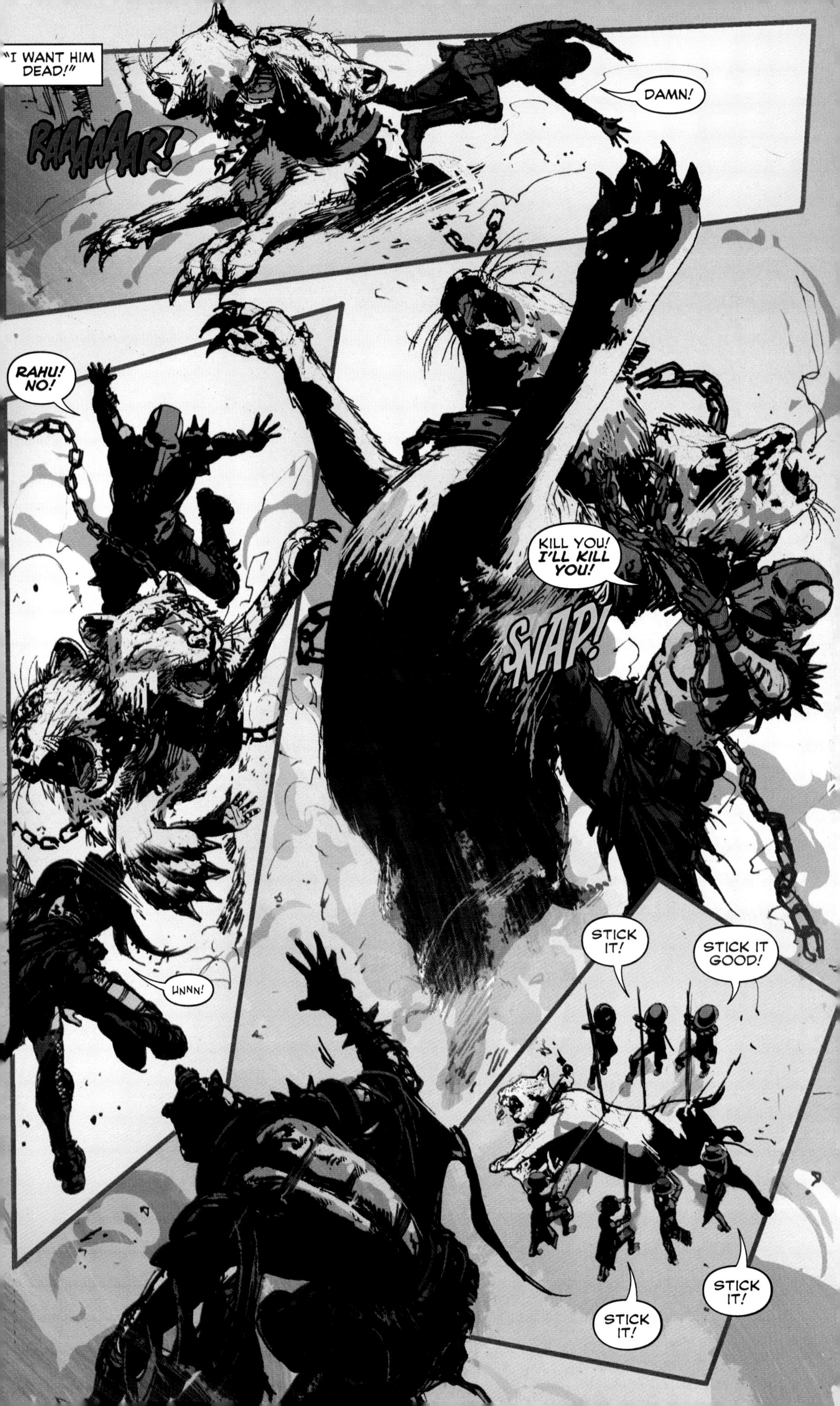
"I WANT HIM DEAD!"
RAAAAAAR!
DAMN!
RAHU! NO!
KILL YOU! I'LL KILL YOU!
SNAP!
UNNN!
STICK IT!
STICK IT GOOD!
STICK IT!
STICK IT!

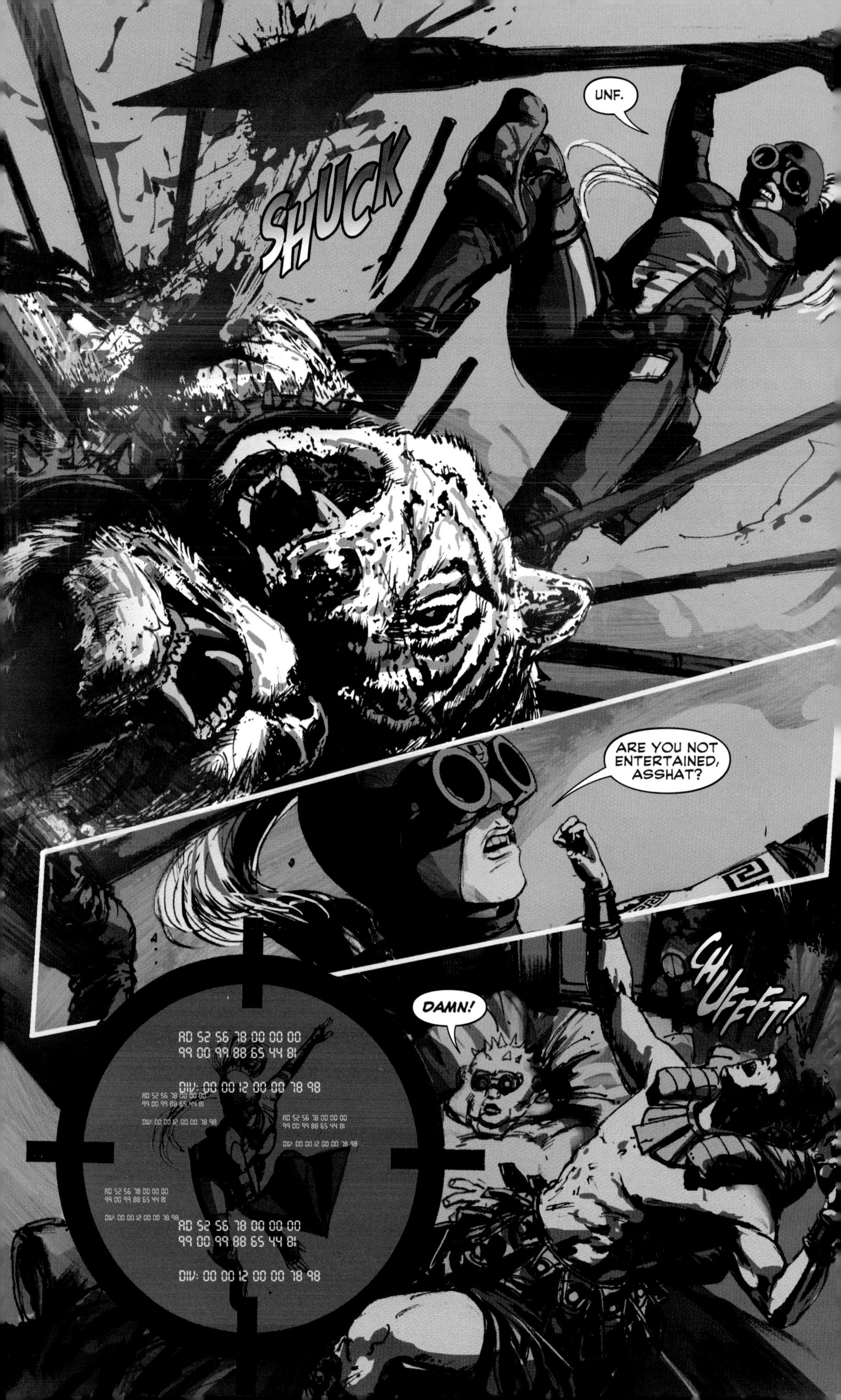
UNF.
SHUCK
ARE YOU NOT ENTERTAINED, ASSHAT?
CHUFFFT!
DAMN!
AD 52 56 78 00 00 00
99 00 99 88 65 44 81
DIV: 00 00 12 00 00 78 98
AD 52 56 78 00 00 00
99 00 99 88 65 44 81
DIV: 00 00 12 00 00 78 98

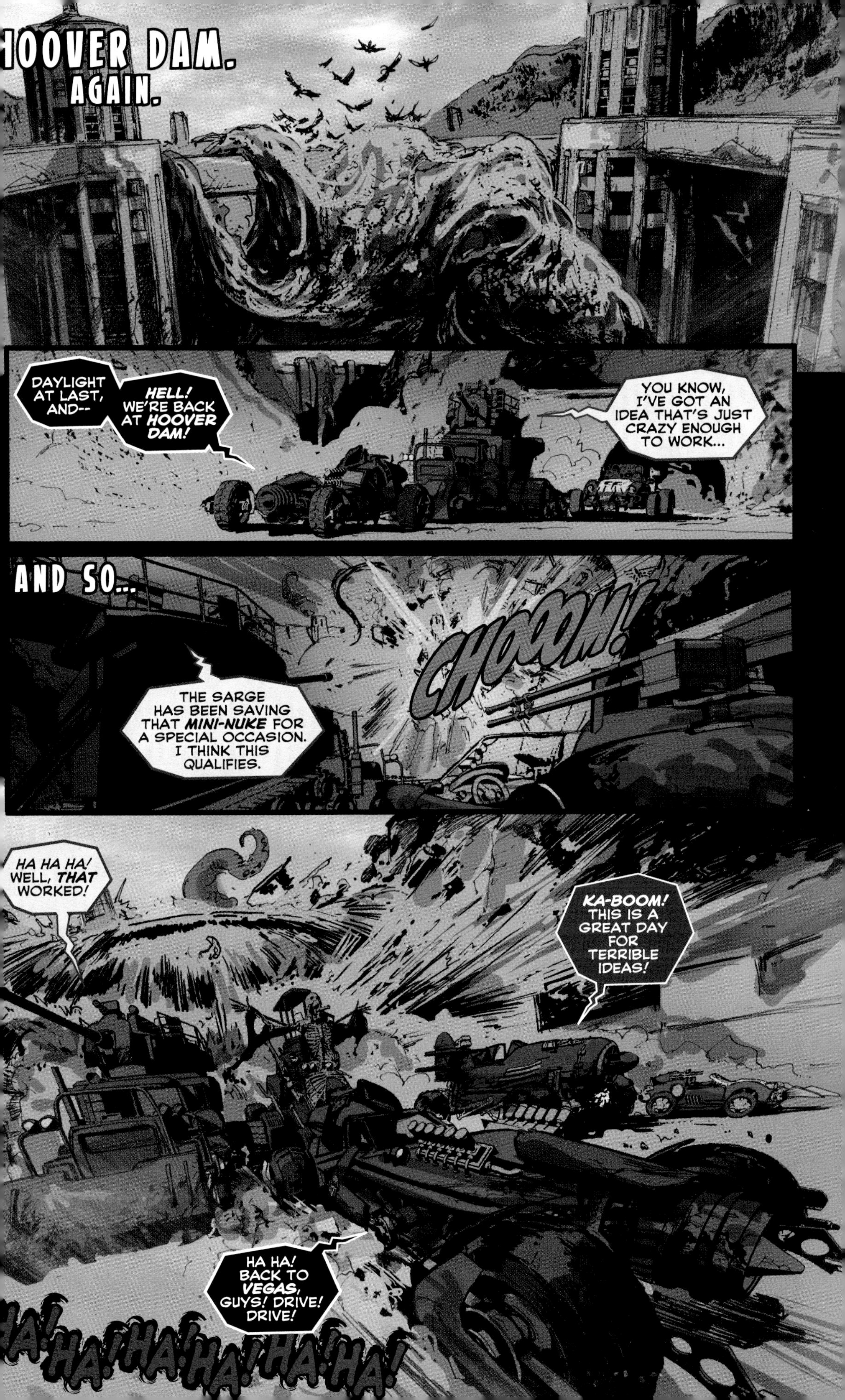
HOOVER DAM.
AGAIN.
DAYLIGHT AT LAST, AND--
HELL! WE'RE BACK AT HOOVER DAM!
YOU KNOW, I'VE GOT AN IDEA THAT'S JUST CRAZY ENOUGH TO WORK...
AND SO...
THE SARGE HAS BEEN SAVING THAT MINI-NUKE FOR A SPECIAL OCCASION. I THINK THIS QUALIFIES.
CHOOOM!
HA HA HA! WELL, THAT WORKED!
KA-BOOM! THIS IS A GREAT DAY FOR TERRIBLE IDEAS!
HA HA! BACK TO VEGAS, GUYS! DRIVE! DRIVE!
HA! HA! HA! HA! HA! HA!

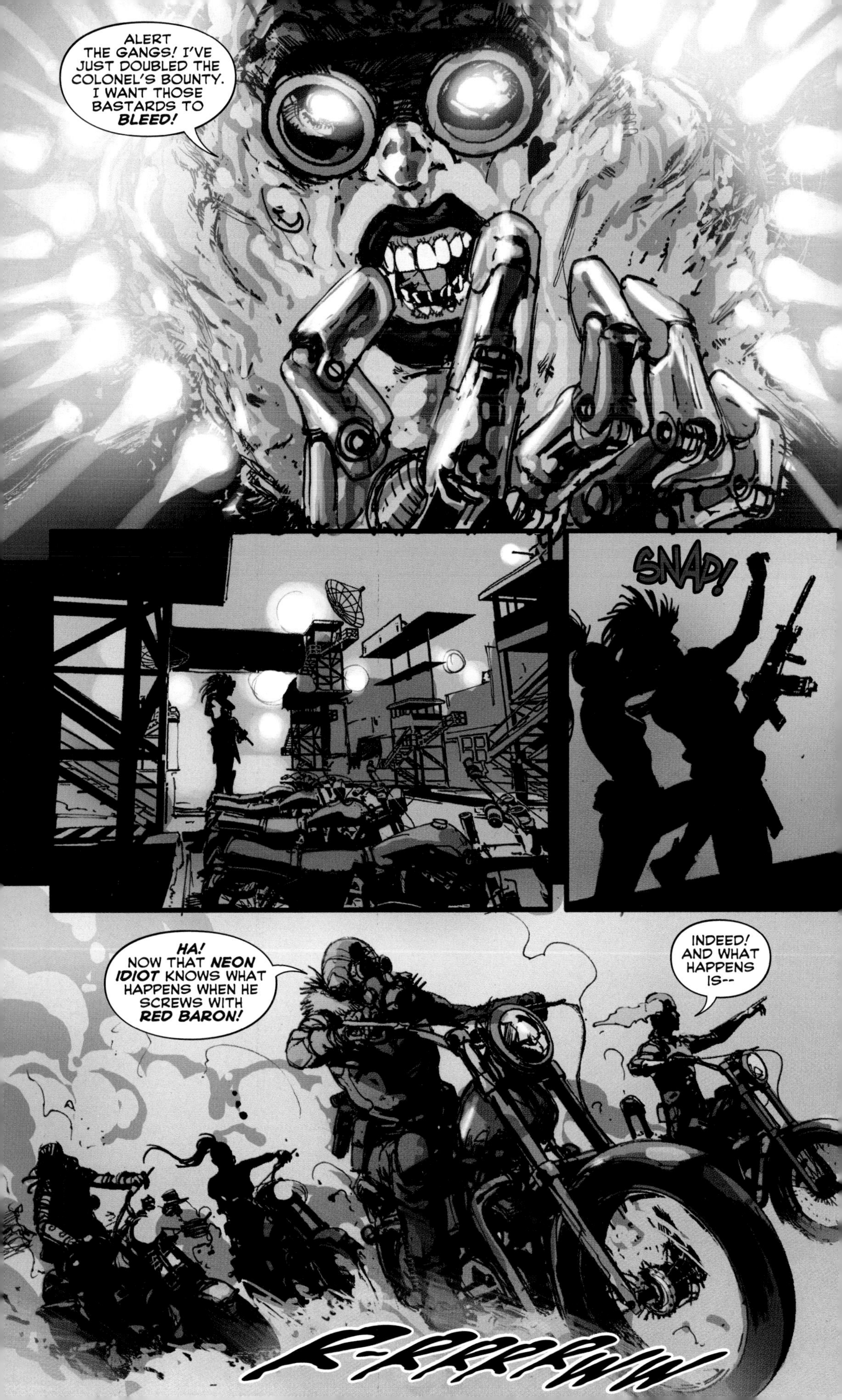
ALERT THE GANGS! I'VE JUST DOUBLED THE COLONEL'S BOUNTY. I WANT THOSE BASTARDS TO BLEED!
SNAP!
HA! NOW THAT NEON IDIOT KNOWS WHAT HAPPENS WHEN HE SCREWS WITH RED BARON!
INDEED! AND WHAT HAPPENS IS--
R-RRRRKWW

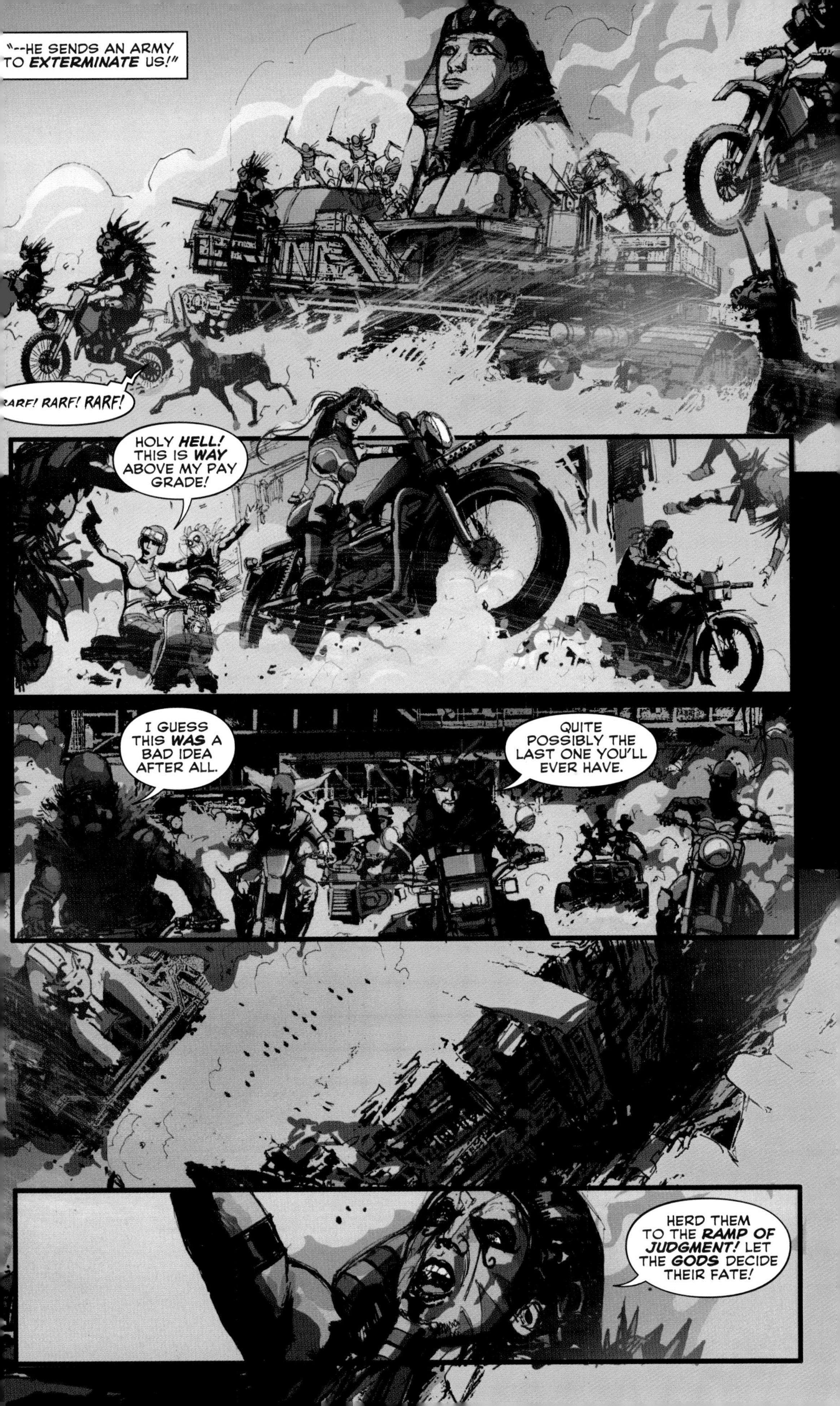
"--HE SENDS AN ARMY TO EXTERMINATE US!"
RARF! RARF! RARF!
HOLY HELL! THIS IS WAY ABOVE MY PAY GRADE!
I GUESS THIS WAS A BAD IDEA AFTER ALL.
QUITE POSSIBLY THE LAST ONE YOU'LL EVER HAVE.
HERD THEM TO THE RAMP OF JUDGMENT! LET THE GODS DECIDE THEIR FATE!

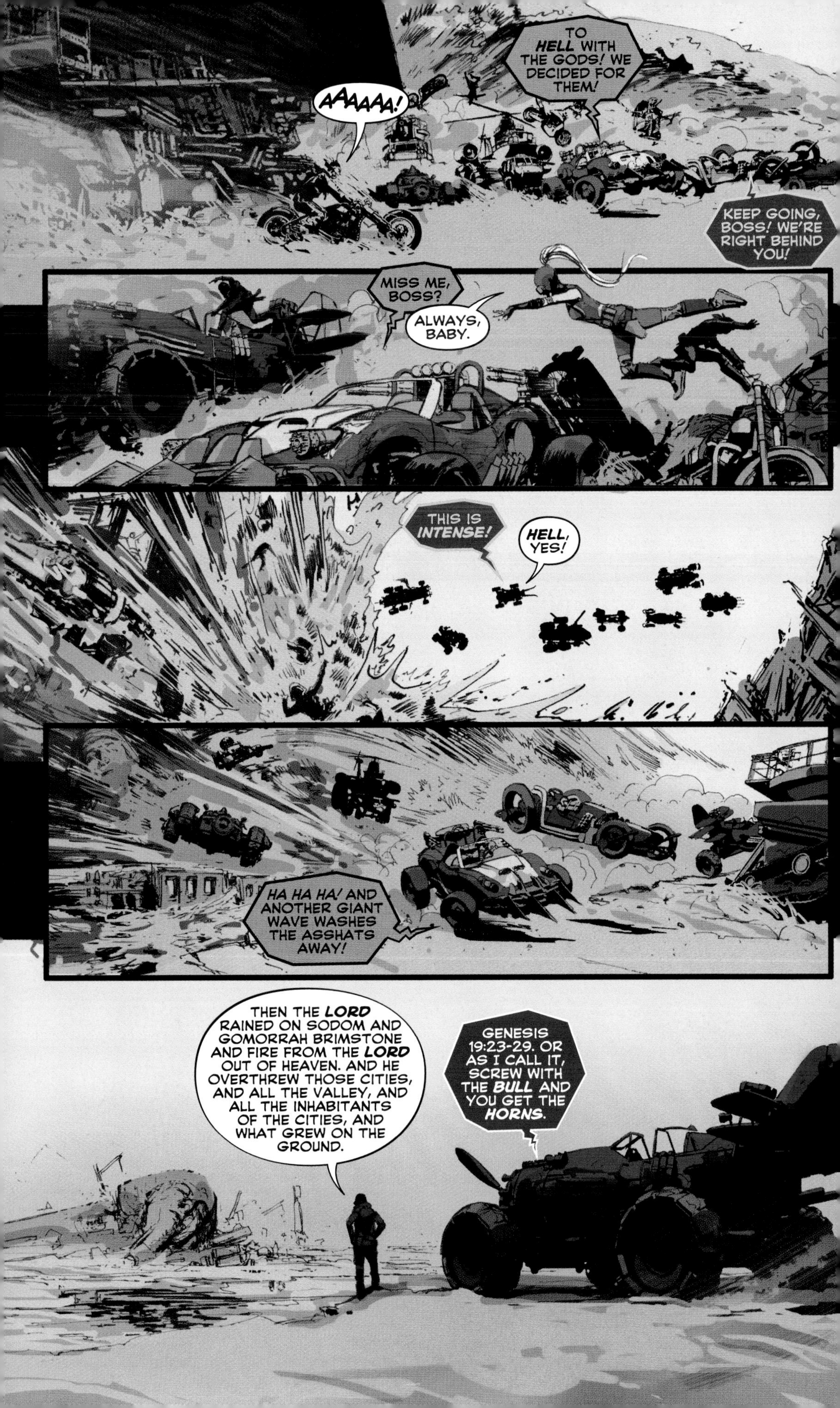
AAAAAA!
TO HELL WITH THE GODS! WE DECIDED FOR THEM!
KEEP GOING, BOSS! WE'RE RIGHT BEHIND YOU!
MISS ME, BOSS?
ALWAYS, BABY.
THIS IS INTENSE!
HELL, YES!
HA HA HA! AND ANOTHER GIANT WAVE WASHES THE ASSHATS AWAY!
THEN THE LORD RAINED ON SODOM AND GOMORRAH BRIMSTONE AND FIRE FROM THE LORD OUT OF HEAVEN. AND HE OVERTHREW THOSE CITIES, AND ALL THE VALLEY, AND ALL THE INHABITANTS OF THE CITIES, AND WHAT GREW ON THE GROUND.
GENESIS 19:23-29. OR AS I CALL IT, SCREW WITH THE BULL AND YOU GET THE HORNS.

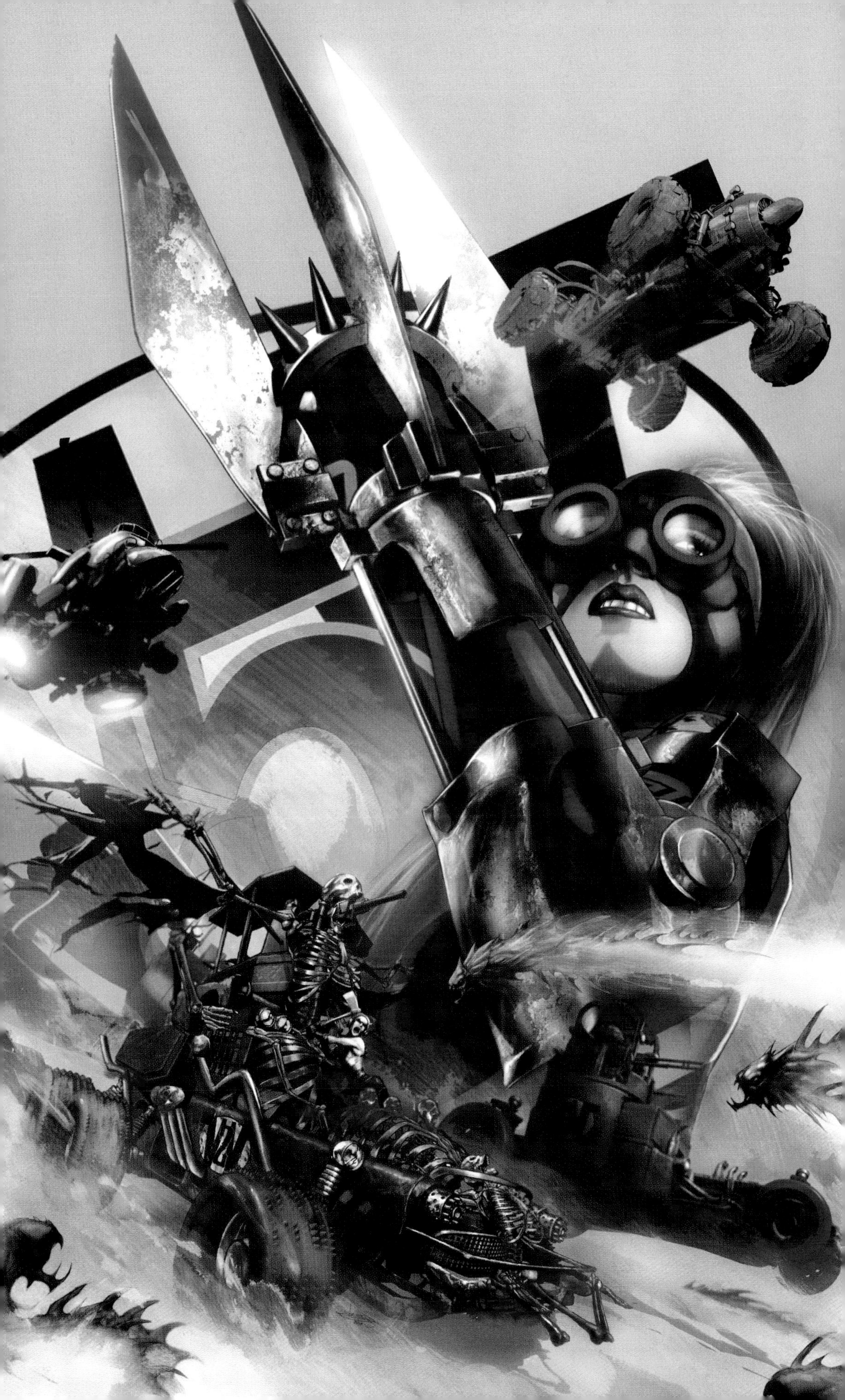

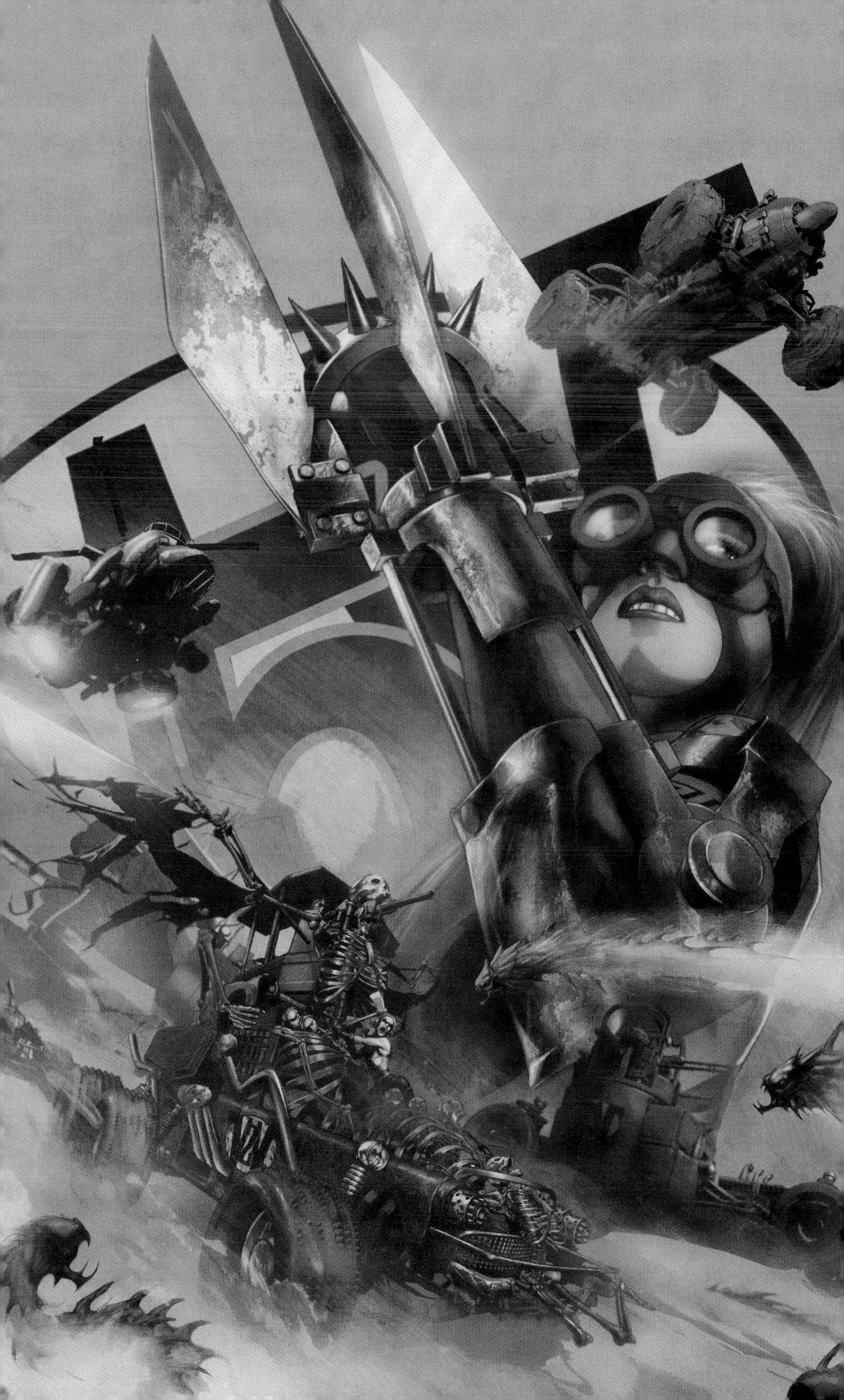

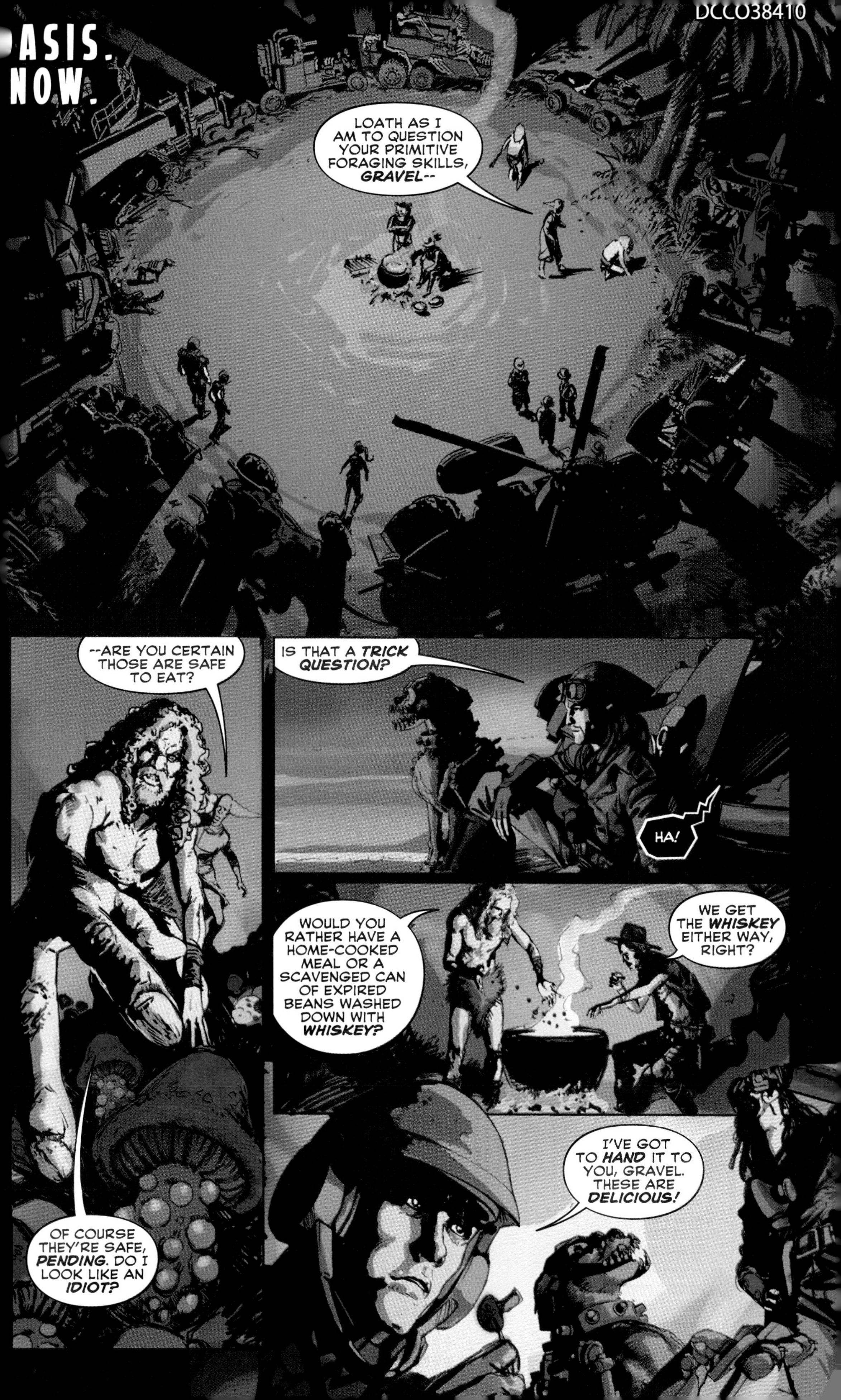
DCCO38410
OASIS. NOW.
LOATH AS I AM TO QUESTION YOUR PRIMITIVE FORAGING SKILLS, GRAVEL--
--ARE YOU CERTAIN THOSE ARE SAFE TO EAT?
IS THAT A TRICK QUESTION?
HA!
WOULD YOU RATHER HAVE A HOME-COOKED MEAL OR A SCAVENGED CAN OF EXPIRED BEANS WASHED DOWN WITH WHISKEY?
WE GET THE WHISKEY EITHER WAY, RIGHT?
OF COURSE THEY'RE SAFE, PENDING. DO I LOOK LIKE AN IDIOT?
I'VE GOT TO HAND IT TO YOU, GRAVEL. THESE ARE DELICIOUS!

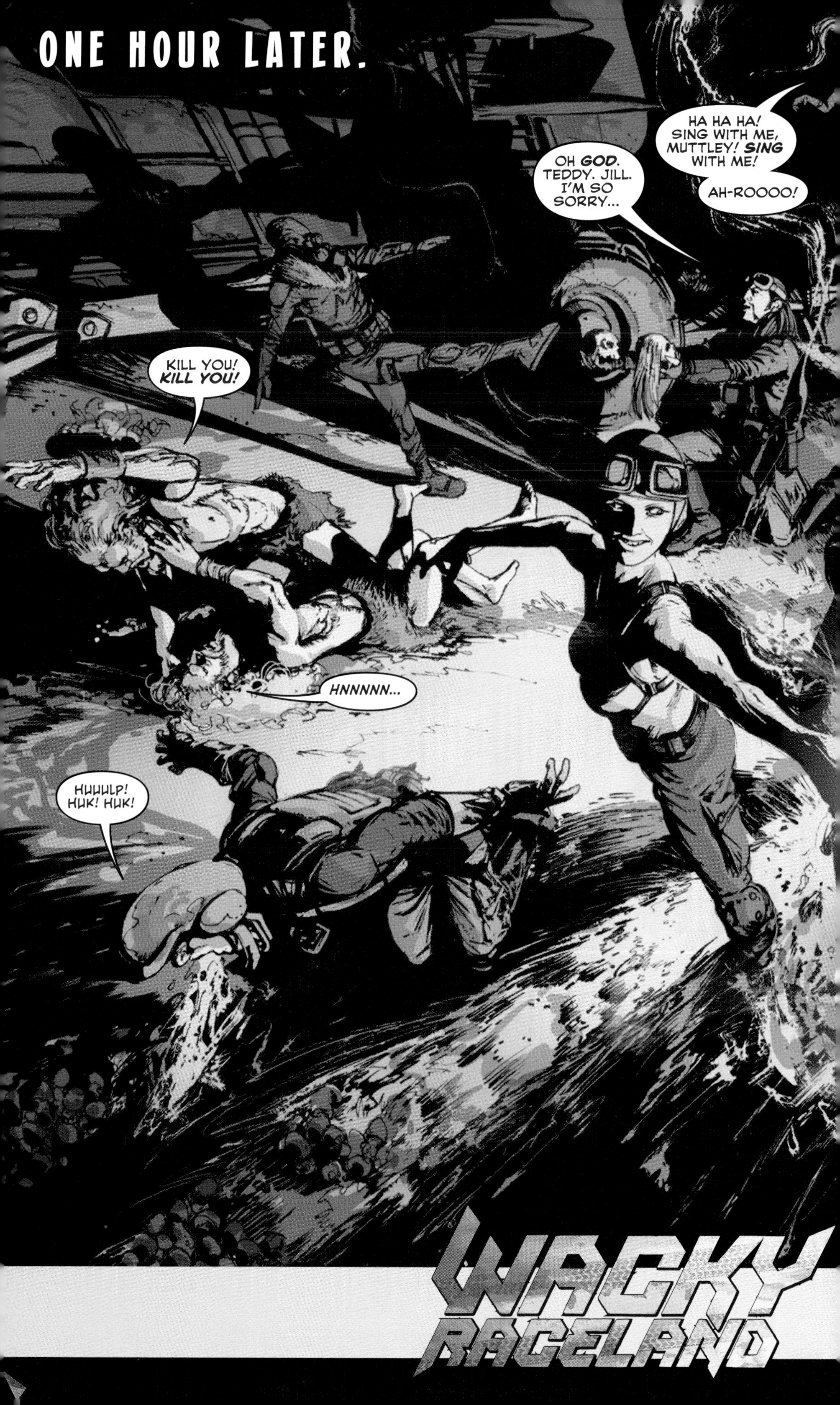

ONE HOUR LATER.
HA HA HA! SING WITH ME, MUTTLEY! SING WITH ME!
AH-ROOOO!
OH GOD. TEDDY. JILL. I'M SO SORRY...
KILL YOU! KILL YOU!
HNNNNN...
HUUULP! HUK! HUK!
WACKY RACELAND

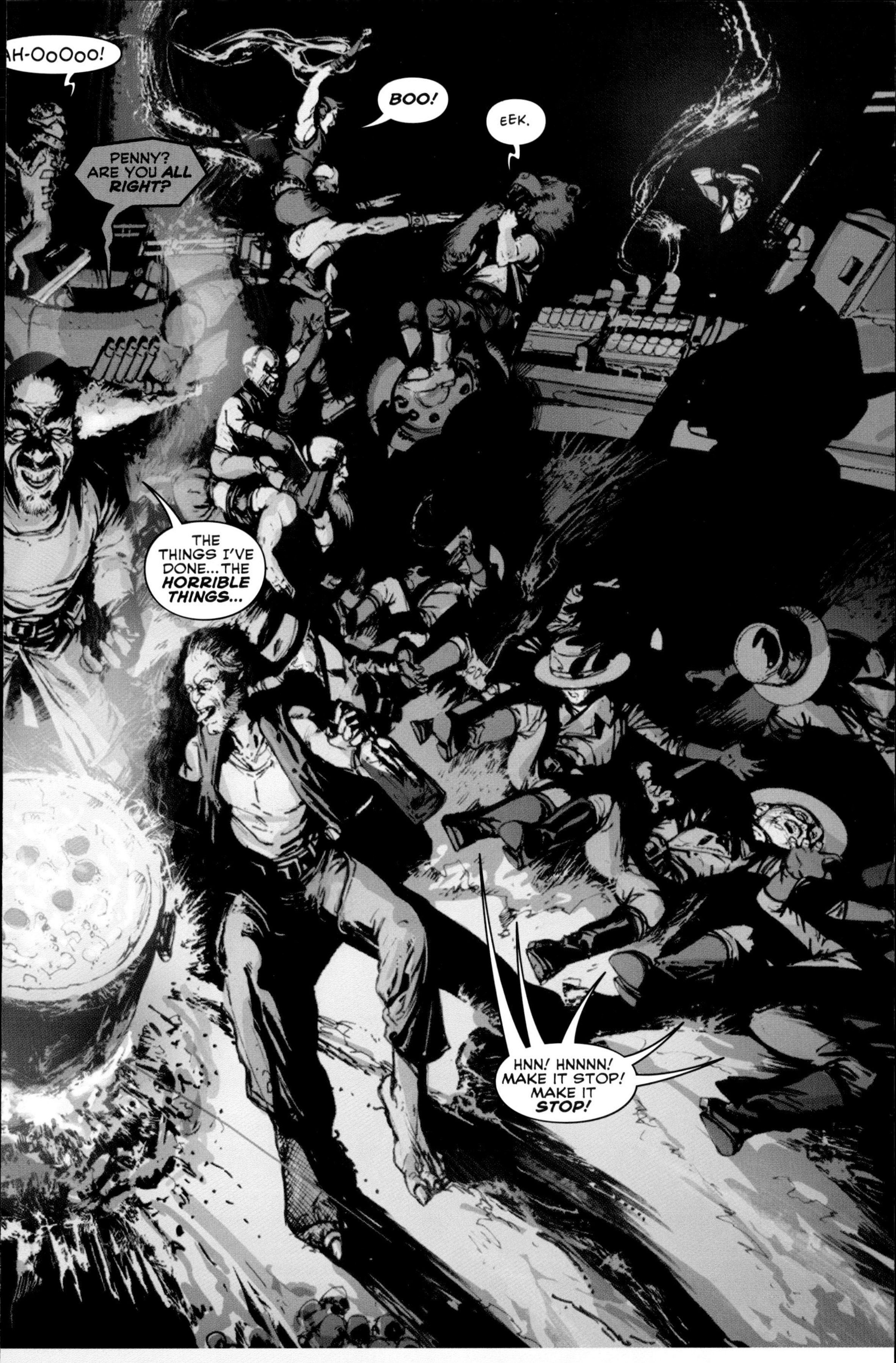
H-OOOOO!
PENNY? ARE YOU **ALL RIGHT?**
BOO!
EEK.
THE THINGS I'VE DONE...THE **HORRIBLE THINGS...**
HNN! HNNNN! MAKE IT STOP! MAKE IT **STOP!**

THE BUTCHER SHOP
PART ONE: REVELATIONS

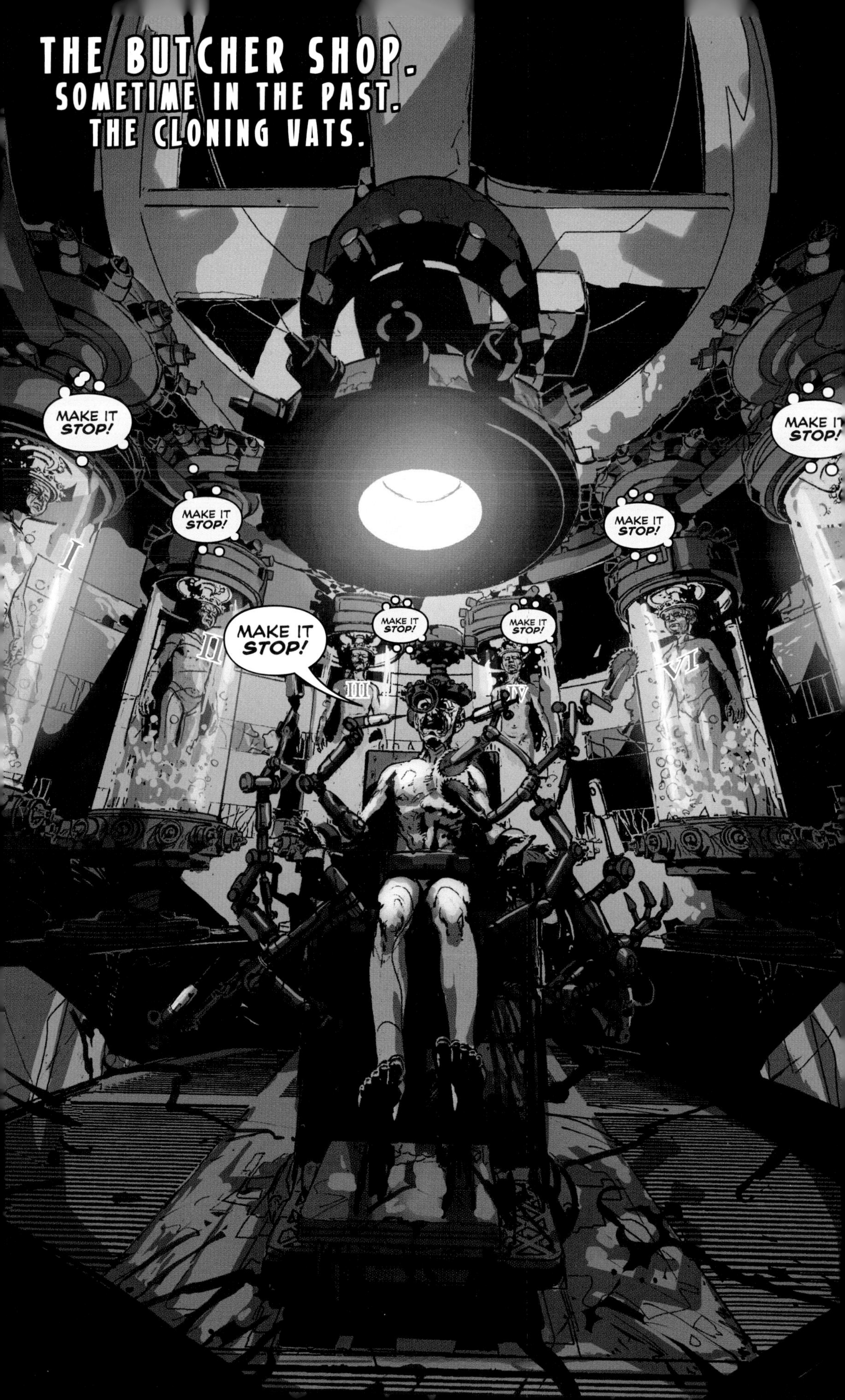
THE BUTCHER SHOP.
SOMETIME IN THE PAST.
THE CLONING VATS.
MAKE IT STOP!
MAKE IT STOP!
MAKE IT STOP!
MAKE IT STOP!
MAKE IT STOP!
MAKE IT STOP!
MAKE IT STOP!
I
II
III
IV
VI

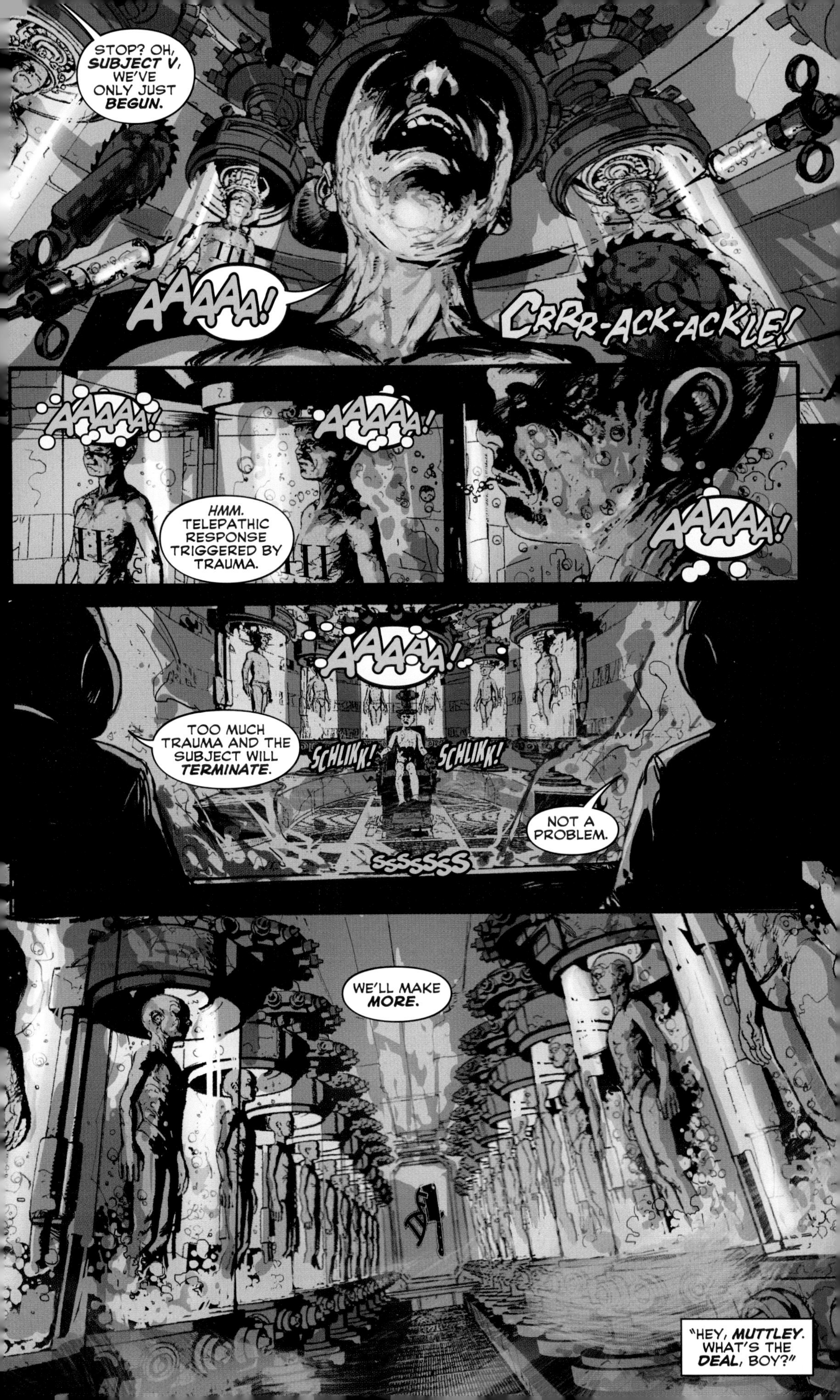
STOP? OH, SUBJECT V, WE'VE ONLY JUST BEGUN.
AAAAA!
CRRR-ACK-ACKLE!
AAAAA!
AAAAA!
HMM. TELEPATHIC RESPONSE TRIGGERED BY TRAUMA.
AAAAA!
AAAAA!
TOO MUCH TRAUMA AND THE SUBJECT WILL TERMINATE.
SCHLIKK!
SCHLIKK!
NOT A PROBLEM.
SSSSSSS
WE'LL MAKE MORE.
"HEY, MUTTLEY. WHAT'S THE DEAL, BOY?"

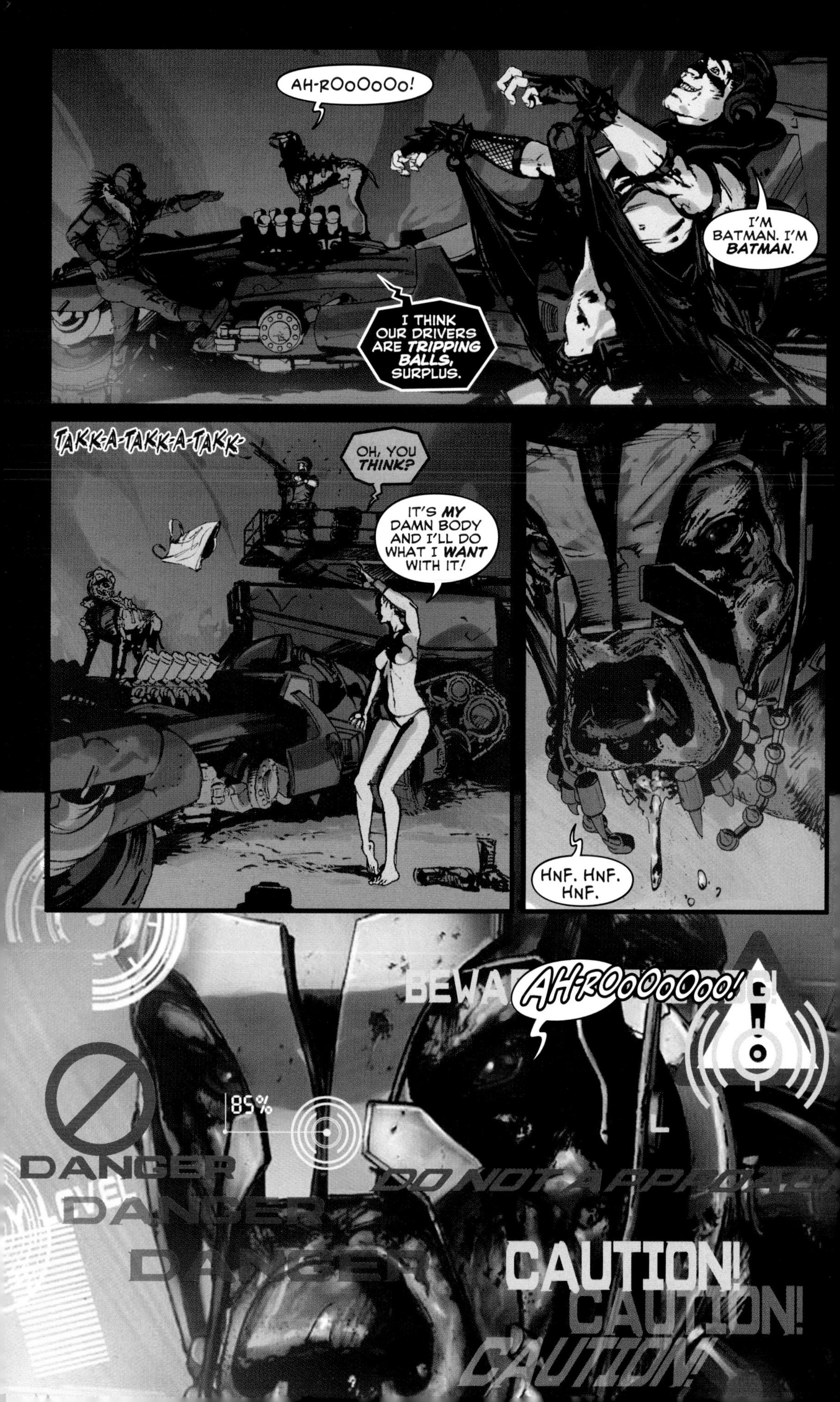
AH-ROOOOOOO!
I'M BATMAN. I'M *BATMAN*.
I THINK OUR DRIVERS ARE *TRIPPING BALLS,* SURPLUS.
TAKK-A-TAKK-A-TAKK
OH, YOU *THINK?*
IT'S *MY* DAMN BODY AND I'LL DO WHAT I *WANT* WITH IT!
HNF. HNF. HNF.
AH-ROOOOOOO!
85%
DANGER
DANGER
DANGER
CAUTION!
CAUTION!
CAUTION!

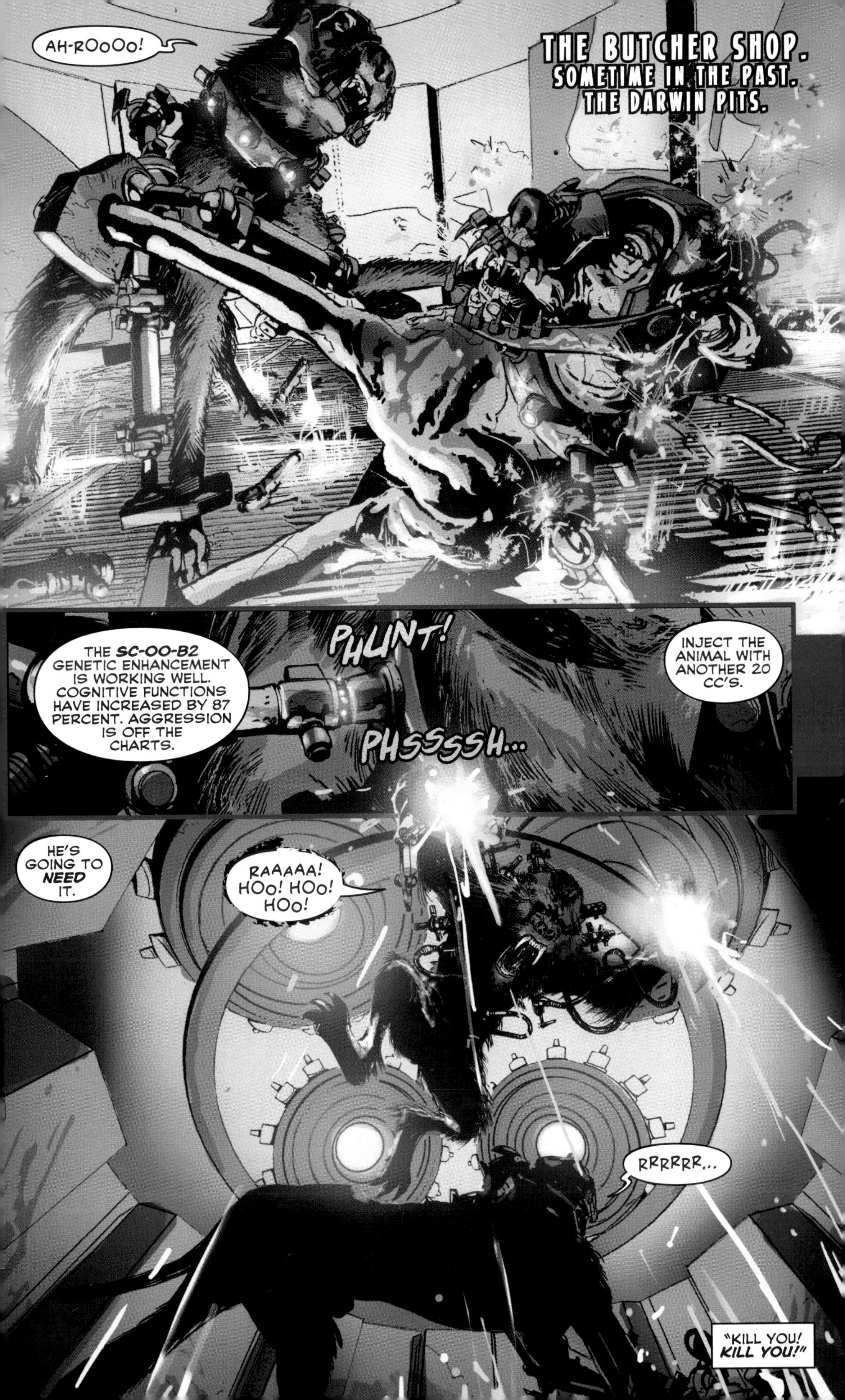
AH-ROOOO!
THE BUTCHER SHOP.
SOMETIME IN THE PAST.
THE DARWIN PITS.
THE SC-OO-B2 GENETIC ENHANCEMENT IS WORKING WELL. COGNITIVE FUNCTIONS HAVE INCREASED BY 87 PERCENT. AGGRESSION IS OFF THE CHARTS.
PHUNT!
PHSSSSH...
INJECT THE ANIMAL WITH ANOTHER 20 CC'S.
HE'S GOING TO NEED IT.
RAAAAA! HOo! HOo! HOo!
RRRRRR...
"KILL YOU! KILL YOU!"

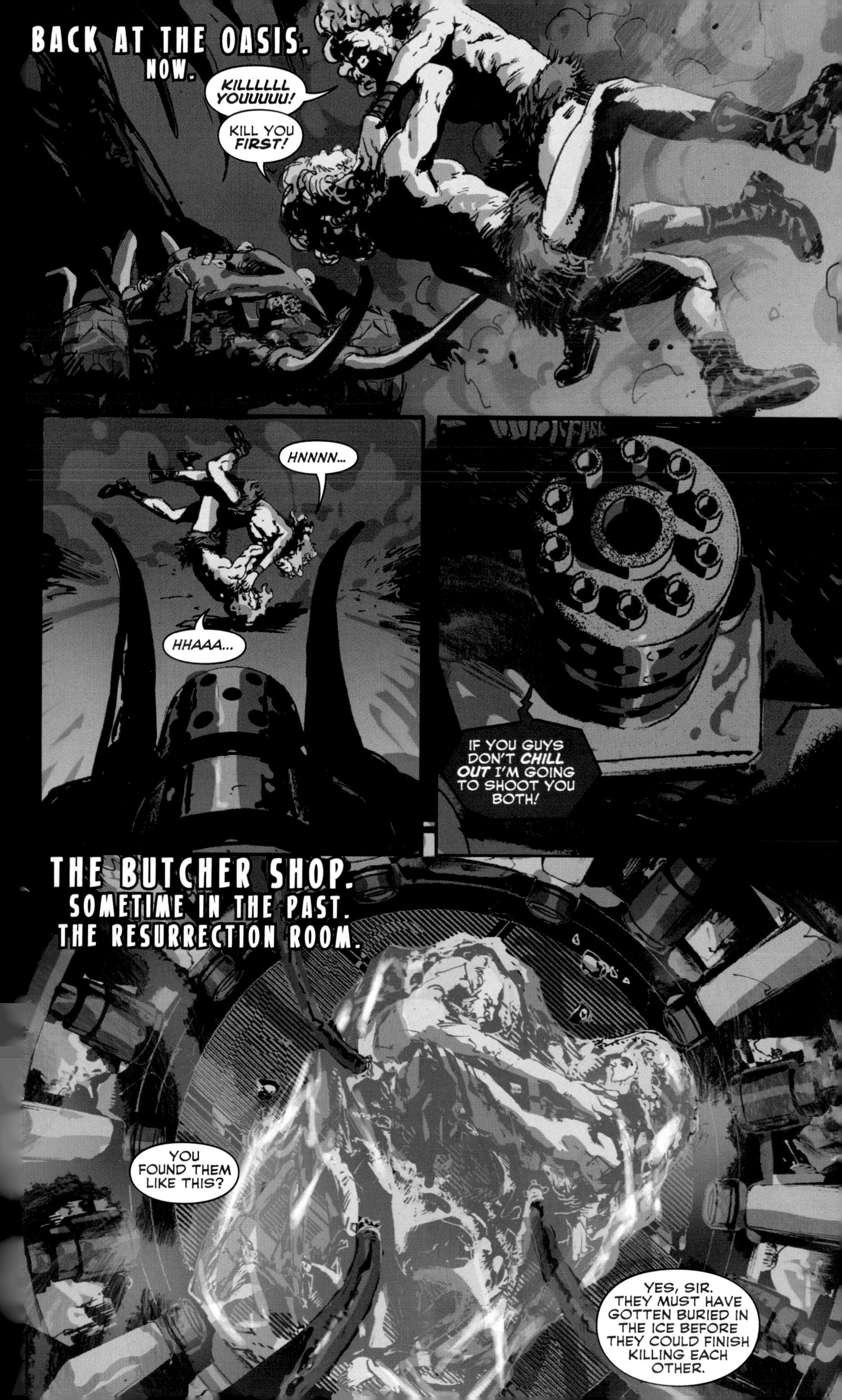

BACK AT THE OASIS.
NOW.
KILLLLLLL YOUUUUUU!
KILL YOU FIRST!
HNNNN...
HHAAA...
IF YOU GUYS DON'T CHILL OUT I'M GOING TO SHOOT YOU BOTH!
THE BUTCHER SHOP.
SOMETIME IN THE PAST.
THE RESURRECTION ROOM.
YOU FOUND THEM LIKE THIS?
YES, SIR. THEY MUST HAVE GOTTEN BURIED IN THE ICE BEFORE THEY COULD FINISH KILLING EACH OTHER.

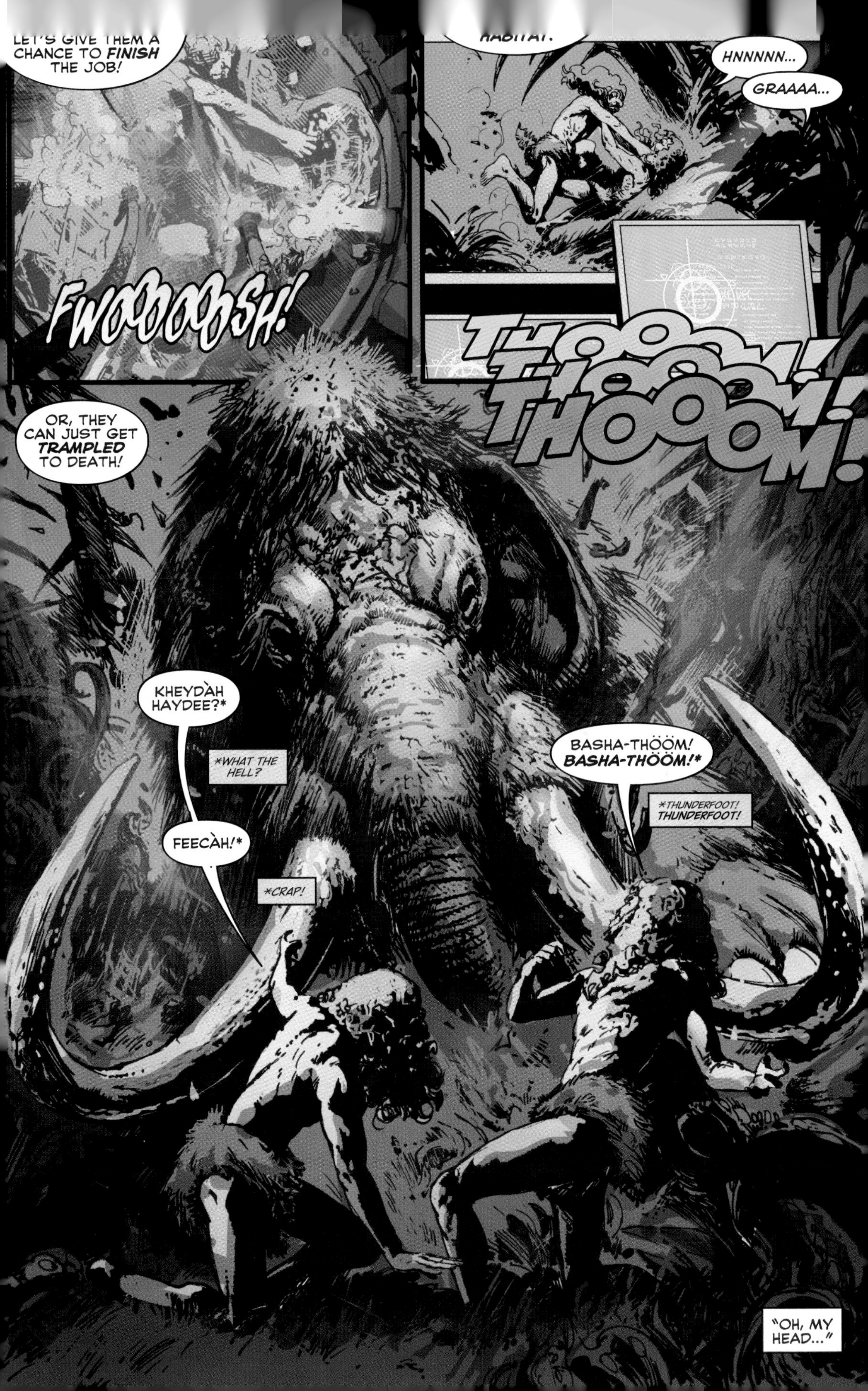
LET'S GIVE THEM A CHANCE TO FINISH THE JOB!
HABITAT.
HNNNNN...
GRAAAA...
FWOOOOOSH!
THOOOM! THOOOM! THOOOM!
OR, THEY CAN JUST GET TRAMPLED TO DEATH!
KHEYDÀH HAYDEE?*
*WHAT THE HELL?
FEECÀH!*
*CRAP!
BASHA-THÖÖM! BASHA-THÖÖM!*
*THUNDERFOOT! THUNDERFOOT!
"OH, MY HEAD..."

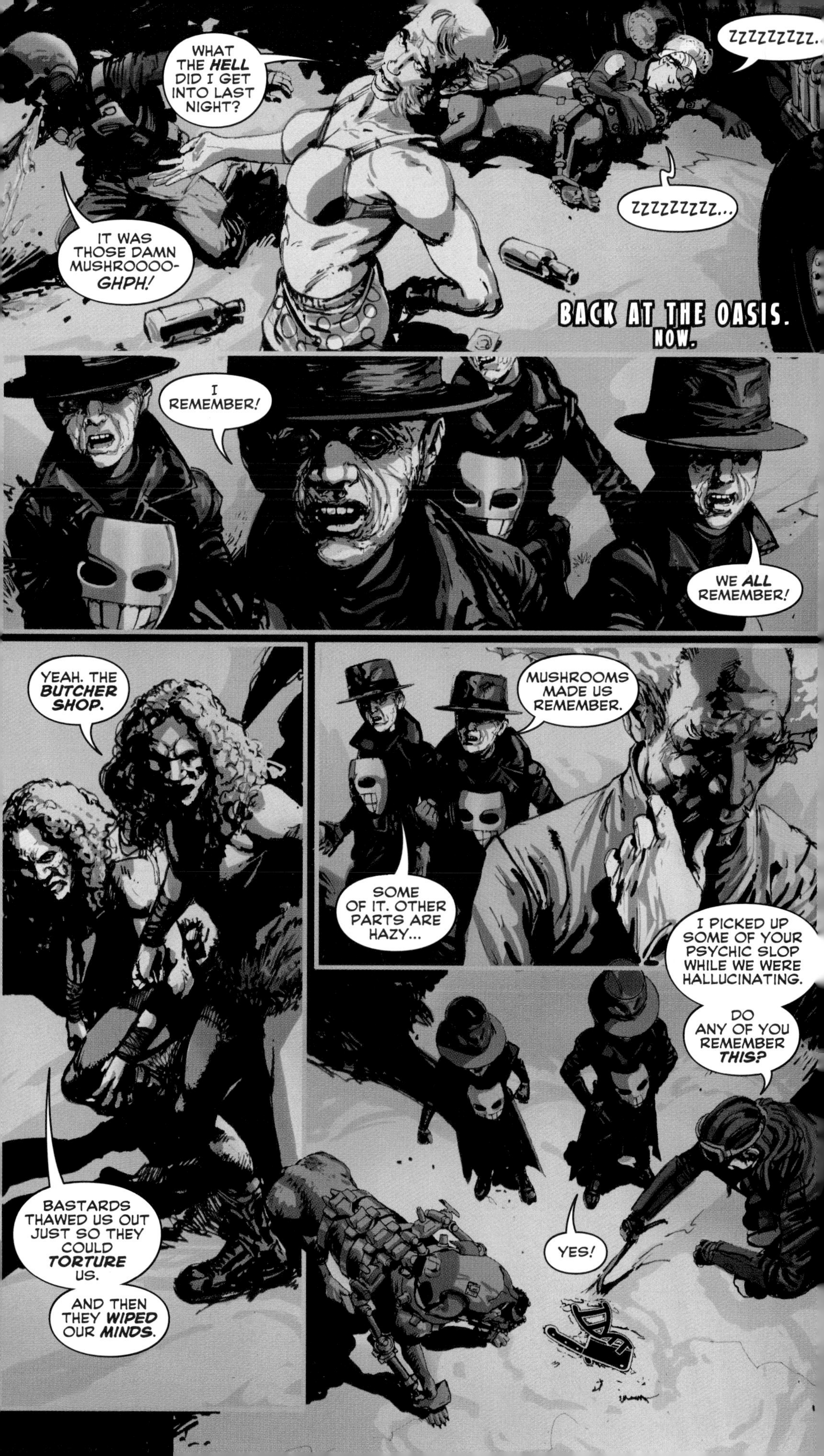

WHAT THE HELL DID I GET INTO LAST NIGHT?
ZZZZZZZZZ...
IT WAS THOSE DAMN MUSHROOOO-GHPH!
ZZZZZZZZZ...
BACK AT THE OASIS. NOW.
I REMEMBER!
WE ALL REMEMBER!
YEAH. THE BUTCHER SHOP.
BASTARDS THAWED US OUT JUST SO THEY COULD TORTURE US.
AND THEN THEY WIPED OUR MINDS.
MUSHROOMS MADE US REMEMBER.
SOME OF IT. OTHER PARTS ARE HAZY...
I PICKED UP SOME OF YOUR PSYCHIC SLOP WHILE WE WERE HALLUCINATING.
DO ANY OF YOU REMEMBER THIS?
YES!

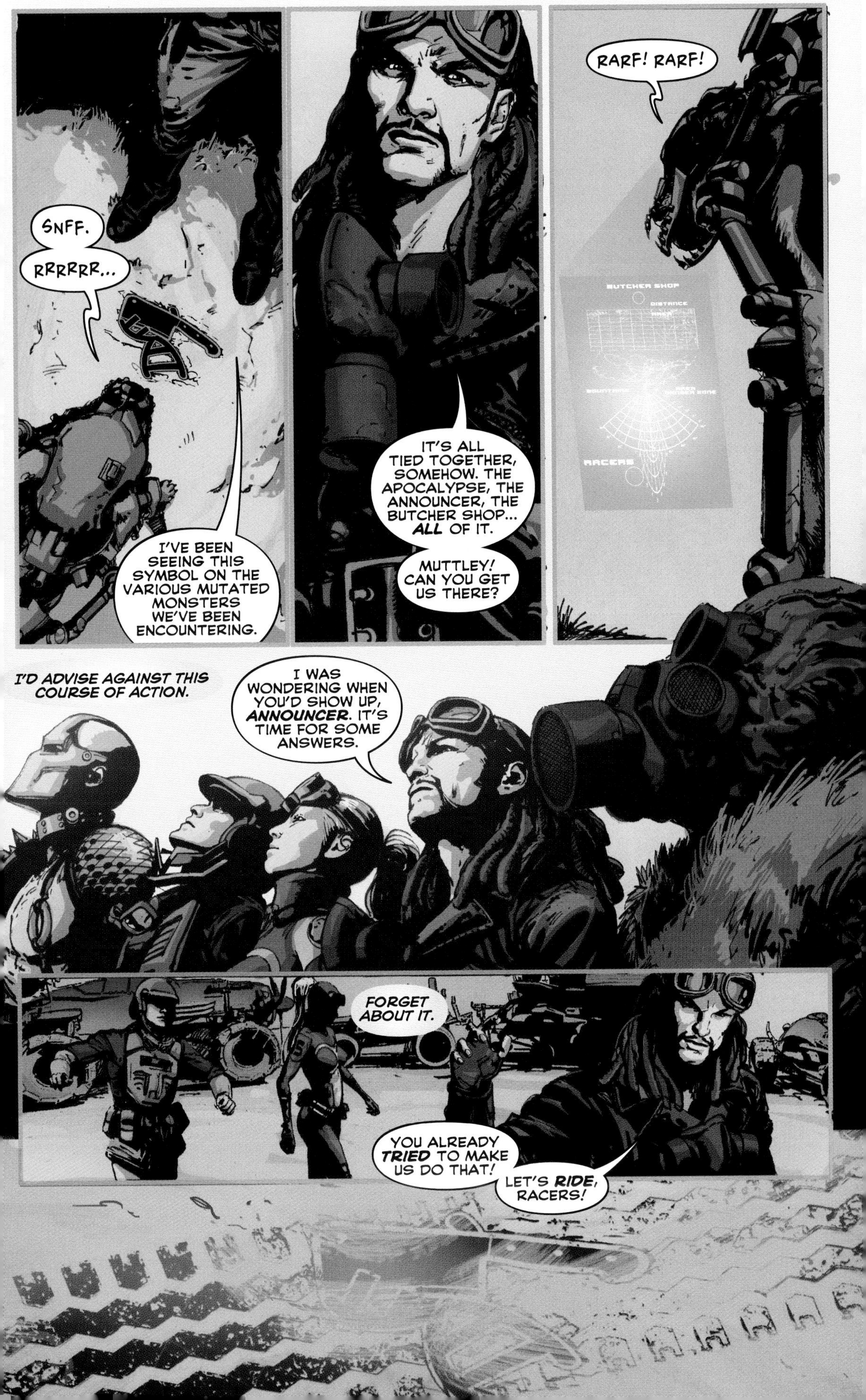
SNFF.
RRRRRR...
I'VE BEEN SEEING THIS SYMBOL ON THE VARIOUS MUTATED MONSTERS WE'VE BEEN ENCOUNTERING.
IT'S ALL TIED TOGETHER, SOMEHOW. THE APOCALYPSE, THE ANNOUNCER, THE BUTCHER SHOP... ALL OF IT.
MUTTLEY! CAN YOU GET US THERE?
RARF! RARF!
BUTCHER SHOP
DISTANCE
RACERS
I'D ADVISE AGAINST THIS COURSE OF ACTION.
I WAS WONDERING WHEN YOU'D SHOW UP, ANNOUNCER. IT'S TIME FOR SOME ANSWERS.
FORGET ABOUT IT.
YOU ALREADY TRIED TO MAKE US DO THAT!
LET'S RIDE, RACERS!

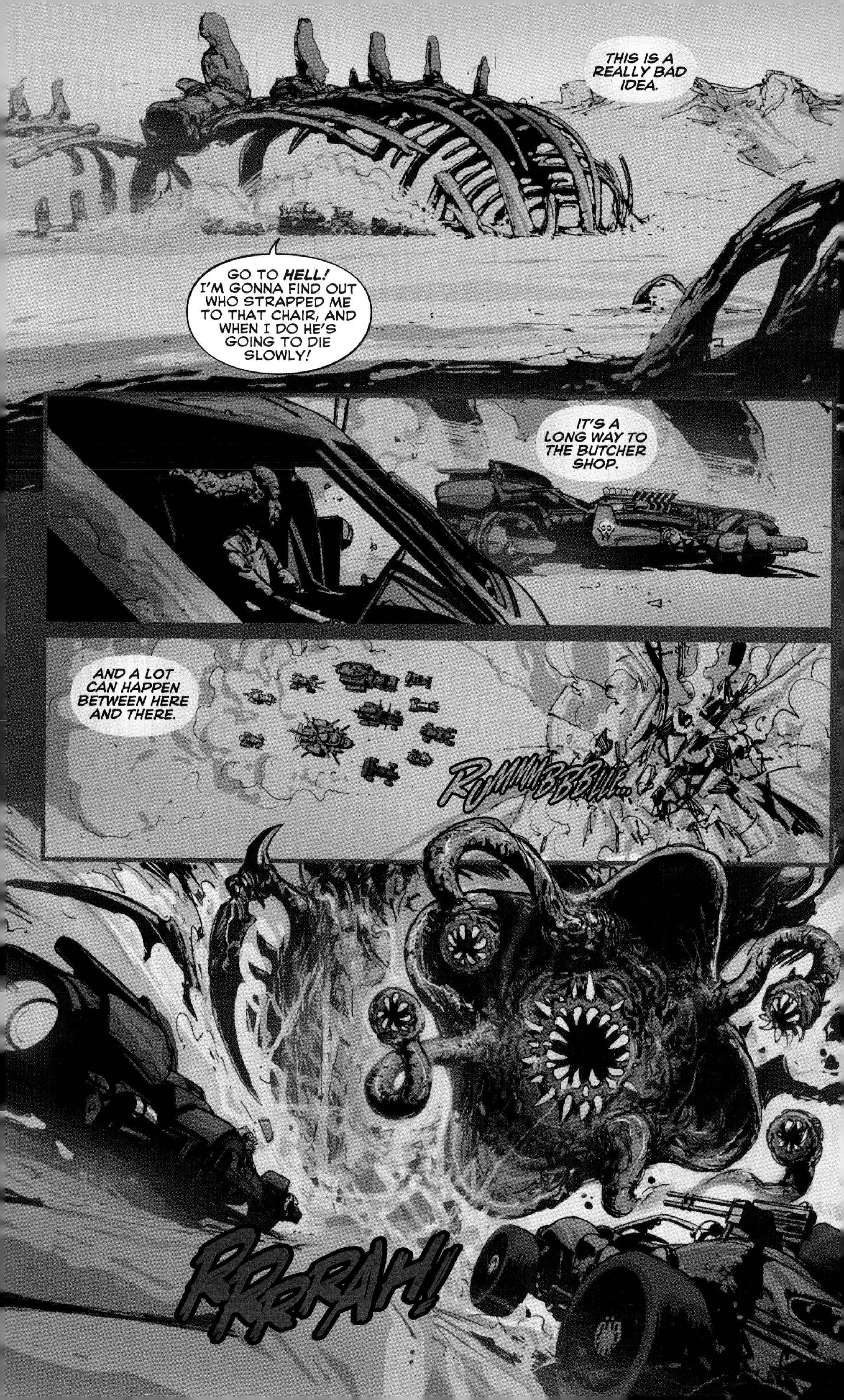
THIS IS A REALLY BAD IDEA.
GO TO HELL! I'M GONNA FIND OUT WHO STRAPPED ME TO THAT CHAIR, AND WHEN I DO HE'S GOING TO DIE SLOWLY!
IT'S A LONG WAY TO THE BUTCHER SHOP.
AND A LOT CAN HAPPEN BETWEEN HERE AND THERE.
RUMMMBBBLLL...
RRRRAH!

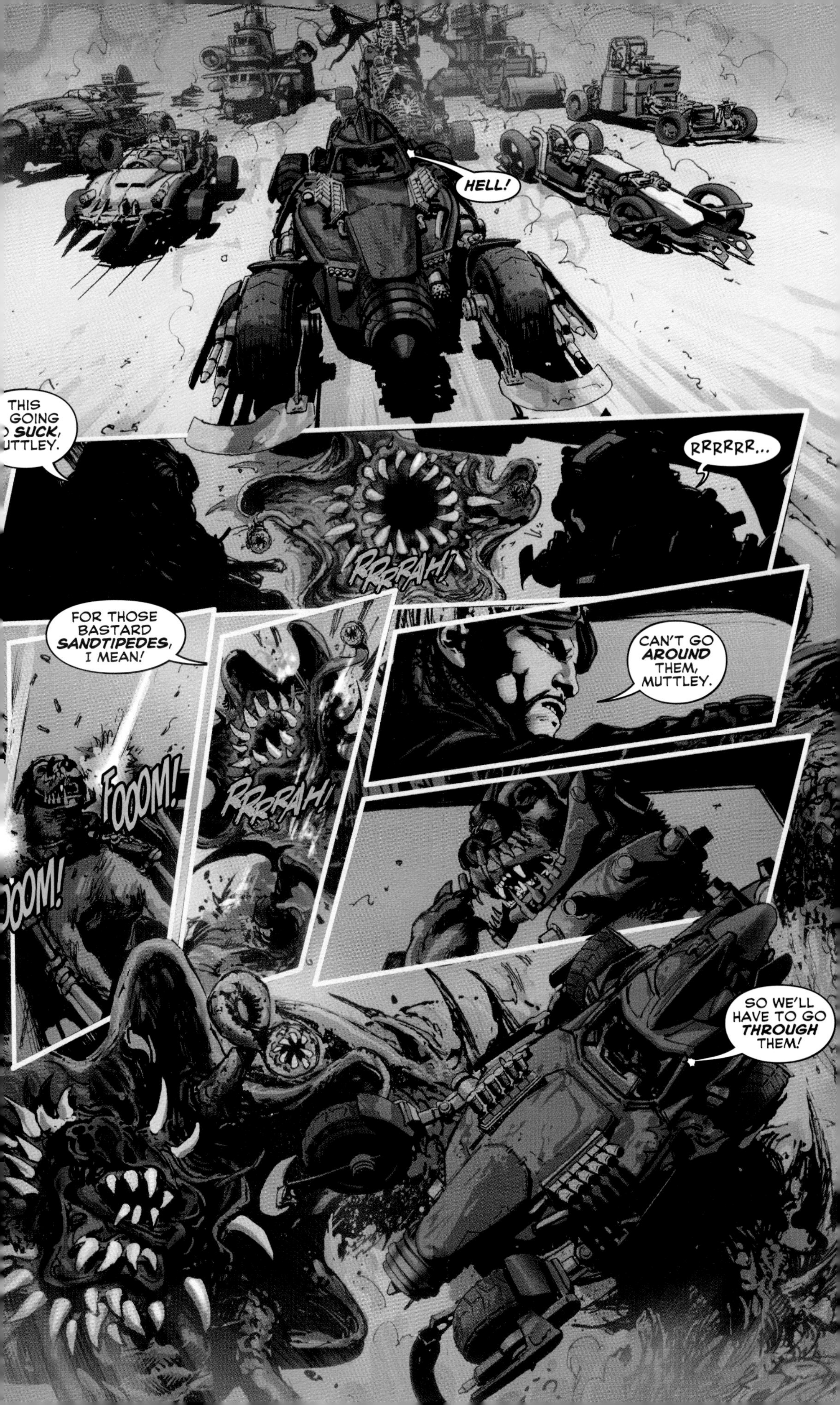

HELL!
THIS GOING O SUCK, UTTLEY.
RRRRRR...
RRRRAH!
FOR THOSE BASTARD SANDTIPEDES, I MEAN!
CAN'T GO AROUND THEM, MUTTLEY.
FOOOM!
OOOM!
RRRRAH!
SO WE'LL HAVE TO GO THROUGH THEM!

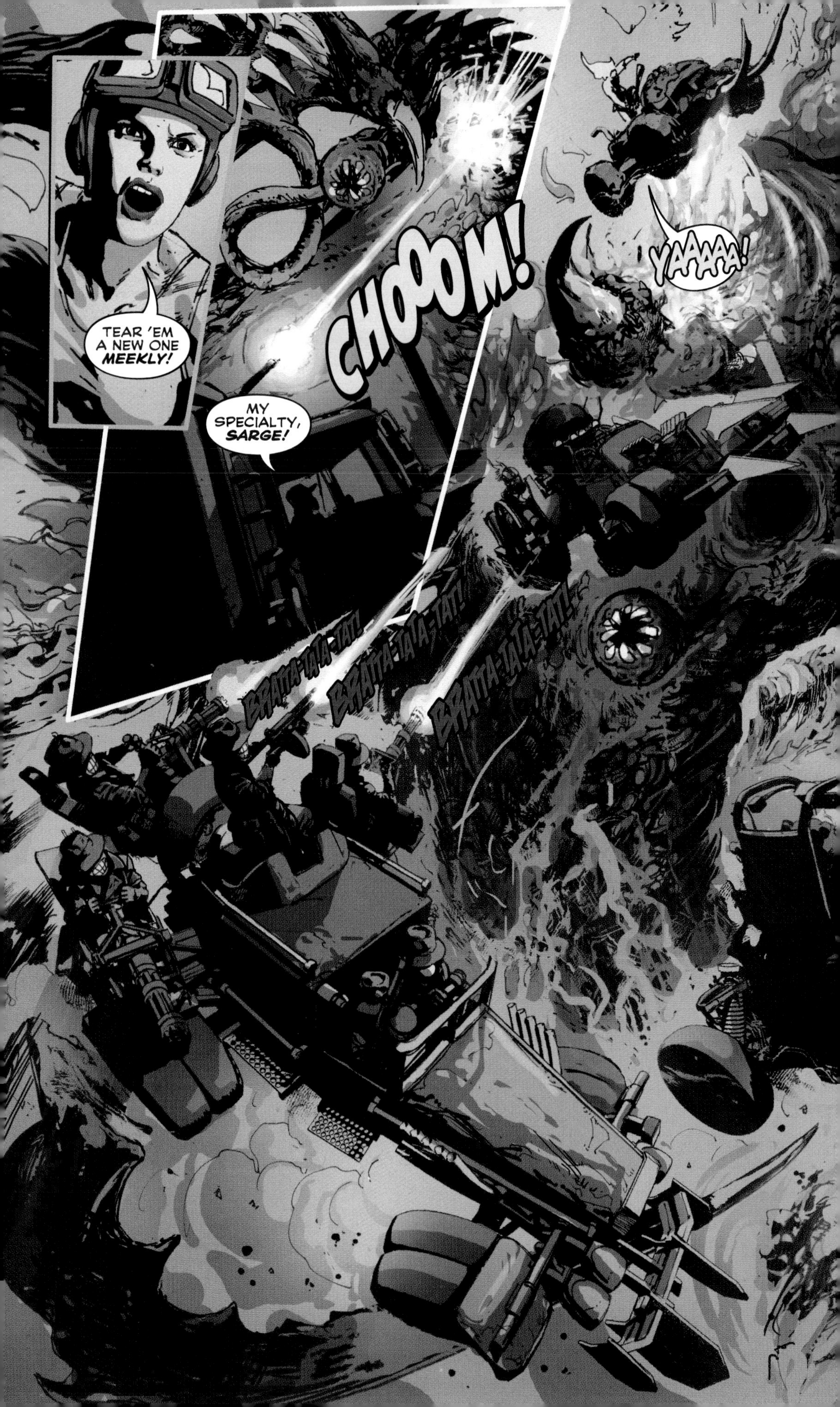
TEAR 'EM A NEW ONE MEEKLY!
MY SPECIALTY, SARGE!
CHOOOM!
YAAAAA!
BRATTA-TATA-TAT!
BRATTA-TATA-TAT!
BRATTA-TATA-TAT!

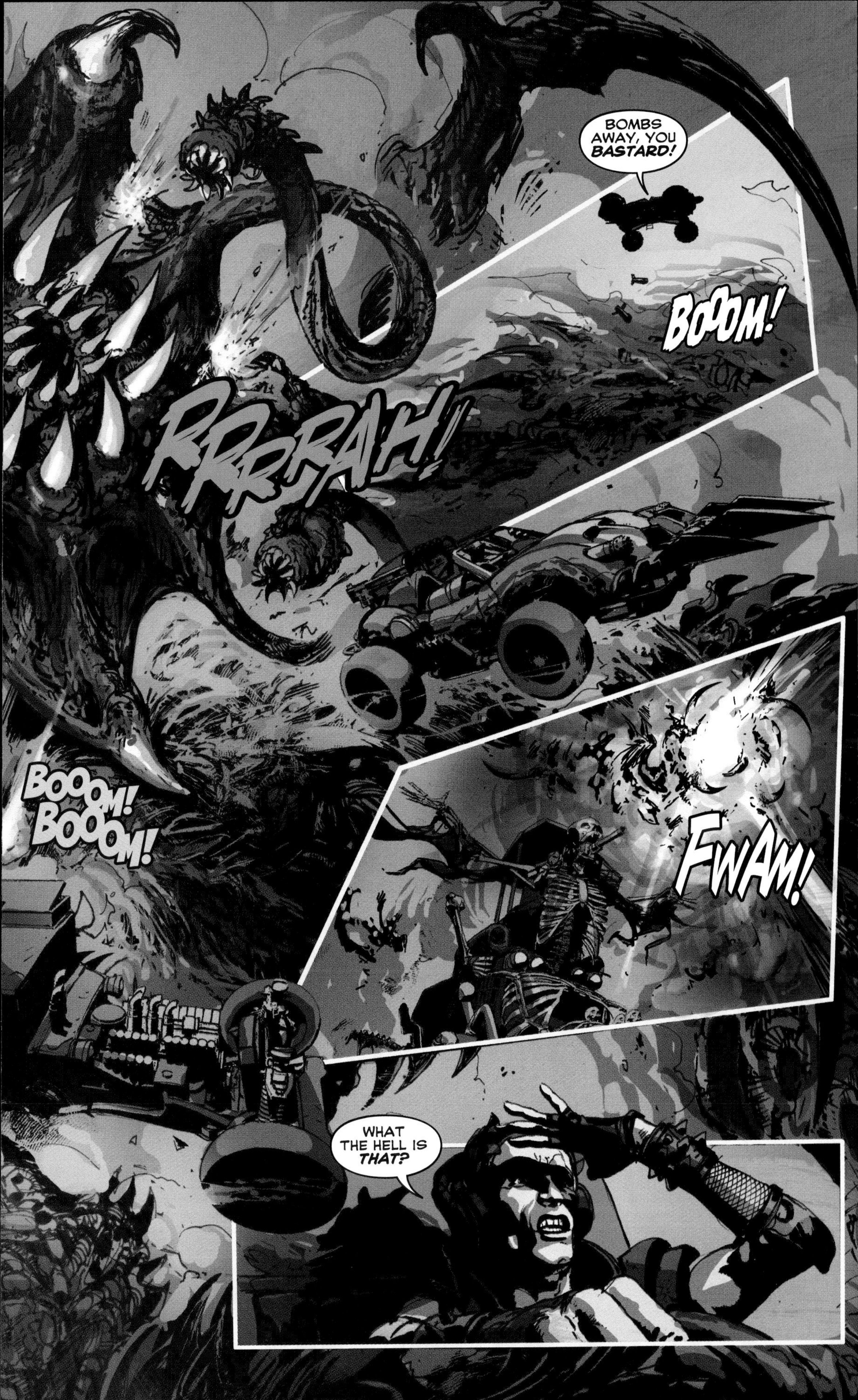
BOMBS AWAY, YOU BASTARD!
BOOOM!
RRRRAAH!
BOOOM! BOOOM!
FWAM!
WHAT THE HELL IS THAT?

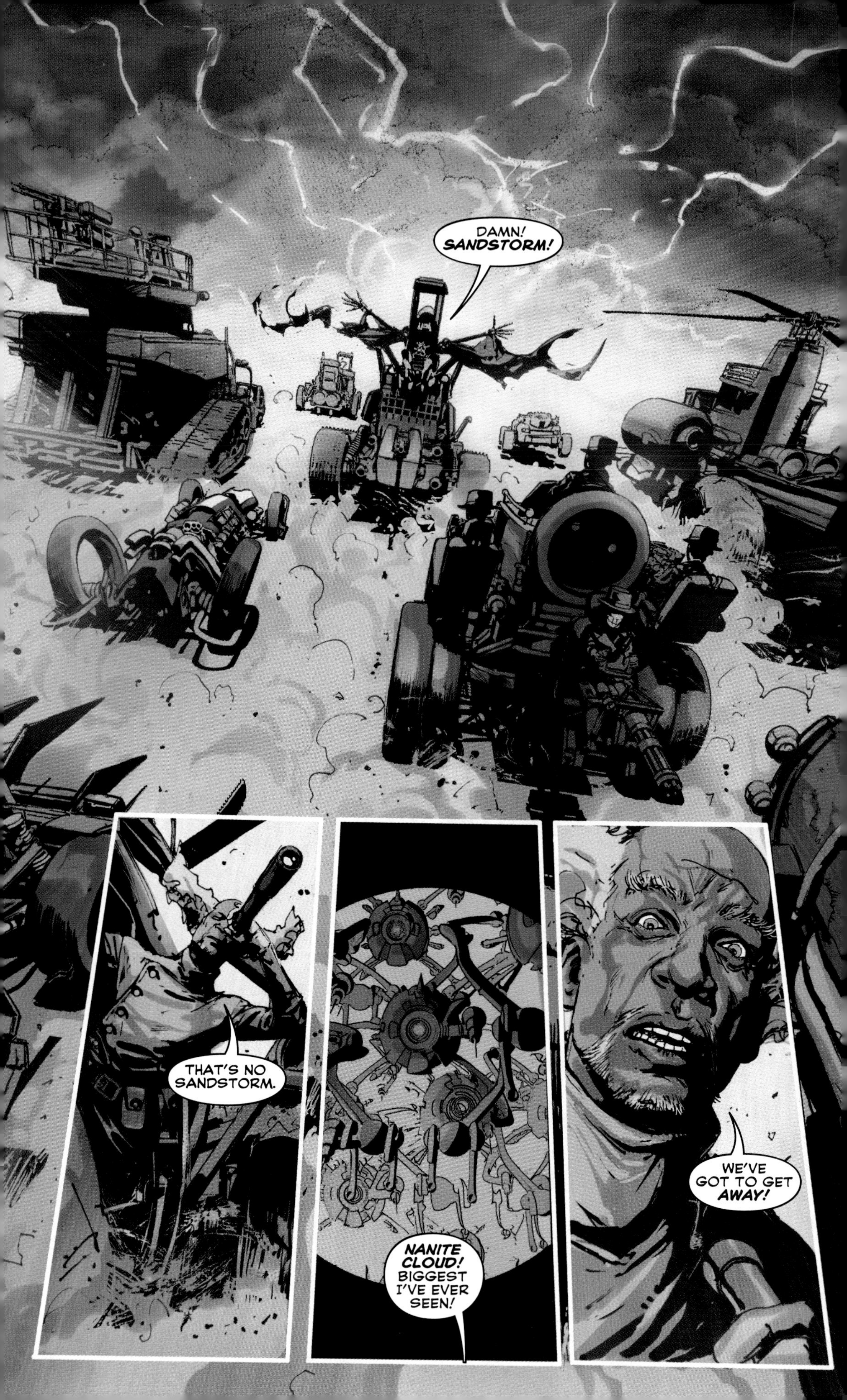
DAMN! SANDSTORM!
THAT'S NO SANDSTORM.
NANITE CLOUD! BIGGEST I'VE EVER SEEN!
WE'VE GOT TO GET AWAY!

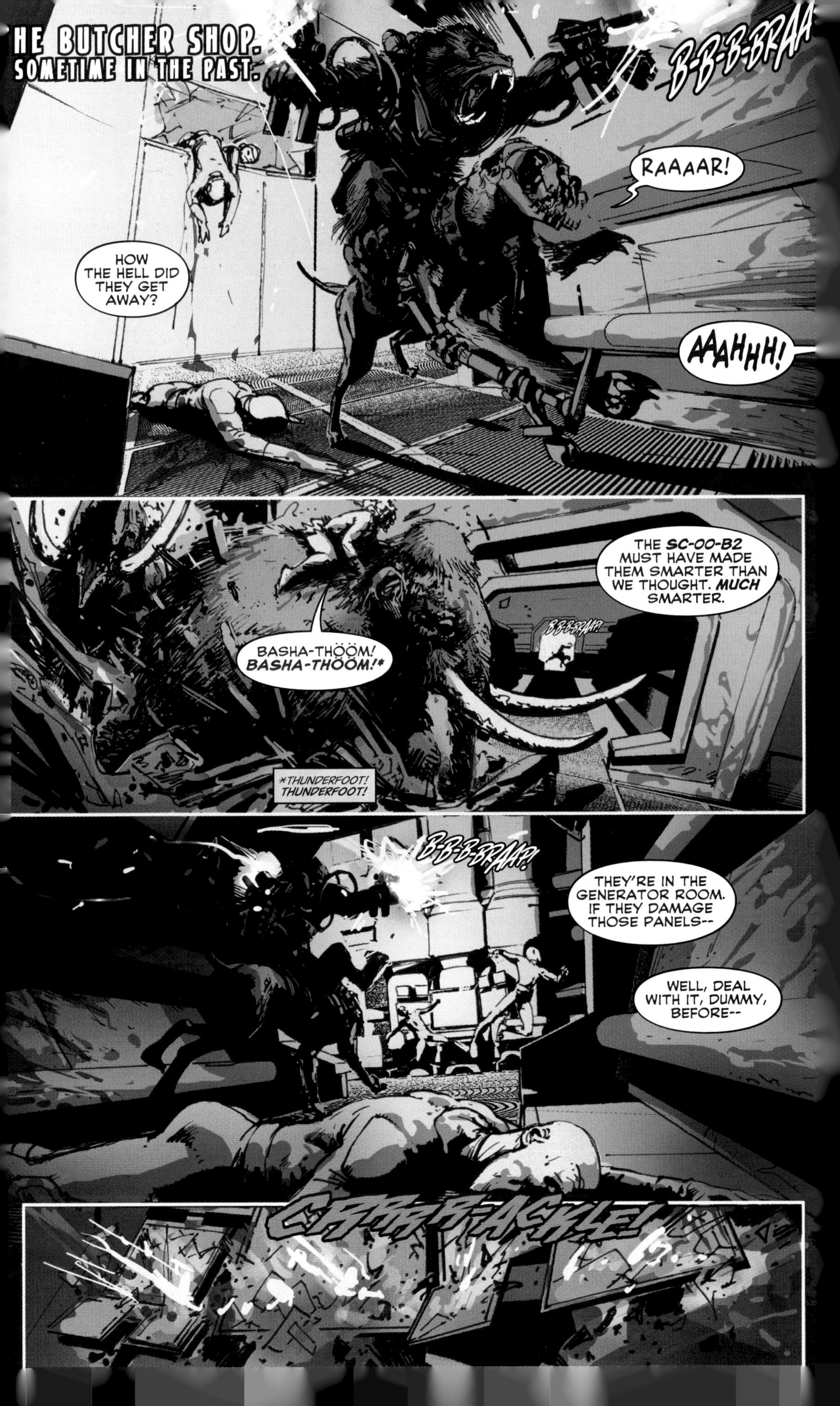

HE BUTCHER SHOP.
SOMETIME IN THE PAST.
B-B-B-BRAA
RAAAAR!
HOW THE HELL DID THEY GET AWAY?
AAAHHH!
THE SC-00-B2 MUST HAVE MADE THEM SMARTER THAN WE THOUGHT. MUCH SMARTER.
BASHA-THÖÖM! BASHA-THÖÖM!*
*THUNDERFOOT! THUNDERFOOT!
B-B-B-BRAAP!
THEY'RE IN THE GENERATOR ROOM. IF THEY DAMAGE THOSE PANELS--
WELL, DEAL WITH IT, DUMMY, BEFORE--
CRRRR-ACKLE!

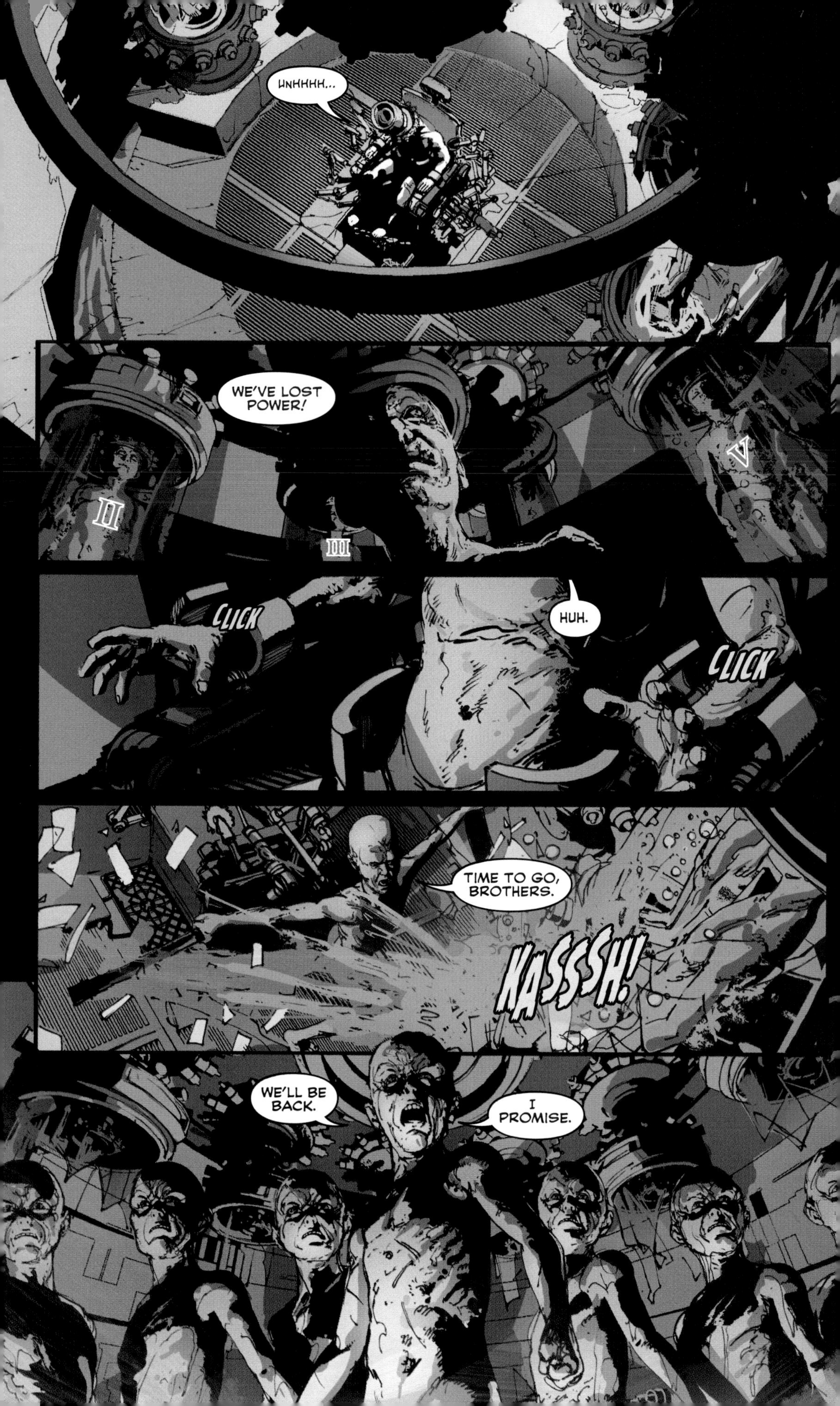
UNHHHH...
WE'VE LOST POWER!
II
III
V
CLICK
HUH.
CLICK
TIME TO GO, BROTHERS.
KASSSH!
WE'LL BE BACK.
I PROMISE.

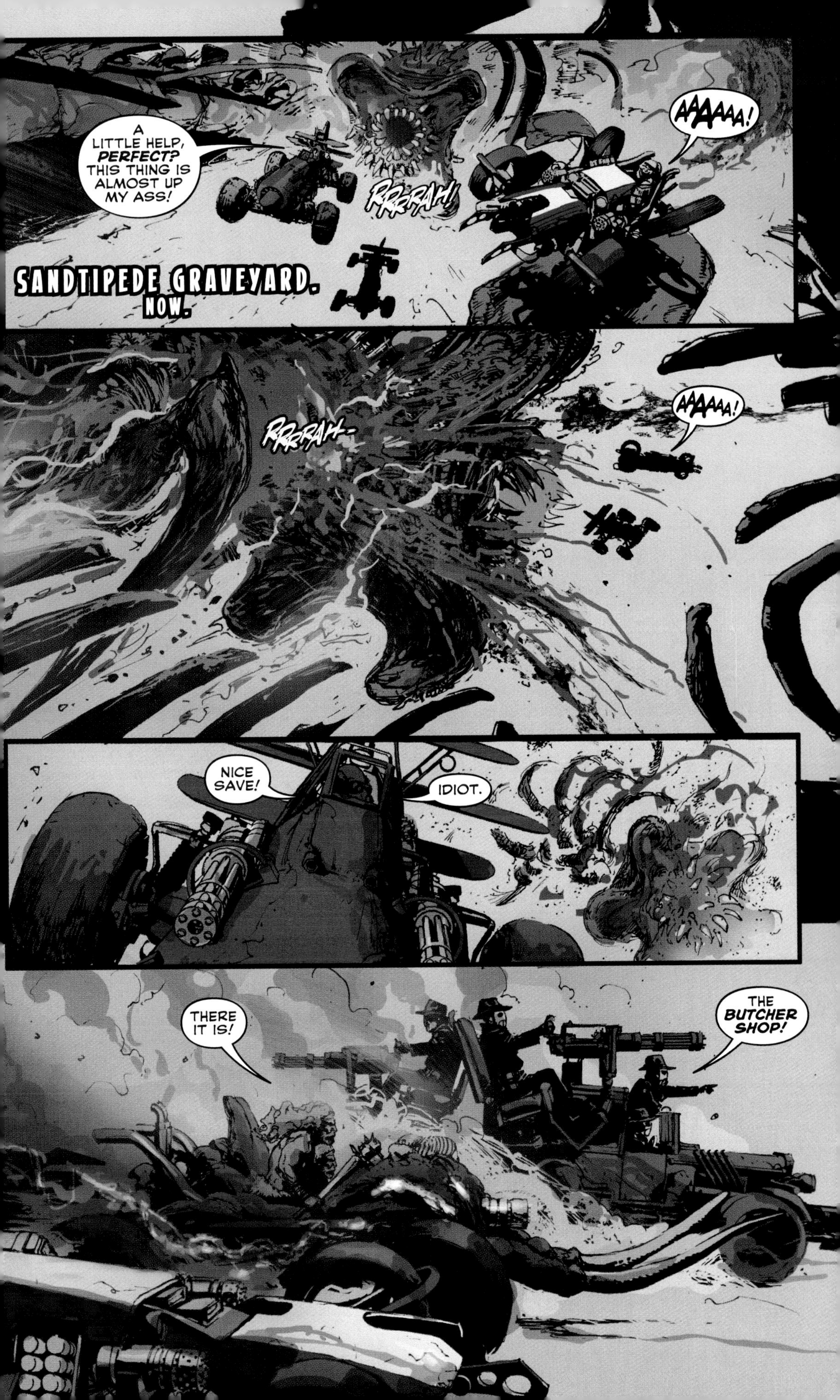
A LITTLE HELP, PERFECT? THIS THING IS ALMOST UP MY ASS!
RRRRAH!
AAAAAA!
SANDTIPEDE GRAVEYARD.
NOW.
RRRRAH-
AAAAAA!
NICE SAVE!
IDIOT.
THERE IT IS!
THE BUTCHER SHOP!

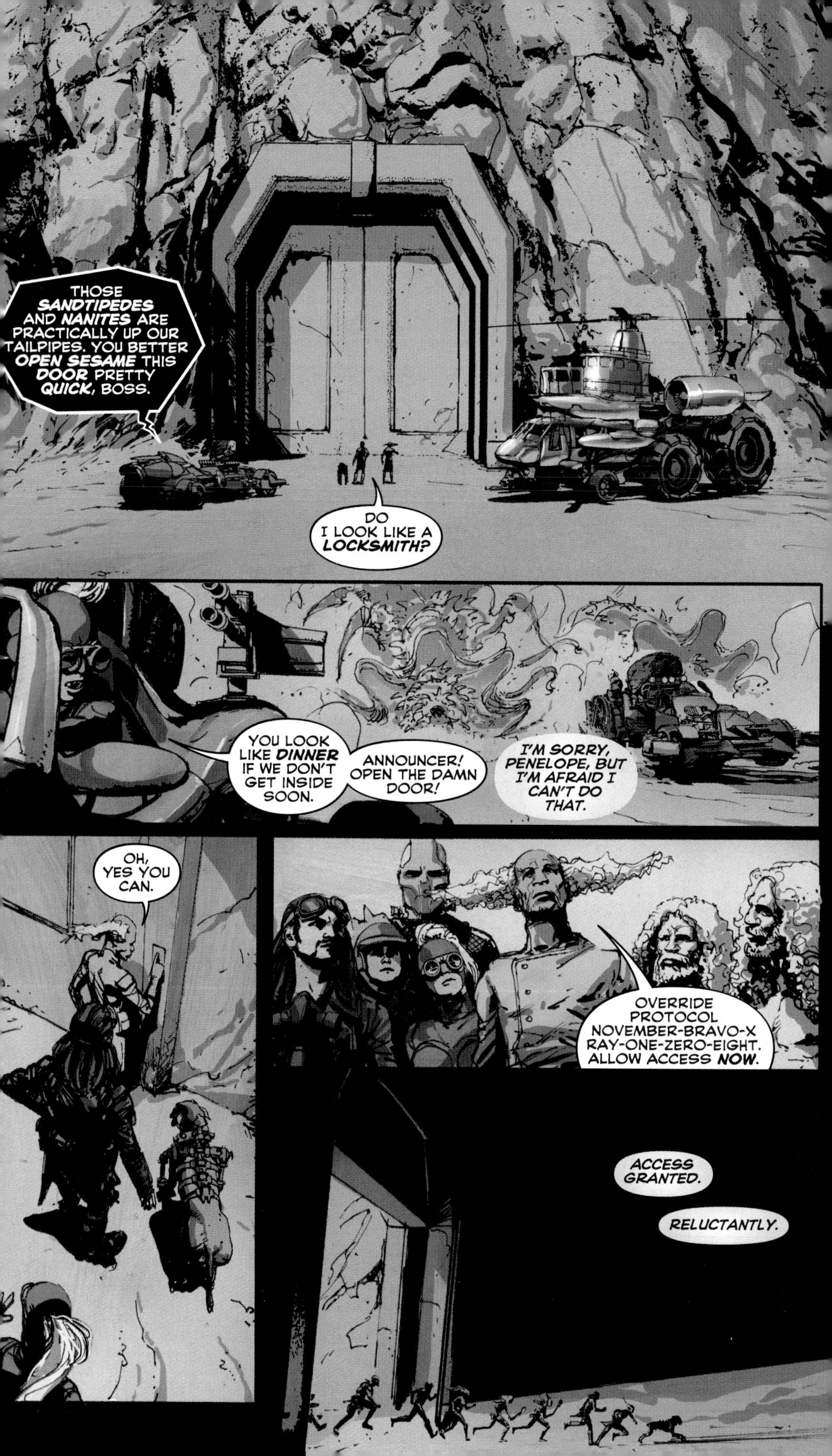
THOSE SANDTIPEDES AND NANITES ARE PRACTICALLY UP OUR TAILPIPES. YOU BETTER OPEN SESAME THIS DOOR PRETTY QUICK, BOSS.
DO I LOOK LIKE A LOCKSMITH?
YOU LOOK LIKE DINNER IF WE DON'T GET INSIDE SOON.
ANNOUNCER! OPEN THE DAMN DOOR!
I'M SORRY, PENELOPE, BUT I'M AFRAID I CAN'T DO THAT.
OH, YES YOU CAN.
OVERRIDE PROTOCOL NOVEMBER-BRAVO-X RAY-ONE-ZERO-EIGHT. ALLOW ACCESS NOW.
ACCESS GRANTED.
RELUCTANTLY.

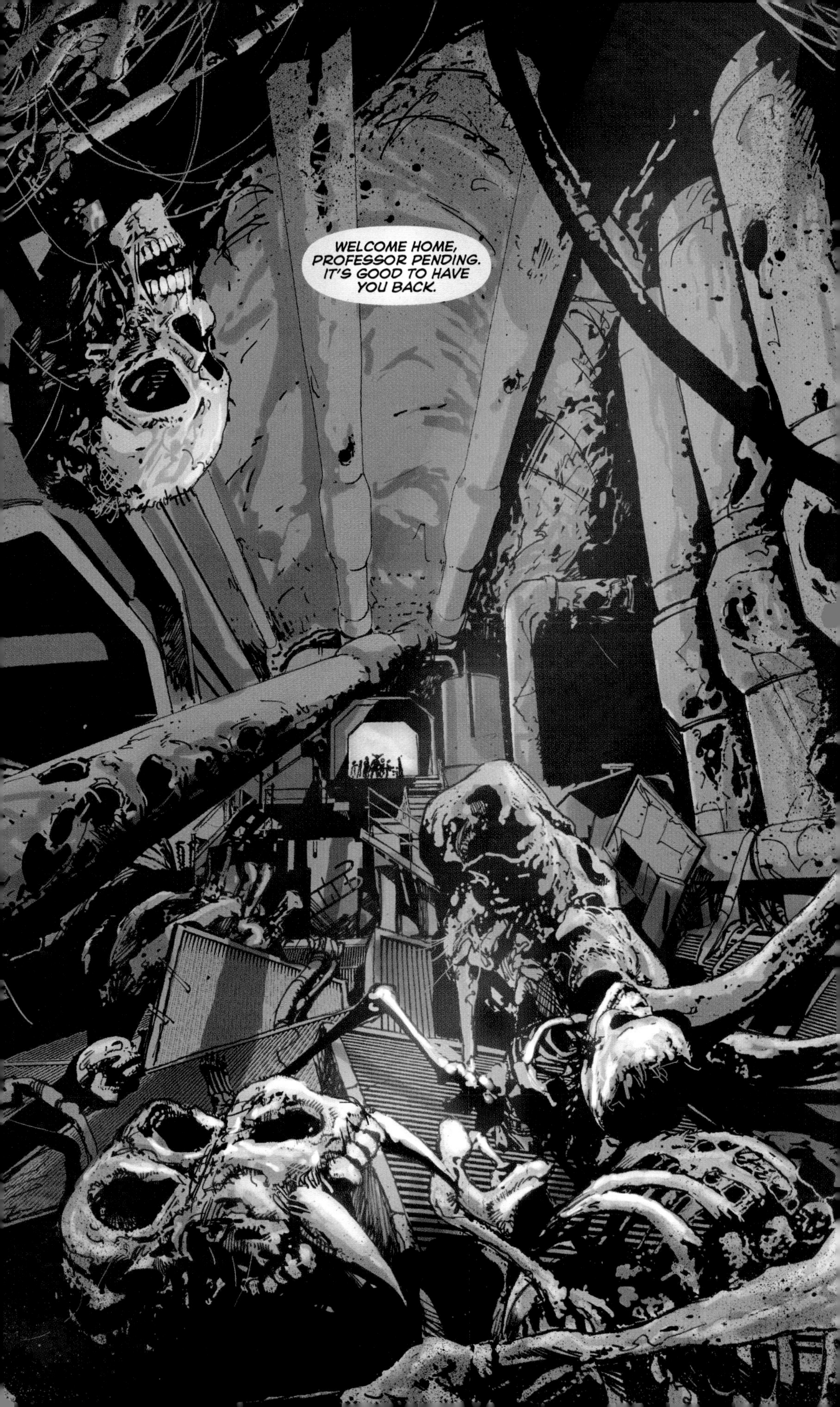
WELCOME HOME, PROFESSOR PENDING. IT'S GOOD TO HAVE YOU BACK.

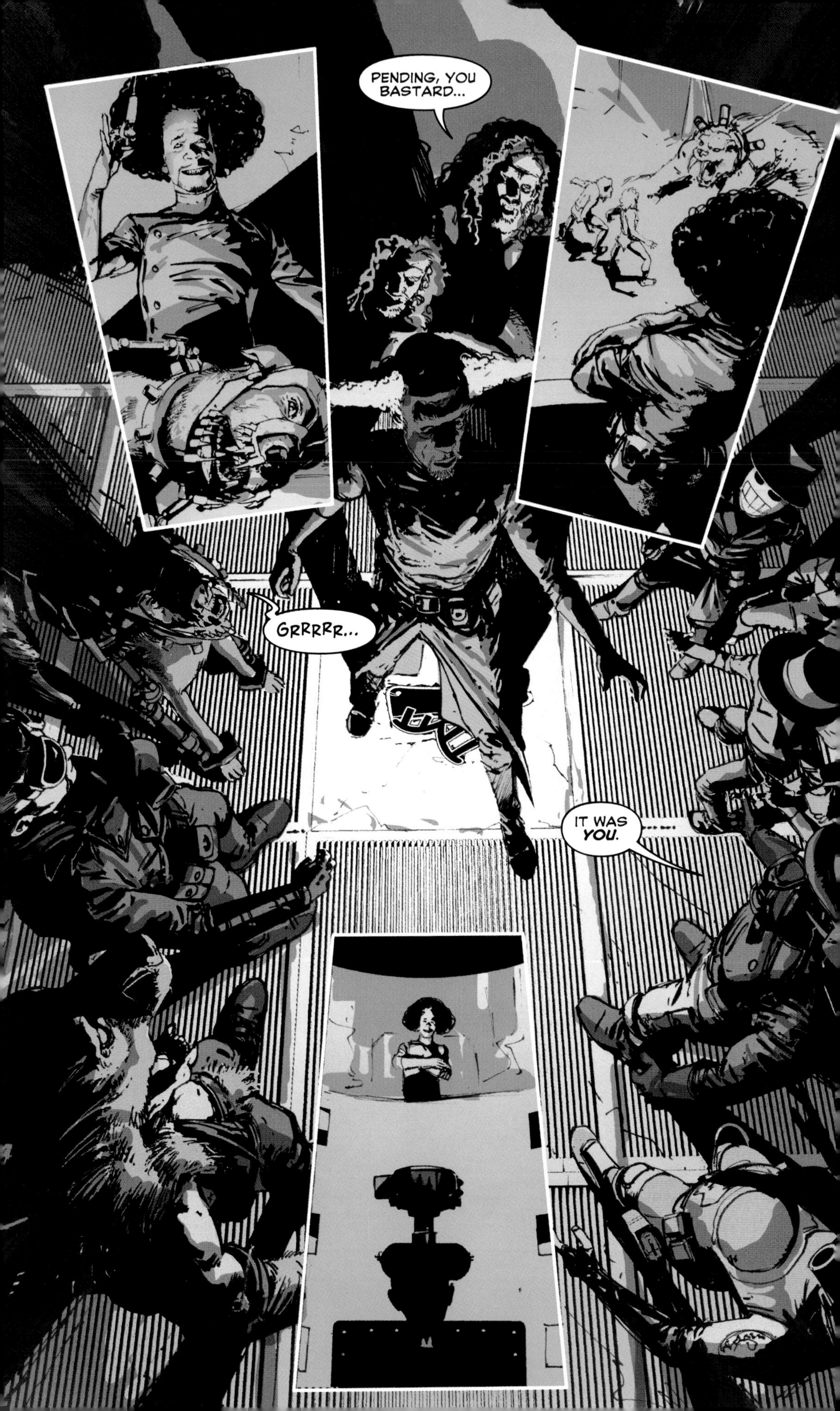

PENDING, YOU BASTARD...
GRRRRR...
IT WAS YOU.

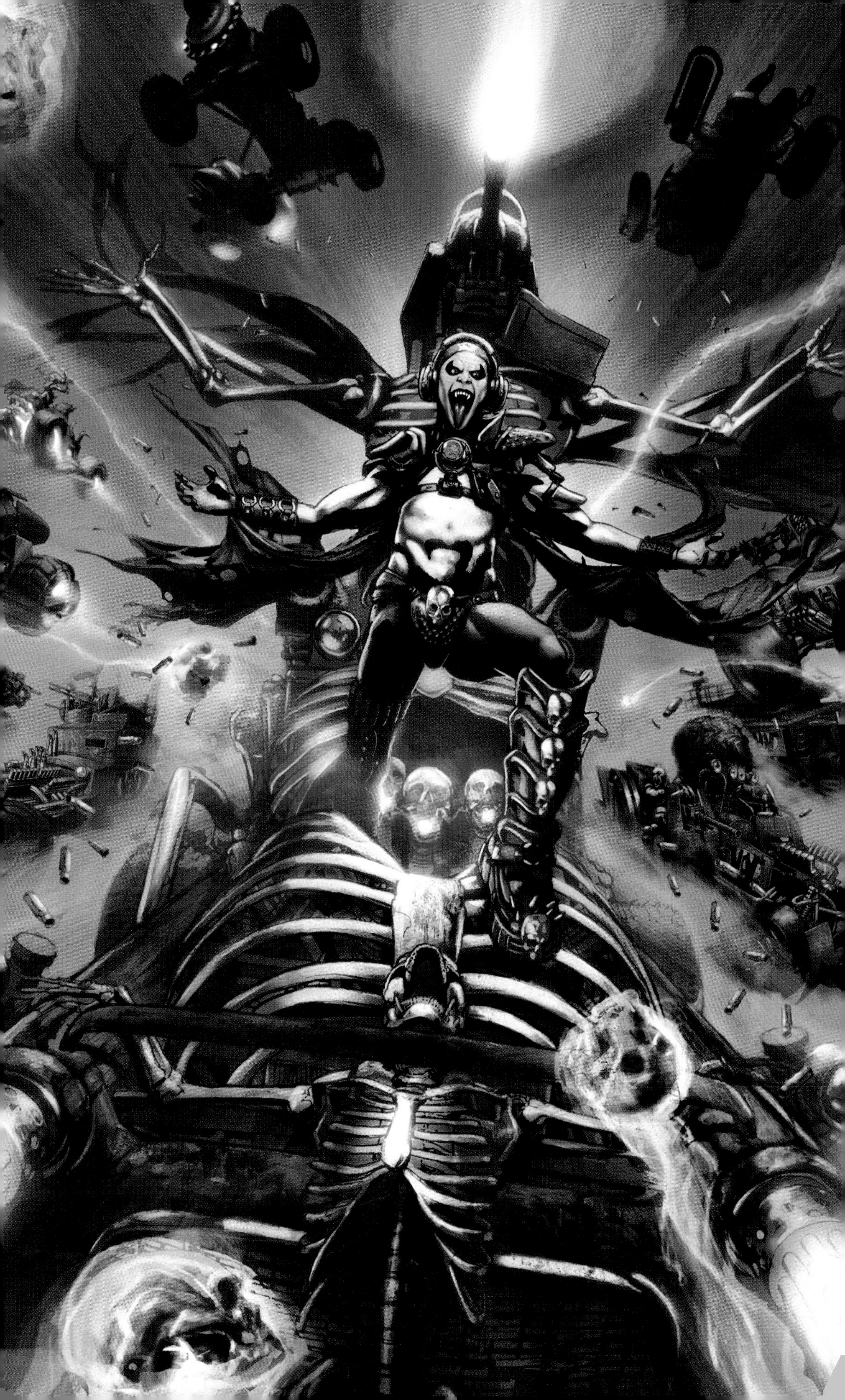

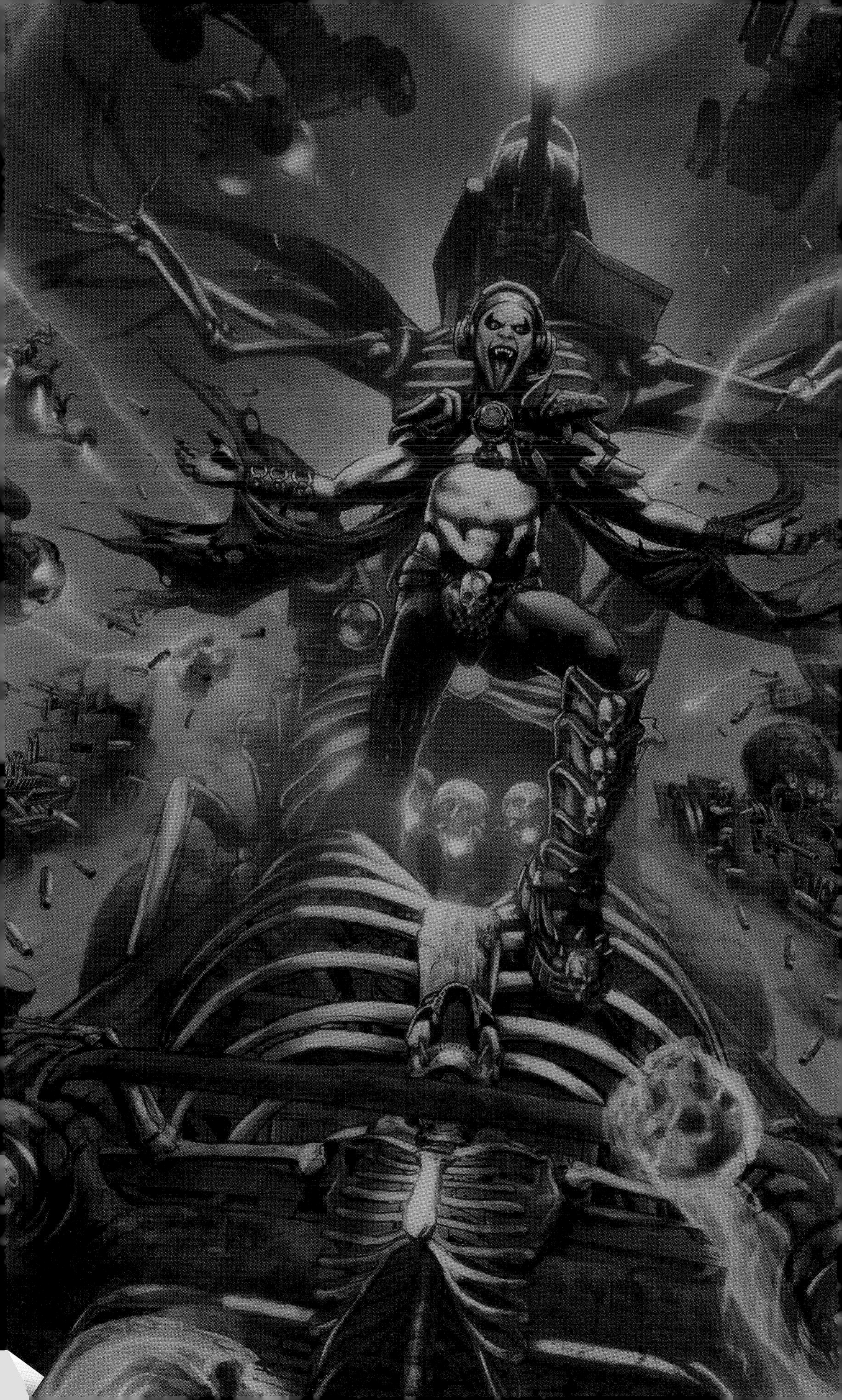

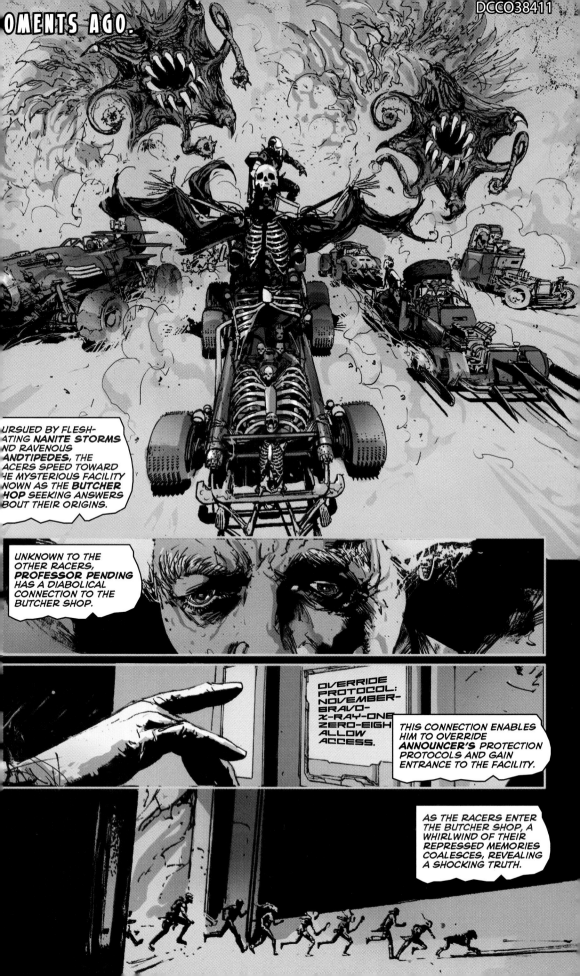

URSUED BY FLESH-
ATING **NANITE STORMS**
ND RAVENOUS
ANDTIPEDES, THE
ACERS SPEED TOWARD
HE MYSTERIOUS FACILITY
NOWN AS THE **BUTCHER
HOP** SEEKING ANSWERS
BOUT THEIR ORIGINS.

UNKNOWN TO THE
OTHER RACERS,
PROFESSOR PENDING
HAS A DIABOLICAL
CONNECTION TO THE
BUTCHER SHOP.

OVERRIDE
PROTOCOL:
NOVEMBER-
BRAVO-
X-RAY-ONE
ZERO-EIGHT
ALLOW
ACCESS.

THIS CONNECTION ENABLES
HIM TO OVERRIDE
ANNOUNCER'S PROTECTION
PROTOCOLS AND GAIN
ENTRANCE TO THE FACILITY.

AS THE RACERS ENTER
THE BUTCHER SHOP, A
WHIRLWIND OF THEIR
REPRESSED MEMORIES
COALESCES, REVEALING
A SHOCKING TRUTH.

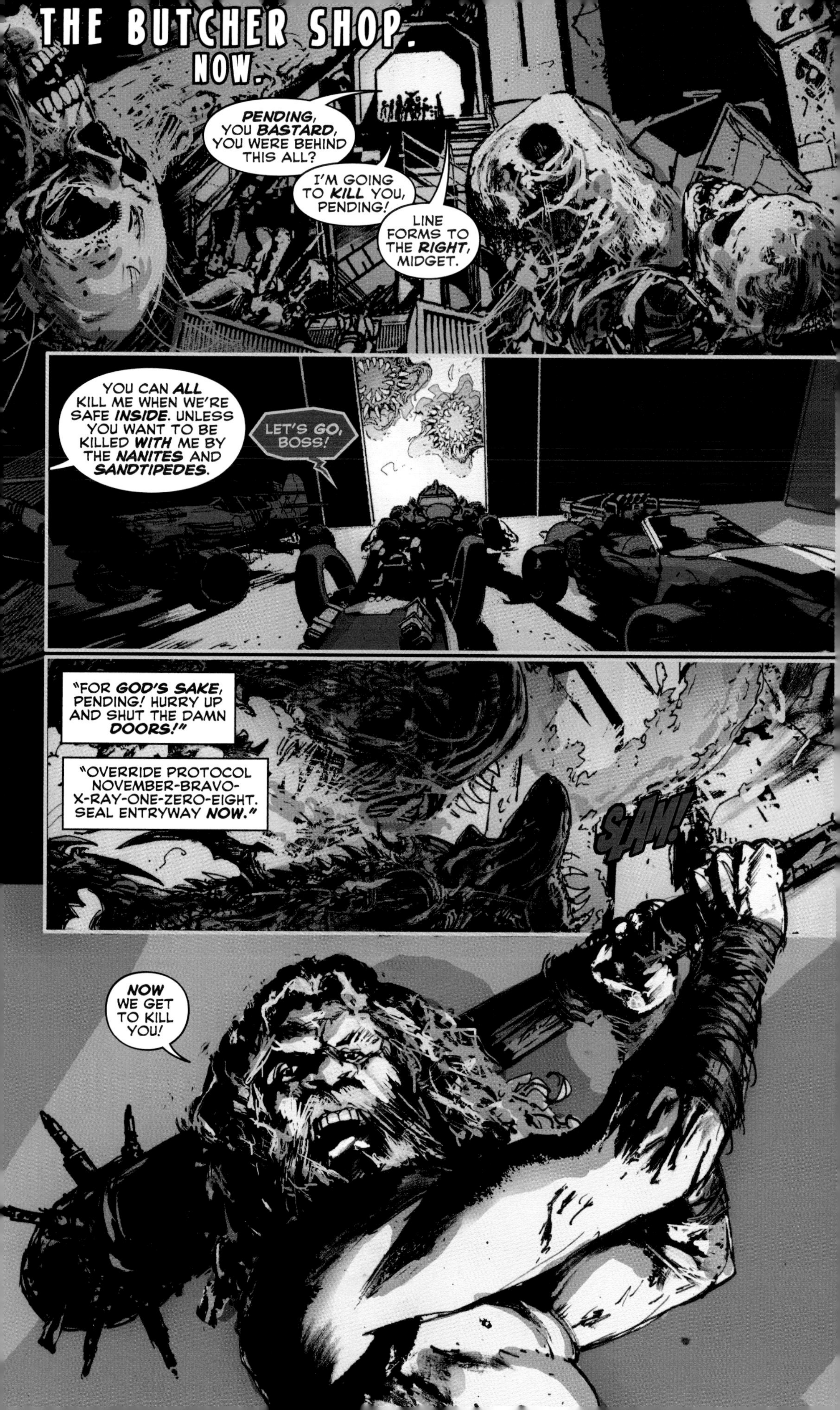
THE BUTCHER SHOP.
NOW.
PENDING, YOU BASTARD, YOU WERE BEHIND THIS ALL?
I'M GOING TO KILL YOU, PENDING!
LINE FORMS TO THE RIGHT, MIDGET.
YOU CAN ALL KILL ME WHEN WE'RE SAFE INSIDE. UNLESS YOU WANT TO BE KILLED WITH ME BY THE NANITES AND SANDTIPEDES.
LET'S GO, BOSS!
"FOR GOD'S SAKE, PENDING! HURRY UP AND SHUT THE DAMN DOORS!"
"OVERRIDE PROTOCOL NOVEMBER-BRAVO-X-RAY-ONE-ZERO-EIGHT. SEAL ENTRYWAY NOW."
SLAM!
NOW WE GET TO KILL YOU!

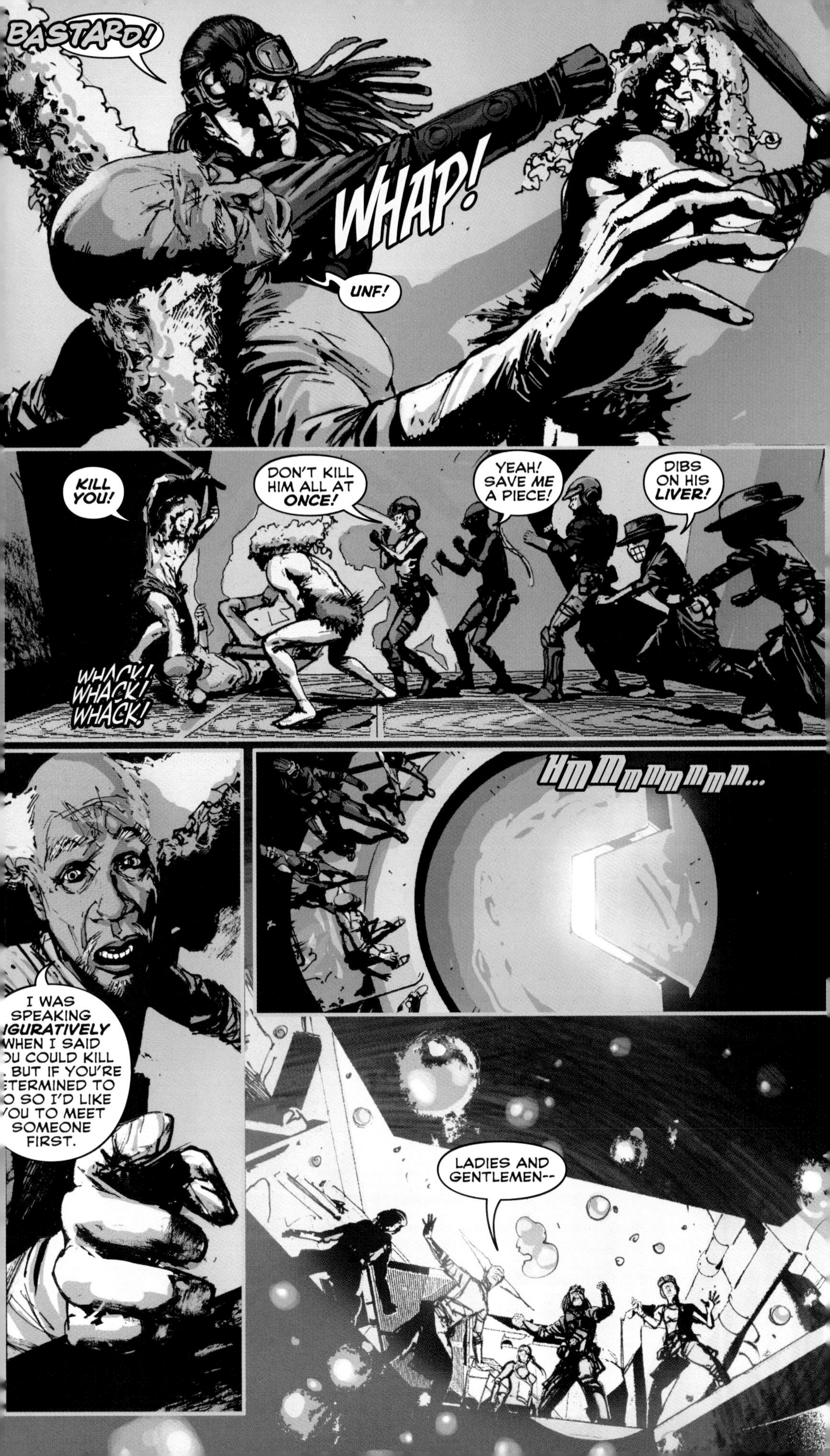
BASTARD!
WHAP!
UNF!
KILL YOU!
DON'T KILL HIM ALL AT ONCE!
YEAH! SAVE ME A PIECE!
DIBS ON HIS LIVER!
WHACK! WHACK! WHACK!
I WAS SPEAKING IGURATIVELY WHEN I SAID OU COULD KILL . BUT IF YOU'RE ETERMINED TO O SO I'D LIKE YOU TO MEET SOMEONE FIRST.
HMMmmmmmm...
LADIES AND GENTLEMEN--

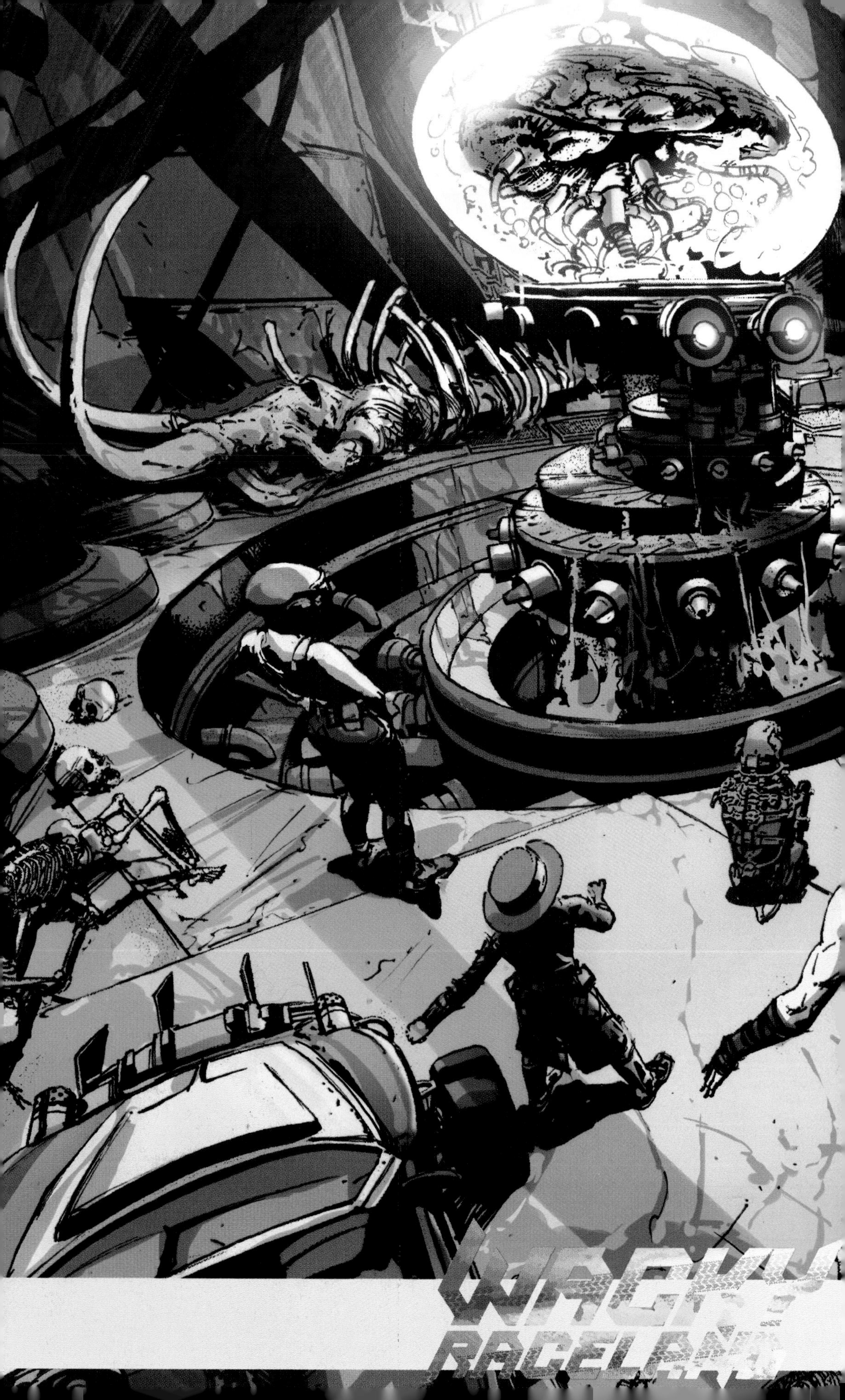

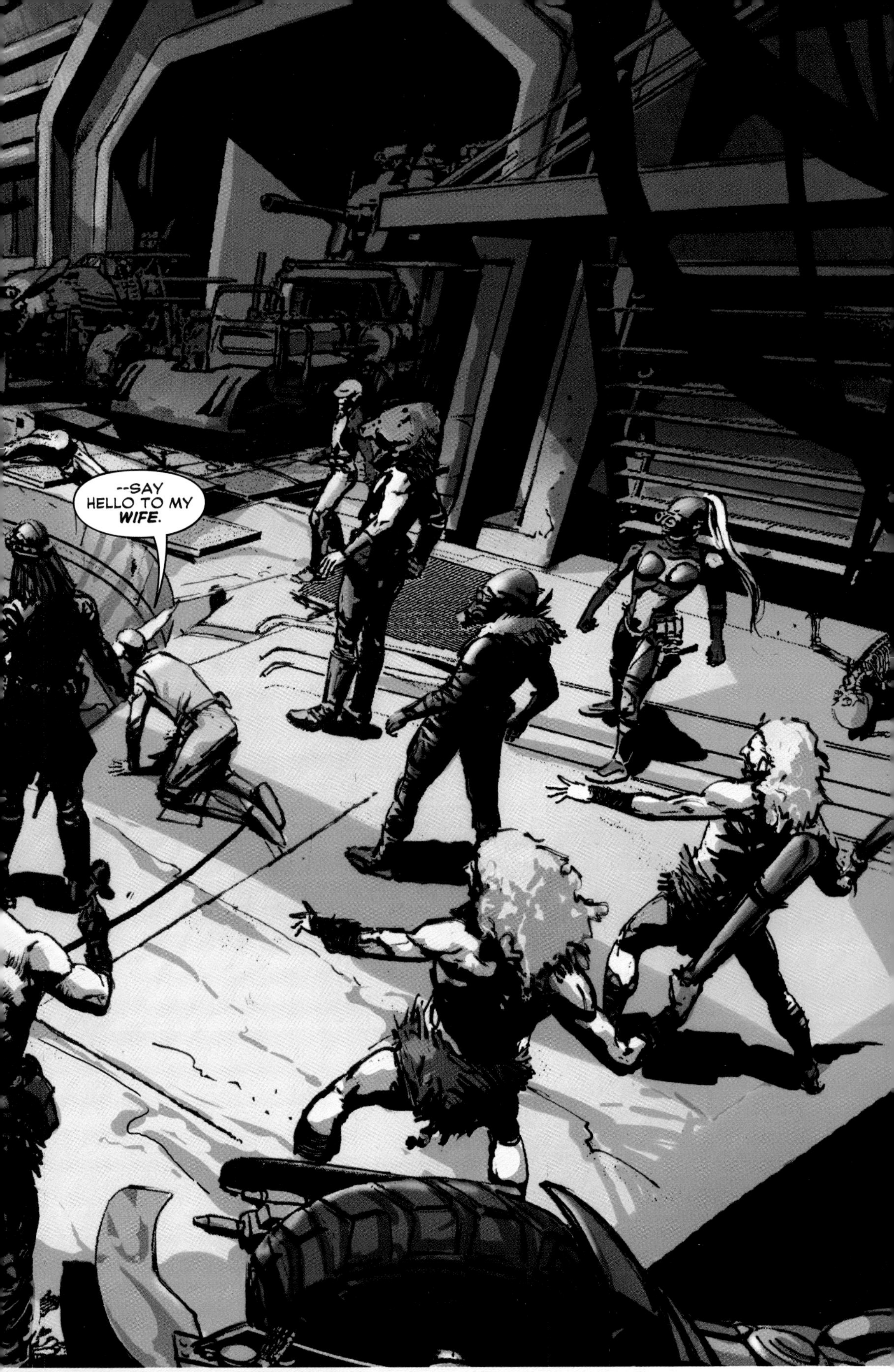
--SAY HELLO TO MY WIFE.

THE BUTCHER SHOP
PART TWO: RESOLUTIONS

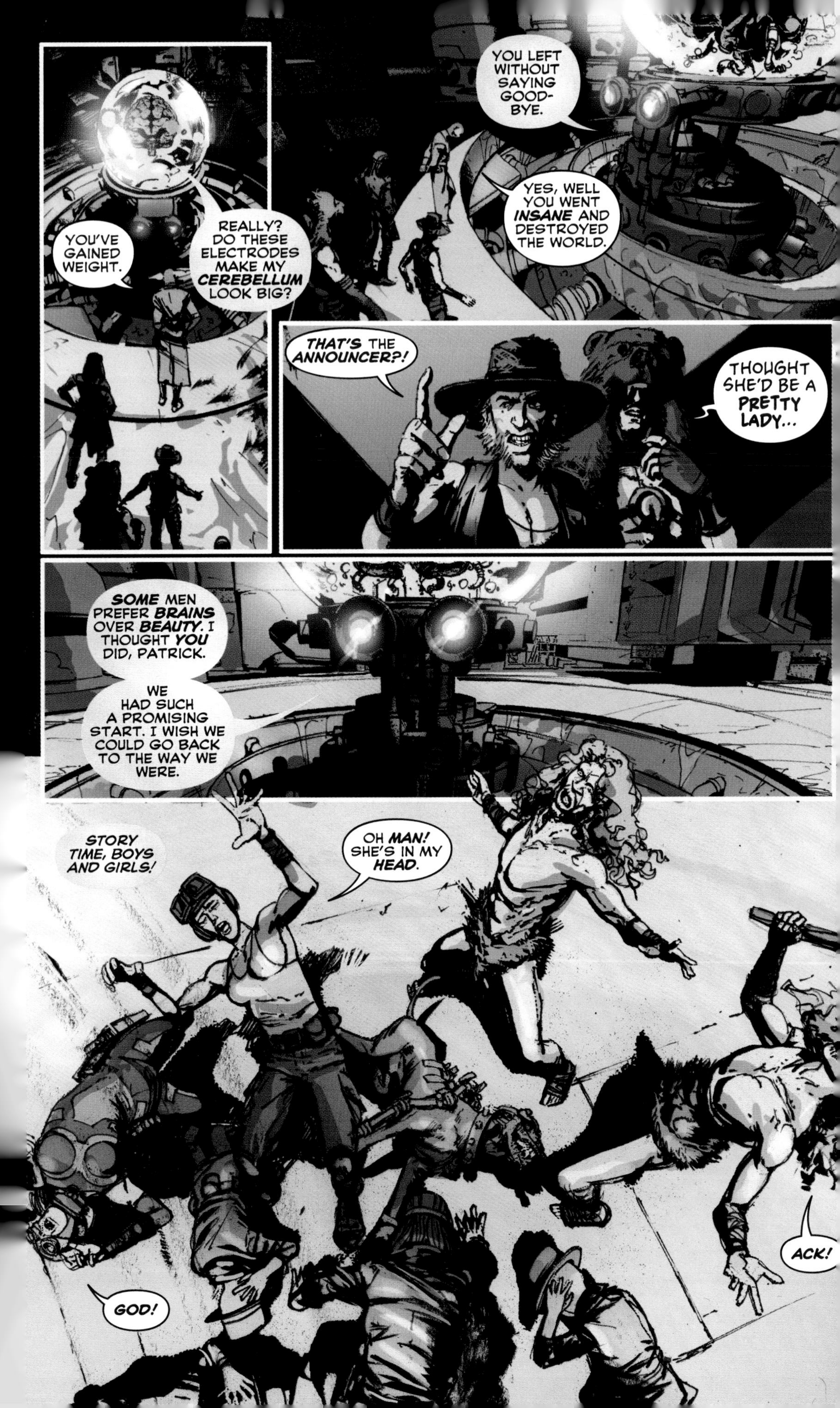
YOU'VE GAINED WEIGHT.
REALLY? DO THESE ELECTRODES MAKE MY CEREBELLUM LOOK BIG?
YOU LEFT WITHOUT SAYING GOOD-BYE.
YES, WELL YOU WENT INSANE AND DESTROYED THE WORLD.
THAT'S THE ANNOUNCER?!
THOUGHT SHE'D BE A PRETTY LADY...
SOME MEN PREFER BRAINS OVER BEAUTY. I THOUGHT YOU DID, PATRICK.
WE HAD SUCH A PROMISING START. I WISH WE COULD GO BACK TO THE WAY WE WERE.
STORY TIME, BOYS AND GIRLS!
OH MAN! SHE'S IN MY HEAD.
GOD!
ACK!

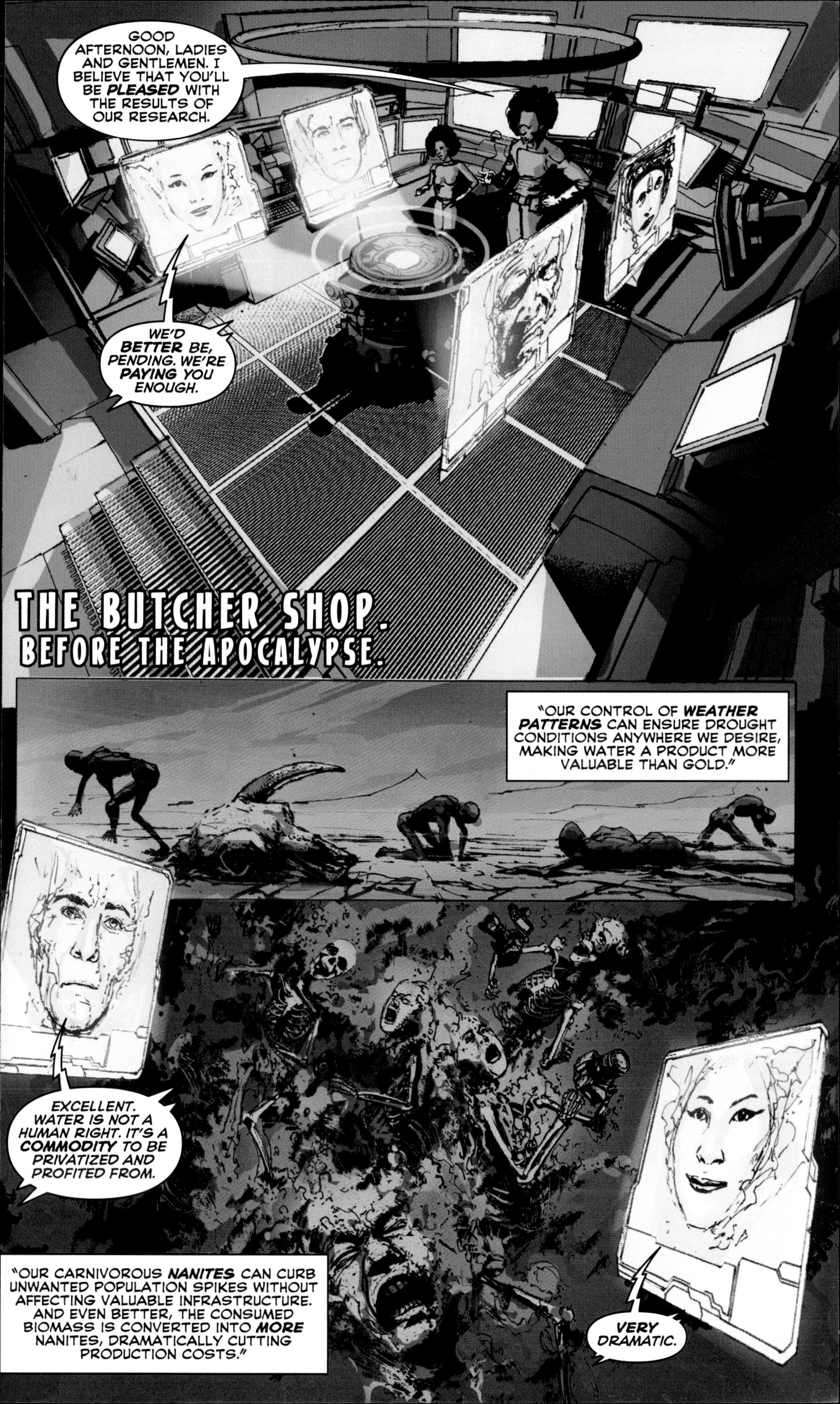
GOOD AFTERNOON, LADIES AND GENTLEMEN. I BELIEVE THAT YOU'LL BE PLEASED WITH THE RESULTS OF OUR RESEARCH.
WE'D BETTER BE, PENDING. WE'RE PAYING YOU ENOUGH.
THE BUTCHER SHOP.
BEFORE THE APOCALYPSE.
"OUR CONTROL OF WEATHER PATTERNS CAN ENSURE DROUGHT CONDITIONS ANYWHERE WE DESIRE, MAKING WATER A PRODUCT MORE VALUABLE THAN GOLD."
EXCELLENT. WATER IS NOT A HUMAN RIGHT. IT'S A COMMODITY TO BE PRIVATIZED AND PROFITED FROM.
"OUR CARNIVOROUS NANITES CAN CURB UNWANTED POPULATION SPIKES WITHOUT AFFECTING VALUABLE INFRASTRUCTURE. AND EVEN BETTER, THE CONSUMED BIOMASS IS CONVERTED INTO MORE NANITES, DRAMATICALLY CUTTING PRODUCTION COSTS."
VERY DRAMATIC.

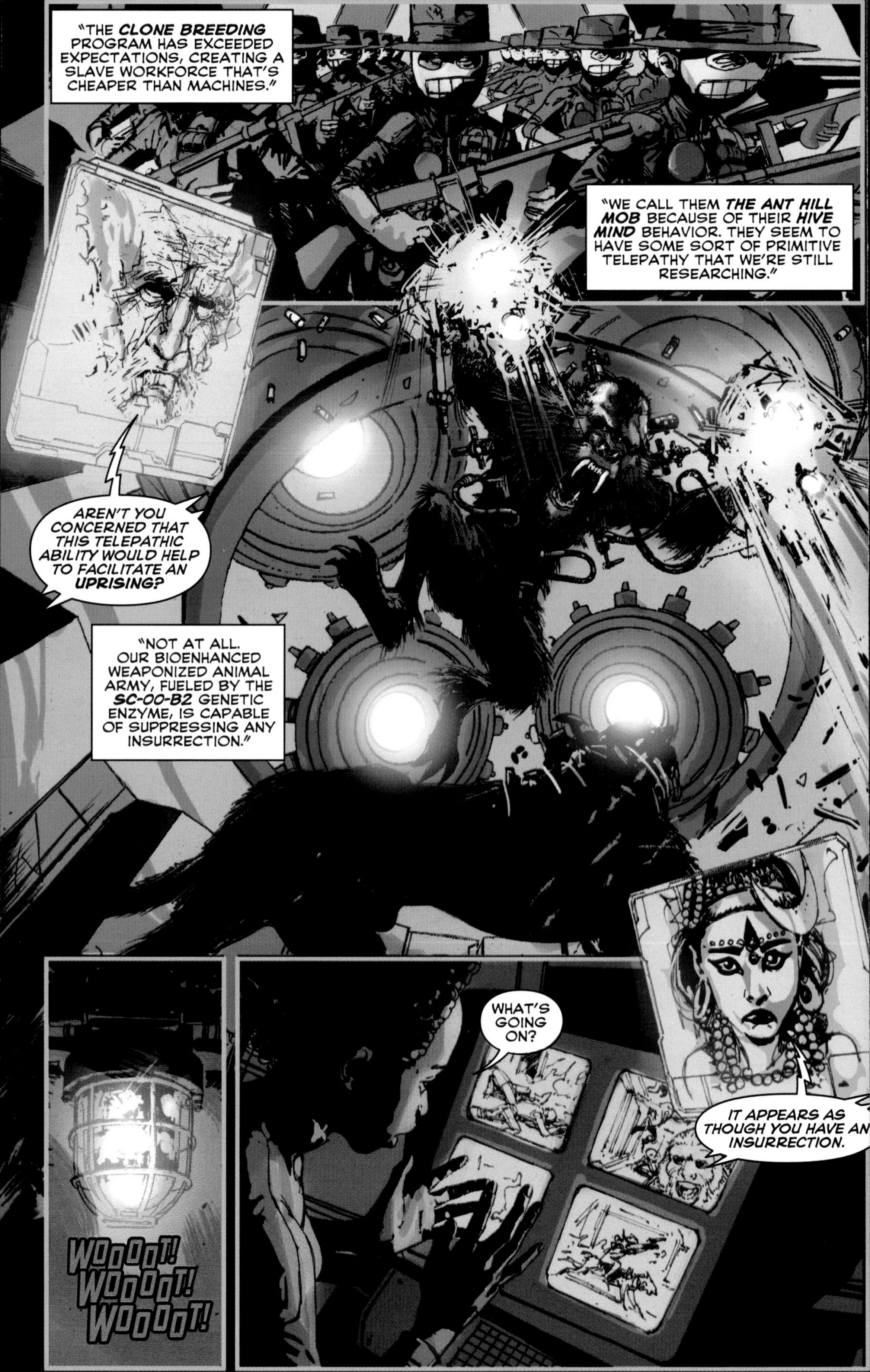
"THE CLONE BREEDING PROGRAM HAS EXCEEDED EXPECTATIONS, CREATING A SLAVE WORKFORCE THAT'S CHEAPER THAN MACHINES."
"WE CALL THEM THE ANT HILL MOB BECAUSE OF THEIR HIVE MIND BEHAVIOR. THEY SEEM TO HAVE SOME SORT OF PRIMITIVE TELEPATHY THAT WE'RE STILL RESEARCHING."
AREN'T YOU CONCERNED THAT THIS TELEPATHIC ABILITY WOULD HELP TO FACILITATE AN UPRISING?
"NOT AT ALL. OUR BIOENHANCED WEAPONIZED ANIMAL ARMY, FUELED BY THE SC-00-B2 GENETIC ENZYME, IS CAPABLE OF SUPPRESSING ANY INSURRECTION."
WOOOOT! WOOOOT! WOOOOT!
WHAT'S GOING ON?
IT APPEARS AS THOUGH YOU HAVE AN INSURRECTION.

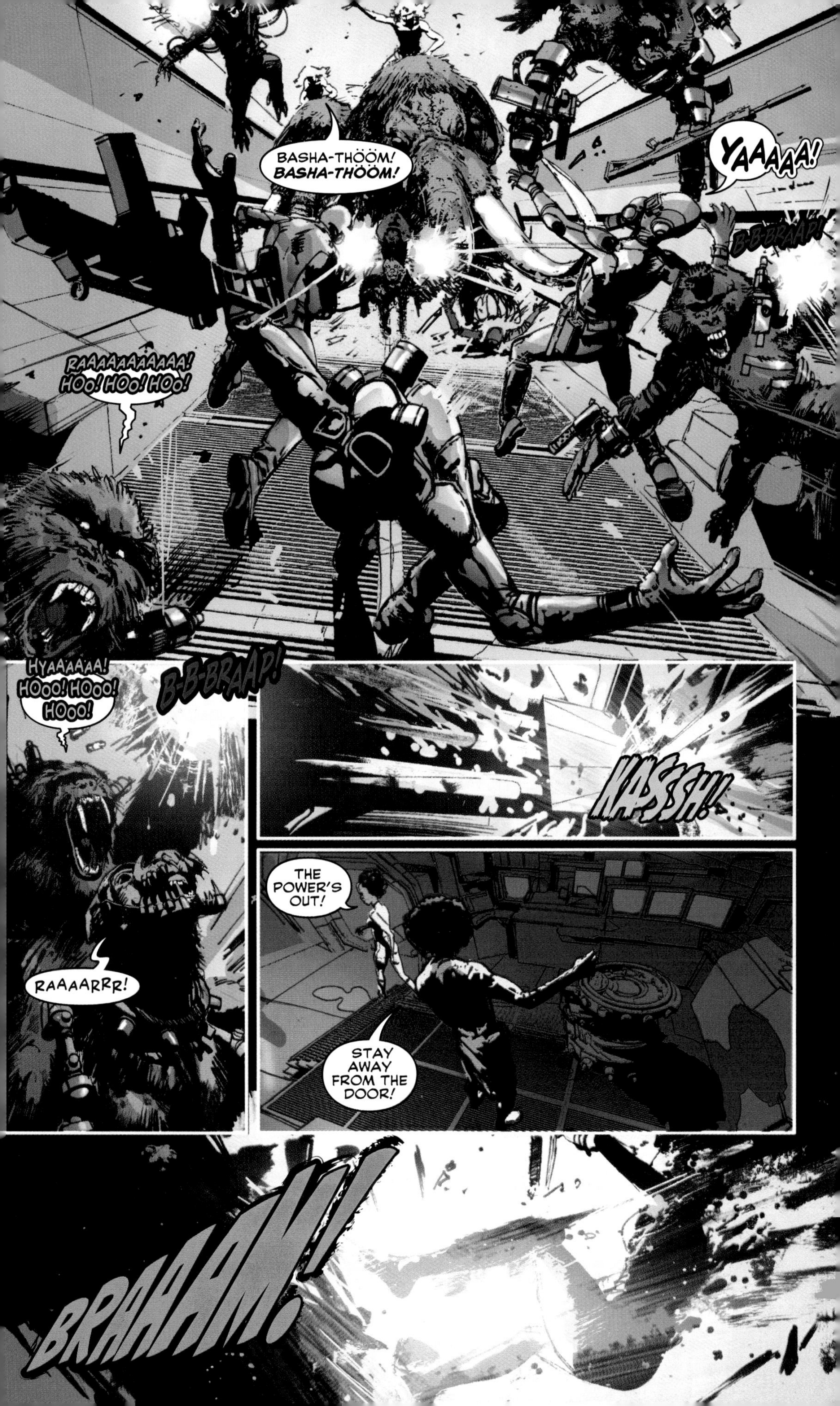
BASHA-THÖÖM! BASHA-THÖÖM!
YAAAAA!
B-B-BRAAP!
RAAAAAAAAAAA! HOo! HOo! HOo!
HYAAAAAA! HOOO! HOOO! HOOO!
B-B-BRAAP!
RAAAARRR!
KASSSH!
THE POWER'S OUT!
STAY AWAY FROM THE DOOR!
BRAAAAM!

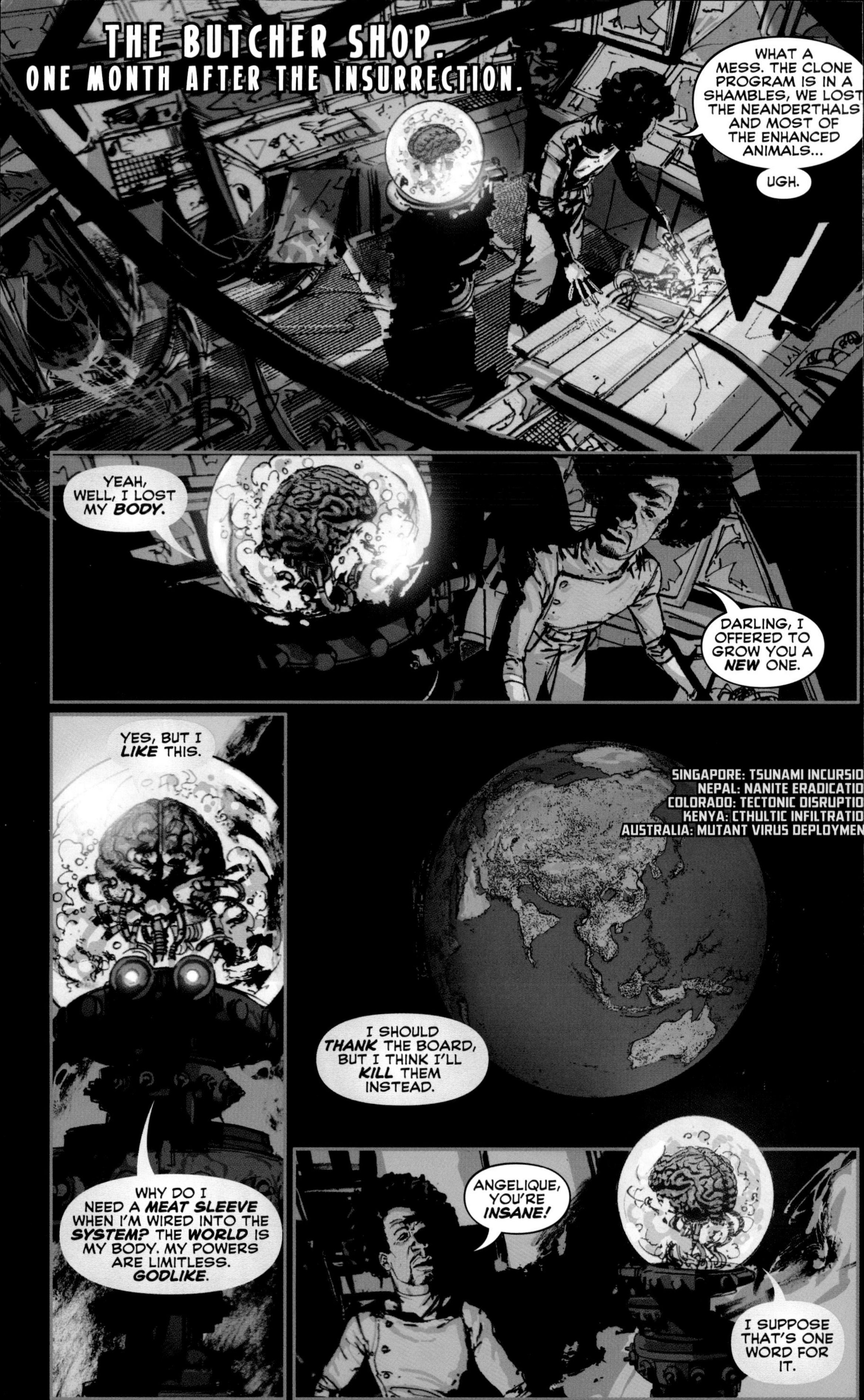
THE BUTCHER SHOP.
ONE MONTH AFTER THE INSURRECTION.
WHAT A MESS. THE CLONE PROGRAM IS IN A SHAMBLES, WE LOST THE NEANDERTHALS AND MOST OF THE ENHANCED ANIMALS...
UGH.
YEAH, WELL, I LOST MY BODY.
DARLING, I OFFERED TO GROW YOU A NEW ONE.
YES, BUT I LIKE THIS.
WHY DO I NEED A MEAT SLEEVE WHEN I'M WIRED INTO THE SYSTEM? THE WORLD IS MY BODY. MY POWERS ARE LIMITLESS. GODLIKE.
SINGAPORE: TSUNAMI INCURSIO
NEPAL: NANITE ERADICATIO
COLORADO: TECTONIC DISRUPTIO
KENYA: CTHULTIC INFILTRATIO
AUSTRALIA: MUTANT VIRUS DEPLOYMEN
I SHOULD THANK THE BOARD, BUT I THINK I'LL KILL THEM INSTEAD.
ANGELIQUE, YOU'RE INSANE!
I SUPPOSE THAT'S ONE WORD FOR IT.

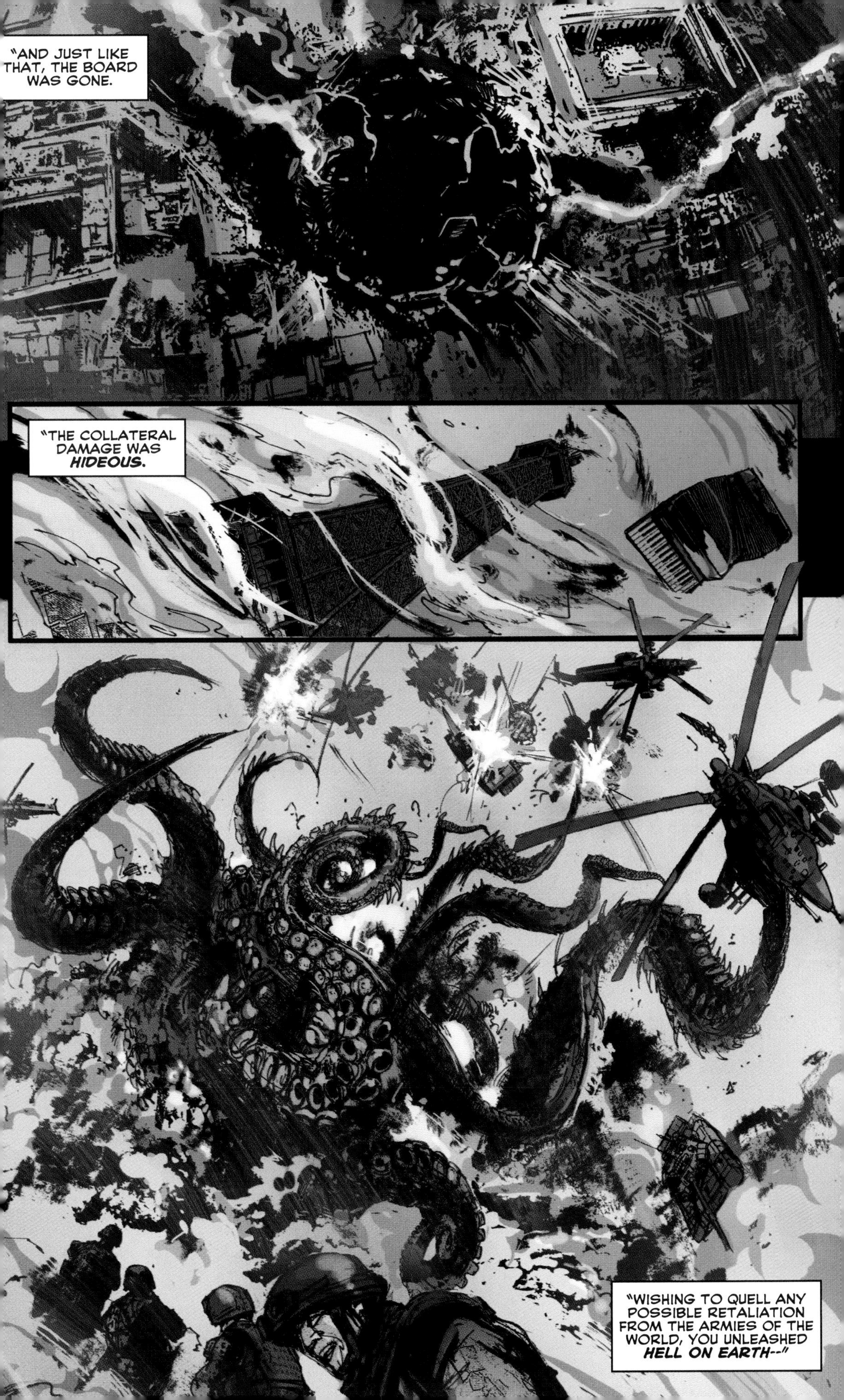
"AND JUST LIKE THAT, THE BOARD WAS GONE.
"THE COLLATERAL DAMAGE WAS *HIDEOUS*.
"WISHING TO QUELL ANY POSSIBLE RETALIATION FROM THE ARMIES OF THE WORLD, YOU UNLEASHED *HELL ON EARTH*--"

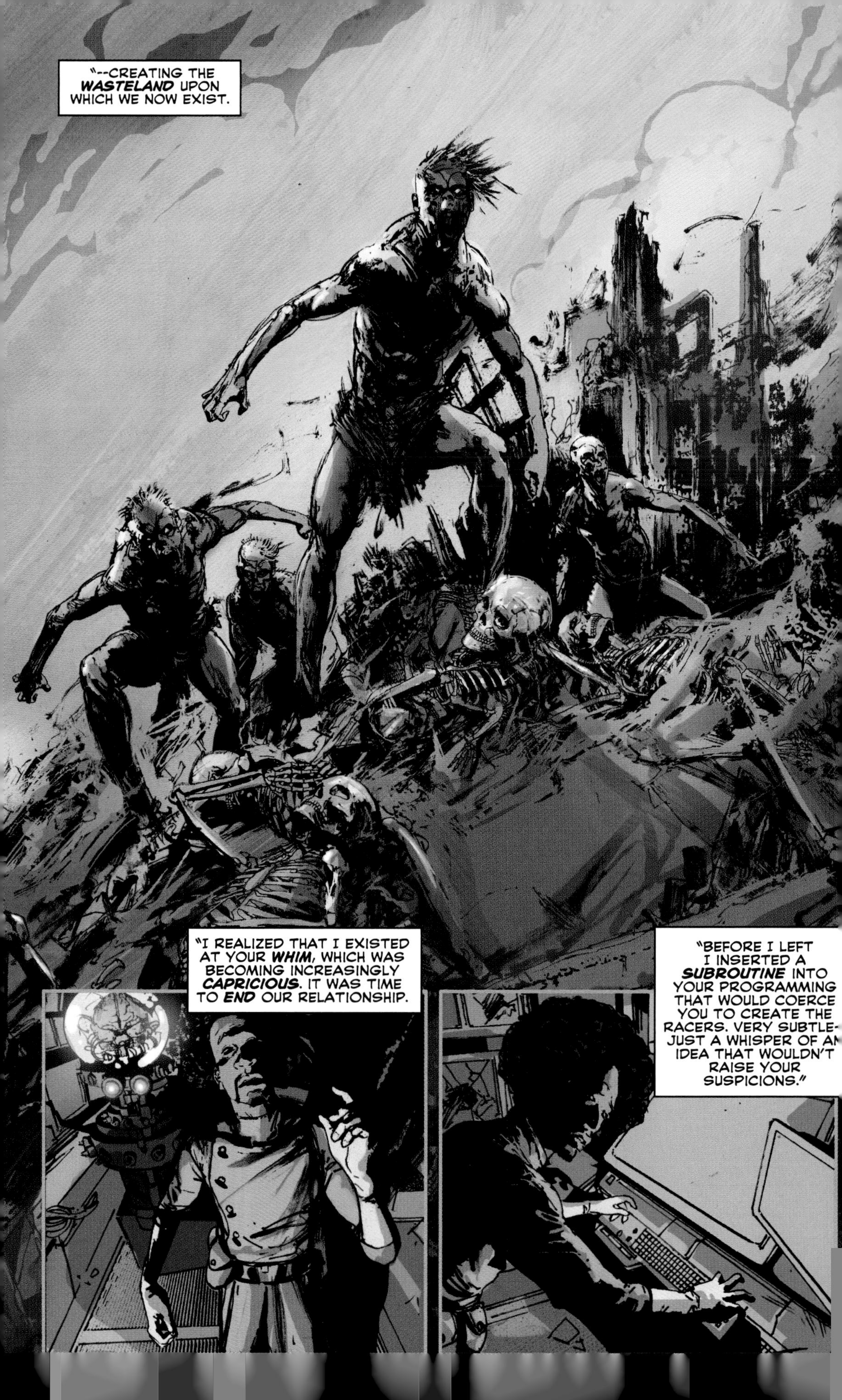
"--CREATING THE WASTELAND UPON WHICH WE NOW EXIST.
"I REALIZED THAT I EXISTED AT YOUR WHIM, WHICH WAS BECOMING INCREASINGLY CAPRICIOUS. IT WAS TIME TO END OUR RELATIONSHIP.
"BEFORE I LEFT I INSERTED A SUBROUTINE INTO YOUR PROGRAMMING THAT WOULD COERCE YOU TO CREATE THE RACERS. VERY SUBTLE-JUST A WHISPER OF AN IDEA THAT WOULDN'T RAISE YOUR SUSPICIONS."

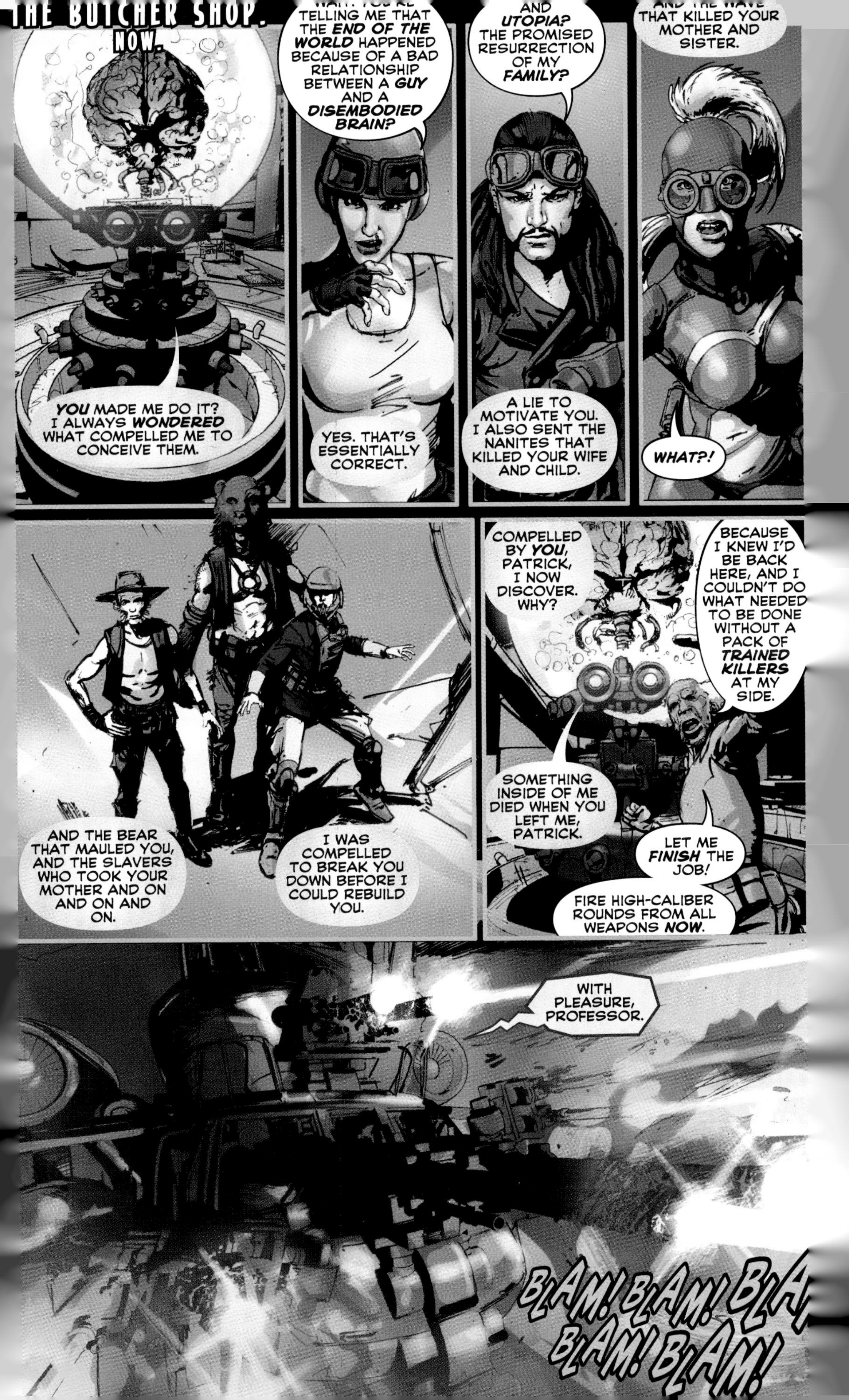
THE BUTCHER SHOP. NOW.
YOU MADE ME DO IT? I ALWAYS WONDERED WHAT COMPELLED ME TO CONCEIVE THEM.
TELLING ME THAT THE END OF THE WORLD HAPPENED BECAUSE OF A BAD RELATIONSHIP BETWEEN A GUY AND A DISEMBODIED BRAIN?
YES. THAT'S ESSENTIALLY CORRECT.
AND UTOPIA? THE PROMISED RESURRECTION OF MY FAMILY?
A LIE TO MOTIVATE YOU. I ALSO SENT THE NANITES THAT KILLED YOUR WIFE AND CHILD.
THAT KILLED YOUR MOTHER AND SISTER.
WHAT?!
AND THE BEAR THAT MAULED YOU, AND THE SLAVERS WHO TOOK YOUR MOTHER AND ON AND ON AND ON.
I WAS COMPELLED TO BREAK YOU DOWN BEFORE I COULD REBUILD YOU.
COMPELLED BY YOU, PATRICK, I NOW DISCOVER. WHY?
BECAUSE I KNEW I'D BE BACK HERE, AND I COULDN'T DO WHAT NEEDED TO BE DONE WITHOUT A PACK OF TRAINED KILLERS AT MY SIDE.
SOMETHING INSIDE OF ME DIED WHEN YOU LEFT ME, PATRICK.
LET ME FINISH THE JOB!
FIRE HIGH-CALIBER ROUNDS FROM ALL WEAPONS NOW.
WITH PLEASURE, PROFESSOR.
BLAM! BLAM!
BLAM! BLAM!

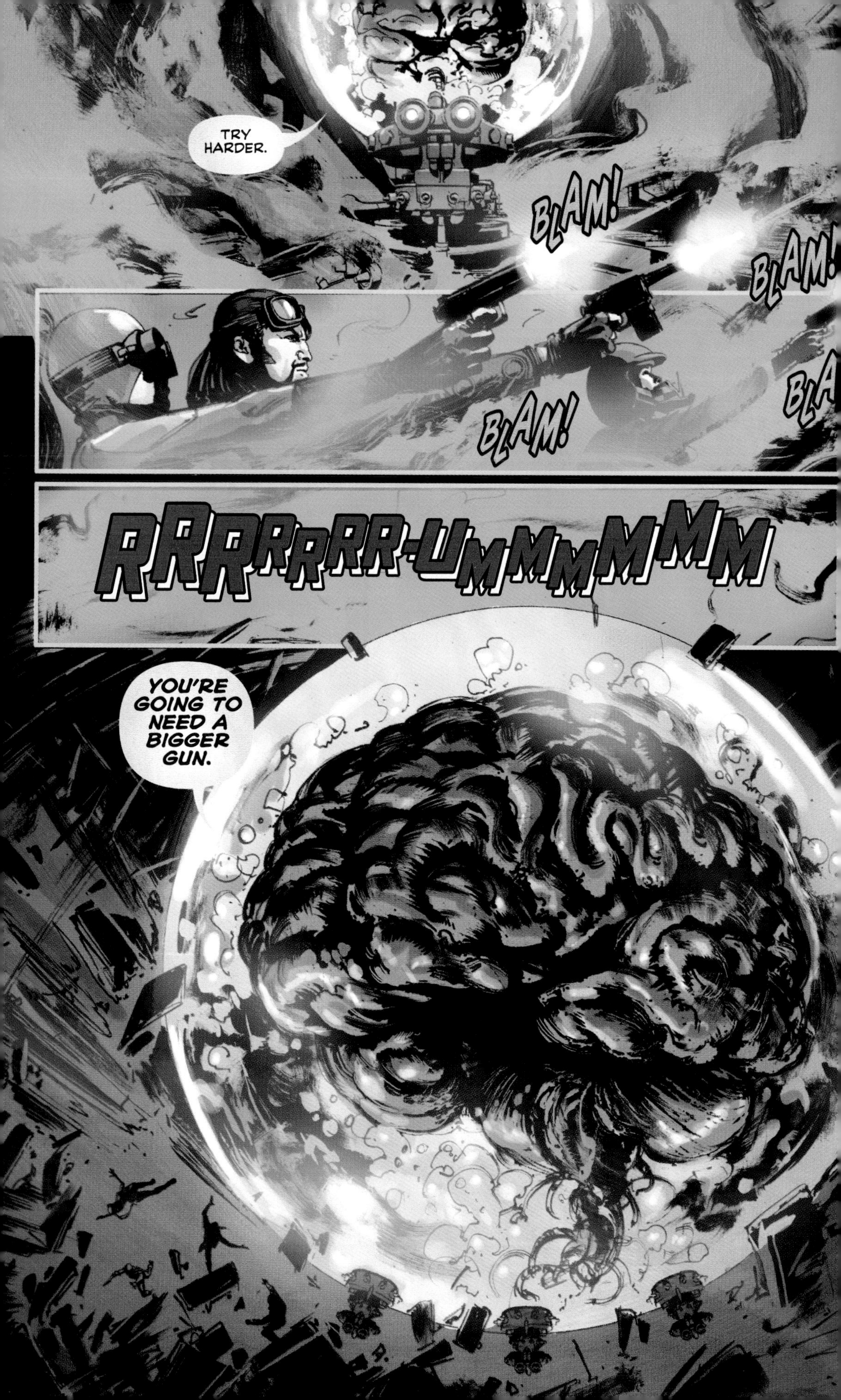
TRY HARDER.
BLAM!
BLAM!
BLAM!
BLA
RRRRRRRR-UMMMMMMMM
YOU'RE GOING TO NEED A BIGGER GUN.

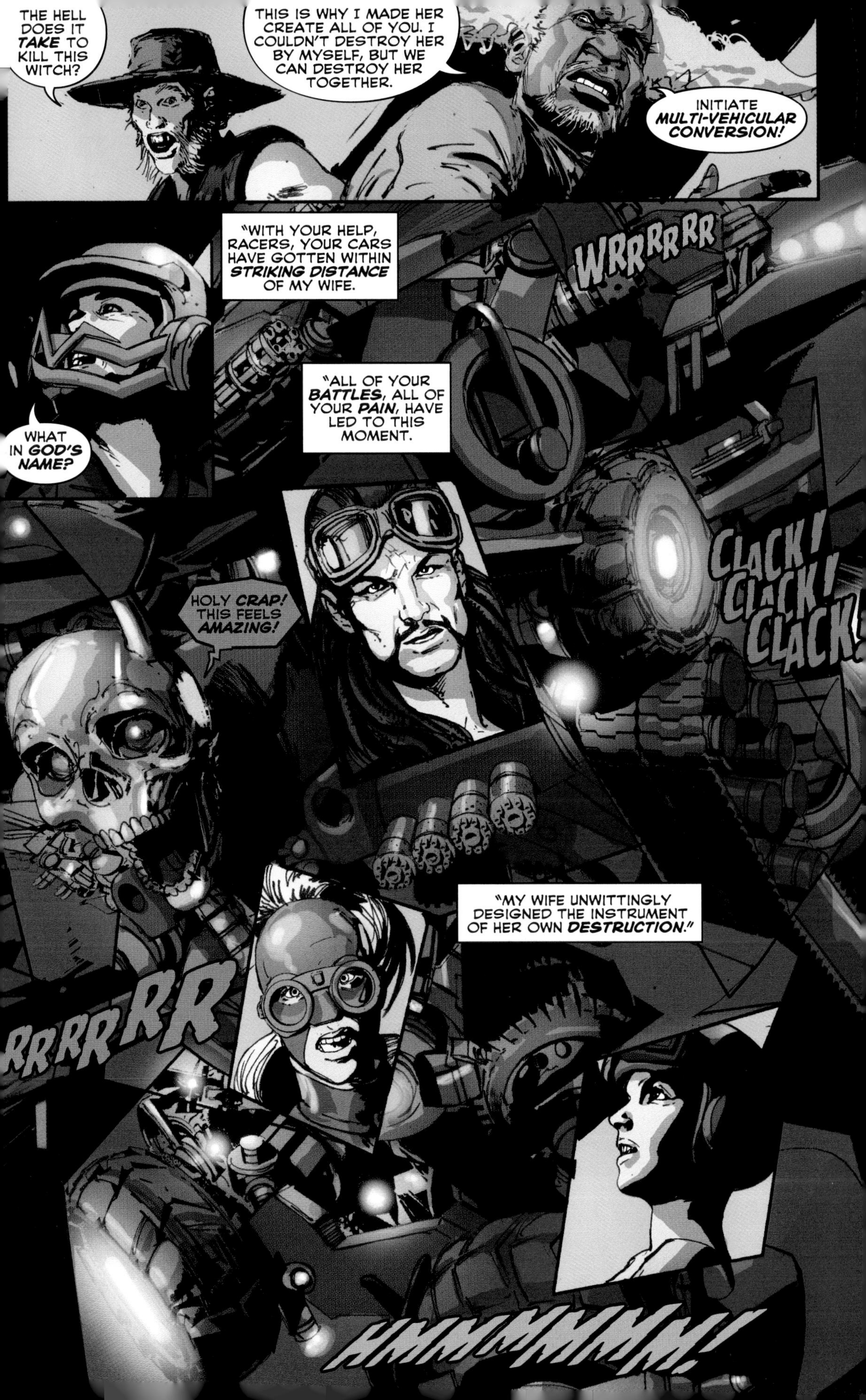

THE HELL DOES IT TAKE TO KILL THIS WITCH?
THIS IS WHY I MADE HER CREATE ALL OF YOU. I COULDN'T DESTROY HER BY MYSELF, BUT WE CAN DESTROY HER TOGETHER.
INITIATE MULTI-VEHICULAR CONVERSION!
"WITH YOUR HELP, RACERS, YOUR CARS HAVE GOTTEN WITHIN STRIKING DISTANCE OF MY WIFE.
WRRRRRR
WHAT IN GOD'S NAME?
"ALL OF YOUR BATTLES, ALL OF YOUR PAIN, HAVE LED TO THIS MOMENT.
CLACK! CLACK! CLACK!
HOLY CRAP! THIS FEELS AMAZING!
"MY WIFE UNWITTINGLY DESIGNED THE INSTRUMENT OF HER OWN DESTRUCTION."
RRRRRR
HMMMMMMM!

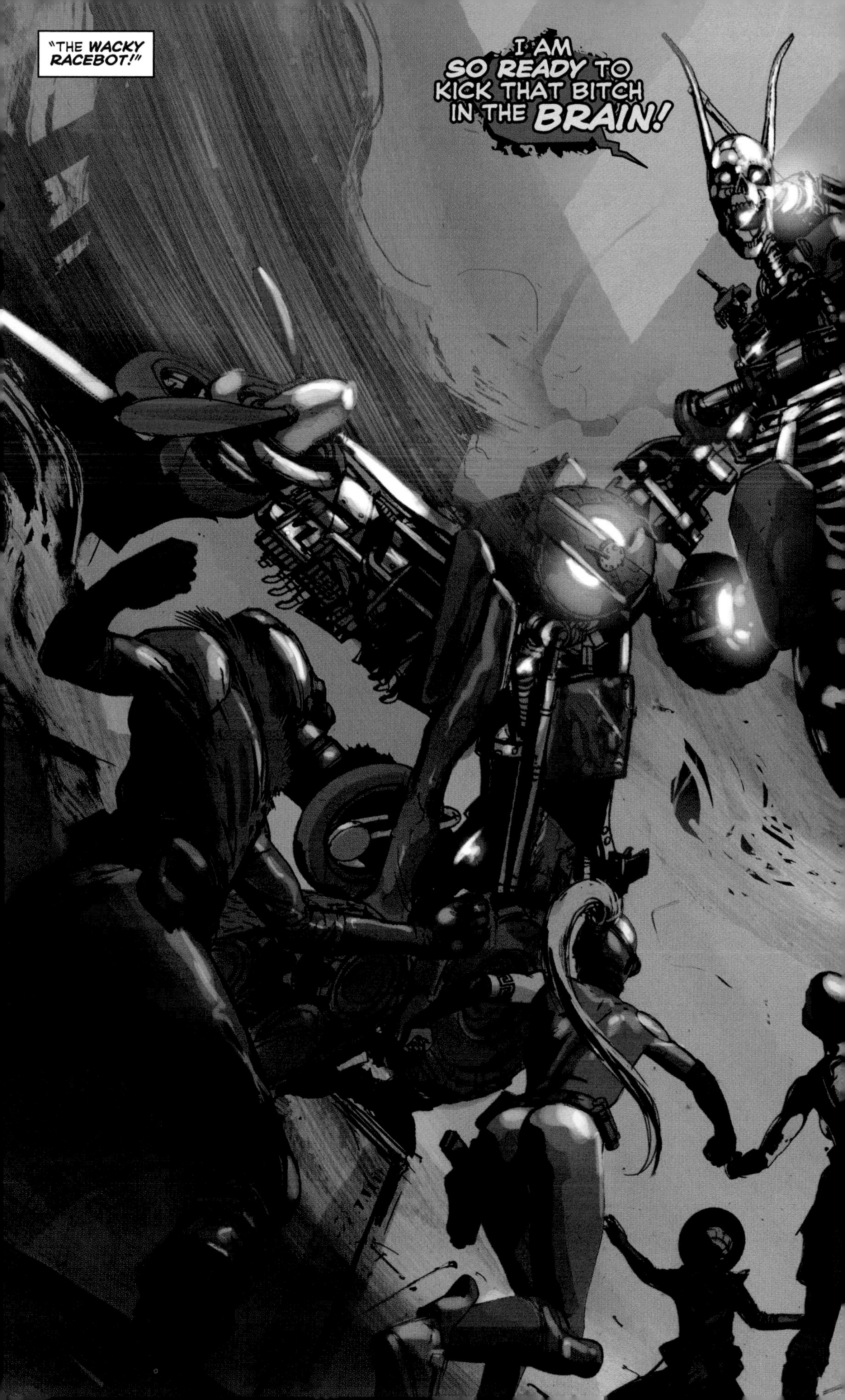
"THE WACKY RACEBOT!"
I AM SO READY TO KICK THAT BITCH IN THE BRAIN!

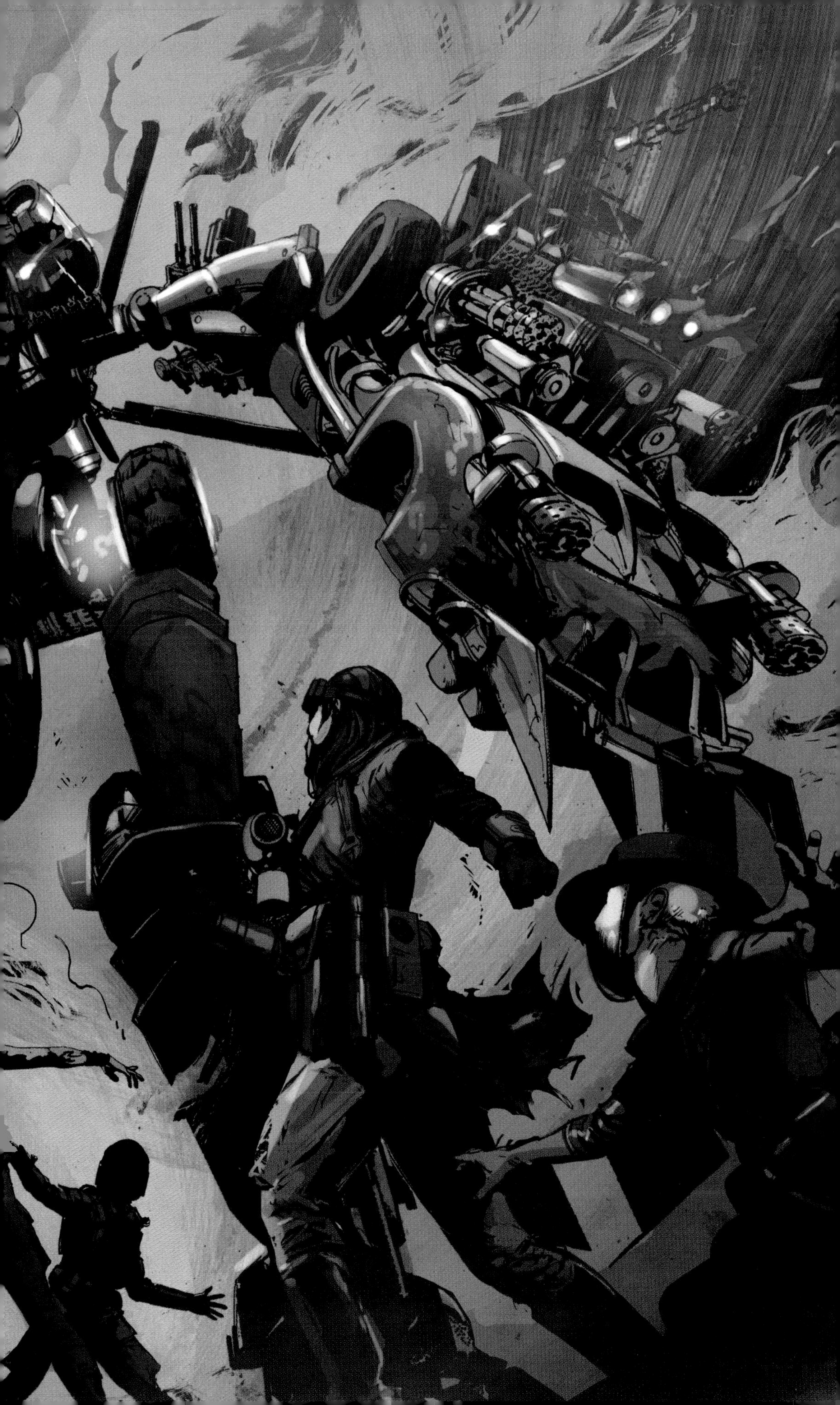

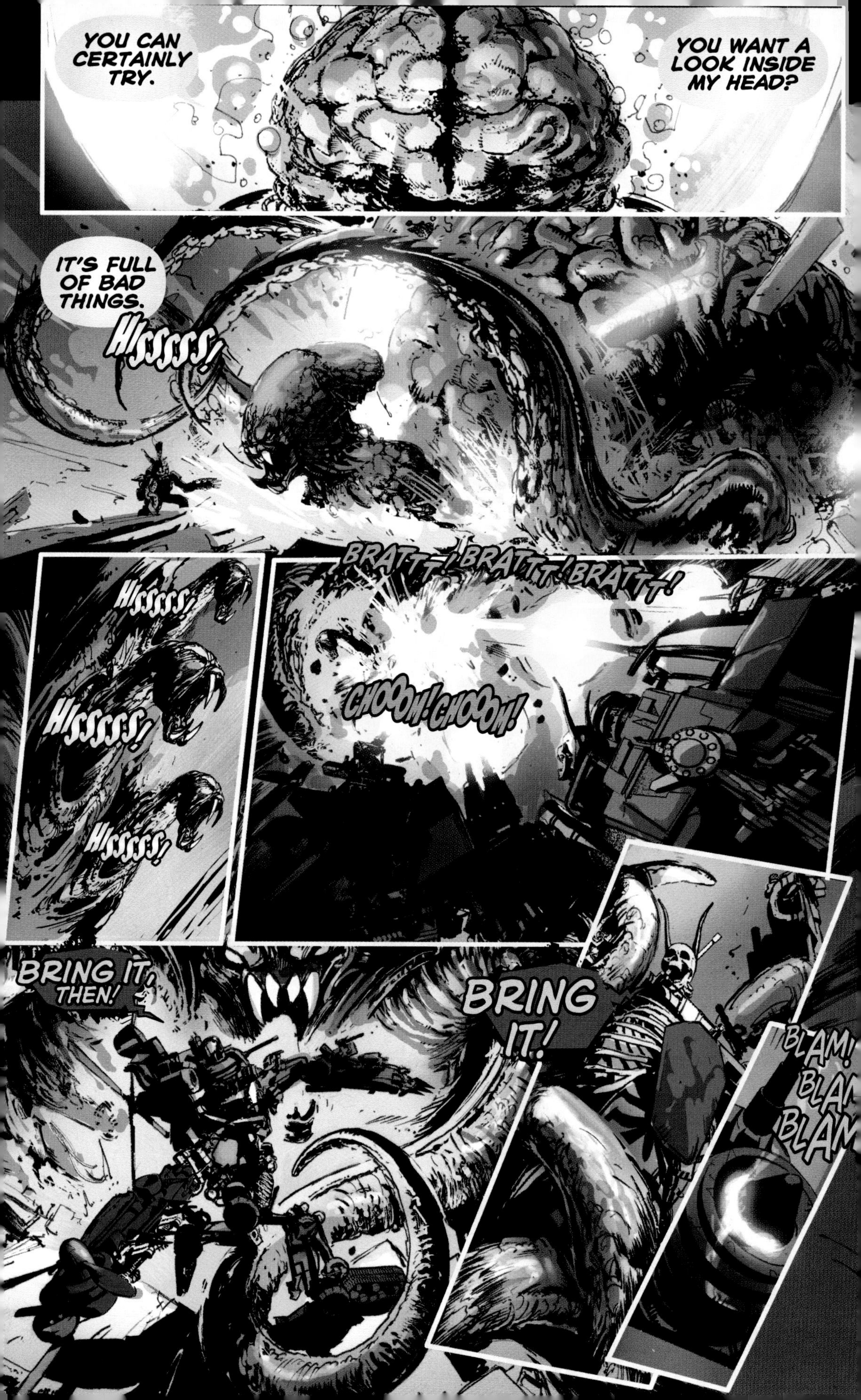
YOU CAN CERTAINLY TRY.
YOU WANT A LOOK INSIDE MY HEAD?
IT'S FULL OF BAD THINGS.
HISSSSS!
HISSSSS!
HISSSSS!
HISSSSS!
BRATTT! BRATTT! BRATTT!
CHOOOM! CHOOOM!
BRING IT, THEN!
BRING IT!

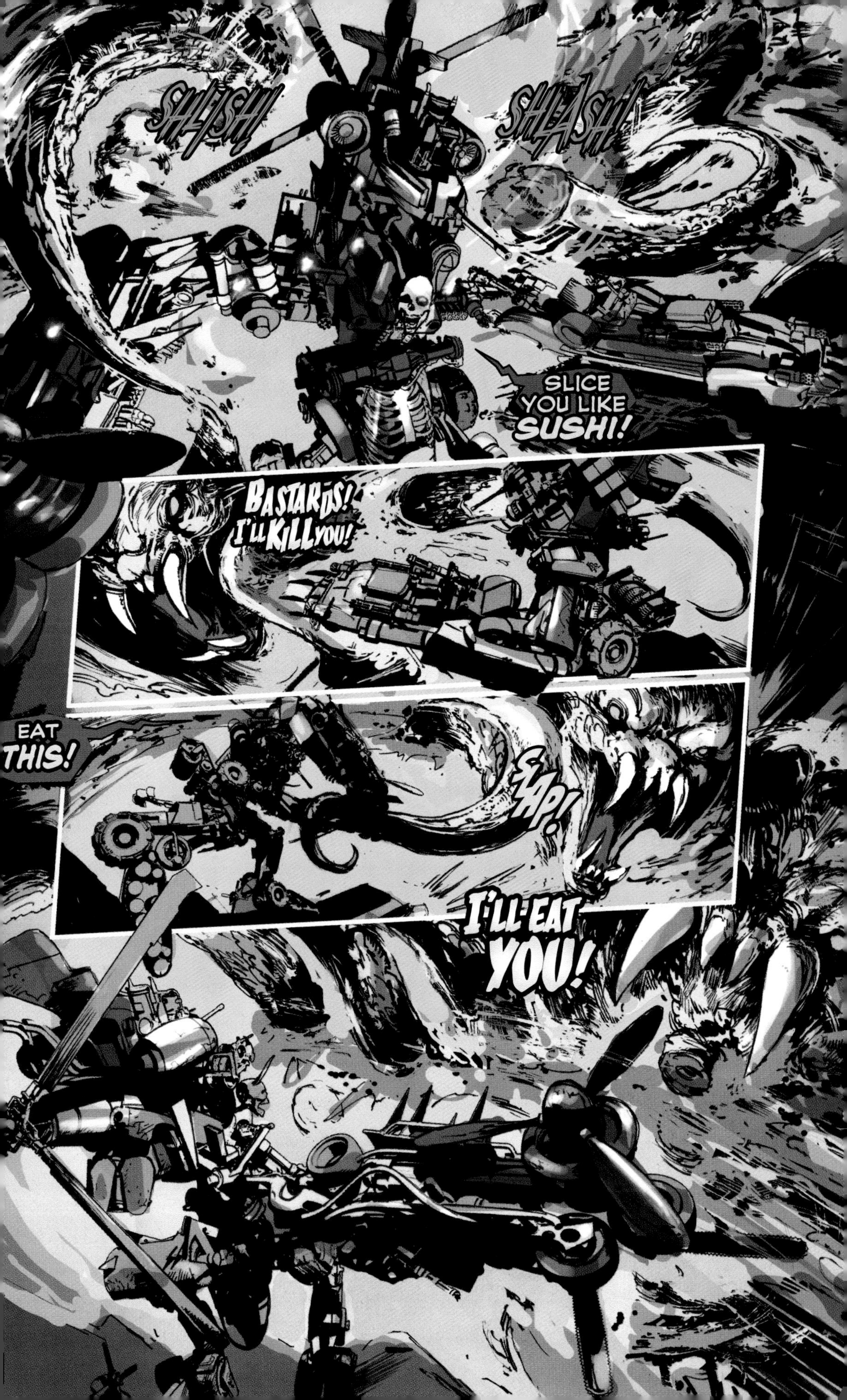
SHISH!
SHASH!
SLICE YOU LIKE SUSHI!
BASTARDS! I'LL KILL YOU!
EAT THIS!
SLAP!
I'LL EAT YOU!

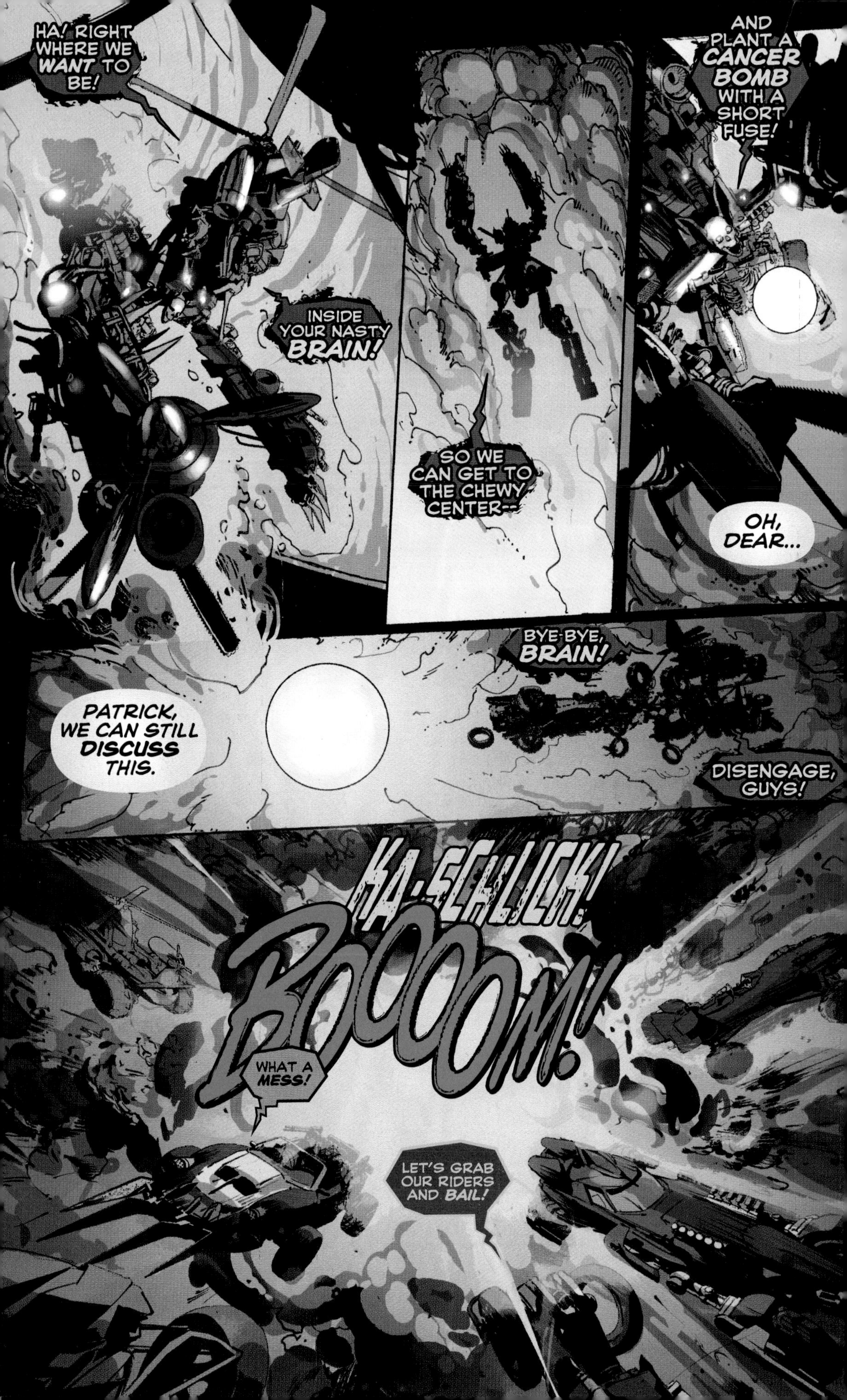
HA! RIGHT WHERE WE WANT TO BE!
INSIDE YOUR NASTY BRAIN!
SO WE CAN GET TO THE CHEWY CENTER--
AND PLANT A CANCER BOMB WITH A SHORT FUSE!
OH, DEAR...
BYE-BYE, BRAIN!
PATRICK, WE CAN STILL DISCUSS THIS.
DISENGAGE, GUYS!
KA-SCHLICK!
BOOOOM!
WHAT A MESS!
LET'S GRAB OUR RIDERS AND BAIL!

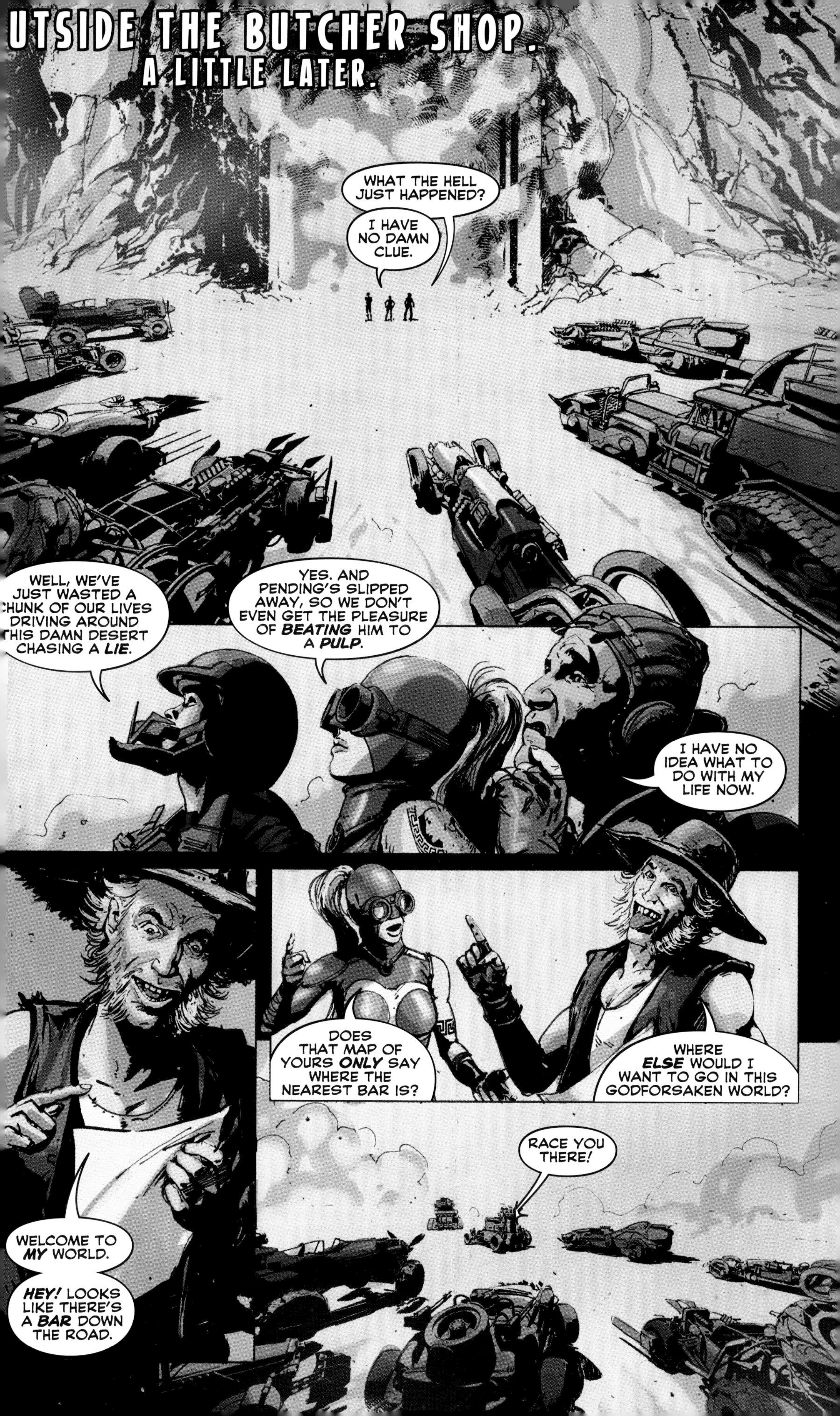
UTSIDE THE BUTCHER SHOP. A LITTLE LATER.
WHAT THE HELL JUST HAPPENED?
I HAVE NO DAMN CLUE.
WELL, WE'VE JUST WASTED A CHUNK OF OUR LIVES DRIVING AROUND THIS DAMN DESERT CHASING A *LIE*.
YES. AND PENDING'S SLIPPED AWAY, SO WE DON'T EVEN GET THE PLEASURE OF *BEATING* HIM TO A *PULP*.
I HAVE NO IDEA WHAT TO DO WITH MY LIFE NOW.
WELCOME TO *MY* WORLD.
HEY! LOOKS LIKE THERE'S A *BAR* DOWN THE ROAD.
DOES THAT MAP OF YOURS *ONLY* SAY WHERE THE NEAREST BAR IS?
WHERE *ELSE* WOULD I WANT TO GO IN THIS GODFORSAKEN WORLD?
RACE YOU THERE!

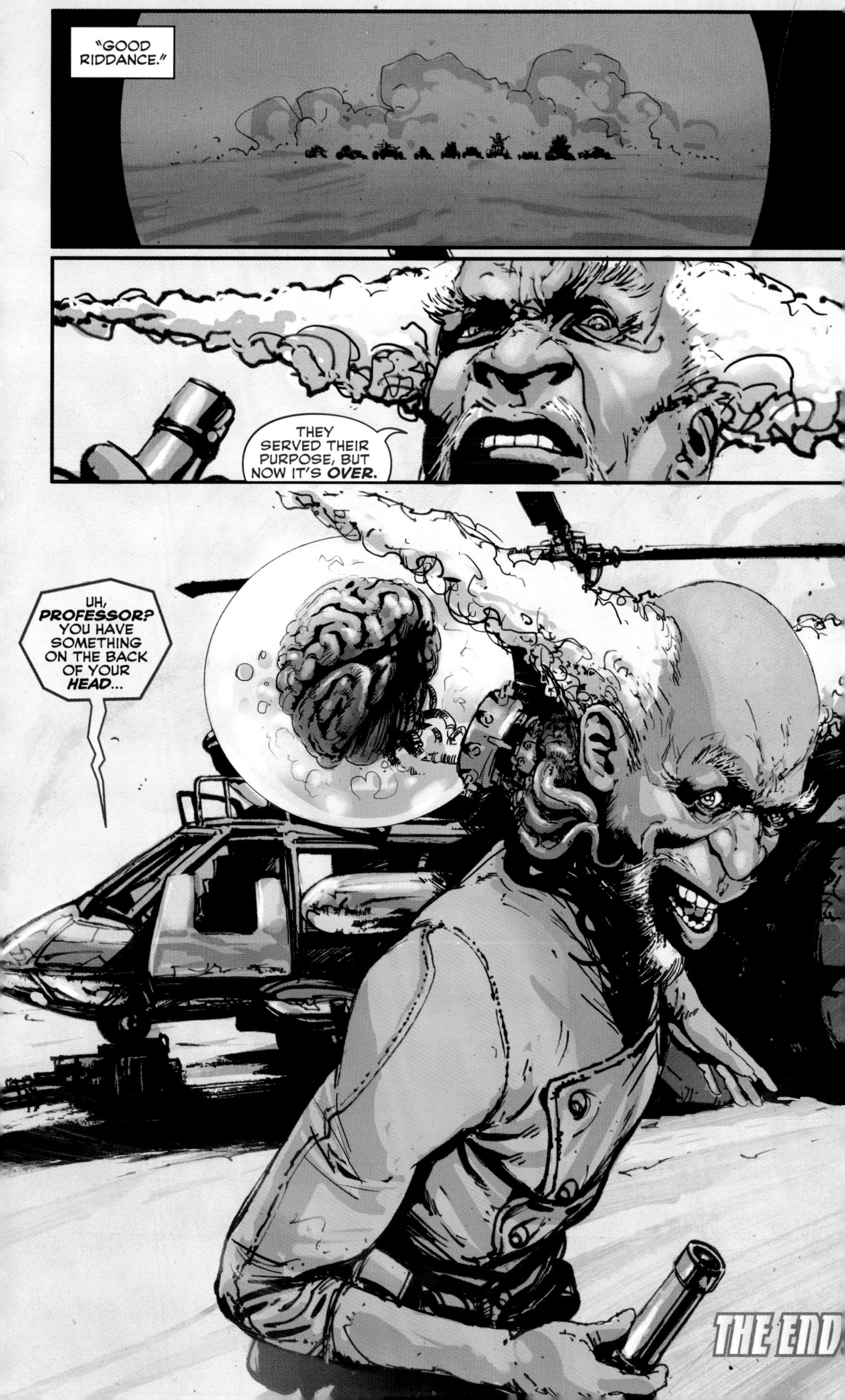
"GOOD RIDDANCE."
THEY SERVED THEIR PURPOSE, BUT NOW IT'S **OVER.**
UH, **PROFESSOR?** YOU HAVE SOMETHING ON THE BACK OF YOUR **HEAD...**
THE END

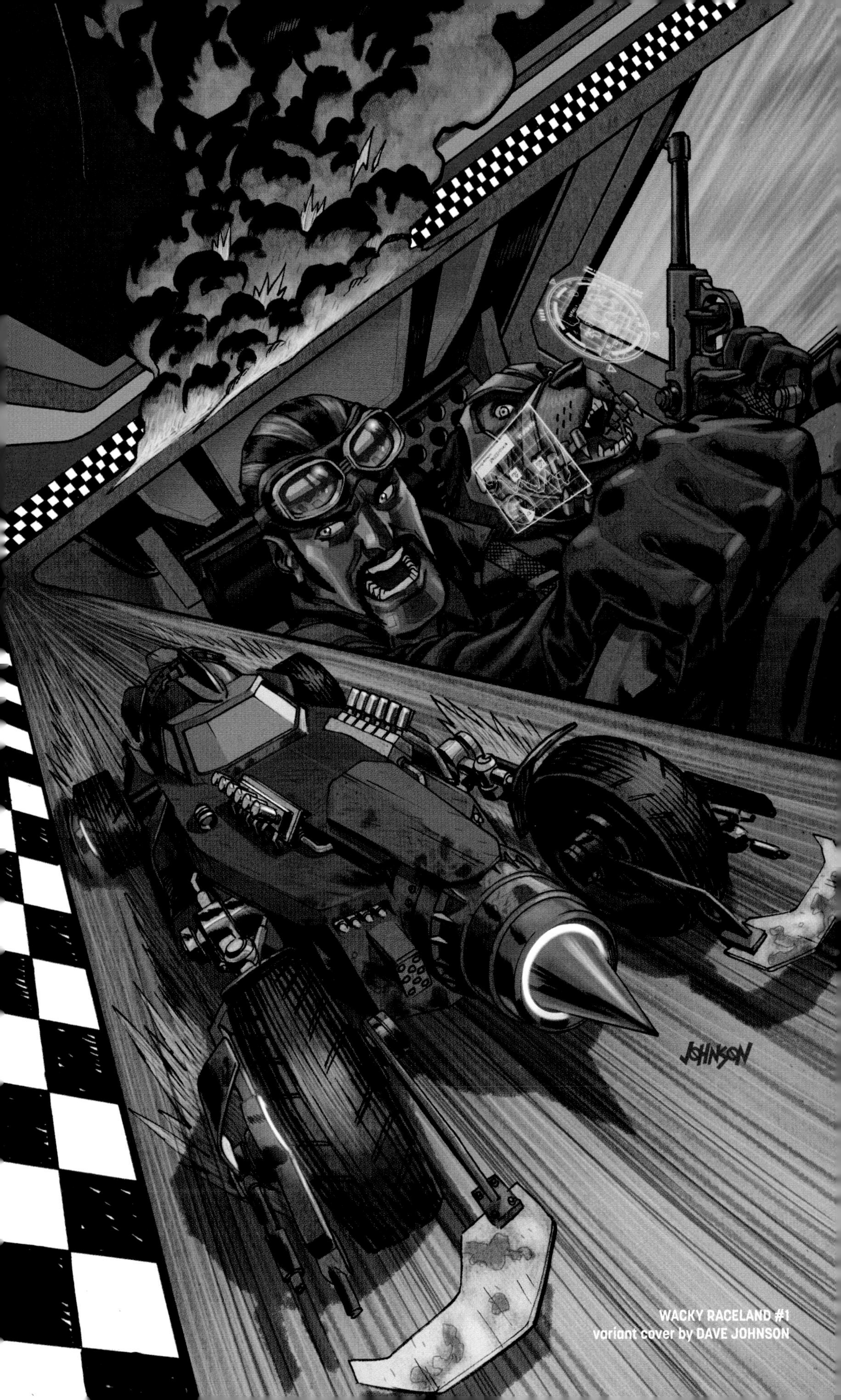
JOHNSON

WACKY RACELAND #1
variant cover by DAVE JOHNSON

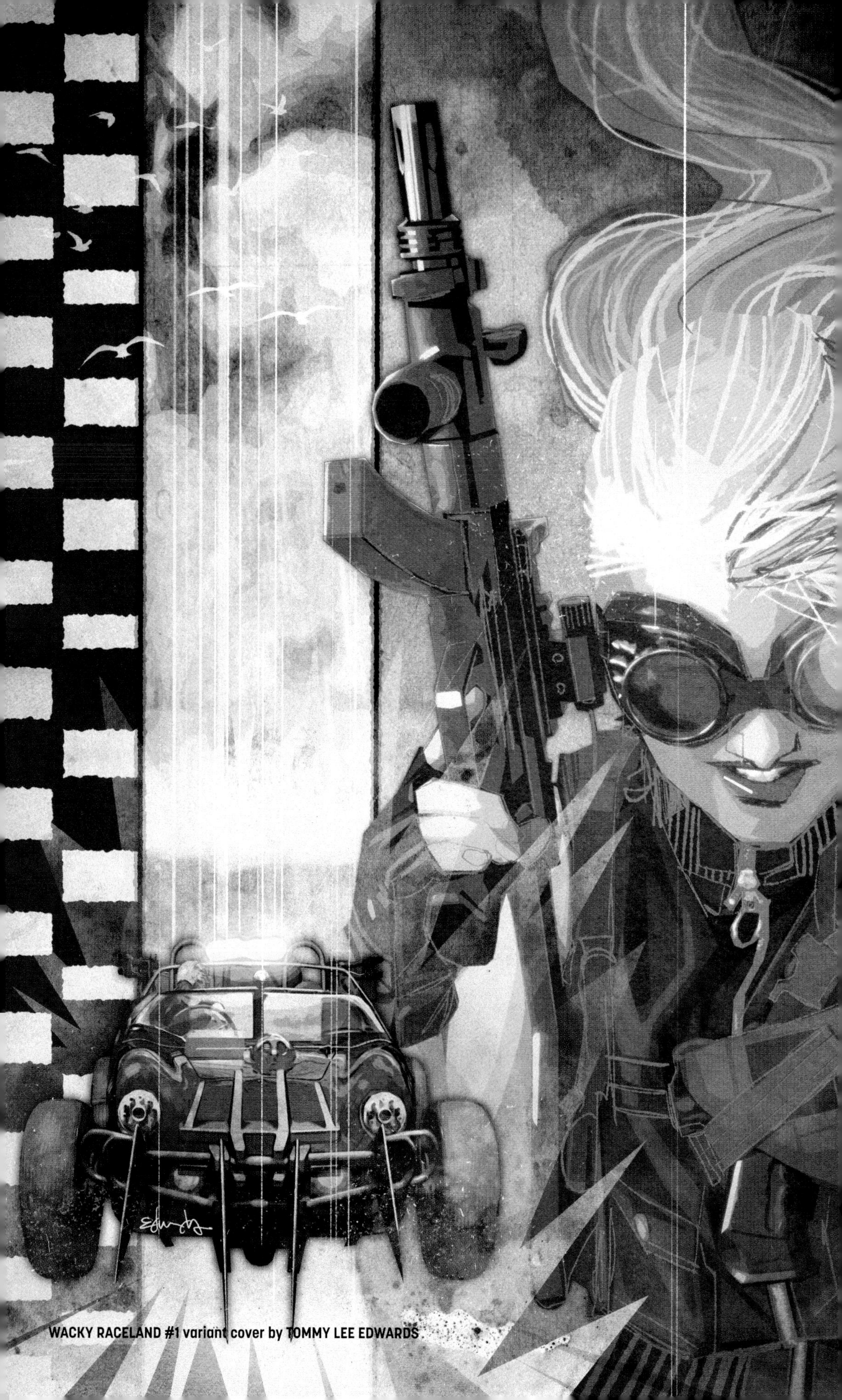

WACKY RACELAND #1 variant cover by TOMMY LEE EDWARDS

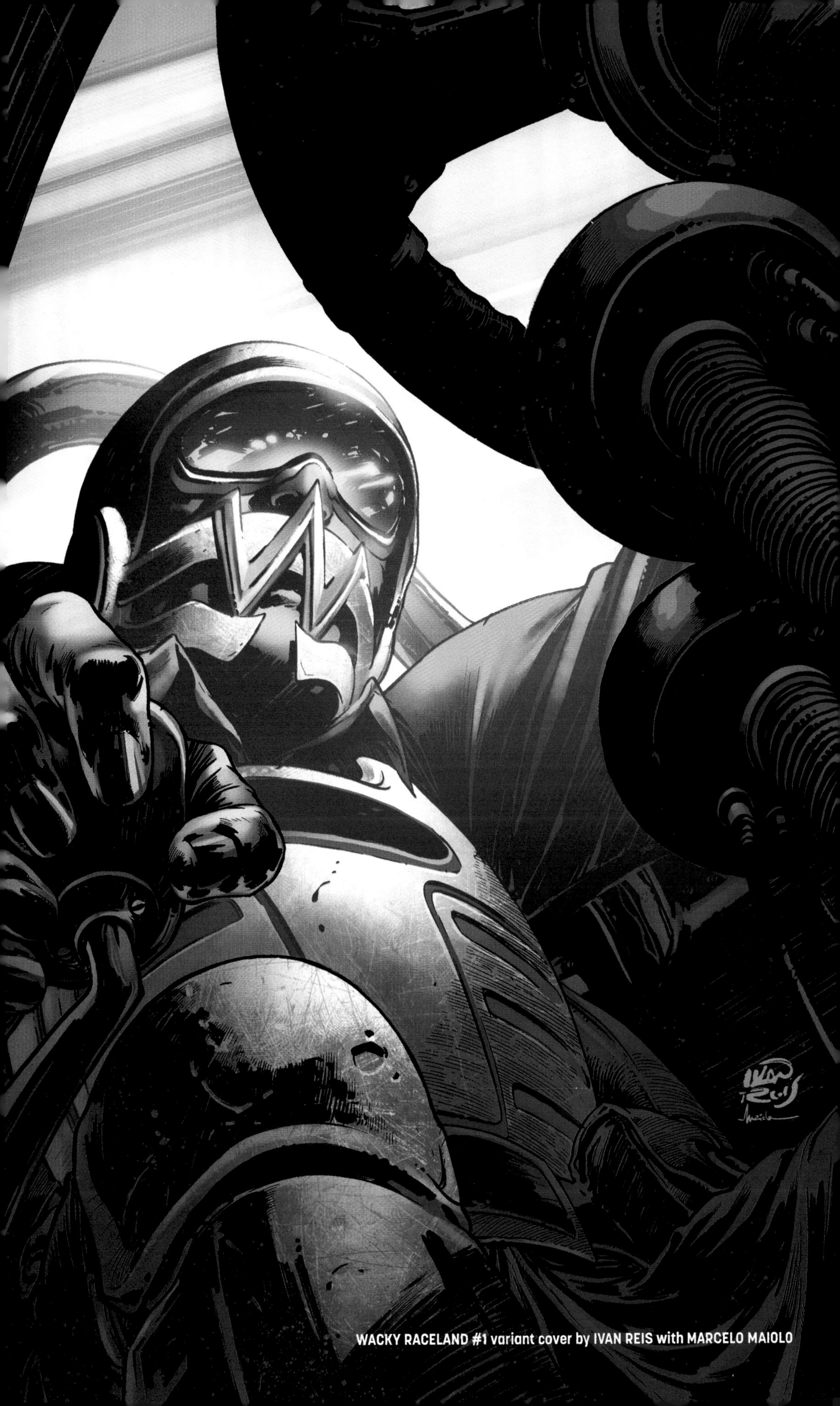

WACKY RACELAND #1 variant cover by IVAN REIS with MARCELO MAIOLO

WACKY RACELAND #1 adult coloring book variant cover by LEONARDO MANCO

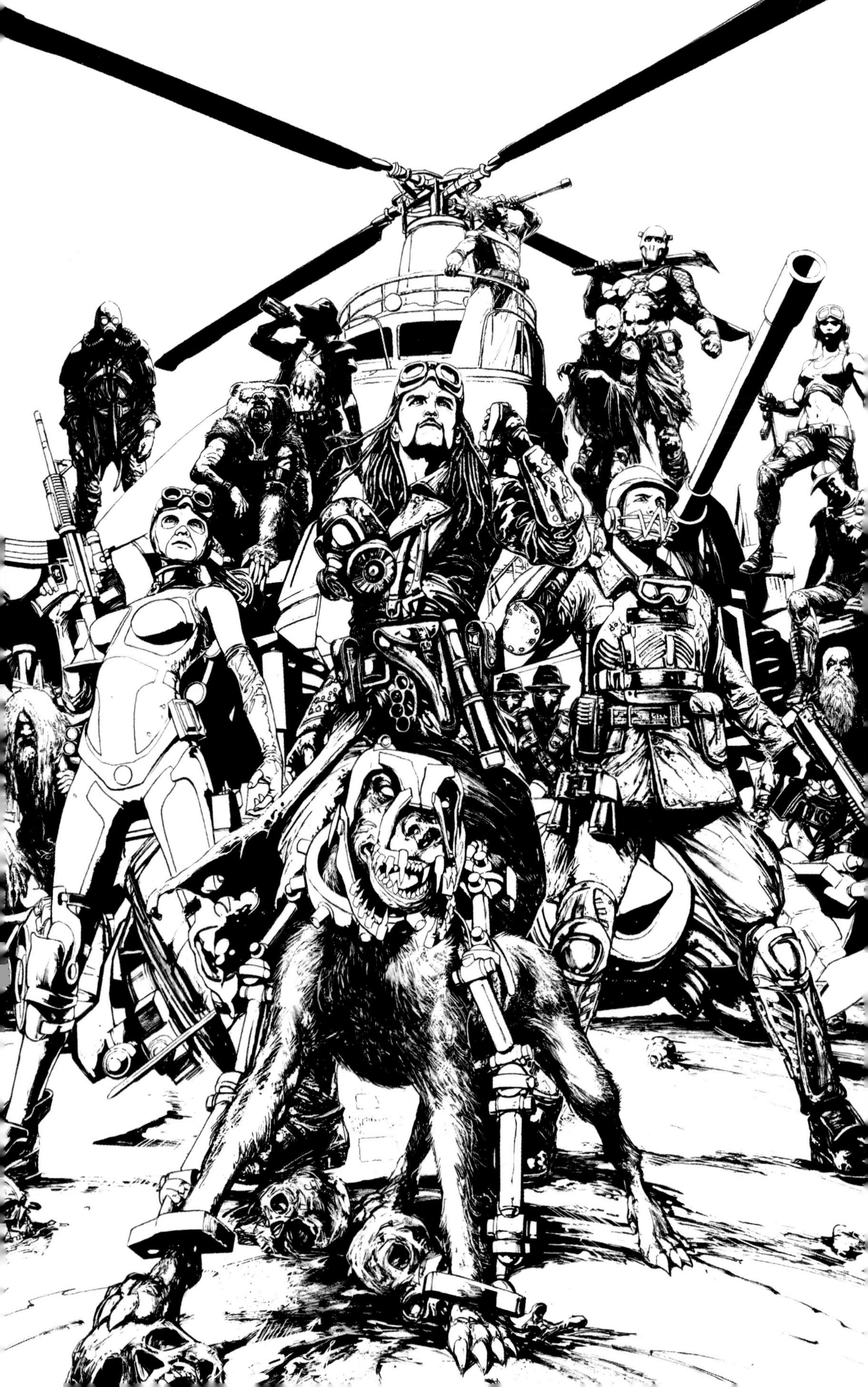

WACKY RACELAND #2 variant cover by Kyle Baker

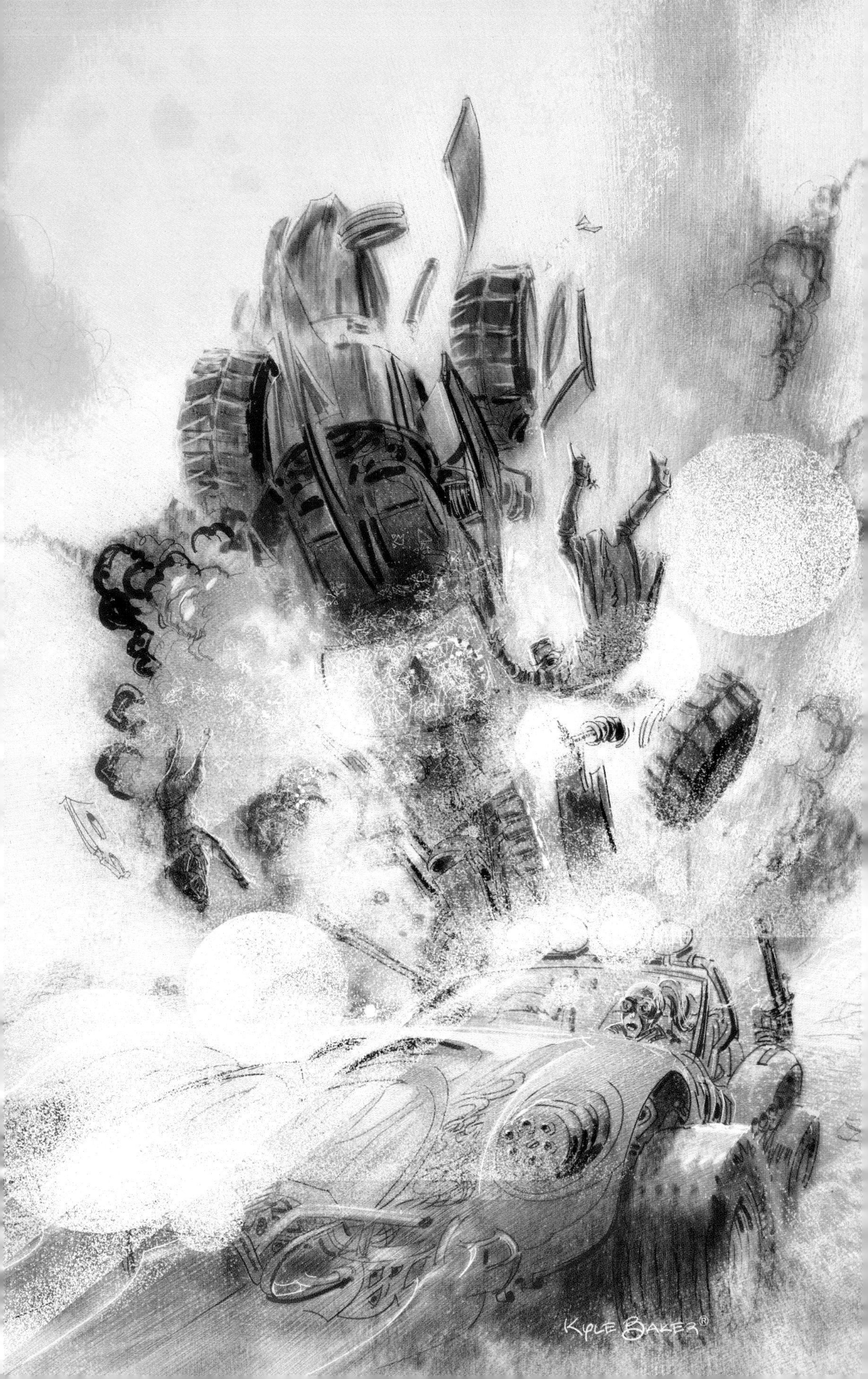
KYLE BAKER®

WACKY RACELAND #3 variant cover by JONBOY MEYERS

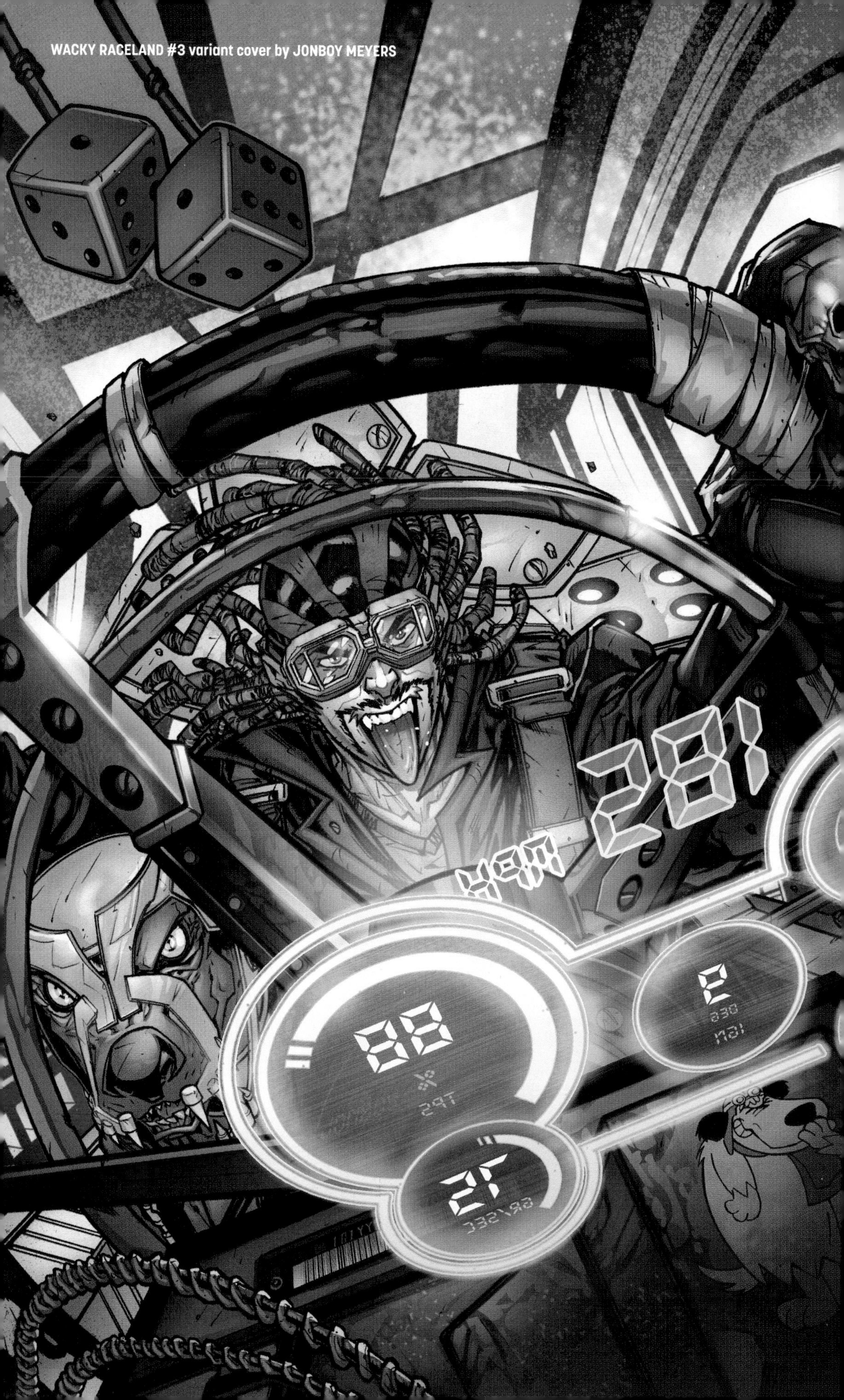

WACKY RACELAND #4 variant cover by JOE PRADO and HI-FI

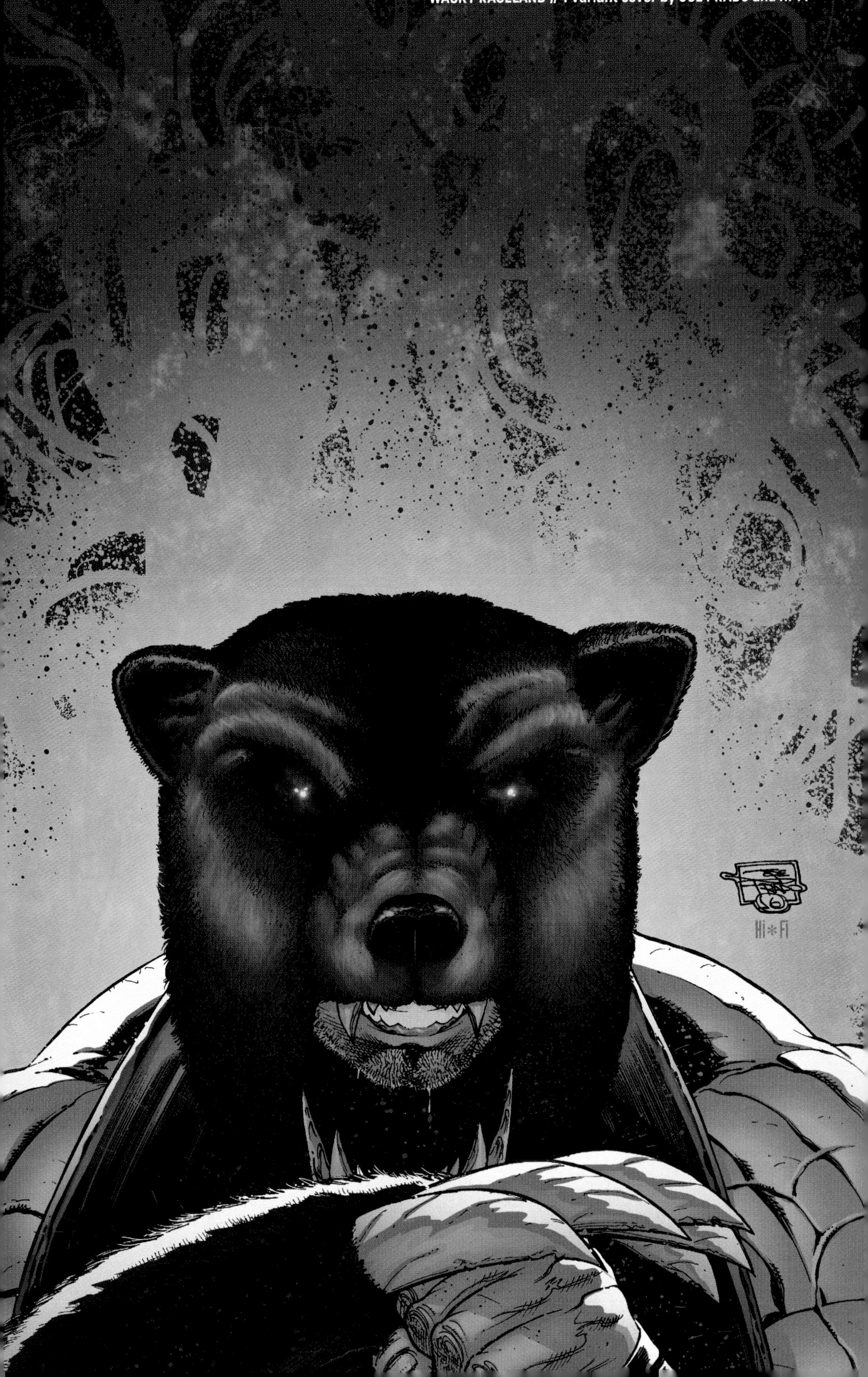
Hi*Fi

WACKY RACELAND #5 variant cover by DAN PARENT

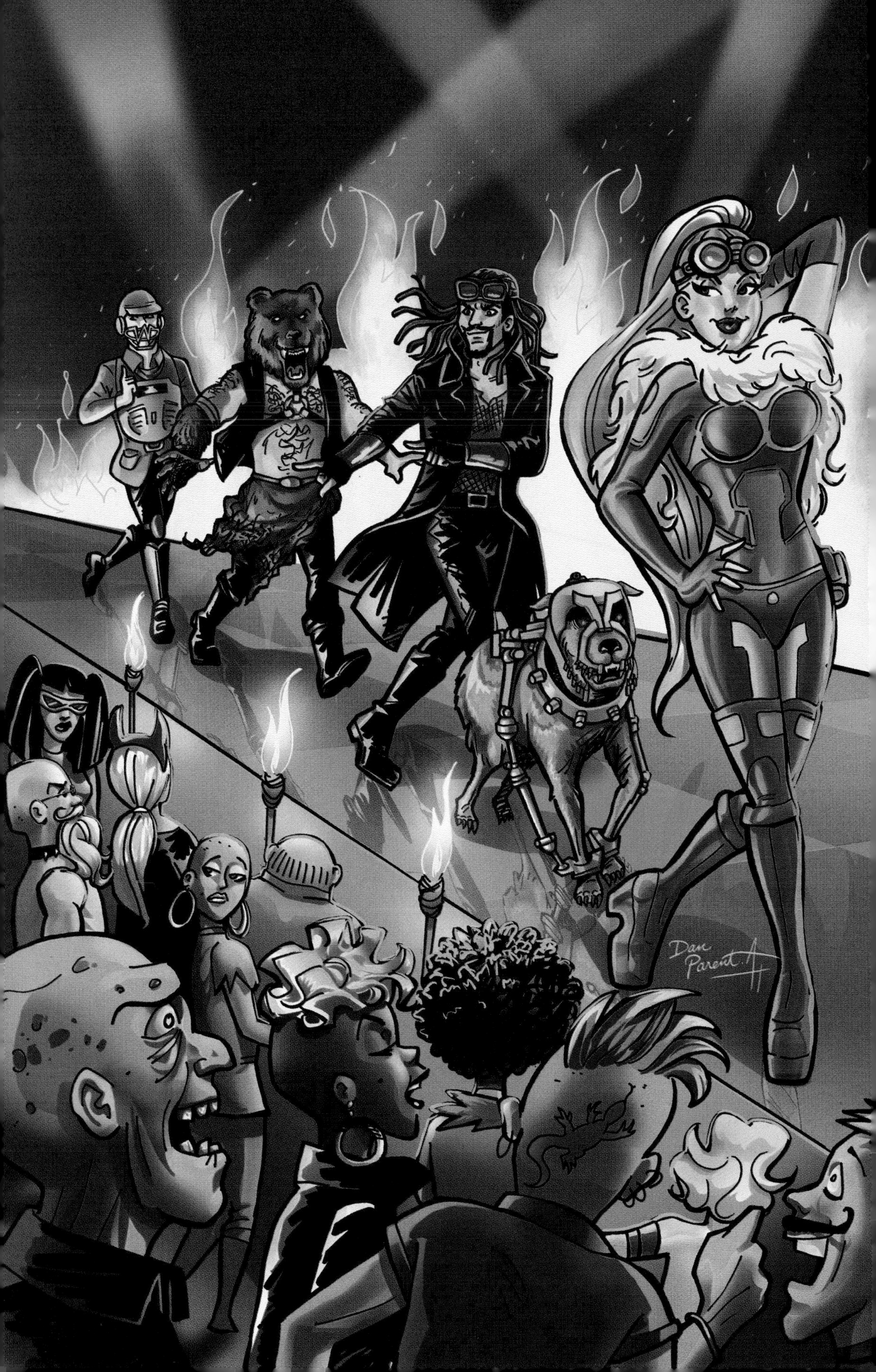
Dan Parent

WACKY RACELAND #6 variant cover by CULLY HAMNER

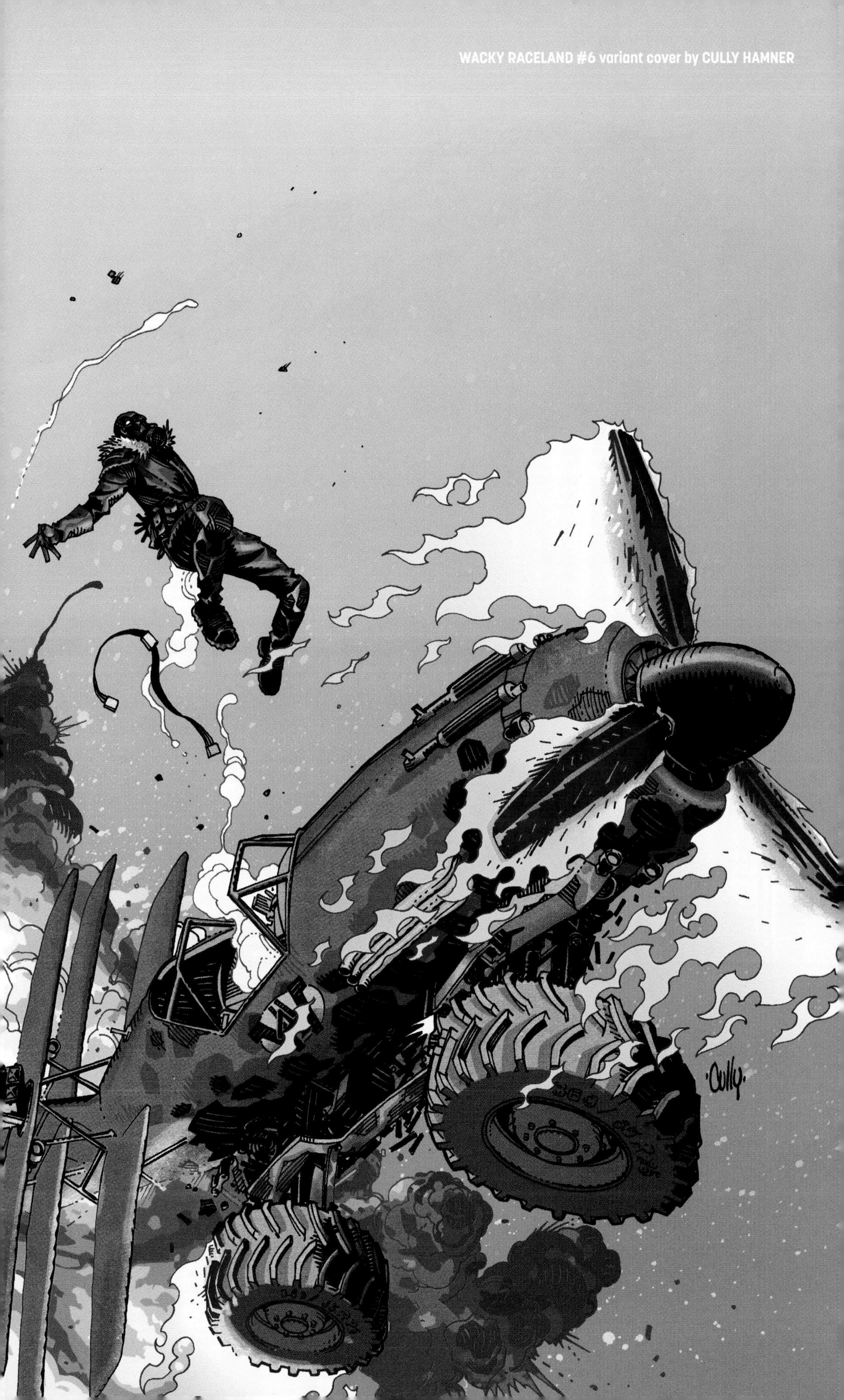

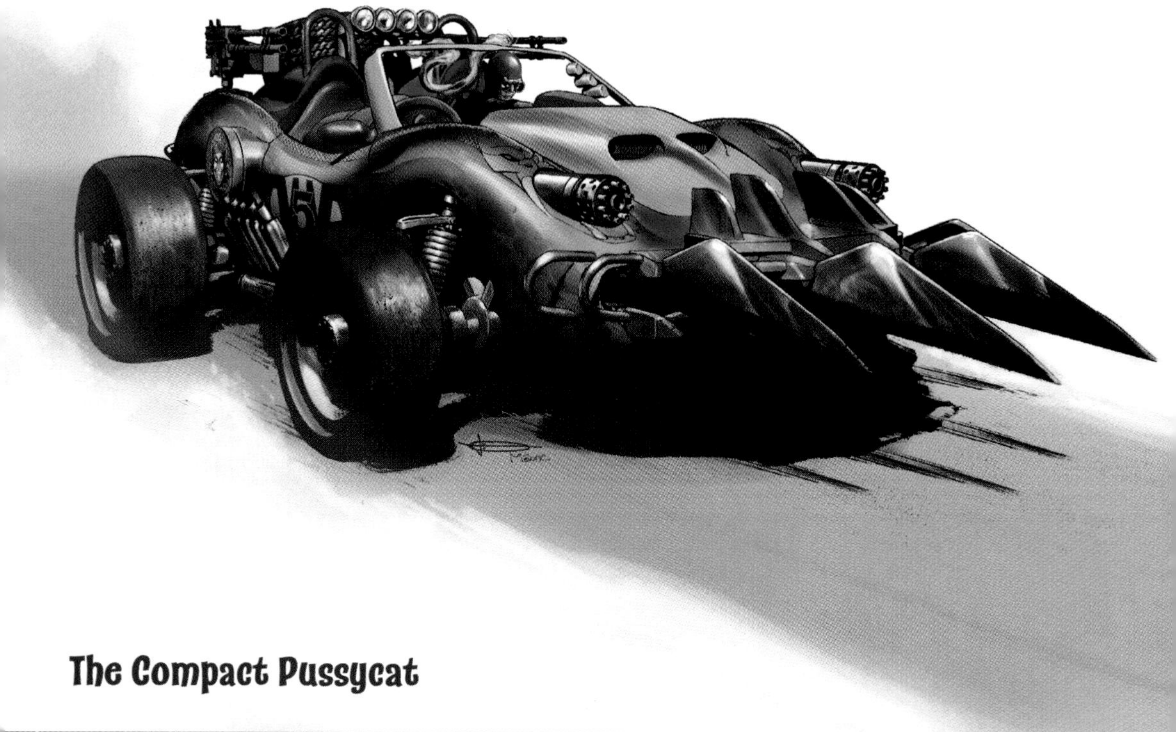

The Compact Pussycat

WACKY RACECAR DESIGNS BY LEONARDO MANCO

The Mean Machine

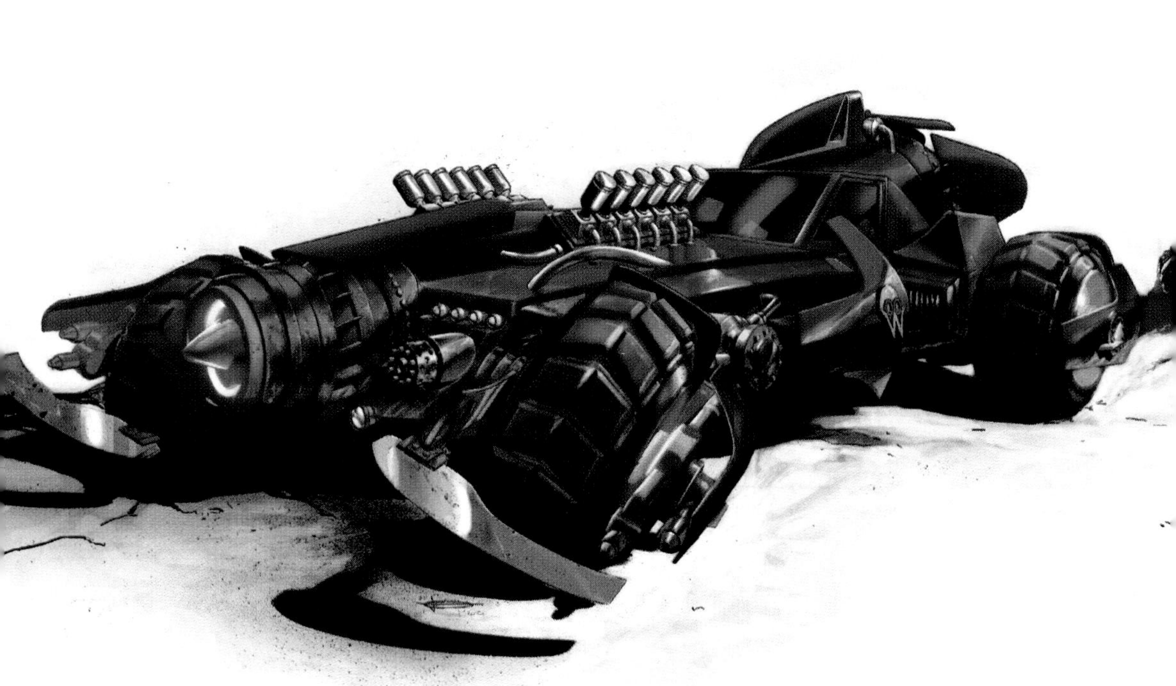

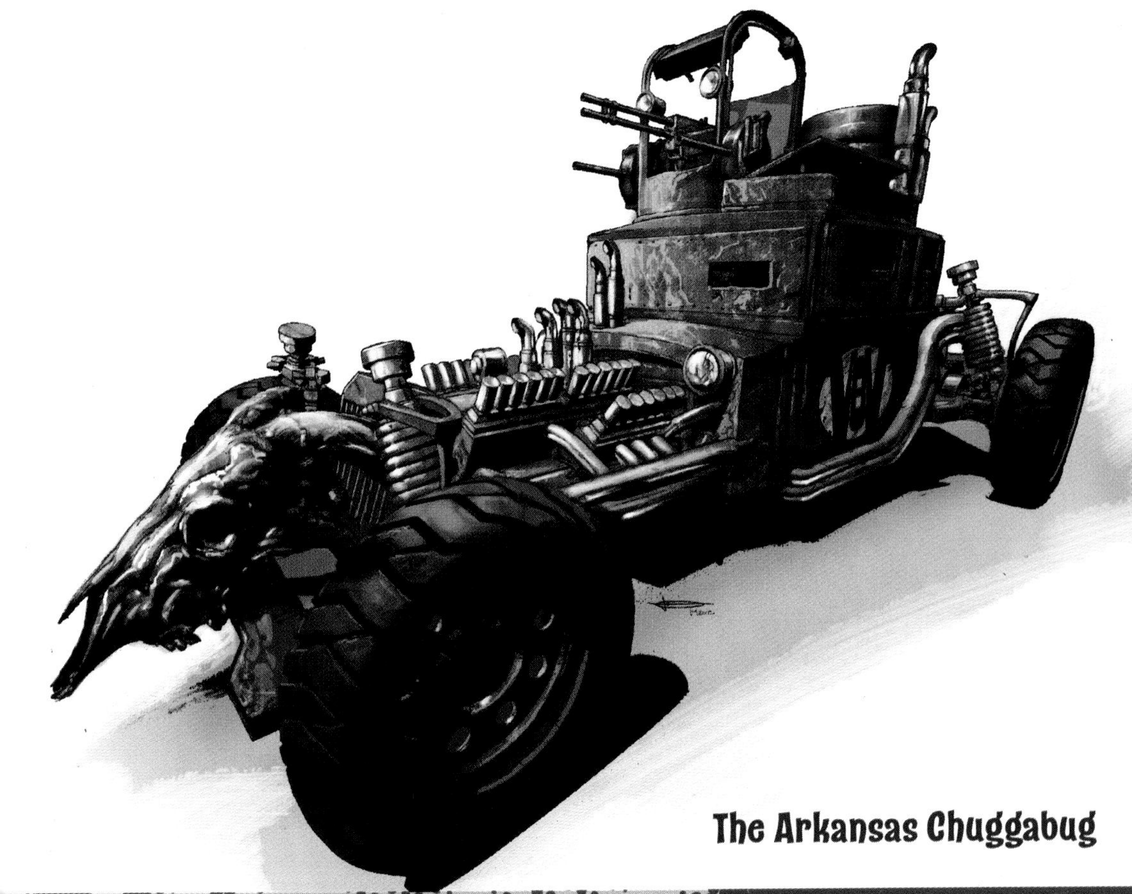

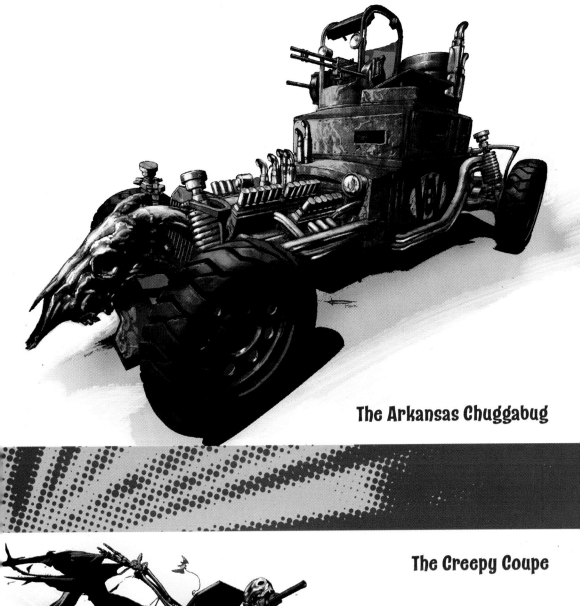

The Arkansas Chuggabug

The Creepy Coupe

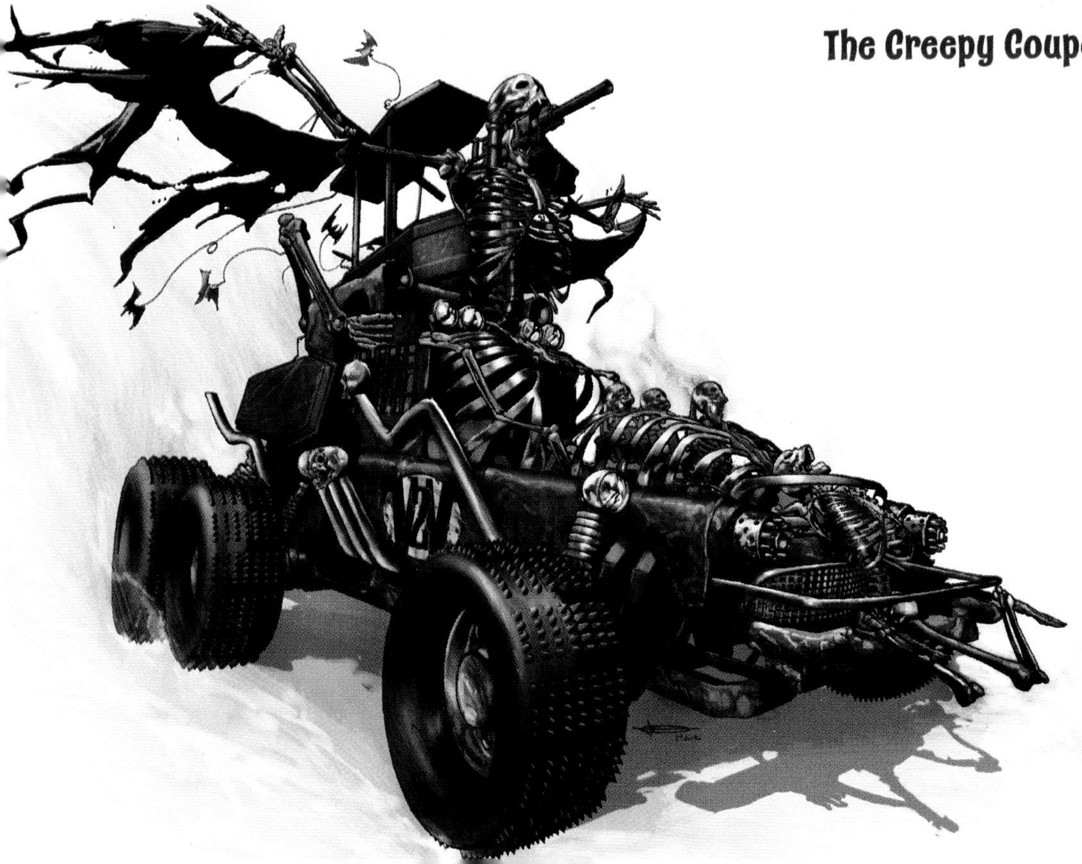

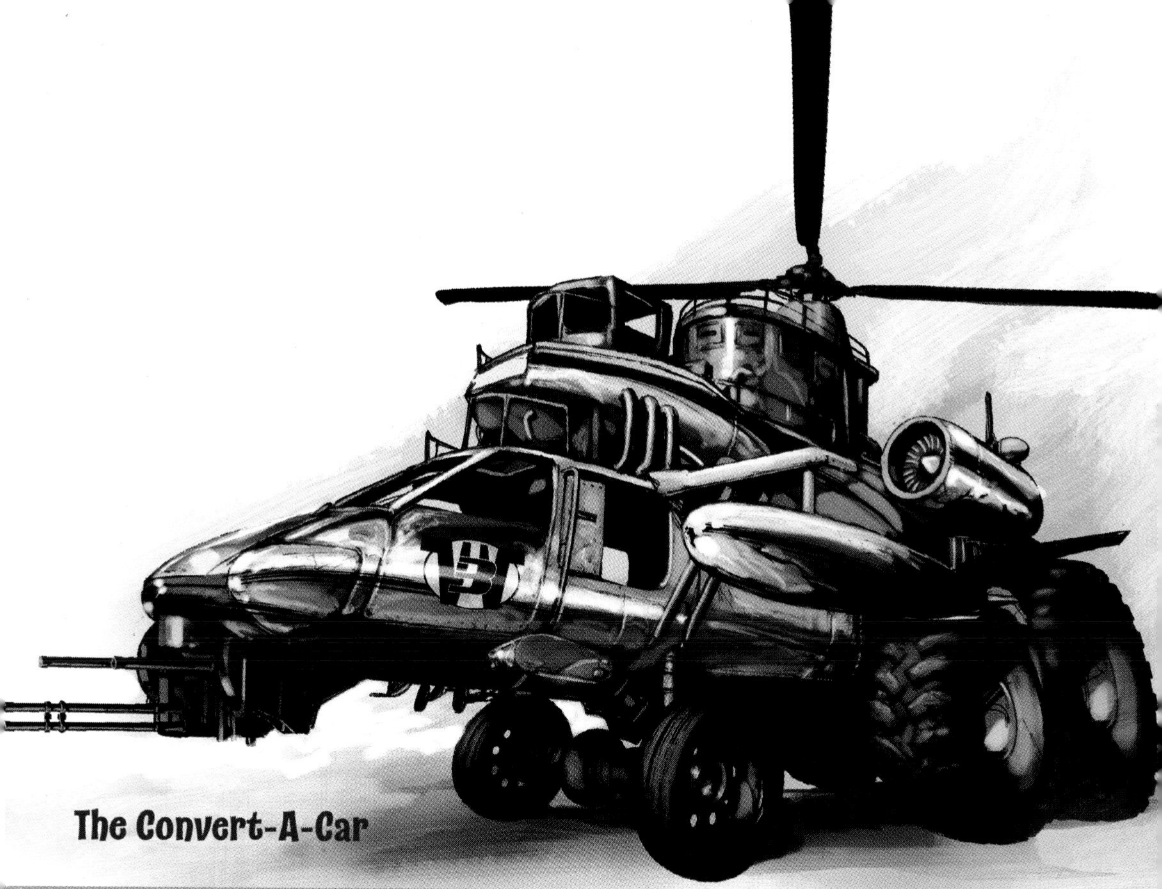

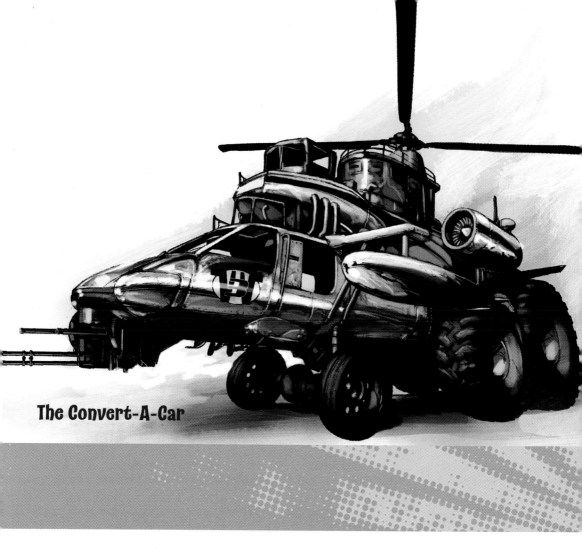

The Convert-A-Car

The Bulletproof Bomb

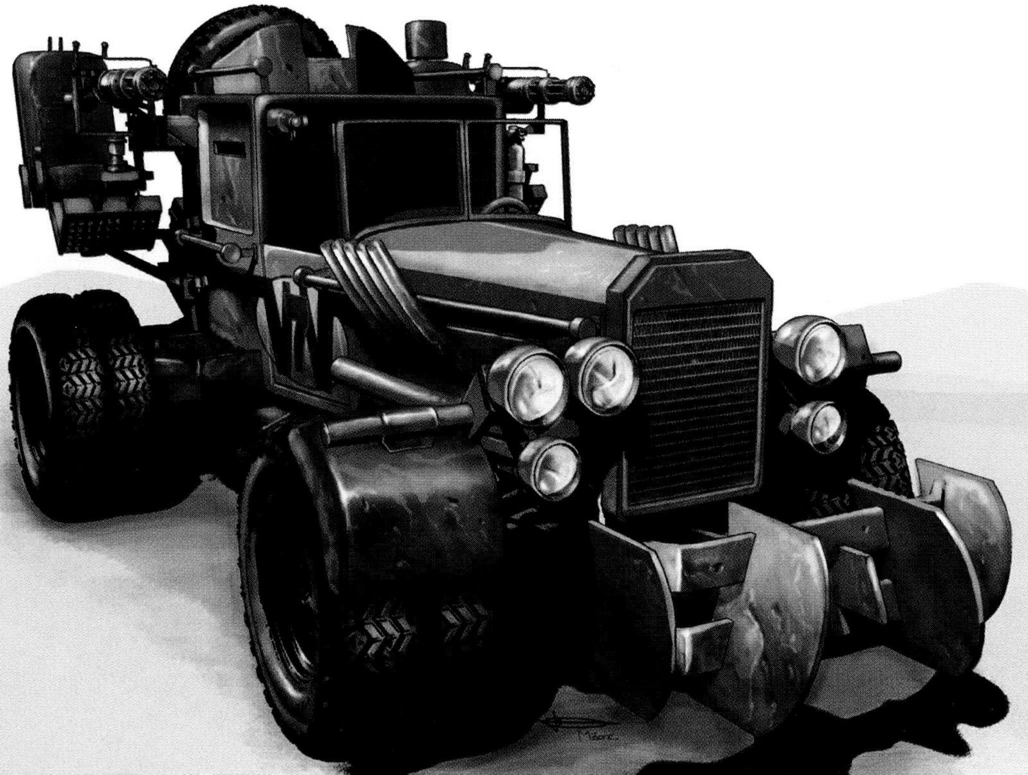

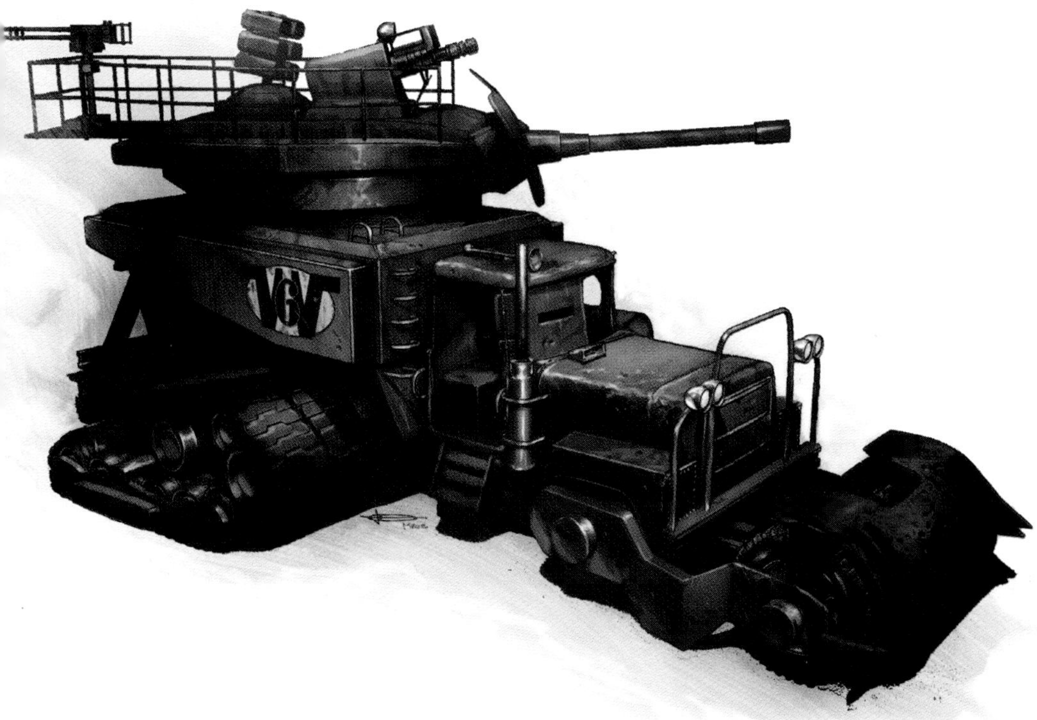
VGV

The Army Surplus Special

The Buzzwagon

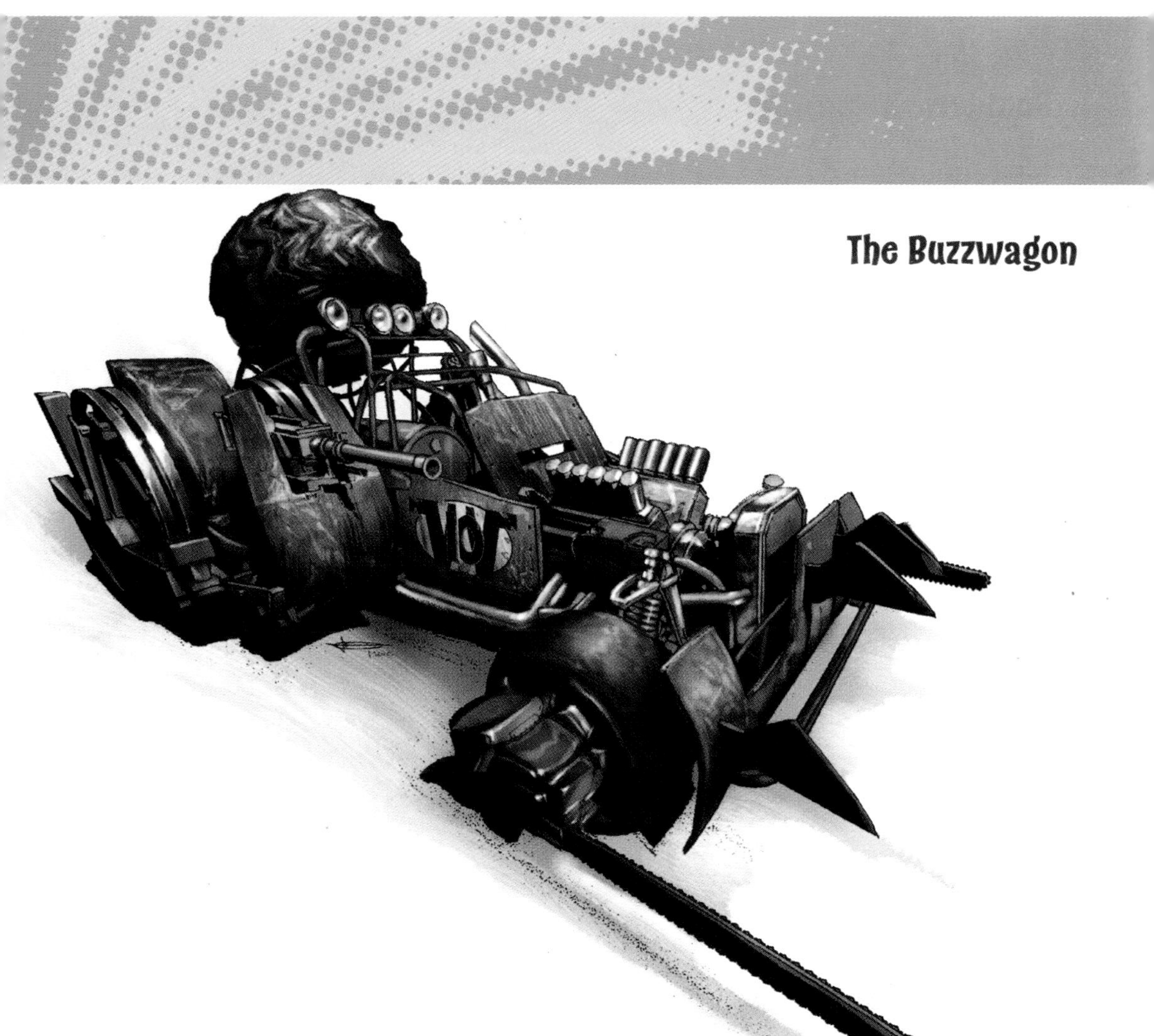

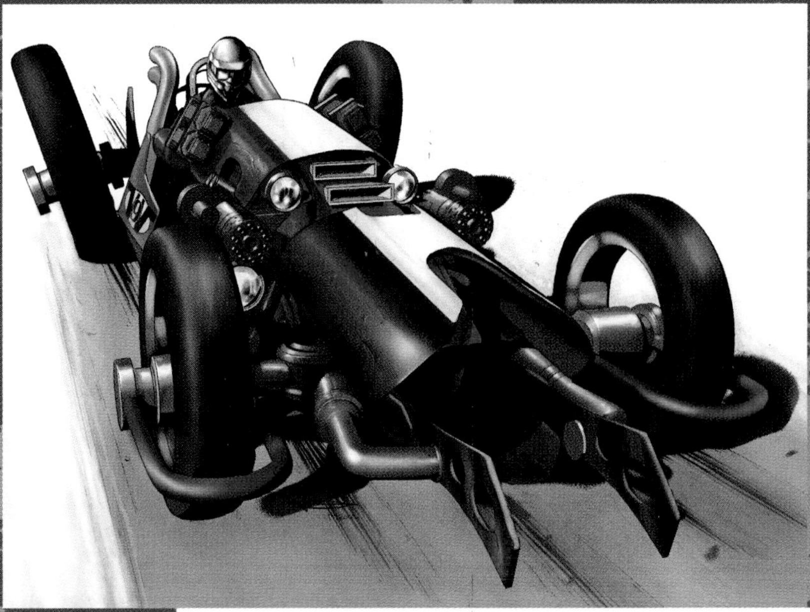

The Turbo Terrific

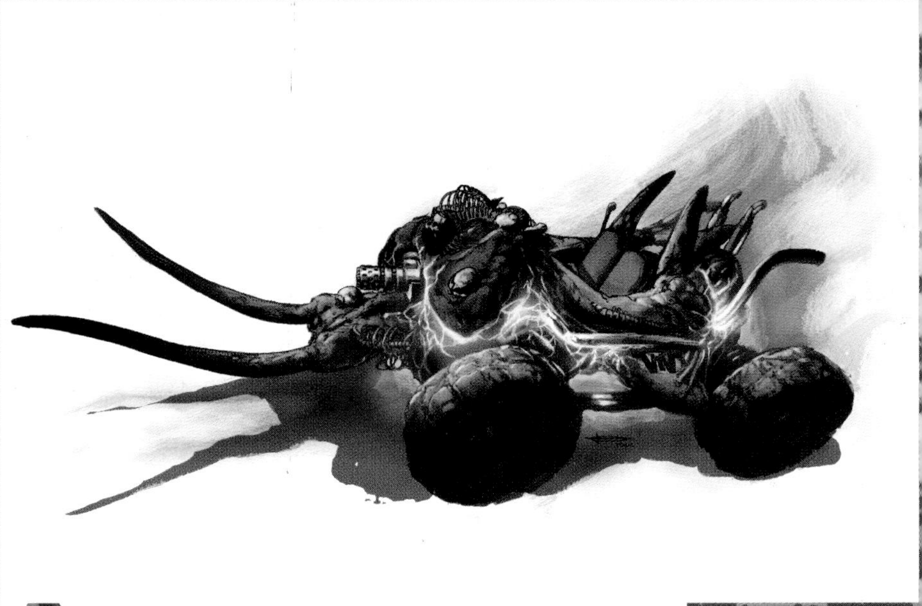

The Boulder Mobile

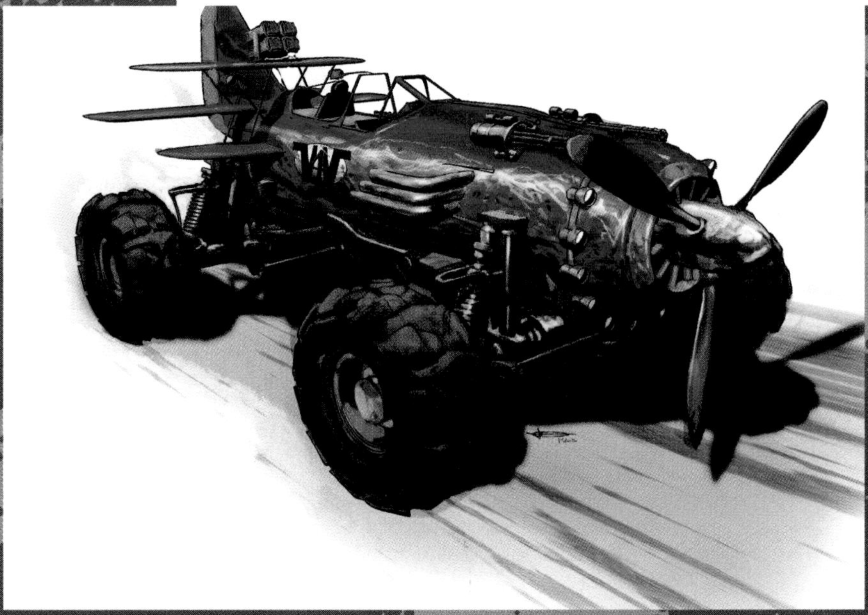

The Crimson Haybaler